To my parents,
Edward and Sari Jay

Contents

Foreword

December, 1971

Dear Mr. Jay,

I have been asked to write a foreword to your book on the history of the Frankfurt Institute of Social Research. Reading your interesting work does not permit me to refuse this request; however, the condition of my health limits me to the short letter form, which should now serve as a foreword. First, my thanks are due you for the care which is demonstrated through all the chapters of your work. Much will be preserved which would be forgotten without your description.

The work to which the Institute devoted itself before its emigration from Germany — one thinks of Friedrich Pollock's book *The Experiments in Economic Planning in the Soviet Union, 1917–1927* or the subsequently published collective work, *Authority and Family* — meant something new in comparison to the then official educational system. It meant the ability to pursue research for which a university still offered no opportunity. The enterprise succeeded only because, thanks to the support of Hermann Weil and the intervention of his son, Felix, a group of men, interested in social theory and from different scholarly backgrounds, came together with the belief that formulating the negative in the epoch of transition was more meaningful than academic careers. What united them was the critical approach to existing society.

Already near the end of the twenties, certainly by the beginning of the thirties, we were convinced of the probability of a National Socialist victory, as well as of the fact that it could be met only through revolutionary actions. That it needed a world war we did not yet envisage at that time. We thought of an uprising in our own country and because of that, Marxism won its decisive meaning for our thought. After our emigration to America via Geneva, the Marxist interpretation of social events remained, to be sure, dominant, which did not mean in any way, however, that a dogmatic materialism had become the decisive theme of our position. Reflecting on political systems taught us rather that it was necessary, as Adorno has expressed it, "not to think of claims to the Absolute as certain and yet, not to deduct anything from the appeal to the emphatic concept of the truth."

The appeal to an entirely other *(ein ganz Anderes)* than this world had primarily a social-philosophical impetus. It led finally to a more positive evaluation of certain metaphysical trends, because the empirical "whole is the untrue" (Adorno). The hope that earthly horror does not possess the last word is, to be sure, a non-scientific wish.

Those who were once associated with the Institute, as far as they are still alive, will certainly be thankful to you for recognizing in your book a history of their own ideas. I feel obliged also in the name of the dead, such as Fred Pollock, Theodor W. Adorno, Walter Benjamin, Franz Neumann, and Otto Kirchheimer, to express to you, dear Mr. Jay, acknowledgment and gratitude for your work.

Cordially,
MAX HORKHEIMER

Montagnola, Switzerland

Introduction

It has become a commonplace in the modern world to regard the intellectual as estranged, maladjusted, and discontented. Far from being disturbed by this vision, however, we have become increasingly accustomed to seeing our intellectuals as outsiders, gadflies, marginal men, and the like. The word "alienation," indiscriminately used to signify the most banal of dyspepsias as well as the deepest of metaphysical fears, has become the chief cant phrase of our time. For even the most discerning of observers, reality and pose have become difficult to distinguish. To the horror of those who can genuinely claim to have suffered from its effects, alienation has proved a highly profitable commodity in the cultural marketplace. Modernist art with its dissonances and torments, to take one example, has become the staple diet of an increasingly voracious army of culture consumers who know good investments when they see them. The avant-garde, if indeed the term can still be used, has become an honored ornament of our cultural life, less to be feared than feted. The philosophy of existentialism, to cite another case, which scarcely a generation ago seemed like a breath of fresh air, has now degenerated into a set of easily manipulated clichés and sadly hollow gestures. This decline occurred, it should be noted, not because analytic philosophers exposed the meaninglessness of its categories, but rather as a result of our culture's uncanny ability to absorb and defuse even its most uncompromising opponents. And finally to mention a third example, it is all too evident in 1972, a few short years after the much ballyhooed birth of an alleged counterculture, that the new infant, if not strangled in the crib, has proved easily domesticated in the ways of its elders. Here too the mechanisms of absorption and cooptation have shown themselves to be enormously effective.

The result of all this is that intellectuals who take their critical function seriously have been presented with an increasingly rigorous challenge to outdistance the culture's capacity to numb their protest. One response has been an ever more frantic flight into cultural extremism, a desire to shock and provoke by going beyond what had previously been the limits of cultural tolerance. These limits, however, have demonstrated an elasticity far greater than anticipated, as yesterday's obscenities are frequently transformed into today's bromides. With the insufficiency of a purely cultural solution in mind, many critical intellectuals have attempted to integrate their cultural protest with its political counterpart. Radical political movements, characteristically of the left, have continued to attract discontented intellectuals in our own time, as they have done traditionally in years past. But this alliance has rarely proved an easy one, especially when the realities of left-wing movements in power have become too ugly to ignore. Consequently, the ebb and flow of radical intellectuals to and from various leftist allegiances has been one of the constant themes of modern intellectual history.

This oscillation stems as well from a more basic dilemma faced only by intellectuals of the left. The elitism of those who confine their extremism solely to the cultural sphere, rejecting its political correlate, does not necessarily engender any particular sense of guilt. For the radical intellectual who chooses political involvement, however, the desire to maintain a critical distance presents a special problem. Remaining apart, not just from society as a whole but also from the movement on whose victory he counts, creates an acute tension that is never absent from the lives of serious leftist intellectuals. The endless self-criticism aimed at exorcising the remnants of elitism, which has characterized the New Left in recent years, bears witness to the persistence of this concern. At its worst, it produces a sentimental *nostalgie de la boue*; at its best, it can lead to an earnest effort to reconcile theory and practice, which takes into account the possibilities for such a unity in an imperfect world.

But what is often forgotten in the desire to purge the phrase "activist intellectual" of its oxymoronic connotations is that intellectuals are already actors, although in a very special sense. The intellectual is always engaged in *symbolic* action, which involves the externalization of his thought in any number of ways. "Men of ideas" are noteworthy only when their ideas are communicated to others through one medium or another. The critical edge of intellectual life comes largely from the gap that exists between symbol and what for want of a better word can be called reality. Paradoxically, by attempting to transform themselves into the agency to bridge that gap, they risk forfeiting the critical perspective it provides. What usually suffers is the quality of their work, which degenerates into propaganda. The critical intellectual is in a sense less *engagé* when he is self-consciously partisan than when he adheres to the standards of integrity set by his craft. As Yeats reminds us, "The intellect of man is forced to choose between / Perfection of the life or of the work." [1] When the radical intellectual too closely identifies with popular forces of change in an effort to leave his ivory tower behind, he jeopardizes achieving either perfection. Between the Scylla of unquestioning solidarity and the Charybdis of willful independence, he must carve a middle way or else fail. How precarious that middle path may be is one of the chief lessons to be learned from the radical intellectuals who have been chosen as the subjects of this study.

The so-called Frankfurt School, composed of certain members of the Institut für Sozialforschung (Institute of Social Research),* can in fact be seen as presenting in quintessential form the dilemma of the left intellectual in our century. Few of their counterparts have been as sensitive to the absorbing power of both the dominant culture and its ostensible opponents. Throughout the Institut's entire existence, and especially in the period from 1923 to 1950, the fear of cooptation and integration deeply troubled its members. Although the exigencies of history forced them into exile as part of the intellectual migration from Central Europe after 1933, they had been exiles in relation to the external world since the beginning of their collaboration. Far from being a source of regret, however, this status was accepted, even nurtured, as the *sine qua non* of their intellectual fertility.

Because of their intransigent refusal to compromise their theoretical integrity at the same time that they sought to identify a social agency to realize their ideas, the adherents of the Frankfurt School anticipated many of the same issues that were to agonize a later generation of engaged intellectuals. Largely for this reason, the work they did in their early years together excited the imaginations of postwar New Leftists in Europe and, more recently, in America as well. Pirated editions of works long since out of print were circulated among an impatient German student movement, whose appetites had been whetted by the contact they had with the Institut after its return to Frankfurt in 1950. The clamor for republication of the essays written in the Institut's house organ, the *Zeitschrift für Sozial-*

* The German spelling of Institut will be used throughout the text to set it apart from any other institute. It will also be used as coterminous with the "Frankfurt School" in the period after 1933. What must be remembered, however, is that the notion of a specific school did not develop until *after* the Institut was forced to leave Frankfurt (the term itself was not used until the Institut returned to Germany in 1950). As will be made clear in the opening chapter, the Weimar Institut was far too pluralist in its Marxism to allow the historian to identify its theoretical perspective with that of the Frankfurt School as it emerged in later years.[2]

forschung (Journal of Social Research), led in the 1960's to the appearance of such collections as Herbert Marcuse's *Negations*[3] and Max Horkheimer's *Kritische Theorie*,[4] to add to the already reissued selections from the writings of other Institut members, such as Theodor W. Adorno, Leo Lowenthal, Walter Benjamin, and Franz Neumann.[5] Although it is not my intention to comment extensively on the Institut's history after its return to Germany, it should be noted that much of the recent attention paid to it was aroused by the reappearance of work done in the relative obscurity of its first quarter century.

Why a history of that period has never before been attempted is not difficult to discern. The Frankfurt School's work covered so many diverse fields that a definitive analysis of each would require a team of scholars expert in everything from musicology to sinology. It would, in short, demand a Frankfurt School all its own. The hazards awaiting the isolated historian are therefore obvious. They were certainly a source of some hesitation on my part before I decided to embark on the project. However, when that decision was behind me and I began to immerse myself in the Institut's work, I discovered that the expertise I lacked in specific disciplines was compensated for by the very comprehensiveness of my approach. For I came to understand that there was an essential coherence in the Frankfurt School's thought, a coherence that affected almost all of its work in different areas. I soon learned that Erich Fromm's discussion of the sado-masochistic character and Leo Lowenthal's treatment of the Norwegian novelist Knut Hamsun illuminated one another, that Theodor W. Adorno's critique of Stravinsky and Max Horkheimer's repudiation of Scheler's philosophical anthropology were intimately related, that Herbert Marcuse's concept of one-dimensional society was predicated on Friedrich Pollock's model of state capitalism, and so on. I also discovered that even when conflicts over issues did develop, as they did, for example, between Fromm and Horkheimer or Pollock and Neumann, they were articulated with a common vocabulary and against a background of more or less shared assumptions. An overview of the Institut's development, despite the superficiality it might entail on certain questions, thus appeared a justifiable exercise.

Moreover, the timing of such a project seemed to me crucial. Although certain of the Institut's members were no longer living — Franz Neumann, Walter Benjamin, Otto Kirchheimer, and Henryk Grossmann, to name the most important — many of the others were still alive, vigorous, and at the stage in their careers when a concern for the historical record was probable. In every case they responded positively to my initial expression of interest in the Institut's history. How much help I received will be apparent in the acknowledgment section that follows.

Despite the aid given me in reconstructing the Institut's past, however, the results should in no way be construed as a "court history." In fact, the conflicting reports I frequently received of various incidents and the often differing estimations of each other's work offered by former Institut colleagues left me at times feeling like the observer at the Japanese play *Rashomon*, not knowing which version to select as valid. My ultimate choices will not please all my informants, but I hope they will be satisfied with my attempts to cross-check as many controversial points as possible. In addition, my own estimate of the Institut's accomplishment ought not to be identified with those of its members. That I admire much of their work cannot be denied; that I have not refrained from criticism where I felt it warranted will, I hope, be equally clear. Remaining faithful to the critical spirit of the Frankfurt School seems much more of a tribute than an unquestioning acceptance of all it said or did.

My only constraint has been dictated by discretion. My access to the extremely valuable Horkheimer-Lowenthal correspondence was qualified by an understandable reluctance on the part of the correspondents to embarrass people who might still be alive. This type of control, which, to be sure, was exercised only infrequently, was the only disadvantage following from my writing about living men. It is rare for the historian to be able to address his questions so directly to the subjects of his study. By so doing, not only have I learned things which the documents could not reveal, but I have also been able to enter into the lives of the Institut's members and appreciate in a more immediate way the impact of their personal experiences as intellectuals in exile. Although the bulk of my text concerns the ideas of the Frankfurt School, I hope that some of those experiences and their relations to the ideas are apparent. For in many ways, both for good and for ill, they were the unique experiences of an extraordinary generation whose historical moment has now irrevocably passed.

Acknowledgments

One of the most gratifying aspects of writing *The Dialectical Imagination* was the opportunity to meet many people who played crucial roles in the history of the Frankfurt School. Included among them were critics as well as defenders of its historical and intellectual record, a record that has always been a stimulus to controversy. I have learned much from both sides and am pleased at this time to be able to acknowledge my debts in print. Equally welcome is the opportunity to thank friends, teachers, and colleagues who provided support of various kinds during all stages of the book's preparation.

Among the former Institut figures who graciously granted me interviews were Max Horkheimer, Herbert Marcuse, Theodor W. Adorno (shortly before his death in the summer of 1969), Erich Fromm, Karl August Wittfogel, Paul Massing, Ernst Schachtel, Olga Lang, Gerhard Meyer, M. I. Finley, and Joseph and Alice Maier. Horkheimer, Marcuse, Fromm, and Wittfogel also took the time to comment on sections of the manuscript after its completion as a doctoral dissertation in history at Harvard. Jürgen Habermas, Alfred Schmidt, and Albrecht Wellmer, of the more recent generation of Frankfurt School adherents, were also willing to submit to my questions. Although we never actually met, Felix J. Weil and I carried on an extensive and spirited correspondence concerning many facets of the Institut, in whose creation he played so important a role. His reactions to sections of the manuscript were invaluable, although our interpretations of certain issues remain somewhat at odds. Gretel Adorno and Gladys Meyer were also very helpful correspondents.

There were three participants in the Institut's history whose cooperation went well beyond anything I might have reasonably expected. Friedrich Pollock spent countless hours with me in Montagnola, Switzerland, in March, 1969, reliving his almost fifty years of involvement with the Institut. After I returned to Cambridge, we maintained a lively correspondence about the progress of my work.

He painstakingly commented on the chapters I was able to submit for his scrutiny before his death in December, 1970. The enormous pride Professor Pollock demonstrated in the Institut's achievement was such that I deeply regret not having been able to present him with a completed manuscript.

Leo Lowenthal was one of the first members of the Frankfurt School with whom I spoke at the beginning of my research. At Berkeley, in the summer of 1968, he gave generously of his time and materials, patiently explaining those references in his valuable correspondence with Horkheimer that had eluded me. In subsequent years, his interest in my work remained keen, and like Pollock he commented with great care and sensitivity on the first drafts of my chapters. Although our interpretations of specific issues were occasionally different, he never sought to impose his views on mine. Since my arrival at Berkeley, he has continued to give support and advice on the completion of the manuscript. Of all the benefits of my research, his friendship has been one of those I value most highly.

Finally, Paul Lazarsfeld offered me constant encouragement and wise counsel throughout the course of my work. Although never a member of the Institut's inner circle, he was interested in its work and peripherally involved in its affairs from the mid-thirties. The documents and letters he had preserved from that time were generously put at my disposal. Moreover, his theoretical distance from the Frankfurt School helped me gain a perspective on its work I might otherwise have lacked.

In short, my debt to the surviving members of the Institut is considerable. Nothing symbolizes this more strikingly than Professor Horkheimer's willingness to compose some prefatory remarks, despite a very serious illness.

No less an acknowledgment of gratitude is due to others who contributed to the making of this book. Of my former teachers, H. Stuart Hughes, who directed the dissertation, warrants a special mention for his many kindnesses throughout the course of my work. I also owe much to Fritz K. Ringer, who first aroused my interest in German intellectual history, for the care and severity with which he criticized the manuscript. To my friends in Cambridge I can only repeat in print what I hope they already know of my deep appreciation. Paul Breines, Michael Timo Gilmore, Paul Weissman, and Lewis Wurgaft did much more to sustain me during my graduate career than read my chapters with a critical eye. I am also very grateful for the advice of newer friends whom I have come to know through a common interest in the Frankfurt School: Matthias Becker, Edward

Breslin, Susan Buck, Sidney Lipshires, Jeremy J. Shapiro, Trent Shroyer, Gary Ulmen, and Shierry Weber. I have also greatly benefited from the opportunity to speak to older scholars concerned with the work of the Frankfurt School, including Everett C. Hughes, George Lichtheim, Adolph Lowe, and Kurt H. Wolff.

My new colleagues at Berkeley have shown me in the short time I have been in their company that considerable vitality can still be found in the old notion of a community of scholars. The book has been improved in particular by the comments of Fryar Calhoun, Gerald Feldman, Samuel Haber, Martin Malia, Nicholas Riasanovsky, Wolfgang Sauer, and Irwin Scheiner. I would also like to express my thanks to William Phillips of Little, Brown, whose unwavering enthusiasm and keen editorial eye have been of great help throughout. My fine typists, Annette Slocombe of Lexington, Massachusetts, and Bajana Ristich and her staff at the Institute of International Studies at Berkeley, were invaluable in getting the manuscript into shape for publication, as was Boris Frankel, who helped me with the index. Finally, it is a particular pleasure to be able to acknowledge the support of the Danforth Foundation, financial and otherwise, which sustained me during my graduate career.

I hope that this list of acknowledgments has not seemed unduly long, for I am anxious to convey the extent to which *The Dialectical Imagination* approached a collective project. Many of the strengths of the text derive from that fact; the weaknesses, alas, are my own responsibility.

M. J.

THE DIALECTICAL IMAGINATION

I

The Creation of the Institut für Sozialforschung and Its First Frankfurt Years

One of the most far-reaching changes brought by the First World War, at least in terms of its impact on intellectuals, was the shifting of the socialist center of gravity eastward. The unexpected success of the Bolshevik Revolution — in contrast to the dramatic failure of its Central European imitators — created a serious dilemma for those who had previously been at the center of European Marxism, the left-wing intellectuals of Germany. In rough outline, the choices left to them were as follows: first, they might support the moderate socialists and their freshly created Weimar Republic, thus eschewing revolution and scorning the Russian experiment; or second, they could accept Moscow's leadership, join the newly formed German Communist Party, and work to undermine Weimar's bourgeois compromise. Although rendered more immediate by the war and rise of the moderate socialists to power, these alternatives in one form or another had been at the center of socialist controversies for decades. A third course of action, however, was almost entirely a product of the radical disruption of Marxist assumptions, a disruption brought about by the war and its aftermath. This last alternative was the searching reexamination of the very foundations of Marxist theory, with the dual hope of explaining past errors and preparing for future action. This began a process that inevitably led back to the dimly lit regions of Marx's philosophical past.

One of the crucial questions raised in the ensuing analysis was the relation of theory to practice, or more precisely, to what became a familiar term in the Marxist lexicon, *praxis.* Loosely defined, *praxis* was used to designate a kind of self-creating action, which differed from the externally motivated behavior produced by forces outside man's control. Although originally seen as the opposite of contemplative *theoria* when it was first used in Aristotle's *Metaphysics*, *praxis* in the Marxist usage was seen in dialectical relation to theory. In fact, one of the earmarks of *praxis* as opposed to mere action was its being informed by theoretical considerations. The goal of revolutionary activity was understood as the unifying of theory and *praxis,* which would be in direct contrast to the situation prevailing under capitalism.

How problematical that goal in fact was became increasingly clear in the postwar years, when for the first time socialist governments were in power. The Soviet leadership saw its task in terms more of survival than of realizing socialist aims — not an unrealistic appraisal under the circumstances, but one scarcely designed to placate socialists like Rosa Luxemburg who would have preferred no revolution at all to a betrayed one. Although from a very different perspective, the socialist leadership in the Weimar Republic also understood its most imperative goal to be the survival of the new government rather than the implementation of socialism. The trade union consciousness, which, as Carl Schorske has shown,[1] permeated its ranks well before the end of the Second Reich, meant the squandering of what opportunities there might have been to revolutionize German society. The split that divided the working class movement in Weimar between a bolshevized Communist Party (KPD) and a nonrevolutionary Socialist Party (SPD) was a sorry spectacle to those who still maintained the purity of Marxist theory. Some attempted a rapprochement with one faction or another. But as demonstrated by the story of Georg Lukács, who was forced to repudiate his most imaginative book, *History and Class Consciousness*, shortly after its appearance in 1923, this often meant sacrificing intellectual integrity on the altar of party solidarity.

When, however, personal inclinations led to a greater commitment to theory than to party, even when this meant suspending for a while the unifying of theory and *praxis,* the results in terms of theoretical innovation could be highly fruitful. It will be one of the central contentions of this work that the relative autonomy of the men who comprised the so-called Frankfurt School of the Institut für Sozialforschung, although entailing certain disadvantages, was one of the primary reasons for the theoretical achievements produced by their collaboration. Although without much impact in Weimar, and with even less during the period of exile that followed, the Frankfurt

School was to become a major force in the revitalization of Western European Marxism in the postwar years. In addition, through the sudden popularity of Herbert Marcuse in the America of the late 1960's, the Frankfurt School's Critical Theory *(Kritische Theorie)* has also had a significant influence on the New Left in this country.

From its very beginning, independence was understood as a necessary prerequisite for the task of theoretical innovation and unrestrained social research. Fortunately, the means to ensure such conditions were available. The idea of an institutional framework in which these goals might be pursued was conceived by Felix J. Weil in 1922.[2] Weil was the only son of a German-born grain merchant, Hermann Weil, who had left Germany around 1890 for Argentina and made a sizable fortune exporting grains back to Europe. Born in 1898 in Buenos Aires, Felix was sent in his ninth year to Frankfurt to attend the Goethe Gymnasium and, ultimately, the newly created university in that city. Except for an important year in Tübingen in 1918–1919, where he first became involved in left-wing causes at the university, Weil remained at Frankfurt until he took his doctorate *magna cum laude* in political science. His dissertation, on the practical problems of implementing socialism,[3] was published in a series of monographs edited by Karl Korsch, who had been one of the first to interest him in Marxism. Drawing upon his own considerable funds inherited from his mother, as well as his father's wealth, Weil began to support a number of radical ventures in Germany.

The first of these was the *Erste Marxistische Arbeitswoche* (First Marxist Work Week), which met in the summer of 1922 in Ilmenau, Thuringia. "Its purpose," according to Weil, was the "hope that the different trends in Marxism, if afforded an opportunity of talking it out together, could arrive at a 'true' or 'pure' Marxism." [4] Among the participants at the week-long session were Georg Lukács, Karl Korsch, Richard Sorge, Friedrich Pollock, Karl August Wittfogel, Bela Fogarasi, Karl Schmückle, Konstantin Zetkin (the younger of two sons of the well-known socialist leader Klara Zetkin), Hede Gumperz (then married to Julian Gumperz, an editor of the Communist *Rote Fahne*, later to Gerhart Eisler and then to Paul Massing),[5] and several wives, including Hedda Korsch, Rose Wittfogel, Christiane Sorge, and Kate Weil. Much of the time was devoted to a discussion of Korsch's yet unpublished manuscript, "Marxism and Philosophy." "The EMA," Weil wrote,[6] "was entirely informal, composed only of intellectuals," and "had not the slightest factional intention or result." Expectations of a *Zweite Marxistische Arbeitswoche* (a Second Marxist Work Week) came to naught when a more ambitious alternative took its place.

With the encouragement of several friends at the University of Frankfurt, Weil's idea of a more permanent institute, which he had conceived during the EMA, became increasingly clarified. One of these friends, Friedrich Pollock, had participated in the discussions in Ilmenau. Born in 1894 in Freiburg, the son of an assimilated Jewish businessman, Pollock had been trained for a commercial career before serving in the war. After its end, no longer interested in business, he became a student of economics and politics at the universities of Munich, Freiburg, and Frankfurt. He was granted a doctorate in 1923 *summa cum laude* from the economics department at Frankfurt with a thesis on Marx's monetary theory. Before the war, in 1911, Pollock had become friends with Max Horkheimer, who later was to emerge as the most important figure in the Institut's history, and who now lent his voice to Pollock's in supporting Weil's plan for an institute of social research.

Horkheimer, Pollock's junior by nine months, was born in 1895 in Stuttgart. At the urging of his father, Moritz, a prominent Jewish manufacturer, he too had had commercial training before entering military service. Horkheimer accepted the advice of his father on such matters as extended visits to Brussels and London, which he took with Pollock in 1913–1914 to learn French and English. But at no time were his interests solely those of the aspiring businessman. There is clear evidence of this in the series of novels he wrote (but left unpublished) during this period in his life. After 1918 he sought more disciplined intellectual training at the same three universities attended by Pollock. Initially working in psychology under the direction of the Gestaltist Adhemar Gelb, he was diverted into another field after news reached Frankfurt that a project comparable to the one in which he was engaged had recently been completed elsewhere. The new field was philosophy and his new mentor Hans Cornelius.

Although Cornelius never had any direct connection with the Institut, his influence on Horkheimer and his friends was considerable, which will become apparent when the elements of Critical Theory are discussed in the next chapter. In 1922 Horkheimer received his doctorate *summa cum laude* under Cornelius's direction with a thesis on Kant.[7] He was "habilitated" * three years later with another

* I am grateful to Dr. Weil for providing a full explanation of this and related German terms (used below) in the academic hierarchical system, as it was around 1920: "A *Privatdozent* was the first step in the academic career. It corresponds to assistant professor in the U.S. To become one, a candidate, usually then serving, after his doctor's degree, as assistant to a full professor, to the dean of the department, or to a *Seminar* (study group), had to submit a new qualifying thesis, the *Habilitationsschrift,* sponsored by two full professors, and then defend it in a *Disputation* before the department consisting of all the full professors. (At Frankfurt University

critical discussion of Kant's work and gave his first lecture as *Privatdozent* in May, 1925, on Kant and Hegel.[8]

Horkheimer's relationship to Pollock was one of the cornerstones of the Institut, and it merits some comment here. An insight into it can be gleaned from a passage in Ludwig Marcuse's autobiography. Marcuse, no relation to Herbert, was the drama critic for a Frankfurt newspaper in the mid-twenties when Cornelius brought his two young protégés to his office. They were "an attractive man, Max Horkheimer, overflowing with warmth, and his reserved, externally austere friend, Fritz Pollock; but one also saw in him a little of what was being guarded behind the reserve." [9] Among the qualities in Pollock to which Marcuse might have alluded was a self-effacing, unquestioning loyalty to Horkheimer, which marked their friendship for the sixty or so years of its duration until Pollock's death in the winter of 1970. With only brief interruptions, the two remained in close proximity for all of their adult lives. Pollock took the role of the pragmatic, prudent realist, often arranging the mundane details of their lives to allow Horkheimer the maximum time for his scholarly pursuits. As a child Horkheimer was highly protected, and during his mature years Pollock often served as buffer between him and a harsh world. Horkheimer, so one observer recalled,[10] was often moody and temperamental. Pollock, in contrast, was steady, even obsessive. The complementarity of their personalities was one of the sources of the Institut's success. That Pollock's own scholarly career suffered to some extent was a price he seemed willing to pay. In the twenties, to be sure, this was a result that was difficult to foresee.

In fact, both men, and probably Weil as well, might have expected successful careers in their respective fields. However, entrance into the highly rigid German university system would have necessitated

there were five such departments: philosophy, law, economics and social sciences, medicine, and natural sciences.) If he passed, the department granted him his *venia legendi,* the 'permission to lecture,' which, however, was limited to a particular field. The *Privatdozent* was not a civil servant *(Beamter)* nor did he receive a salary, only a share in the tuition fees for his course.

"The next step on the ladder was the *Ausserordentliche Professor,* the associate professor. He was a civil servant, with tenure and salary, and also received a share in the tuition fees. He could sponsor *Doktoranden* and participate in the exams, but had no vote in the departmental meetings, although he could speak at these meetings.

"The *Ordentliche Professor,* the full professor, had all the rights of the *Ausserordentliche,* plus the vote in the meetings. But unlike the *Ausserordentliche* he could lecture on any topic he wanted, even outside his field (for example, the holder of a chair for art history could lecture on aerodynamics, if he so wanted). He was, of course, a civil servant with tenure (and usually a large salary), a share in the tuition fees (usually a minimum guarantee) and he was entitled to the services of a university-paid assistant. The full professor's oath of office also conferred German citizenship upon him, if he was a foreigner, unless he previously filed a declination (thus Grünberg chose to remain an Austrian, and, much later, Horkheimer preferred to remain an American)." (Letter of June 8, 1971) confining their broad interests to one discipline. In addition, the type of radical scholarship they hoped to pursue found little favor with the established academic hierarchy. Even the non-Marxist but unconventional Cornelius was very much of an outcast among his colleagues. Accordingly, Weil's idea of an independently endowed institute for social research seemed an excellent way to bypass the normal channels of university life. Such topics as the history of the labor movement and the origins of anti-Semitism, which were neglected in the standard curriculum of German higher education, could be studied with a thoroughness never attempted before.[11] Hermann Weil, Felix's father, was approached with the plan and agreed to an initial endowment providing a yearly income of 120,000 Marks (the equivalent of $30,000 after the inflation had ended). The value of this income has been estimated by Pollock as four times what it would be in 1970. It took approximately 200 Marks (or $50.00) a month to support an unmarried assistant at the Institut. In time the initial grant was supplemented by additional capital gifts from Weil and other sources. To my knowledge, however, there is no evidence to indicate any political contributors, although allegations to this effect were sometimes made by the Institut's detractors in later years. In any event, Hermann Weil's gifts, though not enormous, did permit the creation and maintenance of an institution whose financial independence proved a great advantage throughout its subsequent history.

Although independence, both financial and intellectual, was the goal of the founders, they thought it prudent to seek some affiliation with the University of Frankfurt, itself only recently established in 1914. The original idea of calling it the Institut für Marxismus (Institute for Marxism) was abandoned as too provocative, and a more Aesopian alternative was sought (not for the last time in the Frankfurt School's history). The suggestion of the Education Ministry to call it the Felix Weil Institute of Social Research was declined by Weil, who "wanted the Institut to become known, and perhaps famous, due to its contributions to Marxism as a scientific discipline, not due to the founder's money." [12] It was decided to call it simply the Institut für Sozialforschung. Weil also refused to "habilitate" himself and become a *Privatdozent,* or to consider the possibility of further academic advancement leading to the directorship of the Institut, because "countless people would have been convinced that I 'bought' myself the 'venia legendi' or, later, the chair." [13] Holding a chair as a governmentally salaried full professor at the university was, in fact, a stipulation for the directorship of the Institut as spelled out in the agreement reached with the Ministry of Education.

Weil proposed as candidate an economist from the Technische Hochschule in Aachen, Kurt Albert Gerlach. Weil himself retained control of the Gesellschaft für Sozialforschung (Society of Social Research), the Institut's financial and administrative body.

Gerlach shared with the Institut's founders an aesthetic and political distaste for bourgeois society. He had cultivated the former through connections with the Stefan George circle and the latter through an acquaintanceship with the Fabians gained during several years of study in England. His political inclinations were firmly to the left. Many years later, Pollock would remember him as a non-party socialist,[14] while the British historians F. W. Deakin and G. R. Storry in their study of Richard Sorge wrote: "It is probable that, like Sorge, he was at this time a member of the Communist Party." [15] Whatever the precise nature of Gerlach's politics, when proposed by Weil, he was accepted by the economics and social science department as professor and by the Education Ministry as first head of the Institut. In early 1922, Gerlach wrote a "Memorandum on the Foundation of an Institute of Social Research" [16] in which he stressed the synoptic goals of the Institut. Shortly thereafter, it was announced that he would deliver a series of inaugural lectures on anarchism, socialism, and Marxism. But the lectures were never given, for in October, 1922, Gerlach suddenly died of an attack of diabetes, at the age of thirty-six. (He left his library of eight thousand volumes to Weil, who passed it on to the Institut.)

The search for a successor focused on an older man who would serve as interim director until one of the younger founding members was old enough to acquire a chair at the university. The first possibility was Gustav Mayer, the noted historian of socialism and the biographer of Engels. But the negotiations foundered, as Mayer remembers it, on the demands made by Weil — whom he later dismissed as an *Edelkommunist* (an aristocratic communist) — for total control over the Institut's intellectual life.[17] If this was true, Weil's insistence was certainly short-lived, for the next candidate, who actually got the position, asserted his own domination very quickly. Weil's influence on intellectual questions appears, in fact, never to have been very great.

The final choice for Gerlach's replacement was Carl Grünberg, who was persuaded to leave his post as professor of law and political science at the University of Vienna to come to Frankfurt.[18] Grünberg had been born in Focsani, Rumania, in 1861 of Jewish parents (he later converted to Catholicism to assume his chair in Vienna). He studied jurisprudence from 1881 to 1885 in the Austrian capital, where he subsequently combined a legal and an academic career. In 1909 he became professor at Vienna and in the subsequent year began editing the *Archiv für die Geschichte des Sozialismus und der Arbeiterbewegung (Archive for the History of Socialism and the Workers' Movement)*, popularly known as *Grünbergs Archiv.*

Politically, Grünberg was an avowed Marxist, who has been called "the father of Austro-Marxism" by one observer.[19] This characterization, however, has been disputed by the historian of that movement, who has written that it was true only "insofar as the representatives of Austro-Marxism were his students at the University of Vienna, but not in the sense that Grünberg himself can be counted among the Austro-Marxists, since his work had a primarily historical character and was not devoted to achieving a unity of theory and practice." [20] Grünberg's relative indifference to theoretical questions seems to have persisted after his coming to Frankfurt. Although his journal did contain an occasional theoretical article, such as Karl Korsch's important "Marxism and Philosophy" in 1923 and Georg Lukács's critique of Moses Hess three years later,[21] it was primarily devoted to historical and empirical studies usually grounded in a rather undialectical, mechanistic Marxism in the Engels-Kautsky tradition. Weil's own theoretical interests were never very different, and Grünberg was certainly in agreement with the goal of an interdisciplinary institute dedicated to a radical dissection of bourgeois society. So the problem of Gerlach's successor was satisfactorily resolved by the time the Institut was ready to begin operations. Grünberg, it might be noted in passing, was the first avowed Marxist to hold a chair at a German university.

The official creation of the Institut occurred on February 3, 1923, by a decree of the Education Ministry, following an agreement between it and the Gesellschaft für Sozialforschung. Accepting an invitation by Professor Drevermann of the Senckenberg Museum of Natural Science to use its halls as a temporary home, the Institut immediately began to function, as Weil remembers it, "among open moving boxes filled with books, on improvised desks made of boards, and under the skeletons of a giant whale, a diplodocus, and an ichthyosaurus." [22]

In March, 1923, construction of a building to house its operations at Victoria-Allee 17, near the corner of Bockenheimer Landstrasse on the university campus, was begun. Franz Röckle, Weil's choice as architect, designed a spare, cube-shaped, five-story structure in the *Neue Sachlichkeit* (New Objectivity) style then becoming fashionable in avant-garde Weimar circles. In later years the irony of the Institut's being housed in a building whose architecture reflected the spirit of sober "objectivity" that Critical Theory so often mocked [23] was not lost on its members. Nevertheless, its thirty-six-seat reading room, sixteen small workrooms, four seminar rooms with a hundred places, and library with space for seventy-five thousand volumes served the young Institut well.

On June 22, 1924, the Institut's freshly completed building was officially opened. Grünberg gave the dedicating address.[24] At the outset of his remarks, he stressed the need for a research-oriented academy in opposition to the then current trend in German higher education towards teaching at the expense of scholarship. Although the Institut was to offer some instruction, it would try to avoid becoming a training school for "mandarins" [25] prepared only to function in the service of the status quo. In pointing to the tendency of German universities to become centers of specialized instruction — institutes for "mandarins" — Grünberg was putting his finger on a persistent problem in German history. More than a century before, Wilhelm von Humboldt had attempted to draw a line between "universities" devoted to practical training and "academies" fostering pure research.[26] Over the years, however, the critical "academy" had been clearly shunted aside by the adjustment-oriented university as the model for German higher education. The Institut from its inception was dedicated to countering this trend.

Grünberg continued his remarks by outlining the differences in administration that would distinguish the Institut from other recently created research societies. Rather than collegial in leadership, as in the case of the newly founded Cologne Research Institute of Social Sciences, directed by Christian Eckert, Leopold von Wiese, Max Scheler, and Hugo Lindemann, the Frankfurt Institut was to have a single director with "dictatorial" control. Although the independence of its members was assured, true direction would be exercised in the distribution of the Institut's resources and the focusing of its energies. In subsequent years the dominance of Max Horkheimer in the affairs of the Institut was unquestioned. Although in large measure attributable to the force of his personality and the range of his intellect, his power was also rooted in the structure of the Institut as it was originally conceived.

Grünberg concluded his opening address by clearly stating his personal allegiance to Marxism as a scientific methodology. Just as liberalism, state socialism, and the historical school had institutional homes elsewhere, so Marxism would be the ruling principle at the Institut. Grünberg's conception of materialist analysis was straightforward. It was, he argued, "eminently inductive; its results claimed no validity in time and space," but had "only relative, historically conditioned meaning." [27] True Marxism, he continued, was not dogmatic; it did not seek eternal laws. With this latter assertion, Critical Theory as it was later developed was in agreement. Grünberg's inductive epistemology, however, did not receive the approval of Horkheimer and the other younger members of the group. But in the first few years of the Institut's history Grünberg's approach prevailed. The Grünberg *Archiv* continued to stress the history of the labor movement while publishing an occasional theoretical work, such as Pollock's study of Werner Sombart and Horkheimer's article on Karl Mannheim.[28]

The tone of the Grünberg years, a tone very different from that set after Horkheimer replaced him as director, was captured in a letter sent by a student at the Institut, Oscar H. Swede, to the American Marxist Max Eastman in 1927. The relative orthodoxy of the Institut's Marxism was frustrating to the young Swede, who complained of spending

> hours of exasperating argument in a Marxist Institute with a younger generation settling down to an orthodox religion and the worship of an iconographical literature, not to mention blackboards full of mathematical juggling with blocks of 1000 k + 400 w of Marx's divisions of capital's functions, and the like. God! The hours I've spent listening to the debate of seminaries and student circles on the Hegelian dialektik, with not a single voice to point out that the problems can no longer be solved (if they ever were) by means of straw splitting "philosophical" conceptions. Even the leader [Grünberg], faced with an audience of enthusiastic youth convinced that Relativity is a further installment of bourgeois ideology substituting fluctuating ideas for Newton's absolute materialism, that Freudism [sic] and Bergsonism are insidious attacks from the rear, and that the war can be waged with the sword in one hand and the "Geschichte der Historiko-materialismus" in the other . . . is constantly being brought up against the inherent contradictions in a Marxian M.I.H.[?] and being forced to devise defences against the logical conclusion that we may sit with our arms folded and wait for the millennium to blossom from the dung of the capitalist decay. The fact is that Ec[onomic] determinism cannot produce either fighting or creative forces, and there will be no communism if we have to rely for recruits on the sergeanty of cold, hunger, and low wages.[29]

Ultimately, Swede's impatience with the unimaginative Marxism of the Grünberg years was to be shared by the Institut's later leaders, who were to comprise the Frankfurt School; but during the twenties, little theoretical innovation occurred at what the students were to call the "Café Marx."

Symptomatic of its position were the close ties it maintained with the Marx-Engels Institute in Moscow under the direction of David

Ryazanov.[30] It photostated copies of unpublished manuscripts by Marx and Engels brought over weekly by courier from the SPD's Berlin headquarters and forwarded them to Moscow, where they were included in the collected works, the famous *MEGA (Marx-Engels Historisch-Kritische Gesamtausgabe).*[31]

At the same time, the Institut began to assemble a group of young assistants with a variety of backgrounds and interests. The least important in terms of the Institut's later development, but one of the most fascinating individuals to be associated with it at any time, was Richard "Ika" Sorge. The remarkable story of his espionage for the Russians in the Far East prior to and during the Second World War is too well known to require recapitulation here. Independent Socialist and then Communist after 1918, Sorge was also a doctoral student of Gerlach's at Aachen. He combined his academic activities with such work for the Party as illegal organizing of Ruhr mine workers. In 1921 he married Gerlach's divorced wife, Christiane, which surprisingly did not cost him the friendship of his professor. When Gerlach went to Frankfurt the next year, Sorge followed. After the sudden death of the Institut's projected first director, Sorge remained with the group for a brief time, and was given the task of organizing the library. It was a job he did not relish, and when the Party told him to come to Moscow in 1924, his obedience was uncomplicated by a reluctance to leave Frankfurt. In any case, his connection with the Institut, according to Deakin and Storry, "must have been nominal and a cover" [32] for his work for the Party. It was not until his public exposure as a spy in the 1940's that the others learned of his remarkable undercover career.[33]

Other assistants at the Institut, however, were openly involved with leftist politics, despite the official intention of the founding members to keep it free of any party affiliation. Karl August Wittfogel, Franz Borkenau, and Julian Gumperz were all members of the Communist Party. Political activism as such was thus not in itself a reason for rejection by the group. It could, however, prove a hindrance, as in the case of Karl Korsch, who had been justice minister in the Thuringian SPD-KPD Coalition government in 1923, and continued as a prominent left opposition figure in the KPD until 1926. Wittfogel remembers Korsch's role in the Institut as central during its first years, but the other surviving members have all disagreed with his version of the facts. Korsch did participate in some of the Institut's seminars and wrote occasional reviews for its publications before and after the emigration, but was never offered a full membership.[34] The reasons were no doubt complex, but Korsch's stress on *praxis,* which was to lead him increasingly away from philosophical speculation in later years, certainly played a role. So too did the instability that the others saw in his character.[35]

From time to time the question of Horkheimer's possible membership in the KPD has been raised. But hard evidence to support this view seems unavailable, and there is much in his writings and actions that makes his current denial of membership entirely plausible. During their student days together in Munich in 1919, Horkheimer and Pollock were nonparticipatory witnesses of the short-lived revolutionary activities of the Bavarian literati. Although helping to hide left-wing victims of the white terror that followed, they did not themselves join in the revolution, which they considered premature and inevitably doomed by the lack of objective conditions favoring true social change.[36] Horkheimer's earliest political sympathies were with Rosa Luxemburg, especially because of her critique of Bolshevik centralism.[37] After her murder in 1919, he never found another socialist leader to follow.

In one of the very few concrete political analyses Horkheimer wrote during the pre-emigration period, "The Impotence of the German Working Class," published in 1934 in the collection of aphorisms and short essays known as *Dämmerung*[38] (the German word means both dawn and twilight), he expressed his reasons for skepticism concerning the various workers' parties. The existence of a split between an employed, integrated working-class elite and the masses of outraged, frustrated unemployed produced by capitalism in its current form, he argued, had led to a corresponding dichotomy between a Social Democratic Party lacking in motivation and a Communist Party crippled by theoretical obtuseness. The SPD had too many "reasons"; the Communists, who often relied on coercion, too few. The prospects for reconciling the two positions, he concluded pessimistically, were contingent "in the last analysis on the course of economic processes. . . . In both parties, there exists a part of the strength on which the future of mankind depends." [39] At no time, therefore, whether under Grünberg or under Horkheimer, was the Institut to ally itself with a specific party or faction on the left. In 1931, one of its members characterized its relationship to the working-class movement in these terms:

> It is a *neutral* institution at the university, which is accessible to everyone. Its significance lies in the fact that for the first time everything concerning the workers' movement in the most important countries of the world is gathered. Above all, sources (congress minutes, party programs, statutes, newspapers, and periodicals) . . . Whoever in Western Europe wishes to write on the currents of the workers movement *must* come to us, for we are the only gathering point for it.[40]

When the Institut did accept members who were politically committed, it was solely because of their nonpolitical work. The most important of the activists in its ranks was Karl August Wittfogel.[41] The son of a Lutheran schoolteacher, Wittfogel was born in the small Hanoverian town of Woltersdorf in 1896. Active in the German youth movement before the war, he became increasingly involved in radical politics by its end. In November, 1918, he joined the Independent Socialist party and two years later, its Communist successor. Throughout the Weimar period he directed much of his considerable energy into party work, although he was frequently in hot water in Moscow for the heterodoxy of his positions.

At the same time as his participation in Communist politics deepened, Wittfogel managed to pursue a vigorous academic career. He studied at Leipzig, where he was influenced by Karl Lamprecht, at Berlin, and finally at Frankfurt, where Carl Grünberg agreed to direct his dissertation. He published studies of both bourgeois science and bourgeois society before turning to what was to become his major concern in later years, Asiatic society.[42] As early as 1922 Wittfogel had been asked by Gerlach and Weil to join the Institut they were planning to open. It was not until three years later, however, that he accepted the offer, his wife, Rose Schlesinger, having already become one of the Institut's librarians.

Although his new colleagues respected Wittfogel's contributions to the understanding of what Marx had called the Asiatic mode of production, there seems to have been little real integration of his work with their own. On theoretical issues he was considered naive by Horkheimer and the other younger members of the Institut who were challenging the traditional interpretation of Marxist theory. Wittfogel's approach was unapologetically positivistic, and the disdain was clearly mutual. Symbolic of this was the fact that he had to review one of his own books in 1932 under the pseudonym Carl Peterson, because no one else was interested in taking the assignment.

In 1931, to be sure, his study *Economy and Society in China* was published under the Institut's auspices, but by then he had moved his permanent base of operations to Berlin. Here, among his many other pursuits, he contributed a series of articles on aesthetic theory to *Die Linkskurve*, which have been characterized as "the first effort in Germany to present the foundations and principles of a Marxist aesthetic."[43] Wittfogel, who in the twenties had written a number of plays performed by Piscator and others, developed a sophisticated, Hegelian aesthetic, which anticipated many of Lukács's later positions. It is a further mark of his isolation from his Institut colleagues that it seems to have had no impact whatsoever on Lowenthal, Adorno, or Benjamin, the major aestheticians of the Frankfurt School. To Horkheimer and his colleagues, Wittfogel appeared as a student of Chinese society whose analyses of what he later called "hydraulic society" or "Oriental despotism" they encouraged, but as little else. His activism they found somewhat of an embarrassment; he was no less scornful of their political neutrality.

If Wittfogel cannot be characterized as a member of the Institut's inner circle, either before or after the emigration, the same can be said even more emphatically of Franz Borkenau. Born in 1900 in Vienna, Borkenau was active in the Communist Party and the Comintern from 1921 until his disillusionment in 1929. How he became part of the Institut's milieu has proved difficult to ascertain, although it is probable that he was one of Grünberg's protégés. His political involvement seems to have been as intense as Wittfogel's and his scholarly activity somewhat constrained. Most of his time at the Institut was spent probing the ideological changes that accompanied the rise of capitalism. The result was a volume in the Institut's series of publications released after some delay in 1934 as *The Transition from the Feudal to the Bourgeois World View.*[44] Although now almost completely forgotten, it has invited favorable comparison with Lucien Goldmann's more recent *The Hidden God.*[45] Borkenau's major argument was that the emergence of an abstract, mechanical philosophy, best exemplified in the work of Descartes, was intimately connected to the rise of abstract labor in the capitalist system of manufacturing. The connection was not to be understood as causal in one direction, but rather as a mutual reinforcement. Soon after, an article appeared in the *Zeitschrift für Sozialforschung* critical of Borkenau's central thesis, the only public acknowledgment of his isolation from the others.[46]

The author of the piece, Henryk Grossmann, although a figure in Institut affairs from 1926 until the 1940's, can himself be scarcely described as a major force in its intellectual development. Closer in age and intellectual inclinations to Grünberg than to some of the younger members, Grossmann was born in 1881 in Cracow, then part of Austrian Galicia, of a well-to-do family of Jewish mine owners. Before the war he studied economics at Cracow and Vienna, at the latter with Böhm-Bawerk, and wrote among other things a historical study of Austria's trade policies in the eighteenth century.[47] After serving as an artillery officer in the early years of the war, he held several posts with the Austrian administration in Lublin until the collapse of the Hapsburg Empire in 1918. Choosing to remain in the newly reconstituted Poland after the war, Grossmann was asked to supervise the first statistical survey of its national wealth and was appointed chief of the first Polish census in 1921. In the following year he became professor of economics at Warsaw, a post he held until the Pilsudski government's dislike of his socialism persuaded him to leave in 1925. Grünberg, who had known him in prewar Vienna, then invited him to Frankfurt, where an assistant professorship at the university and an assistantship at the Institut as aide to Grünberg were awaiting him.

An enormously learned man with a prodigious knowledge of economic history, Grossmann is remembered by many who knew him[48] as the embodiment of the Central European academic: proper, meticulous, and gentlemanly. He had, however, absorbed his Marxism in the years when Engels's and Kautsky's monistic materialistic views prevailed. He remained firmly committed to this interpretation and thus largely unsympathetic to the dialectical, neo-Hegelian materialism of the younger Institut members.

One ought not, however, overemphasize Grossmann's insensitivity to Horkheimer's work. On July 18, 1937, for example, he wrote to Paul Mattick that:

> In the last number of the *Zeitschrift* there appeared an especially successful essay of Horkheimer with a sharp, fundamental critique of new (logical) empiricism. Very worthy of being read, because in various socialist circles, Marxist materialism is confused with empiricism, because one shows sympathy for this empiricism as an allegedly antimetaphysical tendency.[49]

Like Wittfogel's and Borkenau's, Grossmann's politics were grounded in a relatively unreflective enthusiasm for the Soviet Union, but although he had been a member of the Polish Communist Party, it seems unlikely that he ever became an actual member of its German counterpart after coming to Frankfurt. Unlike them, he did not experience a later disillusionment with communism, even during his decade or so of exile in America, when many others with similar backgrounds repudiated their past.

Grossmann's quarrel with Borkenau in his *Zeitschrift* article on Borkenau's book was over the timing of the transition from the feudal to the bourgeois ideology — he put it one hundred fifty years before Borkenau — and the importance of technology in effecting the change — Leonardo rather than Descartes was his paradigmatic figure. Nonetheless, Grossmann never questioned the fundamental causal relationship between substructure and superstructure. In his article of 1935 in the *Zeitschrift*, he thus continued to express his allegiance to the orthodoxies of Marxism as he understood them; but this was not totally without variation, as demonstrated by his stress on the technological impetus to change, in opposition to Borkenau's emphasis on capitalist forms of production. A much more important expression of his adherence to the tenets of orthodox Marxism can be found in the series of lectures he gave at the Institut in 1926–1927, which were collected in 1929 as *The Law of Accumulation and Collapse in the Capitalist System*,[50] the first volume of the Institut's *Schriften.*

The question of capitalism's inevitable collapse from within had been the center of controversy in socialist circles, ever since Eduard Bernstein's articles in *Die Neue Zeit* in the 1890's had raised empirical objections to the prophecy of increasing proletarian pauperization. During the next three decades, Rosa Luxemburg, Heinrich Cunow, Otto Bauer, M. J. Tugan-Baranovski, Rudolf Hilferding, and others wrestled with the issue from a theoretical as well as an empirical vantage point. Fritz Sternberg's *Der Imperialismus*, which modified in a more pessimistic direction the Luxemburg thesis that imperialism was only a delaying factor in capitalism's demise, was the last major contribution before Grossmann's. *The Law of Accumulation and Collapse* begins with an excellent analysis of the previous literature on the question. Then, following an exposition of Marx's own views culled from his various writings, Grossmann attempted to build on Otto Bauer's mathematical models a deductive system to prove the correctness of Marx's predictions. The pauperization he pointed to was not that of the proletariat, but that of the capitalists, whose tendency to overaccumulation would produce an unavoidable decline in the profit rate over a certain fixed period of time. Although admitting countertendencies such as the more efficient use of capital, Grossmann confidently asserted that they might mitigate but not forestall the terminal crisis of the capitalist system. The full ramifications of his argument, whose predictions have obviously failed to come true, need not detain us here.[51] Let it be said, however, that the essentially quietistic implications of his thesis, similar to those of all Marxist interpretations that stress objective forces over subjective revolutionary *praxis,* were not lost on some of his contemporaries.[52]

Pollock, the other leading economist in the Institut, was quick to challenge Grossmann on other grounds. Stressing the inadequacy of Marx's concept of productive labor because of its neglect of non-manual labor, Pollock pointed to the service industries,[53] which were becoming increasingly important in the twentieth century. Surplus value might be extracted from workers in these industries as well as from those producing commodities, he argued, which would prolong the life of the system. Grossmann's stand continued basically unchanged, however, and he and Pollock remained at odds on economic questions until Grossmann left the Institut after the Second World War. Carefully read between the lines, Pollock's *Experiments in Economic Planning in the Soviet Union (1917–1927)*,[54] the second volume of the Institut's *Schriften*, gives further evidence of the dispute.

Pollock was invited to the Soviet Union during its tenth anniversary celebrations by David Ryazanov, who had spent some time in Frankfurt in the early 1920's and who continued his relationship by contributing an occasional article to the Grünberg *Archiv*.[55] In the Soviet Union, although admired for his scholarly work as director of the Marx-Engels Institute, Ryazanov was regarded politically as a rather eccentric throwback to the days of pre-Bolshevik social democracy. Despite his frequent criticism of party policy,[56] he survived until Stalin sent him into exile with the Volga Germans a few years after Pollock's visit, a move that has been facetiously described as Stalin's only real "contribution" to Marxist scholarship. Through Ryazanov's friendship, Pollock was able to speak with members of the dwindling opposition within the Bolshevik Party during his trip, in addition to his actual field studies of Soviet planning. The impressions he brought back to Frankfurt after several months were thus not entirely favorable. His book carefully avoided commenting on the political consequences of the Revolution and the forced collectivizations of the 1920's. On the central question he treated — the transition from a market to a planned economy — Pollock was less the enthusiastic supporter than the detached and prudent analyst unwilling to pass judgments prematurely. Here, too, he and Grossmann had cause for disagreement.

Nevertheless, it would be wrong to characterize the general attitude of Institut members in 1927 towards the Soviet experiment as closer to Pollock's skepticism than to Grossmann's enthusiasm. Wittfogel remained as firm as ever in his support, Borkenau had not yet reached his decision to repudiate the Party, and even Horkheimer retained an optimistic hope that humanist socialism might yet be realized in post-Lenin Russia. One of the aphorisms published in *Dämmerung* a few years later expresses Horkheimer's feelings during this period:

> He who has eyes for the meaningless injustice of the imperialist world, which in no way is to be explained by technical impotence, will regard the events in Russia as the progressive, painful attempt to overcome this injustice, or he will at least question with a beating heart whether this attempt still persists. If appearances speak against it, he clings to the hope the way a

cancer victim does to the questionable news that a cure for cancer has probably been found.[57]

Heated *sub rosa* discussions of Pollock's findings did take place, but never broke into print. In fact, after his book was published in 1929, the Institut maintained an almost complete official silence about events in the USSR, broken only by an occasional survey of recent literature by Rudolf Schlesinger, who had been one of Grünberg's students in the twenties.[58] It was really not until a decade later, after the Moscow purge trials, that Horkheimer and the others, with the sole exception of the obdurate Grossmann, completely abandoned their hope for the Soviet Union. Even then, preoccupied with problems that will be discussed later, they never focused the attention of Critical Theory on the left-wing authoritarianism of Stalin's Russia. The lack of available data certainly was one reason, but one ought not to ignore the difficulties involved in a Marxist analysis, however heterodox, of communism's failures.

After all this is said, however, it should also be stressed that Critical Theory as it was articulated by certain members of the Institut contained important, implicit criticisms of the Soviet ideological justification for its actions. Although most of the figures in the Institut's early history already mentioned — Grünberg, Weil, Sorge, Borkenau, Wittfogel, and Grossmann — were unconcerned with the reexamination of the foundations of Marxism to which Horkheimer was becoming increasingly devoted, he was not entirely without allies. Pollock, although primarily interested in economics, had studied philosophy with Cornelius and shared his friend's rejection of orthodox Marxism. Increasingly caught up in the administrative affairs of the Institut after Grünberg suffered a stroke in late 1927, Pollock was nevertheless able to add his voice to Horkheimer's in the Institut's seminars. In the late 1920's he was joined by two younger intellectuals who were to have an increasingly important influence in subsequent years, Leo Lowenthal and Theodor Wiesengrund-Adorno (who was known solely by his mother's name, Adorno, after the emigration).

Lowenthal, born the son of a Jewish doctor in 1900 in Frankfurt, served like the others in the war before embarking on an academic career. At Frankfurt, Heidelberg, and Giessen, he studied literature, history, philosophy, and sociology, receiving his doctorate in philosophy with a thesis on Franz von Baader at Frankfurt in 1923. At the university, he moved in the same radical student circles as Horkheimer, Pollock, and Weil, who had been a friend in secondary school. He had ties as well to the group of Jewish intellectuals surrounding the charismatic Rabbi Nehemiah A. Nobel,[59] which included such figures as Martin Buber, Franz Rosenzweig, Siegfried Kracauer, and Ernst Simon. It was as a member of this latter group, which gave rise to the famed Freies Jüdisches Lehrhaus (Free Jewish House of Learning) in 1920, that Lowenthal came in contact again with a friend from his student days, Erich Fromm, who was later to join the Institut. Lowenthal's own entrance into Institut affairs occurred in 1926, although outside interests limited his involvement. He continued to teach in the Prussian secondary school system and served as artistic adviser to the Volksbühne (People's Stage), a large left-wing and liberal organization. Throughout the late 1920's he wrote critical articles on aesthetic and cultural matters for a number of journals, most prominently the Volksbühne's, and continued to contribute historical pieces on the Jewish philosophy of religion to a variety of periodicals. In addition, he acquired editorial experience that proved useful when the *Zeitschrift für Sozialforschung* replaced *Grünbergs Archiv* as the Institut's organ.

It was as a sociologist of literature and student of popular culture that Lowenthal contributed most to the Institut after he became a full-time member in 1930 (his official title was initially *Hauptassistent* — first assistant — which only Grossmann shared). If it can be said that in the early years of its history the Institut concerned itself primarily with an analysis of bourgeois society's socio-economic substructure, in the years after 1930 its prime interest lay in its cultural superstructure. Indeed, as we shall see, the traditional Marxist formula regarding the relationship between the two was called into question by Critical Theory. Although contributing to the changed emphasis, Lowenthal was less responsible for the theoretical shift than the other important addition to the Institut's circle in the late twenties, Theodor Wiesengrund-Adorno.

Next to Horkheimer, Adorno, as we shall henceforth refer to him, became the man most closely identified with the fortunes of the Institut, which he officially joined in 1938. In the pre-emigration period, however, his energies, always enormous, were divided among a number of different projects, some of which kept him away from Frankfurt. Even after his departure from Europe, when the Institut became the dominant institutional framework within which he worked, Adorno did not confine himself to any one discipline. During his years in secondary school he had been befriended by Siegfried Kracauer, some fourteen years his elder.[60] For over a year he regularly spent Saturday afternoons with Kracauer studying Kant's *Critique of Pure Reason*, lessons he would recall as far more valuable than those he received in his formal university education. Kracauer's approach combined an interest in the ideas themselves with a keen sociology of knowledge. His distrust of closed systems and his stress on the particular as opposed to the universal made a significant impression on his young friend. So too did Kracauer's innovative explorations of such cultural phenomena as the film, which combined philosophical and sociological insights in a way that had little precedent. In later years, both in Germany and in America after both men emigrated, their friendship remained firm. To anyone familiar with Kracauer's celebrated *From Caligari to Hitler*[61] the similarity between his work and certain of Adorno's which will be described later, is strikingly obvious.

However, the young Adorno was interested in more than intellectual pursuits. Like Horkheimer, he combined a rigorous philosophical mind with a sensibility more aesthetic than scientific. Whereas Horkheimer's artistic inclinations led him towards literature and a series of unpublished novels, Adorno was more deeply drawn to music, a reflection of the highly musical environment in which he had been immersed from birth. The youngest of the Frankfurt School's luminaries, Adorno was born in 1903 in Frankfurt. His father was a successful assimilated Jewish wine merchant, from whom he inherited a taste for the finer things in life, but little interest in commerce. His mother seems to have had a more profound effect on his ultimate interests. The daughter of a German singer and a French army officer (whose Corsican and originally Genoese ancestry accounts for the Italian name Adorno), she pursued a highly successful singing career until her marriage. Her unmarried sister, who lived in the Wiesengrund household, was a concert pianist of considerable accomplishment who played for the famous singer Adelina Patti. With their encouragement the young "Teddie" took up the piano and studied composition at an early age, under the tutelage of Bernhard Sekles.

Frankfurt, however, offered little beyond traditional musical training, and Adorno was anxious to immerse himself in the more innovative music issuing at that time from Vienna. In the spring or summer of 1924 he met Alban Berg at the Frankfurt Festival of the Universal German Music Society and was captivated by three fragments from his yet unperformed opera, *Wozzeck*.[62] He immediately decided to follow Berg to Vienna and become his student. Delayed only by his university studies in Frankfurt, he arrived in the Austrian capital in January, 1925. The Vienna to which he moved was less the city of Otto Bauer and Karl Renner, Rudolf Hilferding and Max Adler (the milieu Grünberg had left to come to Frankfurt) than the apolitical but culturally radical Vienna of Karl Kraus and the Schönberg circle. Once there, Adorno persuaded Berg to take him on as a student of composition twice a week and got Eduard Steuermann to instruct him in piano technique. His own compositions seem to have been influenced by Schönberg's experiments in atonality, but not by his later twelve-tone system.[63] In addition to his training Adorno managed to write frequently for a number of avant-garde journals, including *Anbruch*, whose editorship he assumed in 1928, the year he moved back to Frankfurt. He remained at its helm until 1931, despite his renewed academic responsibilities.

Adorno's three years in Vienna were much more than an interlude in his scholarly career. Arthur Koestler, who chanced to be in the same pension with him after his arrival in 1925, remembered Adorno as "a shy, distraught and esoteric young man with a subtle charm I was too callow to discern." [64] To the equally intense but not as highly cultivated Koestler, Adorno presented a figure of magisterial condescension. Even his teacher Berg found Adorno's uncompromising intellectuality a bit disconcerting. As Adorno later admitted, "my own philosophical ballast fell for Berg at times under the category of what he called a fad. . . . I was certainly at that time brutishly serious and that could get on the nerves of a mature artist." [65] His three years in Vienna seem to have eradicated much of his shyness, but new confidence did not mean a significant lessening of his high seriousness or his allegiance to the most demanding of cultural forms. If anything, his frequent attendance at readings by Karl Kraus, that most unrelenting upholder of cultural standards, and his participation in the arcane musical discussions of the Viennese avant-garde only reinforced his predisposition in that direction. Never during the remainder of his life would Adorno abandon his cultural elitism.

In another way as well, the Vienna years were significant in his development. Many years later Adorno would admit that one of the attractions of the Schönberg circle had been its exclusive, coterie-like quality, which reminded him of the circle around Stefan George in Germany.[66] One of his disappointments during his three years in Austria was the dissolution of the circle's unity, which followed after Schönberg's new wife isolated him from his disciples. If this had not happened, it can at least be conjectured, Adorno might not have chosen to return to Frankfurt. Once there, of course, the same cliquish qualities drew him into the orbit of Horkheimer and the younger members of the Institut.

Adorno had known Horkheimer since 1922, when they were together in a seminar on Husserl directed by Hans Cornelius. Both men also studied under the Gestalt psychologist Gelb. In 1924

Adorno had written his doctorate for Cornelius on Husserl's phenomenology.[67] When he returned from Vienna, however, Cornelius had retired and had been replaced in the chair of philosophy by Paul Tillich,[68] after a short interlude during which Max Scheler had held the position. Tillich was a close friend of Horkheimer, Lowenthal, and Pollock, belonging with them to a regular discussion group that included Karl Mannheim, Kurt Riezler, Adolph Löwe, and Karl Mennicke. The *Kränzchen,* as it was called — an old-fashioned word which means both a small garland and an intimate gathering — was to continue in New York for several years, after most of its members were forced to emigrate. Adorno, when he returned to Frankfurt, was welcomed into its company. With Tillich's help he became a *Privatdozent* in 1931, writing a study of Kierkegaard's aesthetics as his *Habilitationsschrift.*[69]

By this time the Institut had undergone significant changes. Grünberg's health after his stroke in 1927 had not appreciably improved, and in 1929, in his sixty-ninth year, he decided to step down as director. He was to live on until 1940, but without any further role in Institut affairs. The three original members of the group were now old enough to be considered for a professorship at the university, the prerequisite for the directorship written into the Institut's charter. Pollock, who had served as interim head of the Institut in all but name before Grünberg came and after Grünberg's illness, was satisfied to remain occupied with administrative affairs. Weil, as noted earlier, had remained a *Privatgelehrter* (private scholar) without being "habilitated" as *Privatdozent* or "*berufen*" as professor.[70] Although continuing to guide the Institut's financial affairs and occasionally contributing an article to *Grünbergs Archiv*,[71] his interests turned elsewhere. In 1929 he left the Institut to move to Berlin, where he worked with two publishing houses, the left-wing Malik Verlag and the more scholarly Soziologische Verlagsanstalt, as well as contributing to the radical Piscator Theater. In 1930 he sailed from Germany for Argentina to tend to the family business, of which, as the oldest of Hermann Weil's two children, he was made the primary owner after his father's death in 1927, a responsibility he very reluctantly assumed. In any event, from 1923 Weil had not been at the center of the Institut's creative work, drawn as he was more to practical than theoretical questions. In later years he would sporadically return to the Institut and faithfully continue to help it financially, but he was never really a prime candidate for its leadership, nor did he intend to be.

Horkheimer was therefore the clear choice to succeed Grünberg. Although he had not been a dominating presence at the Institut during its first few years, his star clearly rose during the interim directorship of his friend Pollock. In 1929, with the support of Tillich and other members of the philosophy department, a new chair of "social philosophy" was established for Horkheimer, the first of its kind at a German university. Weil had convinced the Education Ministry to convert Grünberg's chair in political science, which his father had endowed, to its new purpose. As part of the bargain he promised to contribute to another chair in economics, which Adolph Löwe, a childhood friend of Horkheimer, left Kiel to fill. *The Origins of the Bourgeois Philosophy of History*,[72] a study of Machiavelli, Hobbes, Vico, and other early bourgeois philosophers of history, served as Horkheimer's scholarly credentials for his new position. With the accession of Horkheimer, then only thirty-five, to its directorship in July, 1930, the Institut für Sozialforschung entered its period of greatest productivity, all the more impressive when seen in the context of the emigration and cultural disorientation that soon followed.

In January of 1931, Horkheimer was officially installed in his new post. At the opening ceremonies, he spoke on "The Current Condition of Social Philosophy and the Task of an Institute of Social Research." [73] The differences between his approach and that of his predecessor were immediately apparent. Instead of simply labeling himself a good Marxist, Horkheimer turned to the history of social philosophy to put its current situation in perspective. Beginning with the grounding of social theory in the individual, which had at first characterized classical German idealism, he traced its course through Hegel's sacrifice of the individual to the state and the subsequent breakdown of the faith in an objective totality, which Schopenhauer expressed. He then turned to more recent social theorists, like the neo-Kantians of the Marburg school and the advocates of social totalism like Othmar Spann, all of whom, he argued, had attempted to overcome the sense of loss accompanying the breakdown of the classical synthesis. Scheler, Hartmann, and Heidegger, he added, shared this yearning for a return to the comfort of meaningful unities. Social philosophy, as Horkheimer saw it, would not be a single *Wissenschaft* (science) in search of immutable truth. Rather, it was to be understood as a materialist theory enriched and supplemented by empirical work, in the same way that natural philosophy was dialectically related to individual scientific disciplines. The Institut would therefore continue to diversify its energies without losing sight of its interdisciplinary, synthetic goals. To this end Horkheimer supported the retention of Grünberg's noncollegial "dictatorship of the director."

In concluding his remarks, Horkheimer outlined the first task of the Institut under his leadership: a study of workers' and employees' attitudes towards a variety of issues in Germany and the rest of developed Europe. Its methods were to include the use of public statistics and questionnaires backed up by sociological, psychological, and economic interpretation of the data. To help collect materials, he announced, the Institut had accepted the offer of Albert Thomas, the director of the International Labor Organization, to establish a branch office of the Institut in Geneva. This proved to be the first of several such branches established outside Germany in the ensuing years. The decision to act on Thomas's offer was influenced by more than the desire to collect data, for the ominous political scene in Germany gave indications that exile might be a future necessity. Pollock was thus given the task of setting up a permanent office in Geneva; Kurt Mandelbaum, his assistant, went with him. Once the office was firmly established in 1931, the lion's share of the Institut's endowment was quietly transferred to a company in a neutral country, Holland.

Other changes followed Horkheimer's elevation to the directorship. With its guiding spirit incapacitated, *Grünbergs Archiv* ceased publication, twenty years and fifteen volumes after its initial appearance in 1910. The *Archiv* had served as a vehicle for a variety of different viewpoints both within and outside the Institut, still reflecting in part Grünberg's roots in the world of Austro-Marxism. The need for a journal more exclusively the voice of the Institut was felt to be pressing. Horkheimer, whose preference for conciseness was expressed in the large number of aphorisms he wrote during this period, disliked the mammoth tomes so characteristic of German scholarship. Although a third volume of the Institut's publications series, Wittfogel's *Economy and Society in China*,[74] appeared in 1931, the emphasis was now shifted to the essay. It was through the essays that appeared in the *Zeitschrift für Sozialforschung*, some almost monographic in length, that the Institut presented most of its work to the world in the next decade. Exhaustively evaluated and criticized by the other members of the Institut before they appeared, many articles were almost as much collective productions as individual works. The *Zeitschrift*, in Leo Lowenthal's words, was "less a forum for different viewpoints than a platform for the Institut's convictions,"[75] even though other authors continued to contribute occasional articles. Editorial decisions were ultimately Horkheimer's, although Lowenthal, drawing on his years of relevant experience, served as managing editor and was fully responsible for the extensive review section. One of Lowenthal's first tasks was a trip by plane to

Leopold von Wiese, the doyen of German sociologists, to assure him that the *Zeitschrift* would not compete with his own *Kölner Vierteljahrshefte für Soziologie (Cologne Quarterly of Sociology).*

As Horkheimer explained in the foreword to the first issue,[76] *Sozialforschung* was not the same as the sociology practiced by von Wiese and other more traditional German academicians. Following Gerlach and Grünberg, Horkheimer stressed the synoptic, interdisciplinary nature of the Institut's work. He particularly stressed the role of social psychology in bridging the gap between individual and society. In the first article, which followed, "Observations on Science and Crisis,"[77] he developed the connection between the current splintering of knowledge and the social conditions that helped produce it. A global economic structure both monopolistic and anarchic, he argued, had promoted a confused state of knowledge. Only by overcoming the fetishistic grounding of scientific knowledge in pure consciousness, and by recognizing the concrete historical circumstances that conditioned all thought, could the present crisis be surmounted. Science must not ignore its own social role, for only by becoming conscious of its function in the present critical situation could it contribute to the forces that would bring about the necessary changes.

The contributions to the *Zeitschrift*'s first issue reflected the diversity of *Sozialforschung.* Grossmann wrote once again on Marx and the problem of the collapse of capitalism.[78] Pollock discussed the Depression and the possibilities for a planned economy within a capitalist framework.[79] Lowenthal outlined the tasks of a sociology of literature, and Adorno did the same, in the first of two articles, for music.[80] The remaining two essays dealt with the psychological dimension of social research: one by Horkheimer himself on "History and Psychology,"[81] the second by a new member of the Institut, Erich Fromm.[82] (A full treatment of the Institut's integration of psychoanalysis and its Hegelianized Marxism appears in Chapter 3.) Lowenthal, who had been a friend of Fromm's since 1918, introduced him as one of three psychoanalysts brought into the Institut's circle in the early thirties. The others were Karl Landauer, the director of the Frankfurt Psychoanalytic Institute, which was associated with the Institut, and Heinrich Meng. Landauer's contributions to the *Zeitschrift* were restricted to the review section. (In the first issue he was in very good company: among the other reviewers were Alexandre Koyré, Kurt Lewin, Karl Korsch, and Wilhelm Reich.) Meng, although more interested in mental hygiene than social psychology, helped organize seminars and contributed reviews on topics related to the Institut's interests.

With the introduction of psychoanalysis to the Institut, the Grünberg era was clearly over. In 1932 the publication of a *Festschrift*,[83] collected on the occasion of Grünberg's seventieth birthday the previous year, gave further evidence of the transition. Pollock, Horkheimer, Wittfogel, and Grossmann all contributed articles, but most of the pieces were by older friends from Grünberg's Viennese days, such as Max Beer and Max Adler. The change this symbolized was given further impetus by the acceptance of a new member in late 1932, Herbert Marcuse, who was to become one of the principal architects of Critical Theory.

Marcuse was born in 1898 in Berlin, into a family of prosperous assimilated Jews, like most of the others. After completing his military service in the war, he briefly became involved in politics in a Soldiers' Council in Berlin. In 1919 he quit the Social Democratic Party, which he had joined two years earlier, in protest against its betrayal of the proletariat. After the subsequent failure of the German revolution, he left politics altogether to study philosophy at Berlin and Freiburg, receiving his doctorate at the latter university in 1923 with a dissertation on the *Künstlerroman* (novels in which artists played key roles). For the next six years he tried his hand at book selling and publishing in Berlin. In 1929 he returned to Freiburg, where he studied with Husserl and Heidegger, both of whom had a considerable impact on his thought. During this period Marcuse broke into print with a number of articles in Maximilian Beck's *Philosophische Hefte* and Rudolf Hilferding's *Die Gesellschaft.* His first book, *Hegel's Ontology and the Foundation of a Theory of Historicity*,[84] appeared in 1932, bearing the marks of his mentor Heidegger, for whom it had been prepared as a *Habilitationsschrift.* Before Heidegger could accept Marcuse as an assistant, however, their relations became strained; the political differences between the Marxist-oriented student and the increasingly right-wing teacher were doubtless part of the cause. Without a prospect for a job at Freiburg, Marcuse left that city in 1932. The *Kurator* of the University of Frankfurt, Kurt Riezler, having been asked by Husserl to intercede for Marcuse, recommended him to Horkheimer.

In the second issue of the *Zeitschrift* Adorno reviewed *Hegel's Ontology* and found its movement away from Heidegger promising. Marcuse, he wrote, was tending away from " 'The Meaning of Being' to an openness to being-in-the-world *(Seienden),* from fundamental ontology to philosophy of history, from historicity *(Geschichtlichkeit)* to history." [85] Although Adorno felt that there was some ground still to be covered before Marcuse cast off Heidegger's thrall entirely, the chance for a successful integration of his approach to philosophy with that of the Institut seemed favorable. Horkheimer concurred, and so in 1933 Marcuse was added to those in the Institut who were committed to a dialectical rather than a mechanical understanding of Marxism. He was immediately assigned to the Geneva office.

With the Nazi assumption of power on January 30, 1933, the future of an avowedly Marxist organization, staffed almost exclusively by men of Jewish descent — at least by Nazi standards — was obviously bleak. Horkheimer had spent most of 1932 in Geneva, where he was ill with diphtheria. Shortly before Hitler came to power he returned to Frankfurt, moving with his wife from their home in the suburb of Kronberg to a hotel near the Frankfurt railroad station. During February, the last month of the winter semester, he suspended his lectures on logic to speak on the question of freedom, which was indeed becoming more questionable with each passing day. In March he slipped across the border to Switzerland, just as the Institut was being closed down for "tendencies hostile to the state." The greater part of the Institut library in the building on the Victoria-Allee, then numbering over sixty thousand volumes, was seized by the government; the transfer of the endowment two years earlier prevented a similar confiscation of the Institut's financial resources. On April 13 Horkheimer had the honor of being among the first faculty members to be formally dismissed from Frankfurt, along with Paul Tillich, Karl Mannheim, and Hugo Sinzheimer.[86]

By then all of the Institut's official staff had left Frankfurt. The one exception was Wittfogel, who returned to Germany from Switzerland and was thrown into a concentration camp in March because of his political activities. His second wife, Olga Lang (originally Olga Joffé), herself later to become an expert on Chinese affairs and an assistant at the Institut, worked to secure his release, as did such friends as R. H. Tawney in England and Karl Haushofer in Germany. Wittfogel's freedom was finally granted in November, 1933, and he was permitted to emigrate to England. Shortly thereafter, he joined the others in America. Adorno, whose politics were not as controversial as Wittfogel's, maintained a residence in Germany, although he spent most of the next four years in England, studying at Merton College, Oxford. Grossmann found refuge in Paris for three years and went to England for one more, rather unhappy, year in 1937, before finally coming to the United States. Lowenthal remained in Frankfurt only until March 2, when he followed Marcuse, Horkheimer, and other Institut figures to Geneva, the last to depart before the Institut was closed. Pollock was in effect already in exile when the Nazis came to power, although he was unaware that it was to last for almost two decades and extend to two continents.

In February of 1933 the Geneva branch was incorporated with a twenty-one member board [87] as the administrative center of the Institut. In recognition of its European character it took the name of the Société Internationale de Recherches Sociales (International Society of Social Research), with Horkheimer and Pollock as its two "presidents"; Lowenthal, Fromm, and Sternheim were named their successors the following year.[88] Not only was the "Frankfurt School" now Swiss, but also French and English, as offers of help from friends in Paris and London led to the founding of small branches in those cities in 1933. Celestin Bouglé, a former student of Durkheim and director of the Ecole Normale Supérieure's Centre de Documentation since 1920, suggested to Horkheimer that some space might be found for the Institut in his offices on the Rue d'Ulm. Although a Proudhonist politically (he was an adherent of the Radical Socialist Party) and thus not sympathetic to the Marxist cast of the Institut's work, Bouglé was willing to forget politics in considering the Institut's plight. Maurice Halbwachs, another prominent Durkheimian at the University of Strasbourg, and Georges Scelle, who taught law in Paris when not in the Hague as French advocate at the International Court, joined Bouglé as cosponsors of the move. Further support came from Henri Bergson, who had been impressed with the Institut's work. In London a similar proposal was made by Alexander Farquharson, the editor of the *Sociological Review*, who was able to provide a few rooms in Le Play House. Sidney Webb, R. H. Tawney, Morris Ginsberg, and Harold Laski all added their voices to Farquharson's, and a small office was established that lasted until lack of funds forced its closing in 1936.

In the meantime, the *Zeitschrift*'s Leipzig publisher, C. L. Hirschfeld, informed Horkheimer that it could no longer risk continuing publication. Bouglé suggested as a replacement the Librairie Félix Alcan in Paris. This proved acceptable, and a connection was begun that lasted until 1940, when the Nazis once again acquired the power to intimidate a publisher of the *Zeitschrift.*

With the first issue of the *Zeitschrift* to appear in Paris in September, 1933, the Institut's initial German period was conclusively over. In the brief decade since its founding, it had gathered together a group of young intellectuals with diverse talents willing to coordinate them in the service of social research as the Institut conceived it. The first Frankfurt years were dominated by Grünberg's views, as described earlier, but under his direction the Institut gained structural solidarity and a foothold in Weimar's intellectual life. Although concentrating on research, it helped train students of the caliber of Paul Baran,[89] who in 1930 worked on a projected second volume of Pollock's study of the Soviet economy. Hans Gerth, Gladys Meyer, and Josef Dünner were other students during the pre-emigration years who later made an impact on American social science. (Dünner, it might be noted in passing, wrote a *roman à clef* in 1937, entitled *If I Forget Thee . . .* , in which Institut figures appear under pseudonyms.)[90] In addition, all Institut members participated actively in the discussions about the future of socialism, which attracted such Frankfurt luminaries as Henrik de Man and Paul Tillich. The independence provided by Hermann Weil's generosity allowed the Institut to remain unencumbered by political or academic obligations, even after his death in 1927. It also guaranteed the continuation of its identity in exile, at a time when other German refugee scholars were put through the strain of reestablishing themselves in an alien world without financial backing. An additional $100,000 contributed by Felix Weil, after he rejoined the Institut in New York in 1935, helped keep it financially secure through the thirties.

The sense of a shared fate and common purpose that strikes the observer as one of the Institut's chief characteristics — especially after Horkheimer became director — was transferable to the Institut's new homes partly because of its financial good fortune. It had been the intent of the founding members to create a community of scholars whose solidarity would serve as a microcosmic foretaste of the brotherly society of the future. The *Zeitschrift*, as mentioned earlier, helped cement the sense of group identity; and the common experience of forced exile and regrouping abroad added considerably to this feeling. Within the Institut itself, a still smaller group had coalesced around Horkheimer, consisting of Pollock, Lowenthal, Adorno, Marcuse, and Fromm. It is really their work, rooted in the central tradition of European philosophy, open to contemporary empirical techniques, and addressed to current social questions, that formed the core of the Institut's achievement.

If one seeks a common thread running through individual biographies of the inner circle, the one that immediately comes to mind is their birth into families of middle or upper-middle class Jews (in Adorno's case, only one parent was Jewish). Although this is not the place to launch a full-scale discussion of the Jewish radical in the Weimar Republic, a few observations ought to be made. As noted earlier, one of the arguments employed by Felix Weil and Pollock to persuade the elder Weil to endow the Institut had been the need to study anti-Semitism in Germany. It was not, however, until the 1940's that this task was actually begun. If one were to characterize the Institut's general attitude towards the "Jewish question," it would have to be seen as similar to that expressed by another radical Jew almost a century before, Karl Marx. In both cases the religious or ethnic issue was clearly subordinated to the social. In *Dämmerung*, Horkheimer attacked Jewish capitalists who were against anti-Semitism simply because it posed an economic threat. "The readiness to sacrifice life and property for belief," he wrote, "is left behind with the material basis of the ghetto. With the bourgeois Jew, the hierarchy of goods is neither Jewish nor Christian, but bourgeois. . . . The Jewish revolutionary, like the 'aryan,' risks his own life for the freedom of mankind." [91] Further evidence of their de-emphasis of strictly Jewish as opposed to social oppression was their indifference to Zionism as a solution to the plight of the Jews.[92]

In fact, the members of the Institut were anxious to deny any significance at all to their ethnic roots, a position that has not been eroded with time in most of their cases. Weil, for example, in his extensive correspondence with this author, has heatedly rejected any suggestion that Jewishness — defined religiously, ethnically, or culturally — had any influence whatsoever on the selection of Institut members or the development of their ideas. He has also insisted that the assimilation of Jews in Weimar had gone so far that "discrimination against Jews had retreated completely to the 'social club level,' " [93] with the result that the Institut's neglect of the "Jewish question" was justified by its practical disappearance. That the Institut was founded one year after the foreign minister of Germany, Walter Rathenau, was assassinated largely because of his ethnic roots seems to have had no personal impact on the "assimilated" Jews connected with the Institut. Wittfogel, one of its gentile members, has confirmed this general blindness, arguing that he was one of the few exceptions who recognized the precariousness of the Jews' position, even of those who were most assimilated.[94] What strikes the current observer is the intensity with which many of the Institut's members denied, and in some cases still deny, any meaning at all to their Jewish identities. Assimilated German Jews, as has often been noted, were surprised by the ease with which German society accepted the anti-Semitic measures of the Nazis. Self-delusions on this score persisted in some cases as late as the war. Even so hardheaded a realist as Franz Neumann could write in *Behemoth* that "the German people are the least anti-Semitic of all." [95] His appraisal of the situation seems to have been supported by almost all of his Institut colleagues.

In the face of this vehement rejection of the meaningfulness of Jewishness in their backgrounds, one can only look for indirect ways in which it might have played a role. Certainly the overt impact of Judaism as a system of belief seems to have been negligible. The two possible exceptions to this were Leo Lowenthal and Erich Fromm, both of whom had been active in the group comprising the Frankfurt Lehrhaus. Lowenthal had been one of the contributors to the *Festschrift* dedicated to Rabbi Nobel in 1921, writing on the demonic in religion.[96] He continued to find his way into the pages of such publications as the *Frankfurter Israelitisches Gemeindeblatt* as late as 1930, although by then he had left his truly religious period behind. Still, one would be hard pressed at any time to find echoes of Lowenthal's interest in Judaism in the work he did for the Institut. Fromm, on the other hand, has often been characterized as retaining secular versions of Jewish themes in his work, even after he left Orthodoxy in the mid-twenties.[97] Frequent comparisons have been made between his work and other members of the Lehrhaus group, particularly Martin Buber. What these similarities were will be made clearer in Chapter 3. Only Lowenthal and Fromm (along with Walter Benjamin, who was to write for the *Zeitschrift* in later years) ever evinced any real interest in Jewish theological issues. To the others Judaism was a closed book.

If the manifest intellectual content of Judaism played no role in the thinking of most of the Institut's members, one has to turn to more broadly sociological or cultural explanations. In his recent study of the predominantly Jewish left-wing literati who wrote for the Berlin journal *Die Weltbühne*, Istvan Deak has had to ask similar questions to those that arise in a study of the Frankfurt School. He has correctly noted that the high percentage of Jews on Weimar's left — the *Weltbühne* circle was much larger than the Institut's, but the same correlation still held — was no mere coincidence. It was due, he wrote, "to a specific development: their recognition of the fact that business, artistic, or scientific careers do not help solve the Jewish problem, and that Weimar Germany had to undergo dire transformation if German anti-Semitism was to end." [98] However, the members of the Frankfurt School deny ever having had such a recognition. "All of us," Pollock has written, "up to the last years before Hitler, had no feeling of insecurity originating from our ethnic descent. Unless we were ready to undergo baptism, certain positions in public service and business were closed to us, but that never bothered us. And under the Weimar republic many of these barriers had been moved away." [99] Their radicalism is thus difficult to attribute to a conscious awareness of socialism as the only solution to a keenly felt sense of ethnic oppression.

And yet, for all their claims to total assimilation and assertions about the lack of discrimination in Weimar, one cannot avoid a sense of their protesting too much. If in fact Weimar was an environment in which anti-Semitism was on the wane, which itself seems questionable, it must be remembered that the Institut's members all grew up before the First World War in a very different Germany. Even the most assimilated Jews in Wilhelmian Germany must have felt somewhat apart from their gentile counterparts, and coming to maturity in this atmosphere must surely have left its mark. The sense of role-playing that the Jew eager to forget his origins must have experienced could only have left a residue of bitterness, which might easily feed a radical critique of the society as a whole. This is not to say that the Institut's program can be solely, or even predominantly, attributed to its members' ethnic roots, but merely to argue that to ignore them entirely is to lose sight of one contributing factor.

Once in America, it might be noted parenthetically, the Institut's members became more sensitive to the Jewish question. Adorno, for example, was asked by Pollock to drop the Wiesengrund from his name, because there were too many Jewish-sounding names on the Institut's roster.[100] Paul Massing, one of the few gentiles in their midst, has said that his non-Jewishness was a slight but still significant factor in keeping him apart from his colleagues.[101] Assimilation was paradoxically more difficult in America than it had been in pre-Nazi Germany, at least so many Institut members felt.

Besides the sociological explanation of the effect of their origins, there is a cultural one as well. Jürgen Habermas has recently argued that a striking resemblance exists between certain strains in the Jewish cultural tradition and in that of German Idealism, whose roots have often been seen in Protestant Pietism.[102] One important similarity, which is especially crucial for an understanding of Critical Theory, is the old cabalistic idea that speech rather than pictures was the only way to approach God. The distance between Hebrew, the sacred language, and the profane speech of the Diaspora made its impact on Jews who were distrustful of the current universe of discourse. This, so Habermas has argued, parallels the idealist critique of empirical reality, which reached its height in Hegelian dialectics. Although one cannot draw a very exact line from the Frankfurt School's Jewish antecedents to its dialectical theory, perhaps some predisposition did exist. The same might be argued for its ready acceptance of psychoanalysis, which proved especially congenial to assimilated Jewish intellectuals. (This is not to say, of course, that

Freudianism was a "Jewish psychology," as the Nazis did, but merely to suggest a possible filiation.)

One other important factor must be mentioned. Within the German Jewish community itself, there often raged a struggle between fathers and sons over the content of Judaism and the future of the Jewish people. Sometimes this was resolved in peculiar ways. In her essay on Walter Benjamin, whose conflict with his father was particularly keen, Hannah Arendt has written: "As a rule these conflicts were resolved by the sons' laying claim to being geniuses, or, in the case of numerous Communists from well-to-do homes, to being devoted to the welfare of mankind — in any case, to aspiring to things higher than making money — and the fathers were more than willing to grant that this was a valid excuse for not making a living." [103] As in so many other ways, Benjamin was himself an exception to the rule, as his father refused to support him, but the others were not. Hermann Weil may have been a successful Argentine grain merchant interested more in profits than in revolution, but he was willing to support his son's radicalism with considerable generosity. Nor do Horkheimer's relations with his parents seem to have permanently suffered after the initial friction produced by his decision not to follow his father into manufacturing.[104] The one real period of estrangement that did occur between them followed Horkheimer's falling in love with his father's gentile secretary, eight years his elder. He married her in March, 1926, at about the same time that he began teaching at the university. As Pollock remembered it, "the frictions between Horkheimer and his parents were quite temporary. . . . After a few years of estrangement, there was complete reconciliation and Maidon Horkheimer was accepted with sincerest cordiality." [105] It was apparently much harder for his parents to get used to the idea that Horkheimer was marrying a gentile than that he was becoming a revolutionary.

In fact, one might argue that the strong ethical tone of Critical Theory was a product of the incorporation of the values likely to be espoused in a close-knit Jewish home. In any case, there is little to suggest that the Institut's members carried their rejection of the commercial mentality of their parents into outright personal rebellion. Despite the fervent expressions of solidarity with the proletariat that appeared throughout their work in the pre-emigration period, at no time did a member of the Institut affect the life-style of the working class.

Nowhere are their revolutionary sentiments so clearly articulated as in the work of "Heinrich Regius," the name Horkheimer borrowed from a seventeenth-century natural philosopher to put on the title page of the aphorisms he published in Zurich in the first year of exile. Yet it is in one of the pieces in *Dämmerung*, "A Fable of Consistency," that he implicitly justifies the combination of radical beliefs and a bourgeois standard of living. In the fable, two poor poets are invited to accept a considerable stipend by a tyrannical king who values their work. One is disturbed by the taint on the money. "You are inconsistent," the other answers. "If you so believe, you must continue to go hungry. He who feels one with the poor, must live like them." [106] Agreeing, the first poet rejects the king's offer and proceeds to starve. Shortly thereafter, the other becomes the court poet. Horkheimer finishes his "fairy tale" by cautioning: "Both drew the consequences, and both consequences favored the tyrant. With the general moral prescription of consistency, there seems one condition: it is friendlier to tyrants than to poor poets." [107] And so, the Institut's members may have been relentless in their hostility towards the capitalist system, but they never abandoned the life-style of the *haute bourgeoisie.* It would be easy to term this behavior elitist or "mandarin" — to give Grünberg's word a slightly different meaning — as some of the group's detractors have done. But it seems unlikely that the rejuvenation of Marxist theory to which they so heavily contributed would have been materially advanced by a decision to wear cloth caps.

It is, however, at least arguable that Critical Theory would have been enriched if the members of the Institut had been more intimately involved in practical politics. The example of Lukács, to be sure, suggests that there were pitfalls involved in too close an attachment to one faction or another. But on the other side of the ledger is the case of the Italian Marxist, Antonio Gramsci, whose political experience before his imprisonment by Mussolini in 1926 always served to give his theorizing a concrete quality, which the Frankfurt School's work sometimes lacked. In one sense the Institut's period of exile can be said to have begun before its actual expulsion by the Nazis. After the failure of the German revolution, its members, at least those around Horkheimer, were alienated from all political factions on the left. The SPD was treated with the scorn its craven capitulation before the status quo deserved — in fact, one might argue that the SPD's betrayal of the working class colored the Frankfurt School's subsequent distrust of all "moderate" solutions. The KPD was equally anathema, for its transparent dependence on Moscow and its theoretical bankruptcy. And the pathetic attempts of such left-wing intellectuals as Kurt Hiller and Carl von Ossietzky to transcend the differences between the two parties, or to offer a viable alternative, were rejected for the pipe dreams they quickly proved to be. The result was that the Frankfurt School chose the purity of its theory over the affiliation that a concrete attempt to realize it would have required. That this entailed disadvantages as well as advantages shall be seen in subsequent chapters.

The prudent transfer of the Institut's endowment to Holland in 1931 allowed the continuation of its work without much interruption. The first year in Geneva was a period of readjustment, but not stagnation. The project on the attitudes of workers and employees was not curtailed seriously. Andries Sternheim, a Dutch socialist who had ties to the labor movement, was recommended by someone in Albert Thomas's office to Horkheimer as a prospective member. In Geneva he was admitted as an assistant, and after Pollock's departure for the United States, he became the branch's director. Although of great help in collecting materials for the project, he contributed little to the theoretical work of the Institut, aside from a few contributions to the study of leisure in modern society.[108]

Hampered occasionally by the problems of adjustment to a new publisher, the *Zeitschrift* continued to appear regularly. New names were added to the roster of previous contributors. George Rusche wrote on the relationship between the labor market and criminal punishment,[109] anticipating a book he later published with Otto Kirchheimer's help under the auspices of the Institut. Kurt Mandelbaum (often under the names Kurt or Erich Baumann) and Gerhard Meyer added articles on economics to those written by Pollock and Grossmann.[110] Periodic contributions came from the Paris branch, which attracted such able assistants as Raymond Aron and Georges Friedmann. Paul Ludwig Landsberg, a philosopher for whom the Institut had high hopes that were later dashed by his murder by the Nazis, wrote on race ideology and pseudo-science.[111] American issues were dealt with by Julian Gumperz in a series of articles.[112] The "International" in the Institut's new title was thus clearly evident in the pages of the *Zeitschrift.*

It soon came to mean much more as the Institut began to look elsewhere for a new home. While appreciating its usefulness, Horkheimer and the others never considered the Geneva branch a permanent center of the Institut's affairs. In May, 1933, Grossmann had expressed an anxiety they all shared, when he wrote to Paul Mattick in America that "fascism also makes great progress in Switzerland and new dangers threaten our Institut there as well." [113] Pollock made a trip to London in February, 1934, to appraise the possibility of establishing the Institut in England; but intensive negotiations with Sir William Beveridge, director of the London School of Economics, and Farquharson and his colleagues at the Institute of Sociology convinced him of its unlikelihood. The limited opportunities in England for the refugee scholars who began to stream out of Germany in 1933 have been frequently noted.[114] Of those associated with the Institut, only Borkenau elected to make London his permanent home in exile. He was able to obtain a position teaching international politics in the adult education section of the University of London. A few years later he took time out to visit Spain during the Civil War, which confirmed his already strong dislike for communism and produced one of the classic studies of the war, *The Spanish Cockpit.*[115] By then, his connections with the Institut, except for one last essay in the *Studien über Autorität und Familie (Studies on Authority and Family)* in 1936,[116] had been severed.

In Paris, where the academic establishment was even more impenetrable than in England, the prospects seemed equally limited. Paul Honigsheim, who fled from Cologne and became head of the Institut's Paris branch, has described the cold reception that normally greeted emigrés to France:

> The typical French intellectual, who wanted security and a predictable future for himself and his family, found his way of life threatened by those damn German intellectuals, who did not spend their time drinking apéritifs with their friends but worked twice as hard as the Frenchman. They worked for the sake of God or, if they were not religious believers, for work's sake, which for a true German scholar is almost the same. Accordingly, in contrast to the sympathetic attitude in the United States, the French did not welcome the appointment of German scholars in their midst. Thus it took courage to work openly on behalf of German refugees.[117]

Bouglé, Halbwachs, and their colleagues, Honigsheim stresses, had that courage, but they were in a small minority; as a result, France was ruled out as a possible new home for the Institut's headquarters.

Despite the Institut's Marxist image, at no time was the thought of going eastward to Stalin's Russia seriously entertained, even by Grossmann, who made a short and unsuccessful journey to Moscow in the mid-thirties, or by Wittfogel. The only serious possibility left was America. Julian Gumperz was sent there in 1933 to explore the situation. Gumperz had been a student of Pollock's since 1929 and at one time a Communist Party member, although he later gave it all up, became a stockbroker, and wrote an anti-communist book in the forties;[118] he was born in America and thus was fluent in English. He returned from his trip with a favorable report, assuring Horkheimer and the others that the Institut's endowment, which still brought in about $30,000 a year, would be sufficient to guarantee survival in a country still mired in economic depression.

Over the years, the Institut had made several contacts with prominent figures in the American academic world, such as Charles Beard, Robert MacIver, Wesley Mitchell, Reinhold Niebuhr, and Robert Lynd, all of whom were at Columbia University. Thus when Horkheimer made his first trip to the United States in May, 1934, he was able to gain access to Columbia's patriarchal president, Nicholas Murray Butler. Much to his surprise, Butler offered the Institut affiliation with the university and a home in one of its buildings, at 429 West 117th Street. Horkheimer, fearing he had misunderstood Butler because of his limited command of English, wrote a four-page letter asking him to confirm and clarify his offer. Butler's response was a laconic "You have understood me perfectly!" [119] And so the International Institute for Social Research, as revolutionary and Marxist as it had appeared in Frankfurt in the twenties, came to settle in the center of the capitalist world, New York City. Marcuse came in July, Lowenthal in August, Pollock in September, and Wittfogel soon after. Fromm had been in the United States since 1932, when he came in response to an invitation to lecture by the Chicago Institute of Psychoanalysis. These men were among the first to arrive of that wave of Central European refugee intellectuals who so enriched American cultural life in the decades that followed.[120]

The transition was by no means without its difficulties. Still, in comparison with the members of Alvin Johnson's "university in exile" at the New School for Social Research, who had few or no financial resources to make their resettlement easy, the Institut's members were fortunate. In fact, the tensions that developed between the two refugee groups, although due in part to ideological differences,[121] were also clearly exacerbated by their contrasting financial situations. It should be added, however, that in later years the Institut maintained a strong sense of responsibility to less well-off refugees. When problems did exist for Institut members, they were those of language and cultural adjustment, which plague any immigrant, but not of finances. The most difficult intellectual adjustment, as we shall see later, involved coordinating the philosophically grounded social research practiced by the Institut with the rigorous antispeculative bias of American social science. The use of American empirical techniques that its members learned in exile was an important lesson brought back to Germany after the war, but these skills had not been acquired without considerable hesitancy.

In general, the Institut was not especially eager to jettison its past and become fully American. This reluctance can be gauged by the decision to continue using Félix Alcan as publisher even after leaving Europe. By resisting the entreaties of its new American colleagues to publish in America, the Institut felt that it could more easily retain German as the language of the *Zeitschrift.* Although articles occasionally appeared in English and French and summaries in those languages followed each German essay, the journal remained essentially German until the war. It was in fact the only periodical of its kind published in the language that Hitler was doing so much to debase. As such, the *Zeitschrift* was seen by Horkheimer and the others as a vital contribution to the preservation of the humanist tradition in German culture, which was threatened with extirpation. Indeed, one of the key elements in the Institut's self-image was this sense of being the last outpost of a waning culture. Keenly aware of the relation language bears to thought, its members were thus convinced that only by continuing to write in their native tongue could they resist the identification of Nazism with everything German. Although most of the German-speaking world had no way of obtaining copies, the Institut was willing to sacrifice an immediate audience for a future one, which indeed did materialize after the defeat of Hitler. The one regrettable by-product of this decision was the partial isolation from the American academic community that it unavoidably entailed. Although the Institut began giving lectures in the Extension Division at Columbia in 1936, and gradually developed a series of seminars on various topics,[122] its focus remained primarily on theory and research. Together once again in the security of its new home on Morningside Heights — of the inner circle, only Adorno remained abroad for several years more — the Institut was thus able to resume without much difficulty the work it had started in Europe.

Although sobered by the triumph of fascism in Germany, Horkheimer and the others were still somewhat optimistic about the future. "The twilight of capitalism," wrote "Heinrich Regius" in 1934, "need not initiate the night of humanity, which, to be sure, seems to threaten today." [123] An intensification of their explorations of the crisis of capitalism, the collapse of traditional liberalism, the rising authoritarian threat, and other, related topics seemed the best contribution they could make to the defeat of Nazism. As always, their work was grounded in a social philosophy whose articulation was the prime occupation of Horkheimer, Marcuse, and to a lesser extent, Adorno, during the 1930's. It was here that their reworking of traditional Marxism became crucial. It is thus to the genesis and development of Critical Theory that we now must turn.

II

The Genesis of Critical Theory

> Viewed from the heights of reason, all life looks like some malignant disease and the world like a madhouse.
>
> — GOETHE

> I mistrust all systematizers and I avoid them. The will to a system is a lack of integrity.
>
> — NIETZSCHE

At the very heart of Critical Theory was an aversion to closed philosophical systems. To present it as such would therefore distort its essentially open-ended, probing, unfinished quality. It was no accident that Horkheimer chose to articulate his ideas in essays and aphorisms rather than in the cumbersome tomes so characteristic of German philosophy. Although Adorno and Marcuse were less reluctant to speak through completed books, they too resisted the temptation to make those books into positive, systematic philosophical statements. Instead, Critical Theory, as its name implies, was expressed through a series of critiques of other thinkers and philosophical traditions. Its development was thus through dialogue, its genesis as dialectical as the method it purported to apply to social phenomena. Only by confronting it in its own terms, as a gadfly of other systems, can it be fully understood. What this chapter will attempt to do, therefore, is to present Critical Theory as it was first generated in the 1930's, through contrapuntal interaction both with other schools of thought and with a changing social reality.

To trace the origins of Critical Theory to their true source would require an extensive analysis of the intellectual ferment of the 1840's, perhaps the most extraordinary decade in nineteenth-century German intellectual history.[1] It was then that Hegel's successors first applied his philosophical insights to the social and political phenomena of Germany, which was setting out on a course of rapid modernization. The so-called Left Hegelians were of course soon eclipsed by the most talented of their number, Karl Marx. And in time, the philosophical cast of their thinking, shared by the young Marx himself, was superseded by a more "scientific," at times positivistic approach to social reality, by Marxists and non-Marxists alike.[2] By the late nineteenth century, social theory in general had ceased being "critical" and "negative" in the sense to be explained below.

The recovery of the Hegelian roots of Marx's thought by Marxists themselves was delayed until after World War I for reasons first spelled out by Karl Korsch in the pages of *Grünbergs Archiv* in 1923.[3] Only then were serious epistemological and methodological questions asked about the Marxist theory of society, which, despite (or perhaps because of) its scientific pretensions, had degenerated into a kind of metaphysics not unlike that which Marx himself had set out to dismantle. Ironically, a new understanding of Marx's debt to Hegel, that most metaphysical of thinkers, served to undermine the different kind of metaphysics that had entered "Vulgar Marxism" through the back door of scientism. Hegel's stress on consciousness as constitutive of the world challenged the passive materialism of the Second International's theorists. Here non-Marxist thinkers like Croce and Dilthey had laid the groundwork, by reviving philosophical interest in Hegel before the war. During the same period, Sorel's stress on spontaneity and subjectivity also played a role in undermining the mechanistic materialism of the orthodox adherents of the Second International.[4] Within the Marxist camp, Georg Lukács's *History and Class Consciousness* and Karl Korsch's *Marxism and Philosophy* were the most influential stimulants in the early 1920's to the recovery of the philosophical dimension in Marxism.[5] Much of what they argued was confirmed a decade later, with the revelations produced by the circulation of Marx's long-neglected Paris manuscripts. When, for one reason or another, their efforts faltered, the task of reinvigorating Marxist theory was taken up primarily by the young thinkers at the Institut für Sozialforschung.

On one level, then, it can be argued that the Frankfurt School was returning to the concerns of the Left Hegelians of the 1840's. Like that first generation of critical theorists, its members were interested in the integration of philosophy and social analysis. They likewise were concerned with the dialectical method devised by Hegel and sought, like their predecessors, to turn it in a materialist direction. And finally, like many of the Left Hegelians, they were particularly interested in exploring the possibilities of transforming the social order through human *praxis*.

The intervening century, however, had brought enormous changes, which made the conditions of their theorizing vastly different. Whereas the Left Hegelians were the immediate successors of the classical German idealists, the Frankfurt School was separated from Kant and Hegel by Schopenhauer, Nietzsche, Dilthey, Bergson, Weber, Husserl, and many others, not to mention the systematization of Marxism itself. As a result, Critical Theory had to reassert itself against a score of competitors who had driven Hegel from the field. And, of course, it could not avoid being influenced by certain of their ideas. But still more important, vital changes in social, economic, and political conditions between the two periods had unmistakable repercussions on the revived Critical Theory. Indeed, according to its own premises this was inevitable. The Left Hegelians wrote in a Germany just beginning to feel the effects of capitalist modernization. By the time of the Frankfurt School, Western capitalism, with Germany as one of its leading representatives, had entered a qualitatively new stage, dominated by growing monopolies and increasing governmental intervention in the economy. The only real examples of socialism available to the Left Hegelians had been a few isolated utopian communities. The Frankfurt School, on the other hand, had the ambiguous success of the Soviet Union to ponder. Finally, and perhaps most crucially, the first critical theorists had lived at a time when a new "negative" (that is, revolutionary) force in society — the proletariat — was stirring, a force that could be seen as the agent that would fulfill their philosophy. By the 1930's, however, signs of the proletariat's integration into society were becoming increasingly apparent; this was especially evident to the members of the Institut after their emigration to America. Thus, it might be said of the first generation of critical theorists in the 1840's that theirs was an "immanent" critique of society based on the existence of a real historical "subject." By the time of its renaissance in the twentieth century, Critical Theory was being increasingly forced into a position of "transcendence" by the withering away of the revolutionary working class.

In the 1920's, however, the signs were still unclear. Lukács himself stressed the function of the working class as the "subject-object" of history before deciding that it was really the party that represented the true interests of the workers. As the passage cited from *Dämmerung* in Chapter 1 indicates, Horkheimer believed that the German proletariat, although badly split, was not entirely moribund. The younger members of the Institut could share the belief of its older, more orthodox leadership that socialism might still be a real possibility in the advanced countries of Western Europe. This was clearly reflected in the consistent hortatory tone of most of the Institut's work in the pre-emigration period.

After the Institut's resettlement at Columbia University, however, this tone underwent a subtle shift in a pessimistic direction. Articles in the *Zeitschrift* scrupulously avoided using words like "Marxism" or "communism," substituting "dialectical materialism" or "the materialist theory of society" instead. Careful editing prevented emphasizing the revolutionary implications of their thought. In the Institut's American bibliography[6] the title of Grossmann's book was shortened to *The Law of Accumulation in Capitalist Society* without any reference to the "law of collapse," which had appeared in the original. These changes were doubtless due in part to the sensitive situation in which the Institut's members found themselves at Columbia. They were also a reflection of their fundamental aversion to the type of Marxism that the Institut equated with the orthodoxy of the Soviet camp. But in addition they expressed a growing loss of that basic confidence, which Marxists had traditionally felt, in the revolutionary potential of the proletariat.

In their attempt to achieve a new perspective that might make the new situation intelligible, in a framework that was still fundamentally Marxist, the members of the Frankfurt School were fortunate in having had philosophical training outside the Marxist tradition. Like other twentieth-century contributors to the revitalization of Marxism — Lukács, Gramsci, Bloch, Sartre, Merleau-Ponty — they were influenced at an early stage in their careers by more subjectivist, even idealist philosophies. Horkheimer, who set the tone for all of the Institut's work, had been interested in Schopenhauer and Kant before becoming fascinated with Hegel and Marx. His expression of interest in Schopenhauer in the 1960's,[7] contrary to what is often assumed, was thus a return to an early love, rather than an apostasy from a life-long Hegelianized Marxism. In fact the first book in philosophy Horkheimer actually read was Schopenhauer's *Aphorisms on the Wisdom of Life*,[8] which Pollock gave him when they were studying French together in Brussels before the war. Both he and Lowenthal were members of the Schopenhauer Gesellschaft at Frankfurt in their student days. Horkheimer was also very much interested in Kant at that time; his first published work was an analysis of Kant's *Critique of Judgment*, written for his *Habilitation* under Hans Cornelius in 1925.[9]

If Horkheimer can be said to have had a true mentor, it was Hans Cornelius. As Pollock, who also studied under Cornelius, remembers it, his "influence on Horkheimer can hardly be overestimated."[10] This seems to have been true more from a personal than a theoretical point of view. Although difficult to classify, Cornelius's philosophical perspective was antidogmatic, opposed to Kantian idealism, and insistent on the importance of experience. His initial writings showed the influence of Avenarius and Mach, but in his later work he moved away from their empiriocriticism and closer to a kind of phenomenology.[11] When Horkheimer became his student, Cornelius was at the height of his career, a "passionate teacher . . . in many ways the opposite of the current image of a German university professor, and in strong opposition to most of his colleagues." [12]

Although the young Horkheimer seems to have absorbed his teacher's critical stance, little of the substance of Cornelius's philosophy remained with him, especially after his interest was aroused by readings in Hegel and Marx. What does appear to have made an impact were Cornelius's humanistic cultural concerns. Born in 1863 in Munich into a family of composers, painters, and actors, Cornelius continued to pursue aesthetic interests throughout his life. Talented both as a sculptor and a painter, he made frequent trips to Italy, where he became expert in both classical and Renaissance art. In 1908 he published a study of *The Elementary Laws of Pictorial Art*,[13] and during the war he ran art schools in Munich.

Horkheimer was also certainly attracted by Cornelius's progressive political tendencies. Cornelius was an avowed internationalist and had been an opponent of the German war effort. Although no Marxist, he was considered an outspoken radical by the more conservative members of the Frankfurt faculty. What also doubtless made its impact on Horkheimer was his cultural pessimism, which he combined with his progressive politics. As Pollock recalls, "Cornelius never hesitated to confess openly his convictions and his despair about present-day civilization." [14] A sample of the almost apocalyptic tone he adopted, which was of course shared by many in Weimar's early days, can be found in the autobiographical sketch he wrote in 1923:

> Men have unlearned the ability to recognize the Godly in themselves and in things: nature and art, family and state have only interest for them as sensations. Therefore their lives flow meaninglessly by, and their shared culture is inwardly empty and will collapse because it is worthy of collapse. The new religion, however, which mankind needs, will first emerge from the ruins of this culture.[15]

The young Horkheimer was less eager to embrace so Spenglerian a prognosis, but in time Cornelius's appraisal of the situation increasingly became his own. In the twenties, however, he was still caught up by the revolutionary potential of the working class. Accordingly, his analysis of *The Critique of Judgment* showed little evidence of resignation or despair; instead, it demonstrated his conviction that *praxis* could overcome the contradictions of the social order, while at the same time leading to a cultural renewal. From Kant, however, he took certain convictions that he would never abandon.

Horkheimer's reading of Kant helped increase his sensitivity to the importance of individuality, as a value never to be submerged entirely under the demands of the totality. It also heightened his appreciation of the active elements in cognition, which prevented his acceptance of the copy theory of perception advocated by more orthodox Marxists. What it did not do, however, was to convince him of the inevitability of those dualisms — phenomena and noumena, pure and practical reason, for example — that Kant had posited as insurmountable. In concluding his study, Horkheimer made it clear that although these antagonisms had not yet been overcome, he saw no necessary reason why they could not be. Kant's fundamental duality between will and knowledge, practical and pure reason, could and must be reconciled.[16] In so arguing, Horkheimer demonstrated the influence of Hegel's critique of Kant on his own. Like Hegel, he saw cognitive knowledge and normative imperatives, the "is" and the "ought," as ultimately inseparable.

Because of this and other similarities with Hegel on such questions as the nature of reason, the importance of dialectics, and the existence of a substantive logic, it is tempting to characterize Critical Theory as no more than a Hegelianized Marxism.[17] And yet, on several fundamental issues, Horkheimer always maintained a certain distance from Hegel. Most basic was his rejection of Hegel's metaphysical intentions and his claim to absolute truth. "I do not know," he wrote in *Dämmerung*, "how far metaphysicians are correct; perhaps somewhere there is a particularly compelling metaphysical system or fragment. But I do know that metaphysicians are usually impressed only to the smallest degree by what men suffer."[18] Moreover, a system that tolerated every opposing view as part of the "total truth" had inevitably quietistic implications.[19] An all-embracing system like Hegel's might well serve as a theodicy justifying the status quo. In fact, to the extent that Marxism had been ossified into a system claiming the key to truth, it too had fallen victim to the same malady. The true object of Marxism, Horkheimer argued,[20] was not the uncovering of immutable truths, but the fostering of social change.

Elsewhere, Horkheimer outlined his other objections to Hegel's metaphysics.[21] His strongest criticism was reserved for perhaps the fundamental tenet of Hegel's thought: the assumption that all knowledge is self-knowledge of the infinite subject — in other words, that an identity exists between subject and object, mind and matter, based on the ultimate primacy of the absolute subject. "Spirit," Horkheimer wrote, "may not recognize itself either in nature or in history, because even if the spirit is not a questionable abstraction, it would not be identical with reality." [22] In fact, there is no "thought" as such, only the specific thought of concrete men rooted in their socio-economic conditions. Nor is there "being" as such, but rather a "manifold of beings in the world." [23]

In repudiating identity theory, Horkheimer was also implicitly criticizing its reappearance in Lukács's *History and Class Consciousness.* To Lukács, the proletariat functioned both as the subject and the object of history, thus fulfilling the classical German idealist goal of uniting freedom as an objective reality and as something produced by man himself. In later years Lukács was himself to detect the metaphysical premise underlying his assumption of an identical subject-object in history: "The proletariat seen as the identical subject-object of the real history of mankind is no materialist consummation that overcomes the constructions of idealism. It is rather an attempt to out-Hegel Hegel, it is an edifice boldly erected above every possible reality and thus attempts objectively to surpass the Master himself." [24] These words were written in 1967 for a new edition of a work whose arguments Lukács had long ago seen fit to repudiate. His reasons for that self-criticism have been the source of considerable speculation and no less an amount of criticism. Yet, in pointing to the metaphysical core at the center of his argument, he was doing no more than repeating what Horkheimer had said about identity theory almost four decades before.

To Horkheimer, all absolutes, all identity theories were suspect. Even the ideal of absolute justice contained in religion, he was later to argue,[25] has a chimerical quality. The image of complete justice "can never be realized in history because even when a better society replaces the present disorder and is developed, past misery would not be made good and the suffering of surrounding nature not transcended." [26] As a result, philosophy as he understood it always expresses an unavoidable note of sadness, but without succumbing to resignation.

Yet although Horkheimer attacked Hegel's identity theory, he felt that nineteenth-century criticism of a similar nature had been carried too far. In rejecting the ontological claims Hegel had made for his philosophy of Absolute Spirit, the positivists had robbed the intellect of any right to judge what was actual as true or false.* Their overly

* Throughout its history, "positivism" was used by the Frankfurt School in a loose way to include those philosophical currents which were nominalist, phenomenalist (that is, anti-essen-

empirical bias led to the apotheosis of facts in a way that was equally one-sided. From the first, Horkheimer consistently rejected the Hobson's choice of metaphysical systematizing or antinomian empiricism. Instead, he argued for the possibility of a dialectical social science that would avoid an identity theory and yet preserve the right of the observer to go beyond the givens of his experience. It was in large measure this refusal to succumb to the temptations of either alternative that gave Critical Theory its cutting edge.

Horkheimer's hostility to metaphysics was partly a reaction to the sclerosis of Marxism produced by its transformation into a body of received truths. But beyond this, it reflected the influence of his readings in non-Hegelian and non-Marxist philosophy. Schopenhauer's extreme skepticism about the possibility of reconciling reason with the world of will certainly had its effect. More important still was the impact of three late nineteenth-century thinkers, Nietzsche, Dilthey, and Bergson, all of whom had emphasized the relation of thought to human life.

To Horkheimer,[27] the *Lebensphilosophie* (philosophy of life) they helped create had expressed a legitimate protest against the growing rigidity of abstract rationalism, and the concomitant standardization of individual existence that characterized life under advanced capitalism. It had pointed an accusing finger at the gap between the promises of bourgeois ideology and the reality of everyday life in bourgeois society. The development of the philosophy of life, he argued, corresponded to a fundamental change in capitalism itself. The earlier optimistic belief of certain classical idealists in the unity of reason and reality had corresponded to the individual entrepreneur's acceptance of harmony between his own activities and the functioning of the economy as a whole. The erosion of that conviction corresponded to the growth of monopoly capitalism in the late nineteenth century, in which the individual's role was more overwhelmed by the totality than harmonized with it.[28] *Lebensphilosophie* was basically a cry of outrage against this change. Because of this critical element, Horkheimer was careful to distinguish the "irrationalism"[29] of the philosophers of life from that of their twentieth-century vulgarizers.

In the 1930's, he argued, attacks on reason were designed to reconcile men to the irrationality of the prevailing order.[30] The so-called tragic outlook on life was really a veiled justification for the acceptance of unnecessary misery. *Leben* and *Dienst* (service) had come to be synonymous. What was once critical had now become ideologi-

tialist), empirical, and wedded to the so-called scientific method. Many of their opponents who were grouped under this rubric protested the term's applicability, as for example Karl Popper.

cal. This was also true of the attack on science, which, in the hands of the first generation of *Lebensphilosophen*, had been a justified corrective to the pretensions of scientism, but which by the 1930's had degenerated into an indiscriminate attack on the validity of scientific thought as such. "The philosophic dismissal of science," he wrote in 1937, "is a comfort in private life, in society a lie." [31]

In seeing the irrationalism of the thirties basically as an ideology of passivity,[32] Horkheimer neglected its dynamic and destructive sides, which the Nazis were able to exploit. This was a blind spot in his analysis. But in another way he enriched the discussion of its historical development. In distinguishing between different types of irrationalism, Horkheimer broke with the tradition of hostility towards *Lebensphilosophie* maintained by almost all Marxist thinkers, including the later Lukács.[33] In addition to approving of its antisystematic impulse, Horkheimer gave qualified praise to the emphasis on the individual in the work of both Dilthey and Nietzsche. Like them, he believed in the importance of individual psychology for an understanding of history.[34] While their work in this area was less subtle than the psychoanalysis he hoped to integrate with Critical Theory, he considered it far more useful than the bankrupt utilitarianism that informed liberalism and orthodox Marxism.

What became clear, however, in Horkheimer's discussion of Dilthey's methodology[35] was his rejection of a purely psychological approach to historical explanation. Dilthey's notion of a *Verstehende Geisteswissenschaft* (a social science based on its own methods of understanding and reexperiencing, rather than on those of the natural sciences) did, to be sure, contain a recognition of the meaningfulness of historical structures, which Horkheimer could share. What he rejected was the assumption that this meaning could be intuitively grasped by the historian reexperiencing his subject matter in his own mind. Underlying this notion, he argued, was a Hegelian-like belief in the identity of subject and object. The data of the inner life were not enough to mirror the significant structure of the past, because that past had not always been made consciously by men. Indeed, it was generally made "behind the backs and against the wills" of individuals, as Marx had pointed out. That this need not always be the case was another matter. In fact, Vico was one of Horkheimer's early intellectual heroes;[36] and it was Vico who had first argued that men might understand history better than nature because men made history, whereas God made nature. This, however, was a goal, not a reality. If anything, Horkheimer noted pessimistically, the trend in modern life was away from the conscious determination of historical events rather than towards it. History, therefore, could not simply be "understood," as he claimed Dilthey had hoped, but had to be "explained" instead. Horkheimer did, however, hold out some hope for the attainment of the social conditions that would make Dilthey's methodological vision viable.

Horkheimer's admiration for Nietzsche was equally mixed. In 1935 he argued that Nietzsche was a genuine bourgeois philosopher, as demonstrated by his overemphasis on individualism and his blindness to social questions.[37] Still, Horkheimer was quick to defend Nietzsche against those who sought to reconcile him with the irrationalists of the 1930's. In a long review of Karl Jaspers's study of Nietzsche[38] he castigated the author for trying to "domesticate" Nietzsche for *völkisch* (populist nationalist) and religious consumption. What he valued most in Nietzsche's work was its uncompromisingly critical quality. On the question of certain knowledge, for example, he applauded Nietzsche's statement that a "great truth wants to be criticized, not idolized." [39]

Horkheimer also was impressed by Nietzsche's critique of the masochistic quality of traditional Western morality. He had been the first to note, Horkheimer approvingly commented,[40] how misery could be transformed into a social norm, as in the case of asceticism, and how that norm had permeated Western culture through the "slave morality" of Christian ethics.[41] When it came to the more questionable aspects of Nietzsche's thought, Horkheimer tended to mitigate their inadequacies. The naive glorification of the "superman" he explained away by calling it the price of isolation. Nietzsche's hostility to the goal of a classless society he excused on the grounds that its only champions in Nietzsche's day were the Social Democrats, whose mentality was as pedestrian and uninspired as Nietzsche had claimed. In fact, Horkheimer argued, Nietzsche had been perceptive in refusing to romanticize the working classes, who were even in his time beginning to be diverted from their revolutionary role by the developing mass culture. Where Nietzsche had failed, however, was in his ahistorical belief that democratization inevitably meant the dilution of true culture. He was also deficient in misunderstanding the historical nature of labor, which he absolutized as immutable in order to justify his elitist conclusions. In short, Horkheimer contended that Nietzsche, who had done so much to reveal the historical roots of bourgeois morality, had himself fallen prey to ahistorical thinking.

Towards the third great exponent of *Lebensphilosophie* and one of the Institut's actual sponsors in Paris, Henri Bergson, Horkheimer was somewhat more critical.[42] Although recognizing the trenchant arguments in Bergson's critique of abstract rationalism, he questioned the metaphysical yearnings he detected at its root. Bergson's faith in intuition as the means to discover the universal life force he dismissed as an ideology. "Intuition," he wrote, "from which Bergson hopes to find salvation in history as in cognition, has a unified object: life, energy, duration, creative development. In reality, however, mankind is split, and an intuition that seeks to penetrate through contradictions loses what is historically decisive from its sight." [43] Horkheimer's hostility to the unmediated use of intuition as a means to break through to an underlying level of reality, it might be added, was also extended to the similar efforts of phenomenologists such as Scheler and Husserl.

In an article devoted primarily to Bergson's metaphysics of time, which Bergson himself called "a serious deepening of my works" and "philosophically very penetrating," [44] Horkheimer supported Bergson's distinction between "experienced" time and the abstract time of the natural scientists. But, he quickly added in qualification, Bergson had been mistaken in trying to write a metaphysics of temporality. In so doing he had been led to an idea of time as *durée* (duration), which was almost as abstract and empty as that of the natural sciences. To see reality as an uninterruptible flow was to ignore the reality of suffering, aging, and death. It was to absolutize the present and thus unwittingly repeat the mistakes of the positivists. True experience, Horkheimer argued, resisted such homogenization. The task of the historian was to preserve the memory of suffering and to foster the demand for qualitative historical change.

In all of Horkheimer's writings on the *Lebensphilosophen*, three major criticisms were repeatedly made. By examining these in some detail, we can better understand the foundations of Critical Theory. First, although the philosophers of life had been correct in trying to rescue the individual from the threats of modern society, they had gone too far in emphasizing subjectivity and inwardness. In doing so, they had minimized the importance of action in the historical world. Second, with an occasional exception such as Nietzsche's critique of asceticism, they tended to neglect the material dimension of reality. Third and perhaps most important, in criticizing the degeneration of bourgeois rationalism into its abstract and formal aspects, they sometimes overstated their case and seemed to be rejecting reason itself. This ultimately led to the outright mindless irrationalism of their twentieth-century vulgarizers.

As might be expected, Horkheimer's interest in the question of bourgeois individualism led him back to a consideration of Kant and the origins of *Innerlichkeit* (inwardness).[45] Among the dualistic elements in Kant's philosophy, he noted,[46] was the gap between duty and interest. Individual morality, discovered by practical reason, was internalized and divorced from public ethics. Here Hegel's *Sittlichkeit* (ethics), with its emphasis on bridging the public-private opposition, was superior to Kant's *Moralität* (morality). Despite this, Kant's view was closer to a correct reflection of conditions in the early nineteenth century; for to assume that a harmony could exist at that time between personal morality and public ethics, or between self-interest and a universal moral code, was to ignore the real irrationality of the external order. Where Kant had been wrong, however, was in considering these contradictions immutable. By absolutizing the distinction between the individual and society, he had made a natural condition out of what was merely historically valid, thereby unwittingly affirming the status quo. This was also a failing of the *Lebensphilosophen.* In later years, however, Horkheimer and the other members of the Frankfurt School came to believe that the real danger lay not with those who overemphasized subjectivity and individuality, but rather with those who sought to eliminate them entirely under the banner of a false totalism. This fear would go so far that Adorno could write, in a frequently quoted phrase from *Minima Moralia,* that "the whole is the untrue." [47] But in the 1930's Horkheimer and his colleagues were still concerned with the overemphasis on individuality, which they detected in bourgeois thinkers from Kant to the philosophers of life.

Horkheimer also questioned the moral imperative that Kant had postulated. Although agreeing that a moral impulse apart from egoistic self-interest did in fact exist, he argued that its expression had changed since Kant's time. Whereas in the early nineteenth century it had manifested itself as duty, it now appeared as either pity or political concern. Pity, Horkheimer argued, was produced by the recognition that man had ceased being a free subject and was reduced instead to an object of forces beyond his control.[48] This Kant had not experienced himself, because his time provided greater individual freedom, at least for the entrepreneur. Political action as the expression of morality was also spurned by Kant, who overemphasized the importance of the individual conscience and tended to reify the status quo. In the twentieth century, however, politics had become the proper realm of moral action because, for the first time in history, "mankind's means have grown great enough to present the realization [of justice] as an immediate historical task. The struggle for its fulfillment characterizes our epoch of transition." [49] Both early bourgeois thinkers like Kant and later ones like the *Lebensphiloso-*

phen had failed to appreciate the necessity for political *praxis* to realize their moral visions.

Horkheimer's second major objection to Nietzsche, Dilthey, and Bergson was, as noted above, that they were really hidden idealists. In contrast, Horkheimer proposed a materialist theory of society, but one that was very clearly distinguished from the putative materialism of orthodox Marxism. In one of his most important essays in the *Zeitschrift*, "Materialism and Metaphysics," [50] he set out to rescue materialism from those who saw it simply as an antonym of spiritualism and a denial of nonmaterial existence. True materialism, he argued, did not mean a new type of monistic metaphysics based on the ontological primacy of matter. Here nineteenth-century mechanical materialists like Vogt and Haeckel had been wrong, as were Marxists who made a fetish of the supposedly "objective" material world. Equally erroneous was the assumption of the eternal primacy of the economic substructure of society. Both substructure and superstructure interacted at all times, although it was true that under capitalism the economic base had a crucial role in this process. What had to be understood, however, was that this condition was only historical and would change with time. In fact, it was one of the characteristics of twentieth-century society that politics was beginning to assert an autonomy beyond anything Marx had predicted. Both Leninist and fascist practice demonstrated the change.

Horkheimer also disliked the tendency of vulgar Marxists to elevate materialism to a theory of knowledge, which claimed absolute certainty the way idealism had in the past. In fact, to argue that a materialist epistemology could exhaustively explain reality was to encourage the urge to dominate the world, which Fichtean idealism had most vividly displayed. This was borne out by the fact that monistic materialism as far back as Hobbes had led to a manipulative, dominating attitude towards nature.[51] The theme of man's domination of nature, it might be added parenthetically, was to become a central concern of the Frankfurt School in subsequent years.

Despite the impossibility of attaining absolute knowledge, Horkheimer held that materialism must not succumb to relativistic resignation. In fact, the monistic materialist epistemology of vulgar Marxism had been too passive. Echoing Marx's critique of Feuerbach almost a century before,[52] Horkheimer stressed the active element in cognition, which idealism had correctly affirmed. The objects of perception, he argued, are themselves the product of man's actions, although the relationship tends to be masked by reification. Indeed, nature itself has a historical element, in the dual sense that man conceives of it differently at different times and that he actively works to change it. True materialism, Horkheimer contended, is thus dialectical, involving an ongoing process of interaction between subject and object. Here Horkheimer returned once again to the Hegelian roots of Marxism, which had been obscured in the intervening century. Like Marx, but unlike many self-proclaimed Marxists, he refused to make a fetish of dialectics as an objective process outside man's control. Nor did he see it as a methodological construct imposed like a Weberian ideal type, or a social scientific model, on a chaotic, manifold reality. Dialectics probed the "force-field," to use an expression of Adorno's,[53] between consciousness and being, subject and object. It did not, indeed could not, pretend to have discovered ontological first principles. It rejected the extremes of nominalism and realism and remained willing to operate in a perpetual state of suspended judgment.

Hence the crucial importance of mediation *(Vermittlung)* for a correct theory of society. No facet of social reality could be understood by the observer as final or complete in itself. There were no social "facts," as the positivists believed, which were the substratum of a social theory. Instead, there was a constant interplay of particular and universal, of "moment" * and totality. As Lukács had written in *History and Class Consciousness*:

> To leave empirical reality behind can only mean that the objects of the empirical world are to be understood as objects of a totality, i.e., as the aspects of a total social situation caught up in the process of historical change. Thus the category of mediation is a lever with which to overcome the mere immediacy of the empirical world, and as such it is not something (subjective) foisted onto the objects from outside, it is no value-judgment or "ought" opposed to their "is." *It is rather the manifestation of their authentic objective structure.*[54]

Moreover, the relationship between the totality and its moments was reciprocal. Vulgar Marxists had been mistaken in seeking a reductionist derivation of superstructural, cultural phenomena from their substructural, socio-economic base. Culture, Horkheimer and his colleagues argued, was never epiphenomenal, although it was never fully autonomous. Its relationship to the material substructure of society was multidimensional. All cultural phenomena must be seen as mediated through the social totality, not merely as the reflection of class interests. This meant that they also expressed the con-

* *Das Moment* in German means a phase or aspect of a cumulative dialectical process. It should not be confused with *Der Moment*, which means a moment in time in the English sense.

tradictions of the whole, including those forces that negated the status quo. Nothing, or at least almost nothing, was solely ideological.[55]

In so arguing, it might be added, Horkheimer was closer to Marx himself than the self-styled Marxists who claimed to be orthodox. When discussing the bourgeois state, for example, Marx had not interpreted it solely as the "executive committee of the ruling class," but also as an adumbration, albeit distorted, of the reconciliation of social contradictions that the triumph of the proletariat was to bring about.[56] Engels, likewise, when discussing Realism in literature, had shown an appreciation for the progressive elements in ostensibly reactionary writers like Balzac, because of their ability to portray the concrete totality with all its contradictions. The Institut's extensive work on aesthetic and cultural matters was rooted in the same assumption.

In stressing the totality, Horkheimer correspondingly criticized other social theorists for concentrating on one facet of reality to the exclusion of the others. This led to one of the methodological fallacies the Frankfurt School most frequently attacked: fetishization. More orthodox Marxists within the Institut, such as the economist Henryk Grossmann, were always criticized for their overemphasis on the material substructure of society. The composition of the Institut, with its deliberate diversification of fields, reflected the importance Critical Theory placed on the totality of dialectical mediations, which had to be grasped in the process of analyzing society.

Horkheimer's stress on dialectics also extended to his understanding of logic. Although rejecting the extravagant ontological claims Hegel had made for his logical categories, he agreed with the need for a substantive, rather than merely formal, logic. In *Dämmerung* Horkheimer wrote: "Logic is not independent of content. In face of the reality that what is inexpensive for the favored part of humanity remains unattainable for the others, nonpartisan logic would be as nonpartisan as a book of laws that is the same for all." [57] Formalism, characteristic of bourgeois law (the ideal of the *Rechtsstaat*, which meant judicial universality without relating the law to its political origins), bourgeois morality (the categorical imperative), and bourgeois logic, had once been progressive, but it now served only to perpetuate the status quo. True logic, as well as true rationalism, must go beyond form to include substantive elements as well.

Yet precisely what these elements were was difficult to say. Substantive logic was easier to demand than explain. The agnosticism in Horkheimer's notion of materialism also extended to his views on the possibility of a philosophical anthropology. He dismissed the efforts of Max Scheler, to discover a constant human nature as no more than a desperate search for absolute meaning in a relativist world.[58] The yearning of phenomenologists for the security of eternal essences was a source of self-delusion, a point Adorno and Marcuse were to echo in their respective critiques of Husserl and Scheler.[59]

Accordingly, Critical Theory denied the necessity, or even the possibility, of formulating a definitive description of "socialist man." This distaste for anthropological speculation has been attributed by some commentators to the residual influence of scientific socialism.[60] If "scientific" is understood solely as the antonym of "utopian" socialism, this is true. But in view of the Frankfurt School's hostility towards the reduction of philosophy to science, it seems only a partial explanation. Another possible factor, which Horkheimer himself was to stress in later years,[61] was the subterranean influence of a religious theme on the materialism of the Frankfurt School. It would be an error, in fact, to treat its members as dogmatic atheists. In almost all of Horkheimer's discussions of religion, he took a dialectical position.[62] In *Dämmerung*, to take one example, he argued that religion ought not to be understood solely as false consciousness, because it helped preserve a hope for future justice, which bourgeois atheism denied.[63] Thus, his more recent claim, that the traditional Jewish prohibition on naming or describing God and paradise was reproduced in Critical Theory's refusal to give substance to its utopian vision, can be given some credence. As Jürgen Habermas has noted, German idealist philosophy's reluctance to flesh out its notions of utopia was very similar to the cabalistic stress on words rather than images.[64] Adorno's decision to choose music, the most nonrepresentational of aesthetic modes, as the primary medium through which he explored bourgeois culture and sought signs of its negation indicates the continued power of this prohibition. Of the major figures connected with the Institut, only Marcuse attempted to articulate a positive anthropology at any time in his career.[65] Whether or not the Jewish taboo was actually causal or merely a *post facto* rationalization is difficult to establish with certainty. Whatever the reason, Critical Theory consistently resisted the temptation to describe "the realm of freedom" from the vantage point of the "realm of necessity."

And yet, even in Horkheimer's work there appeared a kind of negative anthropology, an implicit but still powerful presence. Although to some extent rooted in Freud, its primary origins could be found in the work of Marx. In discussing Feuerbach's attempt to construct an explicit picture of human nature, Marx had attacked its atemporal, abstract, antihistorical premises. The only constant, he argued, was man's ability to create himself anew. "Anthropogenesis," to use a later commentator's term,[66] was the only human nature Marx allowed. Here Horkheimer was in agreement; the good society was one in which man was free to act as a subject rather than be acted upon as a contingent predicate.

When Marx seemed to go further in defining the categories of human self-production in the *Economic and Philosophic Manuscripts*, Horkheimer drew back. The central position of labor in Marx's work and his concomitant stress on the problem of alienated labor in capitalist society played a relatively minor role in Horkheimer's writings. In *Dämmerung* he wrote: "To make labor into a transcendent category of human activity is an ascetic ideology. . . . Because socialists hold to this general concept, they make themselves into carriers of capitalist propaganda." [67]

The same was true of Walter Benjamin and Theodor Adorno. To Benjamin, the vulgar Marxist stress on labor "recognizes only the progress in the mastery of nature, not the retrogression of society; it already displays the technocratic features later encountered in Fascism. . . . The new conception of labor amounts to the exploitation of nature, which with naive complacency is contrasted with the exploitation of the proletariat. Compared with this positivistic conception, Fourier's fantasies, which have so often been ridiculed, prove to be surprisingly sound." [68] Adorno, when I spoke with him in Frankfurt in March, 1969, said that Marx wanted to turn the whole world into a giant workhouse.

Horkheimer's antagonism to the fetishization of labor expressed another dimension of his materialism: the demand for human, sensual happiness. In one of his most trenchant essays, "Egoism and the Movement for Emancipation," [69] he discussed the hostility to personal gratification inherent in bourgeois culture. Despite the utilitarianism of a Bentham or a Mandeville, the characteristic ideology of the early bourgeois era was Kantian.[70] Seeing no unity between individual interest and public morality, Kant had posited an inevitable distinction between happiness and duty. Although he gave a certain weight to both, by the time capitalism had become sufficiently advanced, the precedence of duty to the totality over personal gratification had grown to such an extent that the latter was almost completely neglected. To compensate for the repression of genuine individual happiness, mass diversions had been devised to defuse discontent.[71] Much of the Institut's later work on the "culture industry" was designed to show how effective these palliatives were.

But even allegedly revolutionary movements, Horkheimer contended, had perpetuated the characteristic bourgeois hostility to happiness.[72] The fourteenth-century Romans under Cola di Rienzi, and the Florentines in the time of Savonarola, were two clear examples of revolutionary movements that ended by opposing individual happiness in the name of some higher good. Even more strikingly, the French Revolution and especially the Terror illustrated this theme. Robespierre, like Rienzi and Savonarola, confused love for the people with ruthless repression of them. The equality brought by the Revolution, Horkheimer noted, was the negative leveling produced by the guillotine, an equality of degradation rather than dignity. In the twentieth century a similar phenomenon had appeared in fascism. The Führer or Duce expressed in the extreme the typical bourgeois combination of romantic sentimentality and utter ruthlessness. The ideology of duty and service to the totality at the cost of individual happiness attained its ultimate expression in fascist rhetoric. The revolutionary pretensions of the fascists were no more than a fraud designed to perpetuate the domination of the ruling classes.

In contrast to the bourgeois ethic of self-abnegation, Horkheimer upheld the dignity of egoism. During the Enlightenment, Helvetius and de Sade had expressed a protest, however distorted, against asceticism in the name of a higher morality. Even more forcefully, Nietzsche had exposed the connection between self-denial and resentment that is implicit in most of Western culture. Where Horkheimer differed from them was in his stress on the social component in human happiness. His egoistic individual, unlike the utilitarians' or even Nietzsche's, always realized his greatest gratification through communal interaction. In fact, Horkheimer constantly challenged the reification of individual and society as polar opposites, just as he denied the mutual exclusivity of subject and object in philosophy.

The Institut's stress on personal happiness as an integral element in its materialism was further developed by Marcuse in an article he wrote for the *Zeitschrift* in 1938, "On Hedonism." [73] In contrast to Hegel, who "fought against eudaemonism in the interest of historical progress," [74] Marcuse defended hedonistic philosophies for preserving a "moment" of truth in their stress on happiness. Where they traditionally went wrong, however, was in their unquestioning acceptance of the competitive individual as the model of highest personal development. "The apologetic aspect of hedonism," Marcuse wrote, is to be found "in hedonism's abstract conception of the subjective side of happiness, in its inability to distinguish between true and false wants and interests and true and false enjoyments." [75] In upholding the notion of higher and lower pleasures, Marcuse was closer to the Epicurean type of hedonism than to the Cyrenaic, both of which he treated at length in the essay. (He was also in the company of an unlikely ally in the person of John Stuart Mill, who had made a similar distinction in his *Utilitarianism.*) As he explained, "Pleasure in the abasement of another as well as self-abasement under a stronger will, pleasure in the manifold surrogates for sexuality, in meaningless sacrifices, in the heroism of war are false pleasures, because the drives and needs that fulfill themselves in them make men less free, blinder, and more wretched than they have to be." [76]

But, as might be expected, Marcuse denounced the ahistorical belief that the higher forms of happiness could be achieved under present conditions. In fact, so he argued, hedonism's restriction of happiness to consumption and leisure to the exclusion of productive labor expressed a valid judgment about a society in which labor remained alienated. What was invalid, however, was the assumption that this society was eternal. How historical change would come about was of course difficult to predict, because "it appears that individuals raised to be integrated into the antagonistic labor process cannot be judges of their own happiness." [77] Consciousness was therefore incapable of changing itself; the impetus had to come from the outside:

> Insofar as unfreedom is already present in wants and not just in their gratification, they must be the first to be liberated — not through an act of education or of the moral renewal of man but through an economic and political process encompassing the disposal over the means of production by the community, the reorientation of the productive process toward the needs and wants of the whole society, the shortening of the working day, and the active participation of the individuals in the administration of the whole.[78]

Here Marcuse seemed to come perilously close to the stress on objective social development, which more orthodox Marxists had maintained, but which the Institut had attacked by emphasizing the subjective element in *praxis.* In fact, to digress momentarily, the key problem of how change might occur in a society that controlled the consciousness of its members remained a troubling element in much of Marcuse's later work, especially *One-Dimensional Man.*[79]

Whatever the means to achieve true happiness might be, it could only be reached when freedom was also universally attained. "The reality of happiness," Marcuse wrote, "is the reality of freedom as the self-determination of liberated humanity in its common struggle with nature." And since freedom was synonymous with the realization of rationality, "in their completed form both, happiness and reason, coincide." [80] What Marcuse was advocating here was that convergence of particular and general interests usually known as "positive freedom." [81] Individual happiness was one moment in the totality of positive freedom; reason was the other.

The Frankfurt School's stress on reason was one of the salient characteristics of its work.[82] Here its debt to Hegel was most clearly demonstrated. Horkheimer's third major objection to *Lebensphilosophie,* it will be recalled, was that its overreaction to the deterioration of rationality had led to the rejection of reason as such. As Horkheimer would repeat over and over again during his career, rationality was at the root of any progressive social theory. What he meant by reason, however, was never easy to grasp for an audience unschooled in the traditions of classical German philosophy. Implicitly, Horkheimer referred more often than not to the idealists' distinction between *Verstand* (understanding) and *Vernunft* (reason). By *Verstand,* Kant and Hegel had meant a lower faculty of the mind, which structured the phenomenal world according to common sense. To the understanding, the world consisted of finite entities identical only with themselves and totally opposed to all other things. It thus failed to penetrate immediacy to grasp the dialectical relations beneath the surface. *Vernunft,* on the other hand, signified a faculty that went beyond mere appearances to this deeper reality. Although Kant differed from Hegel in rejecting the possibility of reconciling the world of phenomena with the transcendent, noumenal sphere of "things-in-themselves," he shared Hegel's belief in the superiority of *Vernunft* over *Verstand.* Of all the Institut's members, Marcuse was perhaps most drawn to the classical notion of reason. In 1937, he attempted to define it and turn it in a materialist direction in the following way:

> Reason is the fundamental category of philosophical thought, the only one by means of which it has bound itself to human destiny. Philosophy wanted to discover the ultimate and most general grounds of Being. Under the name of reason it conceived the idea of an authentic Being in which all significant antitheses (of subject and object, essence and appearance, thought and being) were reconciled. Connected with this idea was the conviction that what exists is not immediately and already rational but must rather be brought to reason. . . . As the given world was bound up with rational thought and, indeed, ontologically dependent on it, all that contradicted reason or was not rational was posited as something that had to be overcome. Reason was established as a critical tribunal.[83]

Here Marcuse seemed to be arguing for an identity theory, which contrasted sharply with the Frankfurt School's general stress on nonidentity. In fact, in Marcuse's writings the aversion to identity was far fainter than in Horkheimer's or Adorno's.[84] Still, in their work as well, the sanctity of reason and the reconciliation it implied always appeared as a utopian ideal. Jews, after all, may be prohibited from naming or describing God, but they do not deny his existence. In all of the Institut's writings, the standard was a society made rational, in the sense that German philosophy had traditionally defined that term. Reason, as the passage above indicates, was the "critical tribunal" on which Critical Theory was primarily based. The irrationality of the current society was always challenged by the "negative" possibility of a truly rational alternative.

If Horkheimer was reluctant to affirm the complete identity of subject and object, he was more certain in rejecting their strict dualistic opposition, which Descartes had bequeathed to modern thought.[85] Implicit in the Cartesian legacy, he argued, was the reduction of reason to its subjective dimension. This was the first step in driving rationality away from the world and into contemplative inwardness. It led to an eternal separation of essence and appearance, which fostered the noncritical acceptance of the status quo.[86] As a result, rationality increasingly came to be identified with the common sense of *Verstand* instead of the more ambitiously synthetic *Vernunft.* In fact, the late nineteenth-century irrationalists' attack on reason had been aimed primarily at its reduction to the analytical, formal, divisive *Verstand.* This was a criticism Horkheimer could share, although he did not reject analytical rationality out of hand. "Without definiteness and the order of concepts, without *Verstand,*" he wrote, "there is no thought, and no dialectic." [87] Even Hegel's dialectical logic, which Critical Theory embraced, did not simply negate formal logic. The Hegelian *aufheben* meant preservation as well as transcendence and cancellation. What Horkheimer did reject was the complete identification of reason and logic with the limited power of *Verstand.*

Throughout its history, the Institut carried on a spirited defense of reason on two fronts. In addition to the attack by the irrationalists, which by the twentieth century had degenerated into outright obscurantist mindlessness, another and perhaps more serious threat was posed from a different quarter. With the breakdown of the Hegelian synthesis in the second half of the nineteenth century, a new stress on empirically derived social science had developed alongside the increasing domination of natural science over men's lives. Positivism denied the validity of the traditional idea of reason as *Vernunft,* which it dismissed as empty metaphysics. At the time of the Frankfurt School the most significant proponents of this point of view were the Logical Positivists of the Vienna Circle, who were forced to emigrate to the United States at about the same time.[88] In America their impact was far greater than the Institut's because of the congruence of their ideas with the basic traditions of American philosophy. In later years Horkheimer took pains to establish the similarities between such native schools as pragmatism and Logical Positivism.[89]

His first major broadside against Logical Positivism came in 1937 in the *Zeitschrift*.[90] Once again his sensitivity to the changing functions of a school of thought in different historical contexts was evident. Originally, he argued, empiricism as practiced by Locke and Hume contained a dynamic, even critical, element, in its insistence on the individual's perception as the source of knowledge. The Enlightenment empiricists had used their observations to undermine the prevailing social order. Contemporary Logical Positivism, on the other hand, had lost this subversive quality, because of its belief that knowledge, although initially derived from perception, was really concerned with judgments about that perception contained in so-called "protocol sentences." [91] By restricting reality to that which could be expressed in such sentences, the unspeakable was excluded from the philosopher's domain. But even more fundamentally, the general empiricist stress on perception ignored the active element in all cognition. Positivism of all kinds was ultimately the abdication of reflection.[92] The result was the absolutizing of "facts" and the reification of the existing order.[93]

In addition to his distaste for their fetishism of facts, Horkheimer further objected to the Logical Positivists' reliance on formal logic to the exclusion of a substantive alternative. To see logic as an analogue of mathematics, he held, was to reduce it to a series of tautologies with no real meaning in the historical world. To believe that all true knowledge aspired to the condition of scientific, mathematical conceptualization was a surrender to a metaphysics as bad as the one the positivists had set out to refute.[94]

What was perhaps worst of all in Horkheimer's eyes was the positivists' pretension to have disentangled facts from values. Here he detected a falling away from the original Enlightenment use of empiricism as a partisan weapon against the mystifications of superstition and tradition. A society, he argued,[95] might itself be "possessed" and thus produce "facts" that were themselves "insane." Because it had no way to evaluate this possibility, modern empiricism capitulated before the authority of the status quo, despite its intentions. The members of the Vienna Circle might be progressive in their politics, but this was in no way related to their philosophy. Their surrender to the mystique of the prevailing reality, however, was not arbitrary; rather it was an expression of the contingency of existence in a society that administered and manipulated men's lives. As man must reestablish his ability to control his own destiny, so must reason be restored to its proper place as the arbiter of ends, not merely means. *Vernunft* must regain the field from which it had been driven by the triumph of *Verstand.*

What made Horkheimer's stress on reason so problematical was his equally strong antimetaphysical bias. Reality had to be judged by the "tribunal of reason," but reason was not to be taken as a transcendent ideal, existing outside history. Truth, Horkheimer and his colleagues always insisted, was not immutable. And yet, to deny the absoluteness of truth was not to succumb to relativism, epistemological, ethical, or otherwise. The dichotomy of absolutism and relativism was in fact a false one. Each period of time has its own truth, Horkheimer argued,[96] although there is none above time. What is true is whatever fosters social change in the direction of a rational society. This of course once again raised the question of what was meant by reason, which Critical Theory never attempted to define explicitly. Dialectics was superb at attacking other systems' pretensions to truth, but when it came to articulating the ground of its own assumptions and values, it fared less well. Like its implicit reliance on a negative anthropology, Critical Theory had a basically insubstantial concept of reason and truth, rooted in social conditions and yet outside them, connected with *praxis* yet keeping its distance from it. If Critical Theory can be said to have had a theory of truth, it appeared in its immanent critique of bourgeois society, which compared the pretensions of bourgeois ideology with the reality of its social conditions. Truth was not outside the society, but contained in its own claims. Men had an emancipatory interest in actualizing the ideology.

In rejecting all claims to absolute truth, Critical Theory had to face many of the problems that the sociology of knowledge was trying to solve at the same time. Yet Horkheimer and the others were never willing to go as far as Karl Mannheim, who coincidentally shared office space at the Institut before 1933, in "unmasking" Marxism as just one more ideology among others. By claiming that all knowledge was rooted in its social context *(Seinsgebunden),* Mannheim seemed to be undermining the basic Marxist distinction between true and false consciousness, to which Critical Theory adhered. As Marcuse was to write, Critical Theory "is interested in the truth content of philosophical concepts and problems. The enterprise of the sociology of knowledge, to the contrary, is occupied only with the untruths, not the truths, of previous philosophies."[97] Yet curiously, when Horkheimer wrote his critique of Mannheim in the preemigration years,[98] he chose to attack him primarily for the absolutist rather than relativist implications of his sociology of knowledge. Especially unfortunate in this respect, he argued, was Mannheim's "relationism," which attempted to salvage objective truth by arguing that all partial truths were perspectives on the whole. By assuming that such a total truth existed in the synthesis of different viewpoints, Mannheim was following a simplified Gestaltist concept of knowledge.[99] Underlying it all was a quasi-Hegelian, harmonistic belief that one could reconcile all perspectives, a belief whose implications for social change were quietistic. Unlike Marx, who had sought social transformation rather than truth, Mannheim had covertly returned to a metaphysical quest for pure knowledge.[100]

Moreover, Horkheimer charged, Mannheim's concept of the "Being" that determined consciousness was highly undialectical. To Horkheimer, there was always feedback and mediation between base and superstructure.[101] Mannheim, in contrast, had reverted to a kind of dualism of subject and object, which hypostatized both. There was no "objective" reality that individual consciousnesses partially reflected. To argue that there was was to ignore the part played by *praxis* in creating the world.

Praxis and reason were in fact the two poles of Critical Theory, as they had been for the Left Hegelians a century before. The interplay and tension between them contributed greatly to the Theory's dialectical suggestiveness, although the primacy of reason was never in doubt. As Marcuse wrote in *Reason and Revolution*, speaking for the entire Frankfurt School, "Theory will preserve the truth even if revolutionary practice deviates from its proper path. Practice follows the truth, not vice versa."[102] Still, the importance of self-determined activity, of "anthropogenesis," was constantly emphasized in the Institut's earlier writings. Here the influence of *Lebensphilosophie* on Horkheimer and his c lleagues was crucial, although they always understood true *praxis* as a collective endeavor. The stress on *praxis* accorded well with the Frankfurt School's rejection of Hegel's identity theory. In the spaces created by the irreducible mediations between subject and object, particular and universa!, human freedom might be sustained. In fact, what alarmed the Frankfurt School so much in later years was the progressive liquidation of these very areas of human spontaneity in Western society.

The other antipode of Critical Theory, the utopian reconciliation of subject and object, essence and appearance, particular and universal, had very different connotations. *Vernunft* implied an objective reason that was not constituted solely by the subjective acts of individual men. Although transformed from a philosophical ideal into a social one, it still bore traces of its metaphysical origins. Vulgar Marxism had allowed these tendencies to reemerge in the monistic materialism that the Institut never tired of attacking. And yet, as we have seen, even in Critical Theory there were an implicit negative metaphysics and negative anthropology — negative in the sense of refusing to define itself in any fixed way, thus adhering to Nietzsche's dictum that a "great truth wants to be criticized, not idolized."

As thinkers in the tradition of "positive freedom" that included Plato, Rousseau, Hegel, and Marx, they were caught in the basic dilemma that dogged the tradition from its inception. As Hannah Arendt has pointed out,[103] the notion of positive freedom contained an inherent conflict, symbolized by the tension between the Greek political experience and the subsequent attempts of Greek philosophers to make sense of it. From the former came the identification of freedom with human acts and human speech — in short, with *praxis.* From the latter came its equation with that authentic being which was reason. Attempts at an integration have been made ever since. The subtlety and richness of the Institut's effort mark it as one of the most fruitful, even though it too ultimately met with failure.

Before passing on to the methodological implications of Critical Theory, the contributions of other Institut members to its formulation should be made clear. Although Lowenthal and Pollock were concerned primarily with other matters, both intellectual and institutional, they still actively participated in the discussions of the articles submitted for publication in the *Zeitschrift.* More influential, however, were Adorno and Marcuse, both of whom wrote extensively on theoretical issues under their own names. By examining their work individually, we can perhaps further clarify the Institut's philosophical stance. We will do so, however, without commenting on the validity of their analyses of other thinkers; the object is to illuminate Critical Theory, rather than to outline an alternative interpretation.

Insofar as his Institut contributions were concerned, Adorno was occupied in the 1930's almost entirely with the sociology of music. Outside of the *Zeitschrift*, however, he published one long philosophical study and worked at great length on another.[104] In both, his closeness to Horkheimer's position was manifestly revealed. Although the two men did not write collaboratively until the 1940's, there was a remarkable similarity in their views from the first. Evidence of this exists in a letter Adorno wrote to Lowenthal from London in 1934, discussing his response to the recently published *Dämmerung*:

> I have read the book several times with the utmost precision and have an extraordinary impression of it. I already knew most of the pieces; nonetheless, in this form everything appears entirely different; above all, a certain broadness of presentation, which earlier had annoyed me in single aphorisms, now seems obvious as a means of expression — exactly appropriate to the agonizing development of the capitalist total situation whose horrors exist so essentially in the precision of the mechanism of mediation. . . . As far as my position is concerned, I believe I can almost completely identify with it — so completely that it is difficult for me to point to differences. As new and especially essential to me, I would like to mention the interpretation of the problem of personal contingency against the thesis of radical justice, and in general, the critique of static anthropology in all the pieces. Something to discuss would perhaps be the general relation to the Enlightenment.[105]

Here perhaps for the first time Adorno hinted at that more sweeping critique of the Enlightenment which he and Horkheimer together would carry out many years later.

Adorno's earliest major philosophical critique was *Kierkegaard: Construction of the Aesthetic*, written in 1929–1930 and submitted as a *Habilitationsschrift* for Paul Tillich in 1931. Its date of publication ironically fell on the day Hitler took power in 1933. Siegfried Kracauer, with whom Adorno had studied Kant, was the recipient of its dedication; the impact of another close friend, Walter Benjamin, was also evident in Adorno's arguments. Both Benjamin and Tillich were among the book's favorable reviewers.[106] *Kierkegaard* was, however, not a critical or popular success. While partly due to its unapologetically abstruse style and demandingly complex analysis, its minimal effect was also produced by what Adorno was later to call its being "overshadowed from the beginning by political evil." [107]

Whatever its difficulties — all of Adorno's work was uncompromisingly exacting for even the most sophisticated reader — the book did contain many of the themes that were to be characteristic of Critical Theory. The choice of a subject through which Adorno hoped to explore these issues was not surprising in the light of his own artistic inclinations. From the beginning of the book, however, he made it clear that by aesthetics he meant more than simply a theory of art; the word signified to him, as to Hegel, a certain type of relation between subject and object. Kierkegaard had also understood it in a specifically philosophical way. In *Either/Or,* he had defined the aesthetic sphere as "that through which man immediately is what he is; the ethical is that through which he becomes what he becomes." [108] But as Adorno noted in his first of many criticisms of Kierkegaard, "the ethical subsequently withdrew behind his teaching of paradox-religion. In view of the 'leap' of faith, the aesthetic was deprecatingly transformed from a stage in the dialectical process, namely that of the nondecisive, into simple creature-like *(kreatürliche)* immediacy." [109] To Adorno, immediacy, that is, the search for primary truths, was anathema. Like Horkheimer's, his thought was always rooted in a kind of cosmic irony, a refusal to rest somewhere and say finally, Here is where truth lies. Both men rejected Hegel's basic premise of the identity of subject and object.

Ostensibly, Kierkegaard had rejected it as well. Yet to Adorno, Kierkegaard's renowned celebration of subjectivity unwittingly contained an identity theory. "The intention of his philosophy," Adorno wrote, "does not aim towards the determination of subjectivity but of ontology; and subjectivity appears not as its content but as its stage *(Schauplatz)*." [110] Behind all his talk of the concrete, existential individual, there lurked a covert yearning for transcendent truth; "Hegel is turned inward: what for him is world history, for Kierkegaard is the individual man." [111]

Moreover, the ontology posited by Kierkegaard was that of hell, not heaven; despair rather than hope was at the center of his vision. The withdrawal into inwardness that Kierkegaard advocated was really a retreat into a mythical, demonic repetition that denied historical change. "Inwardness," Adorno wrote, "is the historical prison of prehistorical humanity." [112] By rejecting the historical world, Kierkegaard had become an accomplice of the reification he so often denounced; his dialectics were without a material object and were thus a return to the idealism he claimed to have left behind. By denying real history, he had withdrawn into a pure anthropology based on "historicity *(Geschichtlichtkeit):* the abstract possibility of existence in time." [113] Related to this was his concept of *Gleichzeitigkeit,*[114] time without change, which was the correlate of the absolutized self. Here Adorno was making a criticism similar to that leveled by Horkheimer a few years later against Bergson's idea of *durée,* as discussed above.

Along with his analysis of the philosophical implications of inwardness, Adorno included a sociological probe of what he referred to as the bourgeois *intérieur* in Kierkegaard's time. Subjective inwardness, he argued, was not unrelated to the position of *rentier* who was outside the production process, a position held by Kierkegaard himself. In this role he shared the typical petit-bourgeois sense of impotence, which he carried to an extreme by ascetically rejecting the natural self in its entirety: "His moral rigor was derived from the absolute claim of the isolated person. He criticized all eudaemonism as contingent in contrast with the objectless self." [115] It was thus no accident that sacrifice was at the center of his theology; the absolutely spiritual man ended by annihilating his natural self: "Kierkegaard's spiritualism is above all hostility to nature." [116] Here and elsewhere in his book Adorno expressed a desire to overcome man's hostility to nature, a theme that would play an increasing rôle in the Institut's later work.

Although he wrote an occasional article on Kierkegaard in later years,[117] *Kierkegaard: Construction of the Aesthetic* was really Adorno's *Abschied* (farewell) [118] to the Danish philosopher. In 1934 he left the Continent for England, where he studied at Merton College, Oxford. Except for occasional trips back to Germany, he remained in England for the next three and a half years. While continuing his interest in music and producing articles for the *Zeitschrift* on related topics, he found the time to begin a long study of Edmund Husserl, in whose work he had been interested since his doctoral dissertation in 1924. By the time it appeared in 1956, its tone was scarcely less critical than that of his earlier treatment of Kierkegaard. In this work, too, many of the ideas that Horkheimer and Marcuse were simultaneously developing can be found. Although certain sections of the work — the third chapter and the introduction — were not written until the fifties, an examination of *Towards a Metacritique of Epistemology* does give some insight into Critical Theory's attitude towards phenomenology in the thirties.

In his first book, Adorno had singled out Husserl as someone who shared Kierkegaard's stress on the self.[119] Accordingly, he now concentrated on the epistemological aspects of Husserl's work, especially those contained in his early *Logical Investigations*, which was published in three volumes in 1900, 1901, and 1913. He applauded Husserl's desire to go beyond psychologism as an explanation of cognition, but when Husserl spoke of a transcendent subject, Adorno sensed a desire to annihilate the contingent individual. In the same spirit as Kierkegaard, Husserl betrayed a fundamental yearning for ontological certainty. In attacking his "reductive" method, which sought eternal essences through a phenomenological exploration of consciousness, Adorno, like Horkheimer, argued for the importance of mediation *(Vermittlung)*.

Husserl's search for first principles revealed an inherent identity theory, despite his anti-idealistic pretensions. The need for absolute intellectual certainty, Adorno argued, was likely to be a reflex of personal insecurity: "freedom is never given, always threatened. . . . The absolutely certain as such is always unfreedom. . . . It is a mistaken conclusion that what endures is truer than what passes." [120] A true epistemology must end the fetish of knowledge as such, which, as Nietzsche demonstrated, leads to abstract systematizing. The truth was not what was "left over" [121] when a reduction of subject to object, or vice versa, took place. It resided instead in the "force field" [122] between subject and object. Absolute realism and absolute nominalism, both of which could be found in Husserl's work, led to equally fallacious reifications. As Adorno wrote in another article on Husserl, "whoever tries to reduce the world to either the factual or the essence comes in some way or other into the position of Münchhausen, who tried to drag himself out of the swamp by his own pigtails." [123]

By seeking the immutable, Husserl implicitly accepted the reality of the current "administered world." [124] Husserl, Adorno wrote, was "the most static thinker of his period." [125] It was not enough to look for the permanent within the transient, or the archaic within the present. A true dialectics, Adorno argued, was "the attempt to see the new in the old instead of simply the old in the new." [126] Although Husserl had tried to puncture the reified world by means of his reductive method based on intuition *(Wesensschau),* he had failed. Adorno admitted that intuition was a legitimate part of experience, but ought not to be elevated into an absolute method of cognition. In doing just that, Husserl had expressed an unconscious rejection of the "real world," which was "ego-alien" to him.[127] Being could no more be divorced entirely from the facts of perception than it could be equated with them.

From Husserl's epistemology Adorno went on to criticize his mathematical realism and logical "absolutism." The triumph of mathematical thinking in the West, Adorno argued, contained a mythical element. The fetish of numbers had led to a repudiation of nonidentity and a kind of hermetic idealism. Similarly, the reliance on formal logic as a mental absolute contained mythical traces. These modes of thought were also not without social significance. The reification of logic, Adorno asserted, "refers back to the commodity form whose identity exists in the 'equivalence' of exchange value." [128] Instead of formal logic, which perpetuated the false dualism of form and content, Adorno suggested a more dynamic alternative that referred back to Hegel. "Logic," he wrote, "is not Being, but a process that cannot be simply reduced to the pole of 'subjectivity' or 'objectivity.' The self-criticism of logic has as its result dialectics. . . . There is no logic without sentences, no sentences without the synthetic mental function." [129] Formal logic with its laws of contradiction and identity was a kind of repressive taboo that ultimately led to the domination of nature.[130] Adorno also strongly objected to a mimetic theory of perception, and he found it even in Husserl's phenomenology, despite its stress on intentionality. The locus of truth, when correctly understood, he contended, "becomes the mutual dependency, the production through one another *(sich durcheinander Produzieren)* of subject and object, and it should no longer be thought of as static agreement — as 'intention.' " [131] By whatever means, Husserl's attempt to uncover the essential truth, he argued, was in vain: "Only in the repudiation of every such illusion, in the idea of imageless truth, is the lost mimesis preserved and transcended *(aufgehoben),* not in the preservation of its [the truth's] rudiments." [132]

Husserl's tendency to reify the given, Adorno argued, was related to advanced bourgeois society's destruction of *Erfahrung* (experience) and its replacement by administered, lifeless concepts. The disappearance of true experience, which Benjamin had also stressed as a characteristic of modern life,[133] corresponded to the growing helplessness of modern man. To Adorno, phenomenology thus represented the last futile effort of bourgeois thought to rescue itself from impotence. "With phenomenology," he wrote, "bourgeois thought reached its end in dissociated, fragmented statements set against one another, and resigned itself to the simple reproduction of that which is." [134] In doing so, it turned against action in the world: "The denigration of *praxis* to a simple special case of intentionality is the grossest consequence of its reified premises." [135] But worst of all, the assumption of absolute identity and immediacy could well lead to the political domination of an absolute ideology. There was, Adorno suggested, a subterranean connection between phenomenology and fascism — both were expressions of the terminal crisis of bourgeois society.[136]

Among the members of the Frankfurt School Adorno perhaps most consistently expressed abhorrence of ontology and identity theory. At the same time, he also rejected naive positivism as a nonreflective metaphysics of its own, contrasting it with a dialectics that neither denied nor fully accepted the phenomenal world as the ground of truth. Against those who stressed an abstract individualism, he pointed to the social component through which subjectivity was inevitably mediated. He just as strongly resisted the temptation to acquiesce in the dissolution of the contingent individual into a totality, whether of *Volk* or class. Even Walter Benjamin, the friend from whom he learned so much, was not immune to criticism on this score. In an essay he wrote after Benjamin's tragic suicide in 1940, Adorno complained:

His target is not an allegedly overinflated subjectivism but rather the notion of a subjective dimension itself. Between myth and reconciliation, the poles of his philosophy, the subject evaporates. Before his Medusan glance, man turns into the stage on which an objective process unfolds. For this reason Benjamin's philosophy is no less a source of terror than a promise of happiness.[137]

In his persistent stress on nonidentity and contingency, Adorno developed a philosophy that was as "atonal" as the music he had absorbed from Schönberg.[138]

It would be difficult to say the same for the third of the Institut's major theoreticians, Herbert Marcuse. Despite the consistent emphasis on negativity in his work and the pessimism often attributed to it,[139] Marcuse's writing always contained an implicit faith in the possible realization of *Vernunft* in the social world. Late nineteenth-century *Lebensphilosophie* seems to have influenced him less than it did Horkheimer. As Jürgen Habermas has noted,[140] Marcuse was far more receptive to twentieth-century philosophy than were the Institut's other philosophical thinkers. His experiences with Husserl and Heidegger stayed with him, although their influence was much diminished during his years with the Institut. In addition, his style of philosophizing was always more discursive than Horkheimer's or Adorno's, possibly because he did not share their active aesthetic interests. But his style was perhaps also a reflection of his belief that writing in a systematic, nonaphoristic, linear way was an effective way of analyzing and representing reality. Marcuse never stressed the *bilderlos* (imageless) intangibility of the utopian "other" as had the other major figures in the Frankfurt School.

Without suggesting that Marcuse remained the same thinker he had been before 1932, it is still useful to examine his pre-Institut writings for an understanding of his contribution to Critical Theory, as well as his later work, which has sometimes been seen as a return to his Heideggerian period.[141] While Marcuse was at Freiburg, his thinking was heavily imbued with phenomenological categories. At the same time, he was firmly committed to Marxism, although without any specific party affiliation. His efforts to combine the two seemingly irreconcilable systems anticipated similar attempts made by Merleau-Ponty and Sartre after the war. In the first article he published, "Contributions to a Phenomenology of Historical Materialism,"[142] all of Heidegger's special vocabulary—*Sorge* (care), *Geschichtlichkeit* (historicity), *Entschlossenheit* (decisiveness), *Dasein* (being-in-the-world), and so on — was on display. To Marcuse, *Being and Time*, Heidegger's recently published masterwork, was "the moment at which bourgeois philosophy dissolves itself from within and opens the way to a new 'concrete' science." [143] This was so, Marcuse argued, for three reasons: First, Heidegger had shown the ontological importance of history and the historical world as a *Mitwelt*, a world of human interaction. Secondly, by demonstrating that man has a profound concern *(Sorge)* about his true status in the world, Heidegger had correctly raised the question of what constitutes "authentic being." And finally, by arguing that man can achieve authentic being by acting decisively in the world (through *Entschlossenheit*), Heidegger had taken bourgeois philosophy as far as it could go — to the necessity of *praxis.*[144]

It was at this point that Marcuse thought Heidegger had faltered and that Marxism became relevant. The social environment of *Being and Time* was too abstract, and Heidegger's concept of historicity too general, to account for real historical conditions that constrain human action. Marxism answered Heidegger's question about the possibility of authentic being by pointing to the "radical deed." This was Marxism's "basic situation," [145] its moment of self-revelation and self-creation. But what Marx had recognized and Heidegger ignored was the division of society into classes. At the present historical moment, only one class was truly capable of engaging in radical action, of becoming the real historical subject: "The historical deed is only possible today as the deed of the proletariat, because [the proletariat] has the only being-in-the-world *(Dasein)* with whose existence the deed is necessarily given." [146] Only because of its key role in the production process does the proletariat have the potential to perform radical acts. Only through revolution can the historical world be changed, and the possibility of universalizing authentic being beyond the working class be realized.

If, however, Heidegger must be complemented by Marx, so too should Marxism become phenomenological. Dialectics, Marcuse wrote, "must further investigate whether or not the given exhausts itself as such, or contains a meaning that is, to be sure, extra-historical, but inherent in all historicity." [147] Marxism must also abandon its traditional belief that the ideological superstructure was a reflection of the socio-economic substructure. "The old question, what has objective priority, what 'was first there,' spirit or matter, consciousness or being, cannot be decided by dialectical phenomenology and is already meaningless as it is posed."[148] Nor must a dialectical phenomenology try to investigate nature as it does history. Here Engels had been wrong. Natural being was different from historical being; mathematical, nondialectical physics was valid in its own sphere. "Nature," Marcuse wrote, "*has* a history, but *is* not history. Being-there *(Dasein) is* history."[149] Elsewhere, in an article on dialectics, he wrote: "The boundary between historicity and non-historicity . . . is an ontological boundary."[150] This, it should be added, was a point Lukács made in *History and Class Consciousness*, as Marcuse acknowledged; it demonstrated the distance of their thinking from the more "scientific" Marxism of Engels and the orthodox Marxists of the Second International.

This contrast also revealed Marcuse's debt to Dilthey, who had made a similar distinction in his own work. The statement made earlier that Marcuse was less influenced than Horkheimer by late nineteenth-century *Lebensphilosophie* should be understood in the sense that Marcuse was less responsive to its attack on traditional metaphysics. What appealed to Marcuse in Dilthey was precisely Dilthey's merging of history and ontology. In an article titled "The Problem of Historical Reality,"[151] written in 1931, Marcuse praised Dilthey for freeing the *Geisteswissenschaften* (cultural sciences) from the methodology of the *Naturwissenschaften* (natural sciences) and for restoring their philosophical foundation. Dilthey's concept of *Leben* (life) as the basis of historical reality was insightful, Marcuse argued, because of its stress on meaning rather than causality. Since men make their own history, it is unified by the values they have injected into it. Absent from the article were the criticisms that Horkheimer later leveled at Dilthey concerning his implicit idealism and identity theory, for at this time in his career Marcuse approved of the ontological premise of Dilthey's concept of history.

This was demonstrated even more clearly in what Marcuse had intended as his *Habilitationsschrift, Hegel's Ontology and the Foundation of a Theory of Historicity*.[152] Heidegger's influence, which he acknowledged at the very beginning of the work, was pervasive. The contrast between this study and his later treatment of the same subject in *Reason and Revolution* is striking.[153] Here Marcuse accepted the identity of subject and object that was at the center of Hegel's thinking. Being, he interpreted Hegel as saying, is a negative unity, a oneness that persists through all movement and separation. Thus, history is the arena in which being reveals itself. To Marcuse, Hegel's view of history was an anticipation of Heidegger's *Geschichtlichkeit* and Dilthey's *Leben*. In fact, the second half of the study attempted to read *Leben* back into Hegel as the fundamental ontological category of his early writings, including the *Phenomenology of the Spirit* and the *Logic.*

At the end of his discussion, Marcuse treated the relationship between Dilthey's stress on the *Geisteswissenschaften* and Hegel's notion of *Geist.* "Precisely as historical and in its historicity, the inner unity and totality of life is a unity and totality of knowledge," he wrote, "and the action of historical life is essentially determined through this knowledge. Precisely as historical and in its historicity, life becomes spirit. And so Dilthey wrote the sentence through which he most profoundly expressed his closeness to Hegel's intentions: 'Spirit is an historical essence.' "[154] Thus the possibility of a satisfactory historical methodology was rooted in the unity of knowledge and life. Cognition was based on the ultimate identity of subject and object.

What set *Hegel's Ontology* apart from *Reason and Revolution,* which was written after Marcuse had been at the Institut for several years, was its basic indifference to the critical elements in Hegelian philosophy. Marcuse's stress on unity and identity led to a kind of theodicy, which he did not attempt to reconcile with the Marxism he displayed in his other writings. The concept of negation, which was to play such a crucial role in the second Hegel book, was treated in the first as only a moment in the historical differentiation of being. Moreover, because the underlying unity of being was understood to persist throughout time, negation was made to appear as almost an illusion. Nowhere in the book was Hegel treated as having preceded Marx in assailing the irrationality of the existing order. Nowhere was the nonidentity of the actual and the rational stressed, as it would be in *Reason and Revolution.* Nowhere was the importance of mediation in cognition recognized, a recognition that marked Adorno's later treatment of Husserl.

If the early Marcuse, like the Lukács of *History and Class Consciousness,* adhered to an identity theory that Horkheimer and Adorno were attacking, he likewise accepted the possibility of a philosophical anthropology, which they spurned. In addition to his approval of Heidegger's idea of "authentic being," which had anthropological overtones, he expressed considerable excitement over the newly recovered *Economic and Philosophical Manuscripts* of Marx. In a piece he contributed to Rudolph Hilferding's *Die Gesellschaft* in 1932,[155] he argued that it would be a mistake to interpret the philosophical concerns of Marx's early manuscripts as having been "overcome" in the mature writings. The communist revolution, he pointed out, promises more than merely a change in economic relations; it more ambitiously envisions a transformation of man's basic existence through a realization of his essence. Through revolution, man realizes his potential nature in history, which can be understood as the "true natural history of man." [156]

In the article, Marcuse expressed an ambiguous view of man's relation to nature. At one point in his argument[157] he claimed that Marx had sought the unity of man and nature — the very goal that Adorno and Horkheimer were later to emphasize in opposition to Marx. But at the same time, what they disliked in Marx's view of nature, Marcuse himself expressed elsewhere in his article: "All 'nature' (in the widest sense of extrahuman being) is the medium of human life, the life-means [*Lebensmittel*, which also means food] of men. . . . Man cannot simply be subservient to or come to terms with the objective world, he must appropriate it, to make it his own." [158] Clearly implied here was the domination of nature rather than reconciliation with it.

This seeming contradiction is perhaps explained by Marcuse's agreement with Marx that labor *(Arbeit)* was man's means of realizing his essence. Labor, Marcuse contended, was man's nature; it was an ontological category, as Marx and Hegel had both understood, although the former was more perceptive in extending it beyond mental labor.[159] Man, Marcuse asserted, must objectify himself; he must become *an-sich* as well as *für-sich,* object as well as subject. The horror of capitalism was produced by the type of objectification it fostered. Here Marcuse agreed with the analysis of alienated labor in the *Economic and Philosophic Manuscripts*, to which Horkheimer and Adorno rarely referred in their writings. Unalienated labor, he suggested, implied working with others, not against them. Only through social activity might man's "species being" *(Gattungswesen)* be realized. Capitalism, because it prevented this, was a "catastrophe of human essence" demanding a "total revolution." [160]

Significantly, Marcuse's belief in the ontological centrality of labor remained a constant factor in his work after 1933. In *Reason and Revolution* he sought to read Marx's notion of labor back into Hegel: "the concept of labor is not peripheral in Hegel's system, but is the central notion through which he conceives the development of society." [161] In focusing on *Arbeit* as the basic category of human self-realization, Marcuse necessarily de-emphasized an alternative means of self-production that can be found in Hegel's writings, especially his early ones. Jürgen Habermas has recently pointed to the equal importance of this second mode of self-production, "symbolically mediated interaction," that is, language and expressive gestures.[162]

To Marcuse, however, Hegel believed that "language . . . makes it possible for an individual to take a position *against* his fellows and to assert his needs and desires against those of the other individuals. The resulting antagonisms are integrated through the process of labor, which also becomes the decisive force of the development of culture." [163] By tracing the contradictions of society back to a specific type of labor, Marcuse was able to talk of an "essential" change, which would be produced by the overcoming of alienated labor (or the abolition of labor entirely in favor of play, as he was to argue in later works).[164] Because Horkheimer and Adorno were less sure about the ontological significance of labor, they were not as willing to predict an "integration of antagonisms based on overcoming the alienation of labor," which implied a kind of identity theory. As always, they were reluctant to make positive speculations about human nature.

Once Marcuse joined the Institut, the influence of Horkheimer on his work became pronounced. He abandoned Heidegger's vocabulary, as the impact of phenomenology on his thinking began to recede. Descending somewhat from the level of philosophical abstraction, he began to deal with more concrete social and historical issues.[165] He ceased to use Marxism as a positive philosophy answering Heidegger's question about "authentic being" and began employing it more as a critical, dialectical methodology useful in explaining history, not historicity. Even so, Marcuse never engaged in the type of empirical work that the Institut strove to combine with its theorizing. Of all the figures in the Frankfurt School he remained most exclusively concerned with theoretical issues; his *Zeitschrift* articles in the 1930's, for example, included analyses of hedonism, which has been discussed above, the concept of essence, and the relation between philosophy and Critical Theory.

In discussing the function of the concept of essence in various philosophical systems, Marcuse followed Horkheimer in situating each doctrine in its historical setting:

> According to the view characteristic of the dawning bourgeois era, the critical autonomy of rational subjectivity is to establish and justify the ultimate essential truths on which all theoretical and practical truth depends. The essence of man and of things is contained in the freedom of the thinking individual, the *ego cogito.* At the close of this era, knowledge of essence has primarily the function of binding the critical freedom of the individual to pregiven, unconditionally valid necessities.[166]

Husserl's phenomenology, Marcuse argued, was an attempt to rescue bourgeois theory, an attempt that had failed. Scheler, on the other hand, espoused an essentialism that was covertly an ideology of authoritarianism. Materialist theory in contrast "takes up the concept of essence where philosophy last treated it as a dialectical concept — in Hegel's *Logic*." [167] It must relate the concept to dynamic, human *praxis*, as Marx had done. Here, the old Heideggerian Marcuse was clearly gone. In "The Concept of Essence" he wrote:

Since Dilthey, the various trends of *Lebensphilosophie* and existentialism have concerned themselves with the concrete 'historicity' of theory. . . . All such efforts had to fail, because they were linked (at first unconsciously, then consciously) to the very interests and aims whose theory they opposed. They did not attack the presuppositions of bourgeois philosophy's abstractness: the actual unfreedom and powerlessness of the individual in an anarchic production process.[168]

In his essay "Philosophy and Critical Theory," Marcuse clarified the reasons why bourgeois philosophy had been so hermetically isolated: "The philosopher can only participate in social struggles insofar as he is not a professional philosopher. This 'division of labor,' too, results from the modern separation of the mental from the material means of production, and philosophy cannot overcome it. The abstract character of philosophical work in the past and present is rooted in the social conditions of existence." [169] Critical Theory, he argued, is therefore less ambitious than traditional philosophy. It does not think itself capable of giving permanent answers to the age-old questions about man's condition. Instead, it "means to show only the specific social conditions at the root of philosophy's inability to pose the problem in a more comprehensive way, and to indicate that any other solution [lies] beyond that philosophy's boundaries. The untruth inherent in all transcendental treatment of the problem thus comes into philosophy 'from the outside'; hence it can be overcome only outside philosophy." [170]

If Critical Theory was not like philosophy, though preserving many of its insights, neither was it the equivalent of a science, as vulgar Marxists had assumed. "Scientific objectivity as such," Marcuse contended, "is never a sufficient guarantee of truth, especially in a situation where the truth speaks as strongly against the facts and is as well hidden behind them as today. Scientific predictability does not coincide with the futuristic mode in which the truth exists." [171] Instead, Critical Theory must contain a strongly imaginative, even utopian strain, which transcends the present limits of reality: "Without fantasy, all philosophical knowledge remains in the grip of the present or the past and severed from the future, which is the only link between philosophy and the real history of mankind."[172] The stress on fantasy, especially as embodied in great works of art, and the concern with *praxis* were thus the two cardinal expressions of Critical Theory's refusal to eternalize the present and shut off the possibility of a transformed future. Here Marcuse, Horkheimer, Adorno, and the other members of the Institut's inner circle were in complete agreement. In time this was to change, but during the thirties, perhaps the most fruitful decade of the Institut's history, the integration of rational theory, aesthetic imagination, and human action seemed at least a hope, however uncertain and fragile.

The survival of that hope can be read between the lines of the work that occupied Marcuse during his last active years with the Institut, *Reason and Revolution.*[173] Written in large measure to rescue Hegel from his association in American minds with Nazism — the burden of his argument was that Hegel's political theory, including his controversial emphasis on the state, was inherently rationalist, whereas the Nazis were irrationalists in the tradition of organicist romanticism — it also served as the first extensive introduction of Critical Theory to an English-speaking audience.[174] As noted earlier, *Reason and Revolution* demonstrated the distance Marcuse had traveled in the decade since his break with Heidegger; so much so that in most crucial respects, the book agreed with the principles articulated in Horkheimer's *Zeitschrift* essays.

Marcuse, like Horkheimer, was eager to establish the critical, negative thrust of Hegel's rationalism. As he was to do with Freud much later, he was anxious to reverse Hegel's conservative image. He was likewise concerned with the ways in which this radical element had been eliminated in the work of Hegel's positivist successors. In extended critiques of Comte, Stahl, and von Stein, Marcuse sought to expose their conservative political implications, as Horkheimer had done with their twentieth-century positivist descendants. Marcuse also focused on the connections between Marx and Hegel, continuing his earlier analysis of the unity of Marx's early and later work. The Hegelian elements in Marx's thought were not a source of embarrassment to Marcuse as they had been to more "scientific" Marxists, because in his reading, Hegel was already a progressive thinker. "The conception underlying [Hegel's] entire system," he wrote, was that "the given social order, based upon the system of abstract and quantitative labor and upon the integration of wants through the exchange of commodities, was incapable of asserting and establishing a rational community."[175] Even more centrally, as we have seen, Marcuse saw Marx's stress on labor anticipated in Hegel's own work, a point on which he and the Institut members were at variance.

On the other hand, Marcuse was now in full agreement with Horkheimer that the ontological impulse of Hegel's thought, which he had looked on with favor during his Heideggerian period, had been surpassed by Marx's more historical approach:

> The totality in which the Marxian theory moves is other than that of Hegel's philosophy, and this difference indicates the decisive difference between Hegel's and Marx's dialectics. For Hegel, the totality was the totality of reason, a closed ontological system, finally identical with the rational system of history. . . . Marx, on the other hand, detached dialectic from this ontological base. In his work, the negativity of reality becomes a *historical* condition which cannot be hypostatized as a metaphysical state of affairs.[176]

Marcuse also shared Horkheimer's and Adorno's rejection of the assumption that socialism was a necessary outgrowth of capitalism. Like them, he sounded a note of skepticism about the connection between human emancipation and the progress of technology and instrumental rationalism.[177]

Along with this attitude went an acknowledgment of the necessity of voluntarism and *praxis*. Still, like the other members of the Frankfurt School, Marcuse felt that the senior partner in the relationship between theory and practice was clearly the former: "Theory will preserve the truth even if revolutionary practice deviates from its proper path. Practice follows the truth, not vice versa." [178] Even in his later years, when unlike Horkheimer and Adorno he was to look favorably on activist protest, at no time did Marcuse abandon this faith in the primacy of correct theory.

In these ways and others, *Reason and Revolution* was clearly a product of the Frankfurt School. In certain respects, however, Marcuse did reveal a degree of independence from Horkheimer's influence. The difference in their attitude towards the centrality of labor meant that Marcuse hesitated to implicate Marx in his critique of instrumental rationality, in the way that Horkheimer, Adorno, and more recent members of the Frankfurt School were to do.[179] He was also kinder to Marx's successors than they were. Only Bernstein's brand of revisionism came in for criticism; Plekhanov and Lenin were praised for trying to preserve the "critical import of the Marxian doctrine," [180] and Kautsky and the Second International were practically ignored. Moreover, *Reason and Revolution* contained no distinction between Engels's "historical materialism" and the dialectical materialism at the root of Critical Theory. Finally, Marcuse was not as concerned with the conformist, theodicy-like elements in Hegel's identity theory as Horkheimer had been in several of his early essays, a lack of concern perhaps related to his relative indifference to the theological premises of Hegel's thought, which several of his critics were quick to note.[181]

On the whole, however, *Reason and Revolution* was a fitting valedictory for Marcuse, whose association with the Institut was to lessen in the forties as his involvement with governmental service grew. Working with the OSS and the State Department was not precisely what the Frankfurt School had meant when it advocated revolutionary *praxis,* a point that its detractors on the left were to make in subsequent years. Still, like other members of the Institut who worked with the government during the war, Marcuse was faithful to the observation that the unity of theory and practice was only a utopian hope. In the light of the existing alternatives, aiding the war effort against Hitler while maintaining the purity of one's theoretical commitment can scarcely be called a dishonorable compromise. (Later, of course, continuing to work for the American government became increasingly problematical, but Marcuse remained until the Korean War.) The role of the intellectual, the Institut came to believe with growing certainty, was to continue thinking what was becoming ever more unthinkable in the modern world.

If the separation of mental and physical labor could not be overcome by a philosopher's fiat, at least there was useful theoretical work to be done to help bring about the day when the unification of the two might occur (or perhaps to explain why it would not). Although its ultimate relevance to political action was never to be denied, Critical Theory now had to devote itself solely to an examination of social and cultural reality. As a method of social research, however, it would have to be very different from its traditional counterpart. These points were made by Horkheimer in 1937 in one of the most significant of his articles in the *Zeitschrift*, "Traditional and Critical Theory." [182] The objective of traditional theory, he asserted, had always been the formulation of general, internally consistent principles describing the world. This had been true whether they were generated deductively, as in Cartesian theory, inductively, as in the work of John Stuart Mill, or phenomenologically, as in Husserl's philosophy. Even Anglo-Saxon science with its stress on empiricism and verification sought general propositions to test. The goal of traditional research had been pure knowledge, rather than action. If it pointed in the direction of activity, as in the case of Baconian science, its goal was technological mastery of the world, which was very different from *praxis.* At all times, traditional theory maintained a strict separation of thought and action.

Critical Theory differed on several counts. First of all, it refused to fetishize knowledge as something apart from and superior to action. In addition, it recognized that disinterested scientific research was impossible in a society in which men were themselves not yet autonomous; the researcher, Horkheimer argued, was always part of the social object he was attempting to study. And because the society he investigated was still not the creation of free, rational human choice, the scientist could not avoid partaking of that heteronomy. His perception was necessarily mediated through social categories above which he could not rise. In a remark that answered Marshall McLuhan thirty years before McLuhan's recent popularity, Horkheimer wrote, "Let the sentence that tools are extensions of men's organs be turned around, so that organs are also extensions of men's tools," [183] an injunction addressed even to the "objective" social scientist, whether positivist or intuitive. Related to this argument was Horkheimer's objection to Dilthey's methodology of the cultural sciences mentioned above. The historian could not reexperience in his mind that which had never been made by fully autonomous, conscious action.

In discussing the possibility of prediction, Horkheimer used the same argument. Only when society was more rational would it be possible for the social scientist to foretell the future. Vico's insight into the ability of man to understand his history because he made it had yet to be realized, because men do not make their history in the current era. The chances for scientific prediction were thus determined as much socially as methodologically.[184]

In the present society, then, it would be a mistake to see intellectuals as *freischwebende* (free-floating), to use the term Mannheim had taken from Alfred Weber and popularized. The ideal of a "free-floating" intellectual above the fray was a formalistic illusion, which should be discarded. At the same time, it would be equally erroneous to see the intellectual as entirely *verwurzelt,* rooted in his culture or class, as had *völkisch* and vulgar Marxist thinkers.[185] Both extremes misconstrued subjectivity as either totally autonomous or totally contingent. Although definitely a part of his society, the researcher was not incapable of rising above it at times. In fact, it was his duty to reveal those negative forces and tendencies in society that pointed to a different reality. In short, to maintain the formalistic dualism of facts and values, which traditional theories of the Weberian kind so strongly emphasized, was to act in the service of the status quo.[186] The researcher's values necessarily influenced his work; indeed they should consciously do so. Knowledge and interest were ultimately inseparable.

In addition to objecting to the goal of pure knowledge, which informed traditional theory, Horkheimer also rejected the ideal of general principles and verifying or falsifying examples. The general truths Critical Theory dealt with could not be verified or falsified by reference to the present order, simply because they implied the possibility of a different one.[187] There must always be a dynamic moment in verification, one that pointed to the "negative" elements latent in the current reality. Social research must always contain a historical component, not in the rigid sense of judging events in the context of "objective" historical forces, but rather seeing them in the light of historical possibilities. Dialectical social research was receptive to insights generated from man's prescientific experience; as mentioned earlier, it recognized the validity of the aesthetic imagination, of fantasy, as a repository of genuine human aspirations. All valid experience for the social theorist, it held, ought not to be reduced to the controlled observation of the laboratory.

While always keeping the totality of present contradictions and future possibilities in mind, Critical Theory refused to become too general and abstract. It often attempted to grasp the whole as it was embodied in concrete particulars. Not unlike Leibniz, it saw universals present in specific historical phenomena, which were like monads, at once universal and particular. At times its method seemed to emphasize analogy more than cause and effect in the traditional sense. Benjamin's remark that "the eternal is more like lace trimmings on a dress than like an idea," [188] stripped of its theological underpinnings, might have served as a model for Critical Theory, if not for its practitioners' equally strong insistence on the necessity of conceptual explanation. Characteristic of much of the Institut's writing, and Adorno's in particular, was a sometimes dazzling, sometimes bewildering juxtaposition of highly abstract statements with seemingly trivial observations. This is perhaps explained by the fact that unlike traditional theory, which equated "concrete" with "particular" and "abstract" with "universal," Critical Theory followed Hegel, for whom, as George Kline wrote, " 'concrete' means 'many-sided, adequately related, complexly mediated' . . . while 'abstract' means 'one-sided, inadequately related, relatively unmediated.' " [189] By an examination of different concrete phenomena from all the different fields mastered by the Institut's members, it was hoped that mutually fruitful insights could be gained that would help illuminate the whole.

Underlying everything, however, was the goal of social change. In relating research to *praxis,* the Institut was careful to distinguish its approach from that of the pragmatists. This Horkheimer and Adorno made clear in several critiques of the strongly entrenched pragmatist tradition that the Institut encountered in America.[190] Their antipathy towards pragmatism remained strong throughout the rest of their stay in this country. As late as December 21, 1945, Horkheimer could write to Lowenthal:

> You can see from my quotes that I have read not a few of these native products and I have now the feeling to be an expert in it. The whole thing belongs definitely into the period before the First World War and is somehow on the line of empiriocriticism, but much less cultivated than our old Cornelius.

Both pragmatism and positivism, he wrote in a subsequent letter, "share the identification of philosophy and scientism." [191] Although the pragmatists were correct in relating truth to human activity, their understanding of the relationship was too simple, too undialectical:

> The epistemological teaching that truth is life-enhancing, or rather that all 'profitable' thought must also be true, contains a harmonistic deception, if this epistemology does not belong to a totality containing tendencies really leading to a better, life-enhancing condition. Separated from a definite theory of the entire society, every epistemology remains formal and abstract.[192]

Pragmatism ignored the fact that some theories contradict the present reality and work against it, yet are not "false." The implications of pragmatism were thus more conformist than critical, despite its pretensions; like positivism, it lacked a means of going beyond the existing "facts." In making this critique, Horkheimer was performing a valuable service, in that Marxism had been incorrectly reduced to a variant of pragmatism by Sidney Hook and others in the thirties. Yet, as Lowenthal and Habermas were later to note, he missed the dialectical potential in certain strains of the pragmatic tradition.[193]

Dialectical materialism, Horkheimer argued, also had a theory of verification based on practical, historical testing: "Truth is a moment in correct *praxis;* he who identifies it with success leaps over history and becomes an apologist for the dominant reality." [194] "Correct *praxis*" is the key phrase here, indicating once again the importance in the Institut's thinking of theory as a guide to action, as well as a certain circularity in its reasoning. In the desire to unify theory and *praxis,* however, the distance that still necessarily separates them, Horkheimer warned, should not be hastily forgotten. This gap was most clearly shown in the relationship between philosophy and the proletariat. To Marx and Engels, the working class was to be the sole catalyst of the new order. "The *head* of this emancipation is *philosophy,* its *heart* is the *proletariat.* Philosophy cannot be made a reality without the abolition of the proletariat, the proletariat cannot be abolished without philosophy being made a reality." So Marx wrote in his *Critique of Hegel's Philosophy of Right.* But in the twentieth century, Horkheimer argued, material conditions were such that the working classes in advanced industrial societies were no longer automatically suited for this role. The intellectual who slavishly echoed whatever the proletariat seemed to desire was thus abdicating his own true function, which was persistently to stress possibilities transcending the present order. In fact, tension between intellectuals and workers was currently necessary in order to combat the proletariat's conformist tendencies.[195] Thus, Critical Theory did not see itself simply as the expression of the consciousness of one class, which indicated its distance from more orthodox Marxists like Lukács, who consistently stressed class consciousness, even when "imputed" from afar. Instead, it was willing to ally itself with all "progressive" forces willing "to tell the truth." [196]

If the verification of Critical Theory could only come through its relation to "correct *praxis,*" what could this mean when the only class that Marxism declared fit for revolutionary action proved incapable of fulfilling its historical role? In the 1930's the Institut had not fully confronted this problem, although doubts were beginning to appear. "Today," Marcuse wrote in 1934, "the fate of the labor movement, in which the heritage of this philosophy [critical idealism] was preserved, is clouded with uncertainty." [197] As we shall see, the uncertainty continued to grow, except for one dramatic moment during the war when Horkheimer returned temporarily to the optimism of his *Dämmerung* aphorisms.[198]

In the meantime, the Institut began to direct most of its attention towards an effort to understand the disappearance of "negative," critical forces in the world. In effect, this meant a turning away from material (in the sense of economic) concerns, although in the work of Pollock, Grossmann, and others they were not entirely neglected. Instead, the Institut focused its energies on what traditional Marxists had relegated to a secondary position, the cultural superstructure of modern society. This meant concentrating primarily on two problems: the structure and development of authority, and the emergence and proliferation of mass culture. But before such analyses could be satisfactorily completed, a gap in the classical Marxist model of substructure and superstructure had to be filled. The missing link was psychological, and the theory the Institut chose to supply it was Freud's. How the unlikely integration of Marxism and psychoanalysis was brought about is the subject of the next chapter.

III

The Integration of Psychoanalysis

> In psychoanalysis nothing is true except the exaggerations.
>
> — THEODOR W. ADORNO

> If fear and destructiveness are the major emotional sources of fascism, *eros* belongs mainly to democracy.
>
> — the authors of *The Authoritarian Personality*

In the 1970's it is difficult to appreciate the audacity of the first theorists who proposed the unnatural marriage of Freud and Marx. With the recent resurgence of interest in Wilhelm Reich and the widespread impact of Marcuse's *Eros and Civilization*, the notion that both men were speaking to similar questions, if from very different vantage points, has gained credence among many on the left. A generation ago, however, the absurdity of such an idea was rarely disputed on either side of the Atlantic. Although Trotsky had been sympathetic to psychoanalysis, his voice was no longer heard in orthodox Communist circles after 1923, when a taboo descended on Freud and his followers and Pavlovian behaviorism became the new orthodoxy. Within the psychoanalytic movement itself, Siegfried Bernfeld, Otto Fenichel, and Paul Federn had expressed interest in the integration of the two systems, but with little success.[1] Reich, its most vociferous proponent in the late twenties and thirties, met with general ridicule;[2] and by the mid-thirties he had been unceremoniously drummed out of both the Communist Party and the psychoanalytic movement. Conservatives and radicals alike agreed that Freud's basic pessimism about the possibilities for social change were incompatible with the revolutionary hopes of a true Marxist. As late as 1959 Philip Rieff could write: "For Marx, the past is pregnant with the future, with the proletariat as the midwife of history. For Freud, the future is pregnant with the past, a burden of which only the physician, and luck, can deliver us. . . . Revolution could only repeat the prototypal rebellion against the father, and in every case, like it, be doomed to failure." [3]

The Institut für Sozialforschung's attempt to introduce psychoanalysis into its neo-Marxist Critical Theory was thus a bold and unconventional step. It was also a mark of the Institut's desire to leave the traditional Marxist straitjacket behind. In fact, one of the basic divisions between the Grünberg-Grossmann generation of Institut members and their successors, led by Horkheimer, was the contrast in their respective attitudes towards psychology. And in later years, as we shall see, Franz Neumann's general indifference towards psychology was one of the factors preventing his being fully accepted by the Institut's inner circle. When Neumann did finally become interested in Freud, it was near the end of his life, too late to achieve a successful integration of the two traditions.[4]

In contrast, Horkheimer's interest in Freud had extended back into the 1920's. His concern was partly stimulated by Leo Lowenthal, who was actually analyzed by Frieda Fromm-Reichmann in the mid-twenties. In addition, the relationship between psychology and socialism was a topic often discussed in the Frankfurt of those years. A figure of some importance in left-wing university circles after 1929 was the Belgian socialist Henrik de Man, whose *On the Psychology of Marxism* (1927) [5] attempted to replace economic determinism with a more subjectively grounded activism. De Man attacked the utilitarian, interest-oriented psychology he attributed to Marx, stressing instead the irrational roots of radical action. It was rumored at the time that de Man was brought to the Frankfurt faculty as a professor of social psychology to provide a counterweight to the Institut's more orthodox Marxism.[6] Whatever the reason, his coming did not win Horkheimer and the others over to an irrationalist position, which was clearly incompatible with Critical Theory; de Man's later flirtation with fascism would seem to confirm their distrust. What they did share with him, however, was a desire to go beyond the instrumental utilitarianism that permeated vulgar Marxism.

As early as 1927, Adorno, with Horkheimer's encouragement, wrote a lengthy paper in which he related psychoanalysis to Cornelius's transcendental phenomenology.[7] Among the parallels between them that he noted were their shared stress on the connected, symbolically linked structure of the unconscious and their common attempt to start with contemporary experiences to reach those in the past.[8] In the following year, Horkheimer, who had been personally interested in analysis for some time, decided to undergo it himself, selecting as his psychiatrist Karl Landauer, who had been a student of Freud. After a year, the one problem that seriously bothered Horkheimer, an inability to lecture without a prepared text,[9] was resolved and the analysis, which was really more an educational than a therapeutic exercise, ended. Landauer, however, was persuaded to form the Frankfurt Psychoanalytic Institute as a branch of the Southwest German Psychoanalytic Study Group, itself a recent creation in Heidelberg.[10] Opened on February 16, 1929, the Frankfurt Psychoanalytic Institute became the first avowedly Freudian organization to be tied, even indirectly, to a German university. It also maintained a loose connection with Horkheimer and his colleagues, who had been instrumental in securing university approval for the new "guest institute," as it was called. Freud himself wrote two letters to Horkheimer to express his gratitude.[11]

Joining Landauer as permanent members were Heinrich Meng, Erich Fromm, and Fromm's wife, Frieda Fromm-Reichmann.[12] In the first few months of the Psychoanalytic Institute's existence, public lectures were delivered by such luminaries of the movement as Hanns Sachs, Siegfried Bernfeld, Anna Freud, and Paul Federn. Georg Groddeck was also a frequent visitor. Of the four permanent members, Fromm, who had been Lowenthal's friend for over a decade, and who was introduced by him to the Institut, soon established himself as its most important figure. Only he rejoined the Institut für Sozialforschung after its emigration to America, where he soon established himself as one of the most prominent of the so-called Neo-Freudian revisionists. His wife also came to America, but had little to do with the Institut. Landauer went to Amsterdam instead, where he unwisely resisted until it was too late the entreaties of his former colleagues to leave Europe; he died in Belsen during the war. Meng was more fortunate, leaving Frankfurt for Basel, where he established himself as an expert on mental hygiene. It was thus primarily through Fromm's work that the Institut first attempted to reconcile Freud and Marx.

Born in Frankfurt in 1900, Fromm was brought up in an intensely religious milieu. During his adolescence he became strongly attracted to the messianic strains in Jewish thought. "More than anything else," he was later to write, "I was moved by the prophetic writings, by Isaiah, Amos, Hosea; not so much by their warnings and their announcement of disaster, but by their promise of the 'end of days.' . . . The vision of universal peace and harmony between nations touched me deeply when I was twelve and thirteen years old." [13] In his early twenties, Fromm, along with Lowenthal, joined the circle around Rabbi Nobel. He was also instrumental in the formation of the celebrated Freies Jüdisches Lehrhaus, with Georg Salzberger and Franz Rosenzweig. Although Fromm lost the outward trappings of his orthodoxy in 1926 after he was analyzed for the first time in Munich, what might be called an attitude of religiosity remained with him in all his later work.

What he absorbed from his Jewish antecedents was, however, very different from that apparently taken by Horkheimer and Adorno from theirs. Instead of stressing the nonrepresentational quality of truth and the impossibility of defining the essential man, Fromm affirmed the notion of a philosophical anthropology. Like Martin Buber and others in the Lehrhaus circle, he understood man's nature as something created through relatedness to the world and interaction with others. This was to appear most vividly in his later works after his departure from the Institut, but at all times Fromm affirmed the reality of a human nature. It was, however, not a fixed concept like the Roman *natura,* but rather an idea of man's potential nature, similar to the Greek *physis.* Accordingly, Fromm always put great emphasis on the anthropological implications of Marx's *Economic and Philosophic Manuscripts.*[14] Here he was closer to Marcuse, at least before Marcuse's entry into Institut affairs, than to Horkheimer and Adorno. Of those associated with the Frankfurt School, Fromm most often employed Marx's notion of alienation, especially in his post-Institut work.[15] In attempting to ground his vision of a perfected man in man's essential nature, Fromm sought glimpses of that nature in the work of such thinkers as Spinoza[16] and Dewey. And in the 1940's he attempted to go beyond psychology, to an ethical system also based on human nature. Behind the humanistic veneer of his ethics, which were most completely expressed in *Man for Himself* (1947), there lurked a naturalism that some critics found difficult to sustain.[17]

By the forties, Fromm had left not only the Institut behind, but his orthodox Freudianism as well. This did not, of course, mean that he had abandoned all aspects of his earlier position. "I have never left Freudianism," he was later to write,

> unless one identifies Freud with his libido theory. . . . I consider the basic achievement of Freud to be his concept of the unconscious, its manifestations in neurosis, dreams, etc., resistance, and his dynamic concept of character. These concepts have remained for me of basic importance in all my work, and to say that because I gave up the libido theory I gave up Freudianism is a very drastic statement only possible from the standpoint of orthodox Freudianism. At any rate, I never gave up psychoanalysis. I have never wanted to form a school of my own. I was removed by the Interna-

tional Psychoanalytic Association from membership in this Association to which I had belonged, and I am still [1971] a member of the Washington Psychoanalytic Association, which is Freudian. I have always criticized the Freudian orthodoxy and the bureaucratic methods of the Freudian international organization, but my whole theoretical work is based on what I consider Freud's most important findings, with the exception of the metapsychology.[18]

To other observers, however, the jettisoning of the libido theory and other crucial elements in Freud's original thought, such as the Oedipus complex, meant that Fromm had moved far enough away from the essential elements in orthodox theory to justify calling him a thoroughgoing revisionist. Fromm's distinction between Freud's clinical findings and his metapsychology — by which he meant not only Freud's admittedly controversial speculations about instincts of life and death, but also his more widely accepted theory of the libido — did not satisfy those who saw a more intimate connection between the two, including his Institut colleagues.

Although Fromm never entirely ceased his efforts to merge psychoanalysis and Marxism, his later attempts relied less on certain aspects of Freud's work and increasingly on psychological insights that Marx himself had anticipated.[19] When he came to write his intellectual autobiography in 1962, he considered Marx a far more important figure in his own development. "That Marx is a figure of world historical significance," he wrote, "with whom Freud cannot even be compared in this respect hardly needs to be said." [20] The prophetic notion of universal peace that he had learned in his youth led him to appreciate the similar note struck by Marx and to turn away from the less affirmative implications of Freud's thought, although he remained faithful to many Freudian concepts.

Thirty years earlier, however, when Fromm came to the Institut, his attitude towards Freud was very different. After his studies at the universities of Heidelberg, Frankfurt, and Munich, he obtained psychoanalytic training at the Berlin Psychoanalytic Institute. Here he was analyzed by Hanns Sachs and received instruction from such prominent Freudians as Theodor Reik. In 1926 he began to practice clinically himself, although like Sachs and many of the early analysts he was never medically trained as a doctor. The contact he began to have with actual patients was always, so Fromm claimed, an invaluable stimulus to his speculative work, one that the other members of the Institut lacked.[21] Shortly after, his first articles began to appear in orthodox psychoanalytic journals, such as the *Zeitschrift für psychoanalytische Pädagogik*, edited by A. J. Storfer, and Freud's own house organ, *Imago*.

Although his topics often reflected his religious background (for example, a study of the Sabbath),[22] Fromm also displayed an early interest in the development of a social psychology. An article he wrote for *Psychoanalytische Bewegung* in 1931, "Psychoanalysis and Politics," caused considerable controversy in analytic circles. Even more indicative of his desire to enrich his Freudianism with Marxist insights was his first extensive study, *The Development of the Dogma of Christ*,[23] which was stimulated by Theodor Reik's treatment of the same problem. Where Reik had gone wrong, Fromm argued, was in homogenizing the early Christians as a single group with a uniform psychic reality. In doing so, Reik was not unlike theologians such as Harnack: "[Reik] overlooks the fact that the psychological subject here is not a man and is not even a group possessing a relatively unified and unchanging psychic structure, but, rather, is made up of different groups with different social and psychic interests." [24] To Fromm, the basic change in Christian dogma — from the first-century Adoptionist idea of a man becoming God to the fourth-century Homoousian notion of God becoming man — was a product of social change. Only the earlier formulation expressed the rebellious hostility of the first Christians towards authority, the authority of the father. The doctrinal change corresponded to the acceptance of God's authority and a redirection of resentment inwardly, onto the Christians themselves. "The cause for the development," Fromm argued, "lies in the change in the socio-economic situation or in the retrogression of the economic forces and their social consequences. The ideologists of the dominant classes strengthened and accelerated this development by suggesting symbolic satisfactions to the masses, guiding their aggression into socially harmless channels." [25]

In arguing for a sensitivity to the differences between specific social groups, rather than a blanket attribution of ideological doctrines to universal psychic needs, Fromm was asserting in psychological terms what Horkheimer and Marcuse, after his break with Heidegger, were saying about the abstract notion of "historicity." Where he introduced a specifically Freudian component was in his use of psychoanalytic mechanisms as the mediating concepts betwen individual and society — for example, in talking about hostility to authority in terms of Oedipal resentment of the father. This was in fact the use the Institut later made of many of Freud's concepts. In the first issue of the *Zeitschrift* Borkenau was selected to write a review of *The Development of the Dogma of Christ*, which he approvingly called the first concrete example of the integration of Freud and Marx.

In that same issue, Fromm attempted to spell out the basic ground rules for a social psychology.[26] He began by criticizing the notion that psychology applied only to the individual, singling out the early work of Wilhelm Reich for espousing this view.[27] Although attacking the idea of a group or mass soul, Fromm felt that individuals were never entirely isolated from their social situation. The real task was to supplement and enrich the basic Marxist framework, which he accepted as a given. Marxism, he argued, had incorrectly been charged with having a simplistic psychology of acquisitiveness; here he pointed an accusing finger at Bertrand Russell and Henrik de Man for wrongly seeing economic self-interest as the basis of Marx's view of man. In fact, he argued, Marx's psychological premises were few — fewer than Fromm was later to assert himself. Man to Marx has certain basic drives (hunger, love, and so forth), which seek gratification; acquisitiveness was merely a product of specific social conditions. Marxism was, however, in need of additional psychological insights, which such Marxists as Kautsky and Bernstein, with their naive, idealistic belief in inborn moral instincts, had failed to provide.[28] Psychoanalysis could provide the missing link between ideological superstructure and socio-economic base. In short, it could flesh out materialism's notion of man's essential nature.[29]

Fromm, however, had a very definite idea of what constituted the most fruitful aspects of psychoanalysis for a social psychology. At the very beginning of his article,[30] he made clear his rejection of Freud's life and death instinct theory, which he dismissed as an injudicious mixture of biology and psychology. Instead, Fromm adhered to the earlier Freudian dichotomy of erotic and self-preservation drives. Because the former were capable of being displaced, sublimated, and satisfied in fantasies (for example, sadism could be gratified in a number of socially acceptable ways), while the latter could not (only bread could relieve hunger), sexuality was more adaptable to social conditions.[31] The task of an analytical social psychology was to understand unconsciously motivated behavior in terms of the effect of the socio-economic substructure on basic psychic drives. Childhood experiences, Fromm argued, were especially important, because the family was the agent of society. (Fromm's stress on the family remained with him throughout his career, although he was later to modify the orthodox Freudian stress on childhood by arguing that "the analyst must not get stuck in the study of childhood experiences, but turn his attention to the unconscious processes as they exist now." [32] But in the early thirties, he was still close enough to orthodox psychoanalysis to focus on children's formative years.)

Each society, he continued, has its own libidinal structure, a combination of basic human drives and social factors. A social psychology must examine how this libidinal structure acts as the cement of a society and how it affects political authority. Here, it should be added, Fromm was speaking from practical experience. The project to examine workers' authority patterns, which had been announced in Horkheimer's inaugural lecture, was under way, with Fromm directing most of the empirical work. Presupposed in this study, as he explained in the article, was a rejection of the bourgeois norms that most psychologists erroneously absolutized. The prevalent tendency to universalize the experience of the present society, he argued, was most clearly shown in the extension of the Oedipus complex to all human development, when in fact it was restricted to "patriarchal" societies alone.[33] A valid social psychology must recognize that when the socio-economic base of a society changed, so did the social function of its libidinal structure. When the rate of change between the two varied, Fromm argued at the end of the article, an explosive situation might well be created. This was a point that he was to develop at some length in his next major work, *Escape from Freedom*, a decade later.

To give substance to the generalizations of his first *Zeitschrift* essay, Fromm turned his attention next to the problem of character typology.[34] Here again, his basic orientation remained Freudian. For the most part he accepted the psychoanalytic notion of character as the sublimation or reaction formation of fundamental libidinal drives. Building on the ideas of Karl Abraham and Ernest Jones, he began by outlining the oral, anal, and genital character types. Of the three, Fromm expressed a preference for the genital character, which he associated with independence, freedom, and friendliness.[35] He hinted at the hostility towards nongenital character types that marked all his later work and set him apart from Marcuse, who had very different ideas about pregenital "polymorphous perversity."[36] Here, it should be noted, Fromm was closer to Wilhelm Reich, whose own work on character typology was being done at the same time.[37] He also agreed with Reich on the liberating effect of nonrepressed genital sexuality, although never seeing it as sufficient in itself. In later years, however, Fromm's reservations about Reich's views were strengthened; for the Nazis, he came to believe, demonstrated that sexual freedom does not necessarily entail political freedom.[38]

Having established the importance of the basic libidinal roots of character types, Fromm then proceeded to emphasize once again the influence of social factors as mediated through the family. As an example he used the impact of excessively repressive sexual mores, which might prevent the development of a healthy genital sexuality, thus fostering pregenital character types. On the whole, however, he adhered to a fairly orthodox Freudianism: "Since the character traits are rooted in the libidinal structure, they also show relative stability." [39] In concluding the essay, Fromm focused on the relationship between the "capitalist spirit" and anality. Using arguments that have since become commonplace, but that were novel at the time, he related bourgeois rationality, possessiveness, and puritanism to anal repression and orderliness.[40] These traits, he argued, have lasted into the twentieth century, most prominently in petit-bourgeois circles and even in certain proletarian ones, because of a lag between ideology (in the broad sense, which included character types) and socioeconomic change. The relation between the two was one to which Fromm returned in his later study of the Reformation, in *Escape from Freedom.* By then, however, his attitude towards anality and Freud's libido theory in general had undergone a very marked transformation. Although the clinical description of the anal type was unchanged in the later work, Fromm's interpretation was significantly altered.

The change was due almost exclusively to his clinical observations, as mentioned earlier. But there was an intellectual source as well, which helped him to articulate his new perspective. In the midtwenties, Fromm first encountered the work of the nineteenth-century Swiss anthropological theorist Johann Jacob Bachofen. Bachofen's studies of matriarchal culture, which first appeared in the 1860's, had suffered a relative eclipse in the two decades after his death in 1887. The anthropological speculations of Freud, for example, were primarily derived from Sir James Frazer's studies of totemism. Before the decline in interest, however, Bachofen and other theorists of matriarchy, such as Lewis Morgan, were very influential in socialist circles; Engels's *The Origin of the Family* (1884) and Bebel's *The Woman and Socialism* (1883), for example, were both heavily indebted to them.

In the 1920's, matriarchal theory aroused renewed excitement in several different quarters. Antimodernist critics of bourgeois society on the right, such as Alfred Bäumler and Ludwig Klages, were attracted to it for its romantic, naturalistic, anti-intellectual implications. Several of Stefan George's former disciples, repudiating his misogyny, left the George circle in search of the eternal feminine. This was, as E. M. Butler has pointed out,[41] an almost exact repetition of the French St.-Simonians' quest for the "Mystic Mother" almost seventy years before. In more orthodox anthropological circles, in England, Bronislaw Malinowski's studies of matriarchal culture in

Sex and Repression in Savage Society (1927) were used to undermine the universality of Freud's Oedipus complex. Simultaneously, Robert Briffault's *The Mothers: A Study of the Origins of Sentiments and Institutions* (1927) aroused considerable interest.

In psychoanalytic circles, matriarchal theory was also being given new consideration. Wilhelm Reich was among the first to do so. By 1933 he was able to write in *The Mass Psychology of Fascism* that matriarchy was the only genuine family type of "natural society."[42] Fromm was also one of the most active advocates of matriarchal theory. In 1932 he introduced Briffault to the German public in a long review of *The Mothers* in the *Zeitschrift*, which followed an article in English by Briffault himself entitled "Family Sentiments."[43] Fromm was especially taken with Briffault's idea that all love and altruistic feelings were ultimately derived from the maternal love necessitated by the extended period of human pregnancy and postnatal care. Love was thus not dependent on sexuality, as Freud had supposed. In fact, sex was more often tied to hatred and destruction. Fromm also praised Briffault's sensitivity to social factors. Masculinity and femininity were not reflections of "essential" sexual differences, as the romantics had thought. They were derived instead from differences in life functions, which were in part socially determined. Thus, monogamy was economically fostered by the tending of herds, which necessitated movement and the hegemony of the male shepherd. Briffault, Fromm concluded, had gone beyond mere ethnological concerns to enter the tradition of historical materialism itself, as evidenced by his article in the *Zeitschrift* on the importance of economic factors for the development of the family.

In the next issue of the *Zeitschrift* Fromm dealt directly with Bachofen himself.[44] He began by carefully delineating the different elements in matriarchal theory that appealed to right- and left-wing critics of bourgeois society. Bachofen's own confused nostalgia for the past struck a respondent chord on the right. So too did his romanticized view of nature, to which man should submit himself as an infant to its mother.[45] Like the romantics, but unlike Briffault, he absolutized the spiritual differences between man and woman (which, Fromm admitted, did express a legitimate protest against the Enlightenment's "liberation" of women to the status of bourgeois men). Bäumler, Klages, and the other *völkisch* theorists reacted only to Bachofen's naturalistic metaphysics, turning it in the direction of mystical *Schwärmerei* (gushing rapture). What they ignored were his psychosocial insights.

These, on the other hand, were the source of his appeal to the left. Matriarchal society stressed human solidarity and happiness. Its dominant values were love and compassion, not fear and subordination. Both private property and repressive sexuality were absent from its social ethic. Patriarchal society, as Engels and Bebel had interpreted it, was related to class society: both stressed duty and authority over love and gratification. Understood in a certain way, Bachofen's philosophy of history was similar to Hegel's. The advent of patriarchal society corresponded to the break between spirit and nature, the victory of Rome over the Orient.

To Fromm, as might be expected, the socialist reading of Bachofen was more congenial. The importance of studying matriarchal societies, he argued, was not for their historical interest — indeed, their actual existence in the past was not demonstrable — but for the vision they offered of an alternative reality. Like Malinowski, Fromm used matriarchal theory to deny the universality of the Oedipus complex. The strength of this complex in patriarchal societies, he asserted, was partly a result of the son's role as inheritor of the father's property and his position as provider for the father in his old age. This meant that the early education of the son was directed less towards happiness than towards economic usefulness. The love between father and son might well develop into hatred because of the son's fears of failure. The contingency of the love thus produced might well lead to a loss of spiritual security and the reinforcement of duty as the focus of existence.

Maternal love, on the other hand, was unconditional and less responsive to social pressures. In contemporary society, however, the strength of the real mother had eroded. No longer was she seen as the protectress, but rather as someone in need of protection herself. This, Fromm argued, was also true of maternal substitutes, such as the country or *Volk.*[46] Original motherly trust and warmth had been replaced by paternal guilt, anal repression, and authoritarian morality. The advent of Protestantism had increased the sway of the father, as the security of medieval Catholicism with its womb-like church and cult of the Virgin Mother receded in effectiveness.[47] The psychic foundations of capitalism were clearly patriarchal, although paradoxically capitalism had created the conditions for a return to a truly matriarchal culture. This was so because of the abundance of goods and services it provided, which might allow a less achievement-oriented reality principle. Socialism, Fromm concluded, must preserve the promise of this return.

With Fromm's growing interest in Bachofen came a lessening of his enthusiasm for orthodox Freudianism. In 1935 he spelled out the sources of his disillusionment in the *Zeitschrift.*[48] Freud, he argued, was a prisoner of his bourgeois morality and patriarchal values. The emphasis in psychoanalysis on childhood experiences, he went on, served to divert attention from the person of the analyst himself. In a case where the analyst uncritically shared the values of the society, and where the patient's desires and needs were contrary to those values, he tended to arouse the patient's resistance. Theoretically, of course, analysts were supposed to be value-neutral and tolerant of their patient's morals; but in fact, Fromm argued, the ideal of tolerance historically had had two faces.

Fromm's discussion of tolerance[49] is worth examining in some detail, because it expressed an attitude shared by other Institut members, which was later to be repeated in one of Marcuse's most controversial and influential essays.[50] Initially, Fromm wrote, the bourgeois struggle for toleration was directed against social oppression. But when the middle class became socially dominant, tolerance was transformed into a mask for moral laissez-faire. In reality, it was never extended to protect serious threats to the prevailing order. As epitomized in Kant's work, it was applied to thought and speech rather than action. Bourgeois toleration was always self-contradictory: it was consciously relativistic and neutral, but subconsciously designed to preserve the status quo. Psychoanalysis, Fromm suggested, shared the two-faced character of this type of tolerance; the facade of neutrality was often a cover for what Fromm expressly called the doctor's implicit sadism.[51]

Fromm did not, however, take the next step, which Marcuse was later to do. ("Liberating tolerance," Marcuse wrote in 1965, "would mean intolerance against movements from the Right, and toleration of movements from the Left.") [52] Instead, he concentrated on exposing other facets of Freud's patriarchalism. The goal of orthodox psychoanalysis, he argued, was the ability to work, procreate, and enjoy. Freud, however, had stressed the first two over the third, seeing an irreconcilable contradiction between civilization and gratification. His attitude towards political radicals who wanted to construct a society in which gratification was more fully possible was unremittingly hostile. All they were doing, Freud thought, was acting out their Oedipal aggressions towards their fathers.[53] In fact, neurosis had been defined by Freud in terms of the inability to accept bourgeois norms. Further evidence of Freud's inability to transcend his background was his insistence on monetary payment for all therapy. And finally, Fromm argued that in his own person Freud was a classical patriarchal type, authoritarian to both students and patients.[54]

As superior alternatives to Freud, Fromm suggested Georg Groddeck and Sandor Ferenczi. What made them better was their therapeutic innovation of having the analyst face the patient in a one-to-one, more egalitarian relationship. Fromm's abandonment of the Oedipus complex meant that the role of transference was greatly minimized in the technique he now favored. Groddeck and Ferenczi were also less rigid on the question of payment, which they sometimes waived. In contrast to Freud's patricentric, authoritarian, inhumane "tolerance," they offered a therapy that went beyond the short-sighted goal of adjustment to the moral inhumanities of contemporary society. Fromm expressed great regret over the loss to psychoanalysis caused by Ferenczi's early death. In later years he sought to rescue his reputation from the distortions of Ernest Jones, who had described Ferenczi as having become psychotic at the end of his life.[55] Fromm and his wife also remained friends with Groddeck, despite Groddeck's political naiveté — at one time he hoped to get Hitler, whose anti-Semitism he doubted, to sponsor some of his work, only to be disappointed when Hitler came to power.[56]

At the same time as Fromm's disillusionment with Freud grew, so did his estrangement from the other members of the Institut. After contributing a psychological analysis of authority to the *Studien über Autorität und Familie*, a joint research project by the Institut staff published in 1936, Fromm wrote only one more article for the *Zeitschrift*, a study of the feeling of impotency in modern society.[57] In 1939 his connection with the Institut was severed, and he devoted himself more extensively to clinical work, increasingly pursuing the non-Freudian train of his thought. Two years later, *Escape from Freedom*, perhaps his most widely read book, was published. As an explanation of the authoritarianism America was about to fight in the war, it received considerable attention and in time became a classic in its field. Because of the treatment it has received elsewhere,[58] it will be discussed here only for the evidence it provides of Fromm's development away from Freud and the Institut.

As in his earlier *Zeitschrift* articles, Fromm began by accusing Freud of cultural narrowness: "The field of human relations in Freud's sense is similar to the market — it is an exchange of satisfaction of biologically given needs, in which the relationship to the other individual is always a means to an end but never an end in itself." [59] More strongly than ever, he denounced Freud's pessimism and his notion of the death instinct. Here he equated the death instinct with the need to destroy, an interpretation that Marcuse was later to challenge. By so understanding it, Fromm was able to write: "If Freud's assumptions were correct, we would have to assume that the amount of destructiveness either against others or oneself is more or less constant. But what we observe is to the contrary. Not only does the weight of destructiveness among individuals in our culture vary a great deal, but also destructiveness is of unequal weight among different social groups."[60]

Fromm also continued his denigration of Freud's libido theory, while retaining his clinical descriptions. In doing so, he explicitly repudiated the interpretative part of his own work in *The Dogma of Christ*[61] and the libido-oriented character typology he had championed in 1932 in the *Zeitschrift.*[62] His discussion of sado-masochism, one of the central concepts of his theory of irrational authority, sought to purge the concept of any erotic elements. In fact, in his next work, *Man for Himself,* he developed his own typology along very different lines.[63] For the first time in print he acknowledged the similarities between his own thinking and that of Karen Horney and Harry Stack Sullivan,[64] who were revising Freud in a parallel direction. Once again he pointed to the influence of social factors based on the inescapable imperatives of the self-preservation drives. In an appendix he elaborated the concept of "social character" suggested in his earlier works, a concept that he would come to consider his "most important contribution . . . to the field of social psychology."[65] "The social character," he wrote, "comprises only a selection of traits, the *essential nucleus of the character structure of most members of a group which has developed as the result of the basic experiences and mode of life common to that group* [Fromm's italics]."[66]

In all this, Fromm was on familiar ground, which he had covered in one way or another in his earlier articles. What was new in *Escape from Freedom,* however, was a more general interest in what might be called man's "existential" condition. To Fromm, "the main theme of this book" was "that man, the more he gains freedom in the sense of emerging from the original oneness with man and nature and the more he becomes an 'individual,' has no choice but to unite himself with the world in the spontaneity of love and productive work, or else to seek a kind of security by such ties with the world as destroy his freedom and the integrity of his individual self."[67] The notion of alienation, which Fromm had found so suggestive in Marx's early writings, was clearly at the root of his new approach. Isolation and relatedness were now the two poles of his thinking. Neurosis came increasingly to be defined in terms of certain types of interpersonal relations; sadism and masochism, for example, ceased being sexually derived phenomena and became instead strivings that "tend to help the individual to escape his unbearable feelings of aloneness and powerlessness."[68] Their real aim was "symbiosis"[69] with others, which meant the loss of self-integrity and individuality through the dissolution of the self into the other.

In *Escape from Freedom* Fromm distinguished between the isolated atomization of a negative "freedom from" and the "spontaneous activity of the total, integrated personality," [70] of the positive "freedom to." Although taking pains to mention the socio-economic change that would be necessary to end the alienation of "freedom from" and achieve positive "freedom to," he did not lay great stress on the difficulties of this transformation. Increasingly, he came to see the problem of change in optimistic, even moralistic, terms. If there were no inborn drive to destroy, then the dream of the Hebrew prophets, that "vision of universal peace and harmony between nations" that had moved the young Fromm so deeply, might be achieved. In his subsequent writings Fromm emphasized the integration of ethics and psychology. In *Man for Himself* he went so far as to say: "Every neurosis represents a moral problem. The failure to achieve maturity and integration of the whole personality is a moral problem." [71] And in later years he came to appreciate the spiritual teachings of the East, especially the masters of Zen Buddhism,[72] as well as the West.

To be fair to Fromm, however, it should be acknowledged that this was a change in emphasis in his thinking and not an absolute transformation of his position. Reacting to the charge that he had become a Pollyanna, Fromm angrily replied: "I have always upheld the same point that man's capacity for freedom, for love, etc. depends almost entirely on the given socio-economic conditions, and that only exceptionally can one find, as I pointed out in *The Art of Loving*, that there is love in a society whose principle is the very opposite." [73] It is difficult, however, to read his later works without coming to the conclusion that in comparison with Horkheimer and the other members of the Institut's inner circle, who were abandoning their tentative hopes of the twenties and thirties, Fromm was defending a more optimistic position.

Horkheimer and the others had been in general agreement with Fromm's initial contributions to the *Zeitschrift*, even agreeing with his first criticisms of Freud. In fact, Fromm remembers that Karen Horney and Horkheimer were on friendly terms during their first few years as emigrés in New York.[74] Moreover, the Institut had embraced Fromm's hopes for the merger of psychoanalysis and Marxism. In an article entitled "History and Psychology" in the first issue of the Institut's new journal, Horkheimer had argued for the urgency of a psychological supplement to Marxist theory. The motivations of men in contemporary society, he contended, must be understood as both "ideological," in Marx's sense, and psychological. The more society becomes rational, to be sure, the less both these conceptual approaches will be needed to make sense of social reality. But for the present psychological explanation is needed to understand the staying power of social forms after their objective necessity had passed. This must be an individual psychology, Horkheimer agreed with Fromm. No mass soul or group consciousness really exists, although social factors do influence the formation of individual psyches: "Not only the content, but also the strength of the eruptions of the psychic apparatus is economically conditioned." [75]

During the first years of emigration Horkheimer shared Fromm's distaste for the death instinct. As late as 1936, in "Egoism and the Movement for Emancipation," [76] he attacked the resignation it implied. Freud's earlier work, Horkheimer argued, was more dialectical, his later, more biological and positivistic; his belief in a destructive drive was like the medieval attribution of evil to a mythical devil. By missing the historical component in oppression, Freud had absolutized the status quo and become resigned to the necessity of a permanent elite to keep the destructive masses down.

By the late thirties, however, Fromm and the other Institut members began to go along separate paths. The patriarchal-matriarchal distinction Fromm so heavily stressed was never fully accepted by the others. Only Walter Benjamin, who had never met Fromm and was not really a member of the Institut's inner circle, expressed great interest in Bachofen's work.[77] The others were wary of Fromm's dismissal of Freud as a representative of patriarchal thinking. In looking back at the break, Fromm remembers it in terms of Horkheimer's having discovered a "more revolutionary Freud." [78] Because he spoke of sexuality, Horkheimer thought Freud was more of a real materialist than Fromm. Lowenthal, on the other hand, remembers the split as having been produced by Fromm's changed approach, symbolized by the two different parts of *Escape from Freedom*, the social and the "existential." [79] In addition, it is likely that personal differences also played a role. From his writings alone it seems evident that Fromm's sensibility was less ironic than that of the other members of the inner circle, his approach to life less colored by the aesthetic nuances shared by both Horkheimer and Adorno. Adorno's full entry into Institut affairs at about the time Fromm was leaving signified a crucial shift in the tone of the Frankfurt School's work.

Whatever the cause of Fromm's departure, his work became anathema to his former colleagues in the 1940's. After his break, the Institut did not spend much time in its publications discussing the theoretical problems of psychoanalysis. In an article in 1939[80] Horkheimer compared Freud favorably to Dilthey, but without any extensive explanation of the reasons for his preference. Although psychoanalytic categories were used in much of the Institut's work during and after the war, it appears that Horkheimer and the others were less than anxious to publicize their involvement with Freudian theory. In October, 1942, Lowenthal was approached by the eminent ego-psychologist Ernst Kris, who asked him about the Institut's attitude towards Freud. Lowenthal wrote to Horkheimer for advice on how to reply. Horkheimer, who by that time had moved to California, wrote back in an extremely illuminating way. His answer is worth quoting at some length:

> I think you should be simply positive. We really are deeply indebted to Freud and his first collaborators. His thought is one of the Bildungsmächte [foundation stones] without which our own philosophy would not be what it is. I have anew realized his grandeur during the last weeks. You will remember that many people say his original method was particularly adequate to the Viennese sophisticated middle class. This is, of course, totally untrue as a generality, but there is a grain of salt in it which does not do any harm to Freud's work. The greater a work, the more it is rooted in the concrete historical situation. But if you take a close look at this connection between liberalistic Vienna and Freud's original method, you become aware of how great a thinker he was. With the decline of middle-class family life, his theory reached that new stage as expressed in "Jenseits des Lustprinzips" and the following writings. That turn of his philosophy proves that he, in his particular work, realized the changes pointed out in the chapter of the article on Reason [probably part of Horkheimer's "Reason and Self-preservation"] devoted to the decline of the family and the individual. Psychology without libido is in a way no psychology and Freud was great enough to get away from psychology in its own framework. Psychology in its proper sense is always psychology of the individual. Where this is needed, we have to refer orthodoxically to Freud's earlier writings. The set of concepts connected with the *Todestrieb* [the death instinct] are anthropological categories (in the German sense of the word). Even where we do not agree with Freud's interpretation and use of them, we find their objective intention is deeply right and that they betray Freud's great flair for the situation. His development has led him to conclusions not so far from those of the other great thinker of the same period, Bergson. Freud objectively absented himself from psychoanalysis, whereas Fromm and Horney get back to commonsense psychology and even psychologize culture and society.[81]

Expressed in this letter were several fundamental differences of opinion with Fromm. First, Horkheimer denied the accusation that the bourgeois elements admittedly present in Freud's thinking were unequivocally unfortunate. As he had argued in "Traditional and Critical Theory," [82] no thinker can escape his social origins entirely.

"The greater the work, the more it is rooted in the concrete historical situation," he wrote Lowenthal. Thus, Freud's notion of the death instinct had an "objective intention" that was "deeply right," not because it corresponded to a biological universal, but because it expressed the depth and severity of modern man's destructive urges. Second, Freud's putative blindness to the role of the family as agent of society, which Fromm so strongly stressed and which played a part in the Institut's early work on authority, was really a reflection of his sensitivity to the decline of the family in modern life. This was a change that Horkheimer was to discuss at some length in his subsequent work. And finally, Freud had realized that psychology was necessarily the study of the individual. Thus the libido, which implied a stratum of human existence stubbornly out of reach of total social control, was an indispensable concept. It was thus a mistake to sociologize the individual. By the same token, the revisionists were wrong in trying to "psychologize culture and society." Underlying Horkheimer's refusal to collapse psychology into sociology or vice versa was that stress on nonidentity so central to Critical Theory. Not until contradictions were socially resolved could they be methodologically reconciled, a critical point to which Adorno was to return much later in a discussion of "Sociology and Psychology." [83]

It was in fact Adorno who first spelled out in public the Institut's differences with its revisionist former member. On April 26, 1946, he delivered a paper in Los Angeles entitled "Social Science and Sociological Tendencies in Psychoanalysis." [84] It is interesting both for what it says about the Frankfurt School's attraction to Freud and as an anticipation of Marcuse's more widely known castigation of revisionism in *Eros and Civilization.* Adorno addressed himself specifically to Karen Horney's *New Ways in Psychoanalysis* and Fromm's "The Social Limitations of Psychoanalytic Therapy," which had appeared in the *Zeitschrift* eleven years before. Written directly after the war, the paper revealed a bitterness of tone very different from that of the Institut's work in the past.

Adorno began by examining the revisionists' attack on Freud's instinct theory. Instinctivism, he argued, can mean either a mechanical division of the human soul into fixed instincts or a flexible deduction of the psyche from pleasure and self-preservation strivings, with almost infinite variations. Freud's was the latter. The revisionists were thus incorrect in accusing him of being mechanistic, when in fact it was their hypostatization of character types that really deserved that epithet. For all their stress on historical influences, they were less attuned than Freud to the "inner history" of the libido. By overstressing the importance of the ego, they ignored its genetic interaction with the id: "Concretely, the denunciation of Freud's so-called instinctivism amounts to the denial that culture, by enforcing restrictions on libidinal and particularly on destructive drives, is instrumental in bringing about repressions, guilt feelings, and need for self-punishment." [85]

Furthermore, by minimizing the role of childhood experiences (*Erlebnisse,* which were not the same as *Erfahrungen*),* especially the traumas that so strongly affect personality development, the revisionists had constructed a totalistic theory of character. Freud's sensitivity to the importance of traumatic shocks in forming the modern disjointed personality had been lost in the revisionists' work.[86] "The stress on totality," Adorno wrote, "as against the unique, fragmentary impulses, always implies the harmonistic belief in what might be called the unity of the personality, [a unity that] is never realized in our society. It is one of the greatest merits of Freud that he has debunked the myth of this unity." [87] To categorize character types the way Fromm had done was to accept the existence of integrated characters, which was no more than "an ideological cloak for the psychological status quo of each individual." [88]

More generally, the revisionists' vaunted sociological "correction" of Freud really amounted to little more than the smoothing over of social contradictions. By removing the biological roots of psychoanalysis, they had transformed it into a kind of *Geisteswissenschaft* and a means of social hygiene. Their desexualization was part of a denial of the conflict between essence and appearance, of the chasm between true gratification and the pseudohappiness of contemporary civilization. Fromm, Adorno argued, was very wrong to deny the sexual basis of sadism just when the Nazis were displaying it so blatantly. The implications of the revisionists' work, despite their disclaimers, were ultimately conformist; this was especially demonstrated in their increasing moralism. There was no excuse for absolutizing moral norms, Adorno pointed out angrily, when they had been suspect ever since Nietzsche's critique of their psychological roots.

The revisionists, he continued, were also naive in their explanations of the sources of social disorder. To claim as they did that competitiveness was a major cause of conflict in bourgeois society was fatuous, especially in face of the acknowledgment in *Escape from Freedom* that the spontaneous individual had all but vanished. In

* *Erfahrungen* implied a type of integrated experience, which included a sense of the past and expectations of the future — in other words, experience mediated through cultural awareness. The distinction between *Erlebnisse* and *Erfahrungen* played an important role in the Institut's work on mass culture, as we shall see in Chapter 6.

fact, "competition itself never was the law according to which middle-class society operated."[89] The true bond of bourgeois society had always been the threat of bodily violence, which Freud more clearly perceived: "In the age of the concentration camp, castration is more characteristic of social reality than competitiveness."[90] Freud, Adorno argued, belonged to the Hobbesian tradition of bourgeois theorists, whose pessimistic absolutization of the evil in human nature reflected the prevailing reality much better than the affirmative optimism of the revisionists. Freud was not unlike Schopenhauer in identifying civilization with fixation and repetition. The revisionists were once again too sanguine in thinking that true change could explode the repetitive continuum of Western civilization.

Finally, Adorno objected to the stress on love in the revisionists' work. Fromm had attacked Freud for his authoritarian lack of warmth, but true revolutionaries are often called hard and cold. Social antagonisms cannot be wished away; they must be consummated, which inevitably means suffering for someone: "It may well be that our society has developed itself to an extreme where the reality of love can actually be expressed only by the hatred of the existent, whereas any direct evidence of love serves only at confirming the very same conditions which breed hatred."[91] Adorno finished the article with a phrase reminiscent of Walter Benjamin's often quoted remark from his study of Goethe's *Elective Affinities*, "It is only for the sake of the hopeless that we are given hope."[92] "I suspect," Adorno wrote, "that Freud's contempt for men is nothing but an expression of such hopeless love which may be the only expression of hope still permitted to us."[93]

This then was the Institut's attitude towards Freud and Fromm in the 1940's. It was no accident that increased pessimism about the possibility of revolution went hand in hand with an intensified appreciation of Freud's relevance. In a society in which social contradictions seemed unbridgeable and yet paradoxically were becoming more obscured, the antinomies of Freud's thought appeared as a necessary bulwark against the harmonistic illusions of the revisionists. And not only Freud's thought, but its most extreme and outrageous aspects were the most useful. In *Minima Moralia* Adorno expressed this when he wrote in one of his most celebrated phrases, "in psychoanalysis nothing is true except the exaggerations."[94]

In much of the Institut's work during the forties — *The Authoritarian Personality, Dialektik der Aufklärung (Dialectic of the Enlightenment),* Lowenthal's *Prophets of Deceit* — Freud's sobering influence was clearly evident. After the Institut's return to Germany, this influence continued to play a meaningful role in both its theoretical and its empirical work.[95] In 1956 the Institut expressed its appreciation to Freud on the anniversary of his hundredth birthday with a special volume in its new series of *Frankfurter Beiträge zur Soziologie (Frankfurt Contributions to Sociology).*[96] It was, however, left to the member of the Institut's inner circle who had had the least to do with the psychological speculations of the American period to attempt once again to reconcile Freud and Marx in an optimistic direction. In *Eros and Civilization*, Herbert Marcuse sought to rescue that "revolutionary Freud" whom Fromm had dismissed as a myth and whom Horkheimer and Adorno had turned into a prophet of gloom. Although it falls outside the chronological framework of this study, *Eros and Civilization* is a continuation of Critical Theory's earlier interest in Freud, and as such deserves a brief excursus at this point in our narrative.

2

Unlike the other core members of the Institut, Marcuse did not acquire a serious interest in psychoanalysis until he came to America. The early Marcuse was perhaps too much of a rationalist to find anything of great appeal in the murky world of the unconscious. Stressing as he did the potential reconciliation of subject and object, in a way that Horkheimer and Adorno with their emphasis on nonidentity never did, Marcuse was interested less in individual psychology than in the social totality. In the contribution he made to the Institut's early study of authority,[97] he avoided acknowledging the role of the family as agent of society, which Fromm had so strongly advocated and the others had not yet questioned.

And yet, as Paul Robinson has argued,[98] there were subtle adumbrations of his later interest in Freud in much of the work he did in the thirties. For example, in granting the validity of the hedonistic moment in the dialectical totality of reason and happiness, Marcuse had protested against the ascetic tendencies of idealism. In general, sexual repression had been included in his critique of exploitation, which gave it political significance beyond its merely psychological dimension. Furthermore, Marcuse had criticized the bourgeois ideology of love, which raised duty and fidelity above pleasure. He also had attacked the idealist's notion of "personality" [99] in a way anticipating Adorno's later denunciation of the revisionists' idea of character. As early as 1937 he had pointed to the sensual, corporeal element in true happiness, seeing in the most extreme reification of the body an "anticipatory memory" [100] of genuine joy. And finally, Marcuse had recognized the relation between repressed sexuality and aggression, which was to play such a crucial role in *Eros and Civilization*, in his article on hedonism.[101]

It was not, however, until the disturbing implications of the Spanish Civil War and the Moscow purge trials that Marcuse began to read Freud seriously.[102] A growing dissatisfaction with Marxism, even in its Hegelianized form, led him as it had Horkheimer and Adorno to examine the psychological obstacles in the path of meaningful social change. Whereas in their cases it strengthened a deepening pessimism and helped foster a retreat from political activism, in his, it led to a reaffirmation of the utopian dimension of his radicalism. When, after a long period of incubation, *Eros and Civilization* appeared in 1955, it went far beyond the earlier efforts of Critical Theory to merge Freud and Marx. Unlike Horkheimer and Adorno, who used Freud's insights into the profound contradictions of modern man to support their arguments about nonidentity, Marcuse found in Freud, and the later, metapsychological Freud to boot, a prophet of identity and reconciliation. Unlike Fromm, who had basically abandoned the orthodox Freud as an enemy of a new reality principle, Marcuse tried to uncover those elements in psychoanalysis that did in fact look beyond the present system.

It would be beyond the scope of this excursus to deal exhaustively with *Eros and Civilization*, a book of great complexity and richness, but certain observations about its relation to the Institut's previous work can still be made. The first section of it to appear — published separately in *Dissent* in the summer of 1955 — was an attack on the revisionists. Here Marcuse picked up the thread where Adorno had put it down a decade earlier. He began by acknowledging Wilhelm Reich's work as a precedent for his own, but quickly pointed to its inadequacies. To Marcuse, Reich's inability to distinguish between different types of repression prevented him from seeing the "historical dynamic of the sex instincts and of their fusion with the destructive impulses."[103] As a result, Reich was led to a simplistic advocacy of sexual liberation as an end in itself, which finally degenerated into the primitive delusions of his later years.

After curtly dismissing Jung and the psychoanalytic "right wing," Marcuse turned to the neo-Freudians. He opened his discussion of their work with praise for the insights of Fromm's early *Zeitschrift* articles. Marcuse expressed agreement with Fromm's opposition to patriarchal society (he used "patricentric-acquisitive," Fromm's later term for the same phenomenon), comparing it to his own attack on the "performance principle." This he defined as the specific reality principle of the current society under whose rule "society is stratified according to the competitive economic performances of its members." [104] But by the time of Fromm's departure from the Institut, Marcuse argued, the critical edge of his earlier work had been lost. The crucial change came with that increasing devotion to clinical practice that Fromm had so frequently singled out for commendation. In lobbying for the type of happiness-oriented therapy developed by Ferenczi and Groddeck, Fromm had succumbed to the ideology that true happiness could be achieved in this society. But, Marcuse asserted, "in a repressive society, individual happiness and productive development are in contradiction to society; if they are defined as values to be realized within this society, they become themselves repressive." [105]

What Marcuse was saying about psychoanalytic theory and therapy was very similar to what he and the other members of the Institut had so often said about theory and *praxis.* At this stage in Western civilization the two could not be entirely reconciled, although they were not fully independent of one another. To collapse theory completely into *praxis* (or therapy) was to lose its negative, critical quality. By assimilating speculative imagination into therapeutic practice the revisionists were very much like the pragmatists and positivists so disliked by Critical Theory; they were doing what Hegel's successors had done to him, as Marcuse had described in the second part of *Reason and Revolution.* They carried out the assimilation on two fronts. First, they discarded Freud's most daring and suggestive hypotheses: the death instinct, the primal horde, and the killing of the primal father. The archaic heritage that the revisionists mocked was meaningful, Marcuse was to write in his main text, for its "*symbolic value.* The archaic events that the hypothesis stipulates may forever be beyond the realm of anthropological verification; the alleged consequences of these events are historical facts. . . . If the hypothesis defies common sense, it claims, in its defiance, a truth which common sense has been trained to forget." [106] And second, as Adorno had argued in 1946, the revisionists flattened out the conflicts between individual and society, and between instinctual desires and consciousness. In thus returning to pre-Freudian consciousness psychology, they became conformists despite themselves.

Marcuse also repeated Adorno's attack on the revisionists' notion of an integrated personality. In contemporary society, he argued, the possibility of genuine individualism was practically nil: "The individual situations are the derivatives of the *general* fate, and, as Freud has shown, it is the latter which contains the clue to the fate of the individual." [107] Related to this was the inadequacy of the revisionists' moralism: "Freud destroys the illusions of idealistic ethics: the 'personality' is but a 'broken' individual who has internalized and successfully utilized repression and aggression." [108]

With great vehemence, Marcuse attacked the revisionists' mutilation of Freud's instinct theory. Its inner direction, he argued, was originally from consciousness to the unconscious, from the adult personality to childhood experiences, from ego to id, and from individual to genus. In stressing the libido, Freud had developed a materialistic concept of gratification that was opposed to the spiritual and ultimately repressive ideas of the revisionists. In returning to the sexual roots of Freud's theory, Marcuse had once again to consider the Oedipus complex, which Fromm had castigated from his earliest days with the Institut. In the text of *Eros and Civilization* Marcuse mentioned the Oedipus complex infrequently and without according it much importance.[109] But in the *Dissent* article, which served as his epilogue, his attitude was very different. Fromm's attempt to "translate it from the sphere of sex into that of interpersonal relations" [110] was a reversal of the critical thrust of Freud's thought. To Freud, the Oedipal wish was not merely a protest against separation from the child's mother and the painful, alienated freedom it signified to Fromm. It also expressed a profound craving for sexual gratification, for freedom from want, for the mother as woman, not merely as protectress. In fact, Marcuse argued, "it is first the 'sexual craving' for the mother-woman that threatens the psychical basis of civilization; it is the 'sexual craving' that makes the Oedipus conflict the prototype of the instinctual conflicts between the individual and his society." [111] To ignore the libidinal roots of the Oedipus complex, whether it was universal or merely a symbolic expression of this society's deepest problem, was to smooth over the fundamental antagonisms to which it referred.

But even more basic to Marcuse's argument was his protest against the revisionists' rejection of the other instinct of Freud's metapsychological period, Thanatos, the death instinct. It was here that Marcuse went beyond Adorno and Horkheimer as well, and once again sought a utopian integration of Freud and Marx. They had understood the death instinct as a symbolic representation of Freud's sensitivity to the depth of destructive impulses in modern society. Marcuse accepted this interpretation, pointing to the persistence and even intensification of destructive activity which accompanied civilization and which the revisionists tended to minimize. Freud's death instinct captured the ambiguous nature of modern man far more perceptively than the revisionists' implicit faith in progress.

But Marcuse did not end his argument in pessimism as had

Adorno and Horkheimer. The death instinct, as he understood it, did not mean an innate urge to aggression, as it had so often been seen.[112] Freud "did not assume that we live in order to destroy; the destruction instinct operates either against the life instincts or in their service; moreover, the objective of the death instinct is not destruction *per se* but the elimination of the need for destruction." [113] In the text of *Eros and Civilization* Marcuse elaborated on his understanding of the true nature of Thanatos. The real aim of the death instinct was not aggression but the end of the tension that was life. It was grounded in the so-called Nirvana principle,[114] which expressed a yearning for the tranquility of inorganic nature. In this desire, it was surprisingly similar to the life instinct: both sought gratification and the end of desire itself. If the goal of the death instinct was the reduction of tension, then it would cease to be very powerful once the tension of life was reduced. This was the crucial assumption that allowed Marcuse to turn the seemingly pessimistic conclusions of the later Freud in a utopian direction. As he argued, summarizing this point, "if the instinct's basic objective is not the termination of life but of pain — the absence of tension — then paradoxically, in terms of the instinct, the conflict between life and death is the more reduced, the closer life approximates the state of gratification. Pleasure principle and Nirvana principle then converge." [115] In so reasoning, most orthodox adherents of Freud would agree, Marcuse was as much a revisionist as Fromm or Horney, albeit in a different direction.

Thus Marcuse attempted to historicize Thanatos in the best tradition of Critical Theory. Death need not have dominion if life were liberated through the nonrepressive re-eroticization of man's relations to man and nature. This would require, Marcuse argued, a breakdown of the sexual tyranny of the genitals and a return to the "polymorphous perversity" [116] of the child. Here he distinctly went beyond both Freud and Reich, not to mention all three of his former colleagues at the Institut. Only if the entire body were re-eroticized, he argued, could alienated labor, which was grounded in the reification of the nongenital areas of the body, be overcome. A changed society, no longer based on the repressive and antiquated "performance principle," would end historically rooted "surplus repression," thus freeing the individual from his tension-producing alienated labor. Aestheticized play would replace toil; the Nirvana principle and the destruction its inhibition aroused would cease to dominate man's life. Resulting would be the "pacification of existence," [117] the psychological correlate of the identity theory, which, as discussed in the last chapter, was at the root of Marcuse's philosophy.

As was to be expected, Marcuse's bold attempt to read Freud as a revolutionary utopian did not sit well with his former colleagues.[118] Adorno and Horkheimer maintained a tactful silence, but Fromm attempted a rebuttal in subsequent issues of *Dissent.*[119] His line of attack took place on two levels. First, he tried to show that Marcuse had misunderstood Freud and that he lacked any practical experience with psychoanalysis. As he had argued earlier, Fromm claimed that Freud was far more a prisoner of nineteenth-century bourgeois nondialectical materialism than a protester against it. He also sought to discredit Marcuse's understanding of the revisionists, rejecting his tendency to lump them all together without distinguishing the basic differences among them. Fromm claimed, for example, that his own notion of the "productive character" was much more of a challenge to the current society than Marcuse allowed. He further chided Marcuse for being undialectical in his insistence that absolutely no integrated personalities could be produced under present conditions.

The second level of Fromm's rebuttal was more fundamental. Here he tried to restore the unavoidable conflict between sexual gratification and civilization, which Freud himself had so frequently stressed. It was nonsense, Fromm suggested, to think that certain sexual perversions included in Marcuse's advocacy of "polymorphous perversity" could be reconciled with any real civilization. Sadism and coprophilia, to name two, were sick under any circumstances. The goal of complete and immediate gratification that Marcuse sought would make the individual into a system of easily manipulated desires and stimulations, as in Aldous Huxley's *Brave New World.*[120] Love, as apart from sexuality, was not simply ideological, as Marcuse (and Adorno) had suggested, although admittedly its appearance in contemporary society was rare. The negative implications of Marcuse's thinking led to nothing more than nihilistic rejection of the world.

As is often the case with intellectual controversies between former friends and colleagues, the debate went through yet another series of rebuttals and counterrebuttals.[121] And as frequently happens, minor points of difference assumed greater importance than the larger areas of agreement. Marcuse accepted Fromm's charge that he was a nihilist, arguing that the nihilism of the "Great Refusal"[122] was perhaps the only true humanism allowed in the present world. This brought him once again nearer to Horkheimer and Adorno. But the basic thrust of *Eros and Civilization* was clearly in an ultimately affirmative direction. Marcuse's interpretation of the Nirvana principle was really not that far from the sentiment Fromm had expressed years before in *Escape from Freedom* when he wrote: "The drive for life and the drive for destruction are not mutually independent factors but are in a reversed interdependence. The more the drive towards life is thwarted, the stronger is the drive towards destruction; the more life is realized, the less is the strength of destructiveness. *Destructiveness is the outcome of unlived life.*" [123] Marcuse, to be sure, believed that the two instincts could be ultimately reduced to one, whereas Fromm remained a more cautious dualist. Yet in Fromm's dualism the death instinct or the need to destroy was understood solely as a product of the frustration of the life instinct. Later, in *The Heart of Man*, Fromm would formulate his position in the following way:

> This duality . . . is not one of two biologically inherent instincts, relatively constant and always battling with each other until the final victory of the death instinct, but it is one between the primary and most fundamental tendency of life — to persevere in life — and its contradiction, which comes into being when man fails in this goal.[124]

Thus, despite both men's insistence that their positions were miles apart, they seemed to converge on at least the one question of the strength and durability of an instinct to die. Marcuse's most utopian book ended on a note of yea-saying tempered only by an argument Horkheimer had made several decades earlier, concerning the impossibility of redeeming the suffering of those who had died before.[125] Aside from this, it expressed a sanguine confidence far removed from the dark ironies of the other masters of Critical Theory.

IV

The Institut's First Studies of Authority

> The family in crisis produces the attitudes which predispose men for blind submission.
>
> — MAX HORKHEIMER

While the Institut enjoyed the benefits of Nicholas Murray Butler's generosity after 1934, its heart still remained in Europe for several years more. This was demonstrated in a variety of ways. Although returning to Germany was obviously impossible after the Nazi take-over, the rest of the Continent was still accessible until the war. Personal and professional ties drew most of the Institut's members back for occasional visits. The most frequent traveler was Pollock, who made several trips to attend to Institut affairs. The Geneva office, which he had directed until coming to New York, remained open, first under the administrative leadership of Andries Sternheim and then after his return to Holland, under Juliette Favez. The London branch, directed by Jay Rumney, survived only until 1936, but its Parisian counterpart, headed by Paul Honigsheim and Hans Klaus Brill, lasted until the war. One of its chief functions was to act as liaison between the central office in New York and the Librairie Félix Alcan, which continued to publish the *Zeitschrift.* Paris was also important as a way-station for Institut members who were reluctant to leave Europe. Grossmann spent a year there and another in London before coming to New York in 1937. Otto Kirchheimer, a student of politics and law whose contribution to the Institut's work will be discussed in the next chapter, was affiliated with the Paris office for three years after 1934. Gerhard Meyer, the economist, was there from 1933 to 1935; Hans Mayer, the Marxist literary critic, for several years after 1934. Adorno, although spending most of his time in England during the mid-thirties, often took vacations in Paris, where he was able to see an old friend he had introduced to the Institut, Walter Benjamin. Benjamin, as we shall see, had chosen Paris both as the site of his exile and as the controlling metaphor of his work. In the six years he spent there, he developed an attachment to the city that proved fatal in the end.

In addition to its continued personal and institutional links with Europe, the Institut refused to alter its original notion of the audience for whom it was writing. As mentioned in the first chapter, German remained the *Zeitschrift*'s major language until the war. As late as 1940 Horkheimer was able to chide other refugees for their rapid Americanization: "That the German intellectuals don't need long to change to a foreign language as soon as their own bars them from a sizeable readership, comes from the fact that language already serves them more in the struggle for existence than as an expression of truth." [1] Because of the Institut's financial independence, Horkheimer and his colleagues could remain above the "struggle for existence" forced on many of the other emigrés. But Horkheimer's desire to keep the Institut self-consciously German was also rooted in a serious appreciation of the need to maintain a link with Germany's humanist past, a link that might help in the future reconstruction of a post-Nazi German culture. To this end, the Institut's members remained impervious to the entreaties of their new colleagues at Columbia to integrate their work into the American social-scientific mainstream.

On occasion, of course, the *Zeitschrift*'s pages were opened to distinguished American scholars, including Margaret Mead, Charles Beard, and Harold Lasswell.[2] In general, however, the *Zeitschrift* remained a forum for the Institut's own ideas and the findings of much of its empirical work. When new figures appeared, they were usually fellow refugees to whom the Institut had extended a helping hand. In at least one case, that of Ferdinand Tönnies,[3] this was done to aid a distinguished scholar in trouble at the end of a long career. But on the whole the Institut followed a policy that was expressed in one of its mimeographed histories in 1938. Ironic in the light of subsequent events, the statement reads: "It may be said that the Institute has no 'outstanding names' on its staff. The reason for this lies in the belief of the Institute that famous German scholars would easily find positions in American institutions. The case of the younger German refugees is quite different. The Institute has been chiefly concerned with them." [4] Although the Institut's funds were less extensive than some of its disgruntled petitioners imagined, support was extended to some two hundred emigrés. Although a full list has not yet been made public, such names as Fritz Sternberg, Hans Mayer, Paul Lazarsfeld, Fritz Karsen, Gerhard Meyer, and A. R. L. Gurland would be on it. In the ten years after 1934, approximately $200,000 was distributed among 116 doctoral candidates and 14 postdoctoral students.[5] According to Pollock,[6] the methodological or political inclinations of the recipients played no real part in determining the award. The only firm criterion was fervent anti-Nazism. Even positivists like Edgar Zilsel were given support without any attempt being made to coerce them to the Institut's way of thinking.

This is not to say that the Institut indiscriminately accepted the work of people with whom its members disagreed. Ludwig Marcuse, for example, was commissioned in 1938 to write a piece on Father Jahn, the early nineteenth-century romantic sponsor of gymnastic societies. The results of his work were unsatisfactory, so he remembered in his autobiography, for ideological reasons:

> [Horkheimer] was a Hegelian and militant sociologist, believing in the objective spirit, and had expected a study from me which would have worked on Jahn as an illustration of the Left Hegelian science of society. I, on the other hand, belonged at an early age to the diverse opposition: the early Romantics, Stirner, Schopenhauer, Kierkegaard, and Nietzsche. . . . I had a warm inclination towards Pollock and Horkheimer, a high respect for their *Zeitschrift* and their collective volume, *Authority and Family*, which their Institut had published — and was sad not to be able to work with them.[7]

Other refugees such as Henry Pachter[8] have a more bitter recollection of the Institut's process of selecting those it would support, claiming that promises were made that were broken. This the Institut resolutely denies, as it does the accusations made in recent years about the influence allegedly exercised on one beneficiary of a stipend, Walter Benjamin.[9] The validity of these latter allegations will be treated in a subsequent chapter.

Along with the Institut's continued institutional and personal ties to Europe, its reluctance to publish in English, and its concern for other refugee scholars went a strong desire to preserve its own identity apart from the academic structure of Columbia, as it had maintained its independence in Frankfurt. After 1936 the Institut did give courses in the Extension Division and sponsored guest lectures by European scholars such as Harold Laski, Morris Ginsberg, and Celestin Bouglé, which were open to the university community. Still, off in its own building on 117th Street provided by Columbia, the Institut was able to pursue its own work without any pressure from the department with which it was most naturally associated, sociology. This meant that although it maintained friendly ties with Columbia's sociologists, it did not become seriously embroiled in the controversy between the partisans of Robert MacIver and those of Robert Lynd, which split the department in the late thirties.[10] In fact, after the war, when concrete proposals were made to integrate the Institut into the sociology department or Paul Lazarsfeld's newly constituted Bureau of Applied Social Research, they were politely declined. As Horkheimer wrote to Lowenthal in 1942, "Scientific institutions here exercise a constant pressure on their junior members which cannot be compared in the least with the freedom which has reigned in our Institute. . . . People don't want to understand that there can be a group of scholars working under a director not responsible to big business or to mass-culture publicity." [11]

Most importantly, of course, the Institut's European outlook was demonstrated in its work. As to be expected, Critical Theory was applied to the most pressing problem of the time, the rise of fascism in Europe. As Henry Pachter has pointed out,[12] many emigrés without prior political interests or training were compelled by events to study the new totalitarianism. Psychologists like Ernst Kris examined Nazi propaganda, philosophers like Ernst Cassirer and Hannah Arendt probed the myth of the state and the origins of totalitarianism, and novelists like Thomas Mann wrote allegories of Germany's disintegration. Here the Institut was uniquely equipped to make an important contribution. Well before the forced emigration, it had turned its attention to problems of authority. Critical Theory was developed partly in response to the failure of traditional Marxism to explain the reluctance of the proletariat to fulfill its historical role. One of the primary reasons for Horkheimer's early interest in psychoanalysis had been the help it might give in accounting for the psychological "cement" of society. Accordingly, when he assumed the reins of the Institut in 1930, one of the first tasks he announced was an empirical study of the mentality of workers in the Weimar Republic.[13]

Although never actually completed to Horkheimer's satisfaction this was the first real effort to apply Critical Theory to a concrete, empirically verifiable problem. Erich Fromm was the project's director; in later years, Anna Hartock, Herta Herzog, Paul Lazarsfeld, and Ernst Schachtel all contributed to the attempt to complete the study. Approximately three thousand questionnaires were distributed to workers, asking their views on such issues as the education of children, the rationalization of industry, the possibility of avoiding a new war, and the locus of real power in the state. Adolf Levenstein had been the first to use an interpretive questionnaire in 1912,[14] but Fromm's psychoanalytic training allowed him to develop a more sophisticated characterology based on the modified Freudian types he developed in the *Zeitschrift*.[15]

Perhaps the key innovation of the study was the way in which the questionnaire itself was conducted. The answers were taken down verbatim by the interviewers and then analyzed, the way a psychoanalyst listens to the associations of a patient. Certain key words or recurrent patterns of expression were interpreted as clues to the underlying psychological reality beneath the manifest content of the answers. This technique, it might be noted in passing, was very different from that employed in the Institut's collaborative project, *The Authoritarian Personality*, as we shall see when examining that work in Chapter 7. Fromm himself, however, was to turn back to it many years later in the analysis of *Social Character in a Mexican Village*,[16] which he and Michael Maccoby conducted in the late fifties and early sixties.

In general, the interviews disclosed a wide discrepancy between avowed beliefs and personality traits. Approximately 10 percent of the 586 respondents exhibited what was called an "authoritarian" character, a personality syndrome the Institut was to spend much of its subsequent time and energy exploring. Another 15 percent expressed a psychological commitment to antiauthoritarian goals and were thus deemed likely to live up to the revolutionary rhetoric of the left, if circumstances demanded it. The vast majority, however, were highly ambivalent. As a result, the Institut concluded that the German working class would be far less resistant to a right-wing seizure of power than its militant ideology would suggest.

Despite the prescience of its conclusions — the German working class was, in fact, to accept Nazism without any real resistance — the study was never actually published by the Institut. As late as 1939 plans were still afoot to have it appear as *The German Workers under the Weimar Republic*,[17] but with Fromm's departure from the Institut went a major reason for its publication. In later years, Pollock suggested that it was never published because too many of the questionnaires were lost in the flight from Germany.[18] Fromm, however, disputed this claim and argued that Horkheimer and he differed over the value of the work, a quarrel that, in fact, contributed to their break.[19] Some of the project's findings were, however, worked into subsequent studies of authoritarianism, such as *Escape from Freedom*.[20] And the questionnaire it had developed was incorporated into the next major Institut project, the *Studien über Autorität und Familie (Studies on Authority and Family)*.

Before embarking on a discussion of this mammoth work, the fruit of Horkheimer's first five years as director, certain of the theoretical presuppositions of the Institut on the question of authority should be made clear. First, Critical Theory's holistic, syncretic outlook prevented it from developing a theory of specifically *political* authority. To do so would have implied a fetishization of politics as something apart from the social totality. "A general definition of authority," Horkheimer wrote, "would be necessarily extremely empty, like all conceptual definitions which attempt to define single moments of social life in a way which encompasses all of history. . . . General concepts, which form the basis of social theory, can only be understood in their correct meaning in connection with the other general and specific concepts of theory, that is, as moments of a specific theoretical structure." [21]

Reflecting its roots in Marxism, Critical Theory tended to see politics as more epiphenomenal than the socio-economic substructure. Although the Frankfurt School had already begun to question the derivative nature of culture assumed by mechanistic Marxists, it was slower to do the same for politics. Even with the introduction of political scientists such as Franz Neumann and Otto Kirchheimer into the Institut, there was little impetus for the development of an autonomous theory of politics. In fact, only after they left the Institut did Neumann and Kirchheimer develop a sensitivity to the "primacy of politics" in the twentieth century.[22] Until then, they shared an underestimation of the political sphere with the other Institut members, which had been a hallmark of almost all nineteenth-century thought from Marx to the classical economists.[23] Only in the late thirties, when Pollock developed a notion of "state capitalism" that stressed the role of governmental control, did the Institut begin to investigate the political component in political economy. On the whole, however, as Marcuse was later to write, "If there was one matter about which the author of these essays [*Negations*] and his friends were *not* uncertain, it was the understanding that the fascist state was fascist society, and that totalitarian violence and totalitarian reason came from the structure of existing society, which was in the act of overcoming its liberal past and incorporating its historical negation." [24] Because the Institut saw "society" [25] as the fundamental reality, it perceived no need to develop a discrete theory of political authority or obligation. When in fact it did examine such theories, as in the case of Marcuse's analysis of Carl Schmitt,[26] it did so largely to unmask their ideological character. One of the ironies of the Institut's slowness to acknowledge the new primacy of politics was that at this very time, the orthodoxy in the Soviet Union itself had shifted in that direction, stressing political voluntarism rather than objective conditions. Stalin, who was responsible for the theoretical change, was merely ratifying the reality of Soviet practice.[27]

Critical Theory did, however, have an implicit theory of political authority, which was ultimately grounded in its philosophical assumptions. As discussed in Chapter 2, the Hegelian notion of the identity of subject and object, particular and universal, essence and appearance played a key role in the genesis of Critical Theory. Reason, the guiding principle of the Institut's thinking, meant essentially the synthesis of these opposites, the reconciliation of social as well as political antagonisms. In Marcuse's work, identity theory played a greater role than in Horkheimer's. Adorno was at the other end of the spectrum from Marcuse, but still within a Hegelian framework based on the utopian reconciliation of contradictions. Translated into political terms, this meant the classical notion of "positive freedom," combining an end to political alienation with adherence to universally valid rational laws. "The democratic state," Horkheimer wrote in 1942, "should be like the idea of the Greek polis without slaves." [28] Accordingly, the alternative idea of "negative freedom," most often identified with Christian and liberal theorists, was anathema to the Institut. Freedom, as Fromm argued in *Escape from Freedom*,[29] meant "freedom to," not merely "freedom from." And in Marcuse's words, "We know that *freedom is an eminently political concept*. Real freedom for individual existence (and not merely in the liberalist sense) is possible only in a specifically structured polis, a 'rationally' organized society." [30]

There was therefore a type of political authority that might be called legitimate: the authority of reason. It might be noted in passing that insofar as Fromm agreed with this notion, John Schaar's critique of his work, entitled *Escape from Authority*, is misnamed. In an ideal political system, the individual would obey his government because it would truly represent his interests. In fact, the distinction between governed and government would tend to disappear, thereby realizing Marx's withering away of the state as an external apparatus to coerce men. The perfect democracy, or isonomy, which Rousseau among others had espoused, would thus be realized when men followed their own reason. In his more utopian moments Horkheimer went so far as to question all political power. The question of what one should do with power, he wrote during the war, "presupposes the condition which is supposed to disappear: the power of disposition over alienated labor." [31]

In the interim, however, he and the other Institut members were careful to warn against the premature dissolution of political authority. More than once they attacked the anarchists for their impatience.[32] Until a true social transformation occurred, they stressed the necessity of rational authority similar to that exercised by an educator over his pupils. This, however, had been more a possibility during the liberal era than in the present.[33] In the current age of monopoly capitalism, both the free entrepreneur and the autonomous political subject were threatened with liquidation. Thus, the vaunted pluralism of the liberal democracies of the West had degenerated into little more than an ideology. "True pluralism," Horkheimer wrote, "belongs to the concept of a future society." [34] Increasingly, the political authority that dominated modern man was becoming irrational.

In so arguing, it should be noted, the Institut had taken a position very different from that assumed by Max Weber, whose idea of the rationalization of authority came to dominate much American social scientific thinking at about the same time. In *Economy and Society*[35] Weber had developed his well-known tripartite typology of imperative coordination (or legitimate authority): charismatic, traditional, and rational-legal. In general, he saw the ascendancy of rational-legal authority as the secular trend of Western civilization. By rationalization, however, Weber meant something very different from what the Institut did. Briefly, to Weber, rational-legal authority signified obedience to an abstract, consistent system of rules established by agreement or imposition and implemented by a bureaucratic staff. Obligation was to laws, not men. The bureaucracy was composed of officials chosen by regular procedures on the basis of administrative competence. Calculability, efficiency, and impersonality were the basic characteristics of this pattern of authority.

The Frankfurt School did not deny the trend towards bureaucratic rationality and legal formalism (although writing during the era of rising fascism, they could appreciate, as Weber could not, the fragility of the latter). What they did find inadequate was the reduction of rationality to its formal, instrumental side. More Hegelian than Weber, who was schooled in neo-Kantianism, they argued for a substantive rationalism involving ends as well as means. Although Weber had recognized the distinction between formal and substantive rationality,[36] he did not feel, as the Institut did, that socialism would resolve the conflict between them. If anything, so Weber thought, socialism would tighten the screws on the "iron cage" of rationalization. Moreover, by pointing to the frequent incursion of charisma into even the most rationalized systems of authority, Weber demonstrated his sensitivity to the dangers of that combination of rationalized means and irrational ends which was so characteristic of fascism.

The Frankfurt School could be in agreement with this latter observation but not with the former. Where Weber also failed in their eyes was in hypostatizing the distinction between ends and means, a false dichotomy that was further reflected in his belief in the possibility of a "value-free" social science. In addition, the Institut rejected Weber's contention that capitalism was the highest form of socio-economic rationality. As Marxists, they repudiated the notion that an unplanned economy without socialized means of production could be anything but irrational. Accordingly, political authority in a capitalist society could not be rational in the substantive sense of reconciling particular and general interests.[37]

In fact, it was their belief that capitalism in its advanced, monopolistic stage actually decreased the rationality of political authority. The formal, legal rationality that Weber had described corresponded more closely to conditions during the liberal phase of bourgeois society, which were characterized by belief in the *Rechtsstaat* (constitutional state). As capitalism had evolved in a monopolistic direction, liberal political and legal institutions were increasingly replaced by totalitarian ones. Those that remained were little more than the façade for new types of irrational authority. Rationality was itself severely threatened. "The fascist order," Horkheimer wrote during the war, "is the reason in which reason reveals itself as irrational." [38]

However, the transformation from liberalism to totalitarianism was more organic than liberal theorists acknowledged. As Marcuse wrote in his first essay in the *Zeitschrift*: "The turn from the liberalist to the total-authoritarian state occurs within the framework of a single social order. With regard to the unity of this economic base, we can say it is liberalism that 'produces' the total-authoritarian state out of itself, as its own consummation at a more advanced stage of development." [39] In short, fascism was intimately related to capitalism itself. In one of his most frequently quoted phrases, Horkheimer wrote in 1939, "he who does not wish to speak of capitalism should also be silent about fascism." [40] As we shall see, however, when we discuss Franz Neumann's *Behemoth*, the Institut was never fully in agreement about what this relation really was.

Marcuse's article "The Struggle against Liberalism in the Totalitarian View of the State" is worth examining in detail because of the number of points he makes that were subsequently developed in other works by the Institut. The essay is also a model of dialectical thinking, treating totalitarianism as both a reaction to and a continuation of certain trends in liberalism. Originally, Marcuse argued, the totalitarian world view began as a response to the regimenting rationalization of life and the desiccating intellectualization of thought in the nineteenth century. The "anemia" of bourgeois existence was countered by an ideology of heroic vitalism. The arid, brittle quality of nineteenth-century philosophy, both materialist and idealist, produced its corrective in *Lebensphilosophie.* But by the twentieth century the valid insights of Dilthey and Nietzsche had degenerated into a mindless irrationalism, whose function, as Horkheimer often noted,[41] was as a justification for the status quo. Similarly, Marcuse argued, the traditional liberal emphasis on inwardness, its "privatization of reason," [42] and the reduction of freedom to its "negative" dimension gave rise to a universalistic reaction, in which the totality — in Germany, the *Volk* — was made superior to the individual. The facade of a classless society, the ideological *Volksgemeinschaft,* was thus erected on the foundation of continued class rule by the capitalists.

Both a reaction to liberalism and a continuation of one of its assumptions was the totalitarian apotheosis of nature. Liberal economics, Marcuse pointed out, had always been based on the premise of "natural laws." "Here," he wrote, "in the center of the liberalist system, society is interpreted through its reduction to 'nature' in its harmonizing function: as the evasive justification of a contradictory social order." [43] What was new in totalitarianism, however, was the combination of naturalism with irrationalism. Nature had been elevated in *völkisch* thought to a mythic status; the *Volk* was transformed into the central natural reality. Nature, with all its brutality and incomprehensibility, was transformed into the "great antagonist of history," [44] absolutizing the irrationalities of the present order. One of its results was the ethic of self-sacrifice and ascetic denial characteristic of heroic realism.

In attempting to justify this perverse condition, totalitarian theory, as demonstrated in the work of Carl Schmitt, could offer only one solution: "That there is a state of affairs that through its very existence and presence is *exempt* from all justification, i.e., an 'existential,' 'ontological' state of affairs—justification by mere existence." [45] Marcuse's trenchant discussion of political existentialism gave evidence of the distance he had traveled since joining the Institut in 1932. He now argued that Heidegger's position before *Being and Time* was "philosophy's furthest advance" [46] in regaining the concrete subject denied by abstract rationalism from Descartes to Husserl. What followed, however, was a reaction in which abstract anthropology replaced concrete history in order to justify the naturalistic ideology of heroic realism. Marcuse then quoted from Heidegger's notorious pro-Nazi inaugural speech of 1933, "The Self-Assertion of the German University," to show how far existentialism had joined forces with irrational naturalism in glorifying earth and blood as the true forces of history.

The more self-consciously political variation of existentialism, as exemplified by Schmitt, was even more sinister to Marcuse. By reducing politics to existential relationships unencumbered by ethical norms, Schmitt and his ilk had carried the notion of sovereignty to its extreme. "Sovereign," Schmitt had written, "is he who decides on the state of emergency." [47] Sovereignty was thus rooted in the right to make decisions, which was granted to the state. The individual, who had been rescued by earlier *Lebensphilosophie*, was now made subservient to the state. "With the realization of the total-authoritarian state," Marcuse wrote, "existentialism abolishes itself — rather it undergoes abolition." [48] What began philosophically as a protest thus ended politically in capitulation to the dominant forces of society.

There was in all of this one small consolation: "In consciously politicizing the concept of existence, and deprivatizing and deinternalizing the liberalist, idealist conception of man, the totalitarian view of the state represents progress — progress that leads beyond the basis of the totalitarian state, propelling the theory beyond the social order that it affirms." [49] Still, Marcuse stressed, it ought to be recognized that the ideological reconciliation of interests in the *völkisch* state should not be confused with the real reconciliation promised by Marx. As Horkheimer was to write during the war, the fascist *Verstaatlichung* (nationalization) was the opposite of the Marxist *Vergesellschaftlichung* (socialization).[50] It was also a betrayal of the Hegelian notion of the state as the reconciliation of contradictions. In fact, Marcuse argued, anticipating his more extensive discussion in *Reason and Revolution*, the Nazis and Hegel were fundamentally incompatible, despite the popular assumption to the contrary. Critical idealism and existentialism were in reality polar opposites.

In any event, the clearest implication of Marcuse's essay, and one that was shared by other Institut members,[51] was that liberalism along with the economic base that had sustained it was irretrievably dead. The future held only the totalitarian authoritarianism of the right or the liberating collectivism of the left. That a third possibility, what Marcuse was later to call "one-dimensional" society, would emerge from the polarization of the thirties was only dimly perceived by the Institut in the years before the war. Nor did the Frankfurt School allow for the possibility of a retention of certain elements of liberal society in the post-market economy world. By stressing the continuities between liberalism and fascism, which, to be sure, had been ignored by those who saw the latter as a right-wing, reactionary movement instead of the middle-class extremism it was,[52] they tended to minimize the very real differences that separated them. To see the irrationalism of fascist ideology as little more than an affirmation of the status quo was to miss those elements of that status quo — the formal legal safeguards, civil liberties, and so on — which were challenged by that abandonment of rationality. Fascism and liberalism may have been "within the framework of a single social order," but the framework proved large enough to encompass very different political and legal systems.

With these assumptions about the nature of political authority in mind, the *Studien über Autorität und Familie* can now be discussed. Although, as Horkheimer made clear in his introduction,[53] the problem of authority and the family was not at the center of a theory of society, it still deserved serious study because of the family's crucial role in mediating between material substructure and ideological superstructure. In fact, it is not surprising that the Institut's neo-Hegelian Marxism should have led it to an examination of familial relations. For Hegel, the family had been the central ethical institution on which the community was ultimately based.[54] Marx, of course, had had a very different evaluation of the family as it concretely appeared in the society he examined. The bourgeois family, he had argued in *The Communist Manifesto*, was a monument of dehumanized alienation. Unlike Hegel, he felt that a civil society fostering egoistic, exchange-value dominated motivations had invaded the family and distorted its "ethical" side. The reality of the bourgeois family, Marx argued, was its commodity nature; that of the proletarian family was its dissolution through external exploitation. The Institut's own approach, as we shall see, mediated between these two perspectives, although tending increasingly towards Marx's more pessimistic one. It also combined the genetic concerns characteristic of most nineteenth-century students of the family, such as Le Play, Maine, and Bachofen, with the interest in the current function of the family displayed by their twentieth-century successors.[55]

The *Studien* was the product of five years of work carried out by the combined Institut staff, with the exception of Grossmann and Adorno (who did not become an official member until after its completion). In its dedication, it remembered the Institut's major benefactor, Felix Weil, who had helped persuade his father to endow the Institut in the early twenties. It was the first real fruit of the plan announced at Horkheimer's inauguration as professor at Frankfurt to enrich its theoretical perspective with empirical investigations. Although all the information used, with one or two exceptions, was gathered in Europe under the direction of Andries Sternheim, the *Studien* acknowledged the influence of an American forerunner, Robert Lynd's *Middletown*, published in 1929. Horkheimer edited the first part, which consisted of theoretical essays; Fromm the second, devoted to empirical studies; and Lowenthal the third, composed of separate investigations of various related problems. These were followed by extensive bibliographical essays and abstracts in English and French.

Appropriately, in view of the Institut's adherence to the primacy of theory, the initial section of the *Studien* was given over to three long speculative essays by Horkheimer, Fromm, and Marcuse. A fourth, prepared by Pollock on the economics of authority relations, was not finished in time because of his administrative duties. Horkheimer set the tone for the entire volume in his "General Section." He began by establishing the rationale for so closely examining the cultural side of modern society. Although not rejecting the Marxist stress on the centrality of the material substructure, he argued for the reciprocal interaction that inevitably existed between it and the superstructure. Using as examples Chinese ancestor worship and the Indian caste system, he explored the "cultural lag" [56] that often obtains after the original socio-economic cause has disappeared. Ideas and behavioral patterns may have lost their objective — that is, material — justification, but still persist because men are subjectively and emotionally committed to them. Only with this understood could the subtleties of authority relations be adequately appreciated.

The second section of Horkheimer's essay dealt with the historical development of authority in the bourgeois world. Here he expatiated on many of the ideas treated elsewhere in the Institut's work. Horkheimer laid special emphasis on the disparity between the bourgeois ideology of antiauthoritarianism and the increasing submission of the individual to the reified authority of an irrational socio-economic order. He was careful, however, to argue against the total antiauthoritarianism of Bakunin and other anarchists who misunderstood the material preconditions necessary for true freedom. Only when general and particular interests were reconciled would the formalistic opposition of authority and reason hypostatized by the anarchists be finally overcome. "Anarchism," Horkheimer wrote, "and authoritarian statism both belong to the same cultural epoch." [57]

With this as a background, Horkheimer turned to the function of the family in the process of socialization. Here he drew a distinction between the family in the era of bourgeois liberalism and its contemporary counterpart. In the former, the father enjoyed the authority that accompanied his objective role as economic provider, in addition to his other sources of authority, such as physical superiority over his children. To this extent, he was both the natural and the rational head of his household. With the undermining of his objective social power in the late capitalist era, however, his authority had become increasingly ideological and irrational. The working class family was particularly susceptible to this crucial change because of its precarious economic condition. With the decline of the father's authority went a transfer of his "metaphysical" aura to social institutions outside the family. These institutions now enjoyed the immunity from criticism that the early bourgeois father had to some extent earned. Misfortune was thus blamed on personal inadequacy or natural causes rather than on social ones. Acceptance of impotence as inevitable, rather than active self-assertion, was the result.[58]

This part of Horkheimer's analysis was in the same spirit as Marx's critique of the bourgeois family, although it was enriched by a more developed psychological understanding of interpersonal relations. However, Horkheimer did not entirely reject Hegel's alternative notion of the family as a preserve of ethical resistance against social dehumanization. Where he criticized Hegel was for his shortsighted hypostatization of the opposition between family and civil society. Antigone's relationship to her brother, which Hegel interpreted as a symbol of the inevitable antagonism between family and society, was to Horkheimer a foretaste of the rational society of the future.[59] He did, however, agree with Marx's observation that the "negative," critical thrust of familial life and conjugal love had been seriously eroded in bourgeois society more than Hegel had grasped. In the twentieth century this trend was even more pronounced. For example, simply to oppose a matriarchal principle in Bachofen's sense to the current patriarchal society would be to ignore the subtle transformation of the woman's role in modern life. As Strindberg and Ibsen had illustrated in their plays, so Horkheimer argued, the emancipation of women in bourgeois society proved less of a liberation than once assumed. Women in most cases had adapted to the system and become a conservative force through their total dependence on their husbands. In fact, children learned to obey the prevailing order at their mother's knee, despite the potential for an alternative social system implicit in the traditional matriarchal ethic of warmth, acceptance, and love.

In short, Horkheimer recognized a dialectical relationship between family and society, at once reinforcing and contradictory, but with the negative element on the decline. Thus the essay ended on a pessimistic note: "The education of authoritarian characters . . . does not belong to transient appearances, but to a relatively lasting condition. . . . The dialectical totality of generality, particularity, and individuality proves now to be the unity of mutually reinforcing forces."[60] The major implication of his essay, and that of the *Studien* as a whole, was the transformation of the family's role in the process of socialization. Because of the decline of the "negative," countersocial function of the family, individuals were more directly socialized by other institutions in the society. As we shall see when examining the Institut's discussion of mass culture, these alternative agents of socialization were instrumental in creating a type of "authoritarian personality" more subtle and resistant to change than any in premodern societies. The crisis of the family was to be a topic appearing again and again in subsequent work by Institut members and others, such as the psychologist Alexander Mitscherlich,[61] who were influenced by them.

The second essay in the theoretical section of the *Studien*, Fromm's "Social Psychological Section," also had considerable resonance in future Institut work. In the mid-thirties, as explained in Chapter 3, Fromm's attitude towards orthodox psychoanalysis was very much in flux. As a consequence, his essay expressed a certain ambivalence towards Freud. It began with the acknowledgment that Freud's theory of mass psychology and the superego was the best starting point for a general psychological analysis of authority. Having said this, however, Fromm quickly pointed to the shortcomings he saw in psychoanalytic theory. Freud, he argued, sometimes assigned the reality principle to the rational ego, sometimes to the superego, whereas in a healthy society it ought to belong only to the former. Freud was also too simplistic in his notion of identification as the primary source of the superego, although identification was a useful analytical tool.[62] He was especially wrong, Fromm continued, in basing the child's identification with his father solely on the Oedipus complex and fear of castration. There were other specifically socio-economic factors, he argued, which also affected the authority relationship.

In fact, the progress of society itself was a major influence on the relative strength of the ego and superego in repressing the socially dangerous impulses of the id. With the development of the productive powers of mankind, human control of nature, both within and outside man, had grown. This meant the increase of man's capacity to create a rational society ruled by his ego, rather than by his traditionally formed superego. Freud, however, had neglected the active side of ego development and overstressed its adaptive quality.[63] With a strengthened ego, Fromm continued, freedom from irrational anxiety would be maximized and authority derived from the superego lessened. If, on the other hand, social conditions were out of phase with the productive powers, the development of a strong ego would be hindered, leading to a regression to irrational authority rooted in the superego. As Ferenczi had demonstrated, the loss of ego in hypnotic situations led to an authority relation between therapist and patient that was clearly irrational.

Fromm, however, was not completely satisfied with the loss of ego as an explanation of the ardor with which some people embraced authority. Nor was he willing to accept an innate drive for subordination, such as that postulated by McDougall or Vierkandt.[64] Instead, he attempted to integrate his historical causation with psychosexual concepts derived largely from Freud. Anticipating his later argument in *Escape from Freedom*, he offered the sado-masochistic character as the core of the authoritarian personality. In 1936 he grounded it primarily in sexuality, whereas in his later formulation it was based on the "existentialist" categories of alienation and symbiotic relatedness.[65]

Fromm agreed with Freud that both masochism and sadism were part of a unified character syndrome, adding that authoritarian societies based on hierarchy and dependency increased the likelihood of its appearance. Masochism in such societies, he argued, manifested itself in the passive acceptance of "fate," the force of "facts," "duty," "God's will," and so on.[66] Although difficult to explain fully, the pleasures of inferiority were derived negatively from its liberation of the individual from his anxiety, positively from his feeling of participation in power. They were also related, Fromm argued, to a weakening of heterosexual, genital sexuality and a regression to pregenital, especially anal, libidinous stages. Homosexual identification with the powers above, more often spiritual than corporeal, was another characteristic of sado-masochistic authoritarianism. This latter aspect of the syndrome was especially pronounced in patriarchal cultures in which men were presumed to be inherently superior to women and were thus transformed into the objects of masochistic love.

Fromm concluded his essay by discussing types of reactions against authority. Here he distinguished between "rebellions," which simply replace one irrational authority with another without signifying a real change in underlying character, and "revolutions," which did reflect such a change. The latter, which Fromm admitted were far less frequent, implied an ego strong enough to withstand the blandishments of irrational sado-masochistic authority. In rational, democratic societies, the leaders who did emerge enjoyed an authority based on capability, experience, and disinterestedness rather than metaphysical, innate superiority. Therefore, not all antiauthoritarian impulses were justified. "Rebellions" were pseudo-liberations in which the individual was really seeking a new irrational authority to love, even when he seemed most antagonistic to all authority. The resentful anarchist and the rigid authoritarian were thus not as far apart as they might appear at first glance. This accounted for the sudden embrace of authority that often characterized the seemingly libertarian anarchist.

Fromm's contribution to the *Studien*'s theoretical section struck an optimistic note in its support for the possibility of reconciling a strong individual ego, mature heterosexual genital sexuality, and a rational, democratic society. As discussed in the previous chapter, his adherence to this position in the following years, combined with his diminution of the importance of sexuality, increasingly distanced him from other Institut members. Horkheimer and Adorno, as we shall see, began to question the nature-dominating, rational ego that Fromm had so strongly supported. And Marcuse, as we have already seen, rejected the notion of heterosexual genitality as the standard of psychic health most compatible with the good society. In the thirties, however, all Institut members accepted the general contours of Fromm's psychosocial utopia with little qualification.

Marcuse, who was to become Fromm's most outspoken opponent in the fifties, was not yet a serious student of Freud. The essay that he contributed to the *Studien*'s theoretical section was a rather straightforward intellectual history of theories of authority. This and the bibliographical essay he also wrote for the volume[67] demonstrated not only his indifference to psychology, but also his noninvolvement with the Institut's empirical work based on psychological categories. Of all the members of the Frankfurt School, Marcuse was least empirically inclined, a fact that his critics in later years never tired of rehearsing.[68]

In his "Intellectual Historical Section," Marcuse developed many of the points made elsewhere in *Zeitschrift* articles. He began by stressing once again the intrinsic connection between freedom and authority, which bourgeois theorists had so often failed to acknowledge. Instead, he pointed out, they posited the notion of negative freedom, most characteristically formulated by Kant, which meant the separation of inner and outer selves. Internal autonomy was preserved at the cost of external heteronomy. The antiauthoritarian pretensions of bourgeois theory masked the metaphysical sanction it gave to the prevailing social order. And under capitalism this order remained inevitably irrational.[69]

In the series of brief intellectual historical sketches that followed, Marcuse outlined the classic forms of negative freedom as they appeared in the thought of the Reformation and of Kant. Missing, however, were such theorists in between as Hobbes, Locke, Hume, and Rousseau, whose thinking rarely appeared in any of the Institut's discussions of "bourgeois" theory.[70] What followed instead were sections devoted to challengers of the bourgeois notion of freedom from both the left and right: Hegel, Burke, Bonald, de Maistre, Stahl, and Marx himself. Marcuse finished by turning to the transformation of the liberal ideas of freedom and authority into their totalitarian successor. Here he focused on the work of Sorel and Pareto, whose theories of elitism, he argued, anticipated both the fascist "leader principle" and the Leninist notion of the party. The core of totalitarian theory, Marcuse continued, was irrational formalism. The source of authority was no longer grounded in universal law or social preeminence, but was understood instead to be derived from "natural" or racial right. The substance of totalitarian theory was entirely without positive content; all its concepts were counterconcepts, such as antiliberalism or anti-Marxism. The bourgeois preserve of internal, "negative" freedom had been liquidated, leaving only obedience to heteronomous authority.

All three of the essays in the theoretical section were obviously prepared in coordination with each other. All posited the increasing irrationality of the social order and the concomitant decline of rational authority, political or otherwise. All expressed, on the other hand, a certain confidence in the possibility of a social order in which general authority and particular interest might be reconciled. And finally, all shared the dismay, most strongly voiced in Horkheimer's essay, that the family was rapidly ceasing to be an agent on the side of this possibility.

To add weight to these conclusions, the *Studien* next presented a report of the Institut's empirical work. Although a source of reinforcement and modification, these investigations were never really the essential justification for the Institut's theoretical speculations. Critical Theory, as we have explained earlier, was unremittingly hostile to pure induction as a methodology. "Moreover," Horkheimer and the others explained, "as our experience in this field was limited and the answering of questionnaires meets with special difficulties in Europe, these empirical investigations took on largely the character of an experiment. Nowhere have the results been generalized. The questionnaires were not considered numerous enough to be statistically conclusive. They were intended only to keep us in contact with the facts of daily life and were destined to serve primarily as material for typological conclusions."[71] Fromm, to be sure, felt more positively about their validity,[72] but Horkheimer's views prevailed.

Yet, fragmentary and inclusive as the empirical studies were, they provided valuable methodological experience, which aided the Institut in all its subsequent investigations of authority. Except for a brief preliminary report on the psychic state of the unemployed in America, all the empirical work discussed in the *Studien* had been done in Europe, directly before the expulsion from Germany or immediately thereafter in other countries. The most extensive was based on the questionnaires Fromm had developed to test the psychological status of workers and clerical employees. Although, as mentioned before, some 586 of the three thousand original questionnaires were salvaged, there seemed sufficient variation to support a tripartite division of psychological types: authoritarian, revolutionary, and ambivalent. (Significantly, the antithesis of the "authoritarian" type was called "revolutionary". By the time of *The Authoritarian Personality*. after the Institut had been in America for over a decade, it had changed to the "democratic," a shift of emphasis that reflected the dampening of the Institut's revolutionary fervor.) The quantitative generalizations drawn from the material by Fromm and Lazarsfeld were not, however, published nor was an attempt made to correlate it with the subsequent performance of the German working class when the Nazis came to power.

Other studies were similarly modest in their conclusions. Only a third of the answers to a survey of German physicians' attitudes towards sexual morality, conducted in 1932, were received. Thus, although representative examples were given, followed by some observations from Holland by Karl Landauer, no attempt was made to generalize the material. Caution was also displayed in analyzing a dual study of youthful authority patterns, although here the evidence was more extensive. Surveys had been conducted both of experts on youth in various countries and of adolescents themselves. The former were summarized by Andries Sternheim and a new member of the Institut's junior staff, Ernst Schachtel, who had been a friend of Fromm's since their student days in Heidelberg.[73] Jay Rumney added a brief description of a separate study of English experts conducted by the London branch of the Institut, which was still in progress. These were followed by reports on surveys of adolescents in Switzerland, France, and England. Käthe Leichter directed the Swiss investigations, with the methodological advice of a refugee from

Vienna who was soon to become more deeply involved in Institut affairs, Paul Lazarsfeld. Less complete were the investigations made in Paris, reported by Jeanne Bouglé and Anne Weil, and London, described once again by Rumney. The final contributions to the *Studien*'s empirical section were reports of preliminary studies of the effects of unemployment in France and America, which anticipated a later work by Mirra Komarovsky to which we shall soon return.

From his own project on the workers' authoritarianism, Fromm was able to draw certain methodological conclusions.[74] First was the necessity of treating the totality of answers, rather than isolated ones, as the basis for analysis. The goal, as stated earlier, was the uncovering of the respondents' underlying character types, which were revealed only through the complete set of their answers and in comparison with other sets. This, however, required something more than inductive generalization. In Fromm's words, "as much as the formation of types is influenced and should be permanently differentiated by the material of the investigation, the types cannot be exclusively acquired from classification, but presuppose a developed psychological theory." [75] The sado-masochistic character he had described earlier was the product of such a theory. To correlate the evidence from the questionnaires with a theoretical model, Fromm admitted, required interpretive skill, but if done with sufficient deliberation it need not lead to distortions of the material. Other supporting evidence, even graphology, which Schachtel attempted to use with mixed results, might be adduced with effect.

Once correlations between certain specific answers and the more general character types could be established, these might be related to other data such as social class or religious belief. The important point, however, was that behind all the empirical operations there must be a global theory. The most fruitful, Fromm implied, was of course Critical Theory. In fact, as Schachtel was to argue at some length in a subsequent *Zeitschrift* article,[76] American personality tests were inadequate precisely because of their antitheoretical basis. Besides this more general conclusion, more specific ones followed, but clearly the Institut's empirical efforts were still at a relatively primitive stage, at least in comparison with its later work, where content analysis and projective tests were introduced to good advantage.

The *Studien*'s third section, edited by Lowenthal, included sixteen studies, many of almost monographic length.[77] Because of lack of space in the volume itself, which still totaled more than nine hundred pages, many of these were presented as abstracts, and because of a similar problem here they cannot be treated separately. Several of the essays dealt specifically with the effects of economics on the family, which had been neglected in the theoretical section. Others treated legal questions involving familial relations in various countries. Strikingly absent in this section, as in the *Studien* as a whole, was a study of anti-Semitism and its relation to authoritarianism. This was perhaps a reflection of the Institut's general minimization of the Jewish problem, which has been noted earlier. Pollock, when questioned about it, replied "one didn't want to advertise that." [78] It perhaps also corresponded to the Institut's unwillingness to draw unnecessary attention to the overwhelmingly Jewish origins of its members. Whatever the cause, the neglect was not long-lived. In 1939 Horkheimer published an essay on "The Jews and Europe," [79] one of his most despairing, and the Institut began to draw up plans for a major study of anti-Semitism. Although never completed as initially conceived, this plan served as a forerunner of the "Studies in Prejudice" directed in part by the Institut in the forties, several of which dealt with the problem of anti-Semitism. The objective that the Institut's founders had used to help persuade Hermann Weil to endow the Institut in the early twenties was thus not really achieved until two decades later, long after the Institut had first attempted to explore authoritarianism in the *Studien.* Yet without the experience provided by the first collaborative effort of the Institut, it is unlikely that its subsequent work on this question, as on many others, would have proceeded in quite the same way.

Although the *Studien* was an important link in the Institut's own development, its impact on the outside world was mixed. Largely because of its appearance in German, the American academic community was slow to assimilate its findings and methodology. This process was not abetted by the extremely hostile review the work received in the New School's journal, *Social Research,* at the hands of Hans Speier.[80] Not only did the Institut's Marxist tinge arouse the New School's ire, but so did its enthusiasm for Freud. Max Wertheimer, the founder of Gestalt psychology, was the doyen of the New School's psychologists from 1934 until his death in 1943. His disdain for psychoanalysis was echoed in Speier's disparaging review. As noted in the previous chapter, the integration of Marx and Freud was still a butt of ridicule in the 1930's, and not only at the New School. The reception of the *Studien* suffered accordingly.

The Institut's interest in the issue of authoritarianism did not, however, wane following the completion of the *Studien.* As the Nazi threat grew, so did the intensity of the Institut's attempt to understand it. The results were of sufficient richness to warrant a discussion of their own, which will occupy us in the next chapter. Before focusing on the German case, however, the full range of the Institut's explorations of authoritarianism must be made clear. In fact, one of the key elements in the Institut's interpretation of Nazism was the belief that the phenomenon could not be isolated from general trends in Western civilization as a whole.

Even more ambitiously, the Institut attempted to situate the crisis of Western civilization in a global context. Here it relied on its experts in non-European affairs to broaden the scope of its work. The methodology that they used, however, tended to diverge from that employed in the *Studien.* This was especially true of the work of Karl August Wittfogel, whose distance from Critical Theory has already been stressed. Despite the gap between his approach and Horkheimer's, his studies of China appeared in the *Zeitschrift* during the 1930's with some regularity.[81] Enriched by almost three years of research in the Far East after 1935, Wittfogel's work continued to be based on more orthodox Marxist premises than those of the Institut's inner circle. Although sponsored in his research by the Institut, he also received support from the Rockefeller Foundation and the Institute of Pacific Relations. In the forties Wittfogel became increasingly independent of the Institut, both ideologically and financially. But in the several years after his return from China, his connection was prized as a link to the American academic world. The Institut's short historical accounts of those years always included extensive mention of his work, and he was prominently featured in the Institut's lecture series at Columbia's Extension Division. After his third marriage in 1940 to Esther Goldfrank, however, his role in the Institut diminished gradually, until it finally withered away in 1947.

The other major contributor to the Institut's non-European studies of authority was one of its founders, Felix Weil. Although Weil never broke with the Horkheimer group on ideological or political grounds, he too was little affected by Critical Theory. In 1944 his *Argentine Riddle*,[82] an analysis of the country he had known from birth, was published in New York, although not under Institut auspices. As in Wittfogel's more formidable studies of Chinese history, there was little evidence of the effect of the *Studien*'s methodology.

The first American study to show the Institut's methodological influence was Mirra Komarovsky's *The Unemployed Man and His Family*,[83] published in 1940. An outgrowth of research conducted in Newark in 1935–1936, it was a collaborative effort with Paul Lazarsfeld's Research Center of the University of Newark.[84] Lazarsfeld, who had received Institut support for sponsoring the project, wrote the introduction and helped with the typological classifications, which he had previously outlined in the *Zeitschrift.*[85] The project used qualitative rather than quantitative techniques to explore the effects of the Depression on familial life.

Substantively, the study dealt with the impact of unemployment on fifty-nine families recommended by the Emergency Relief Administration. Various members of the family were subjected to a series of interviews designed to reveal changes in familial relationships. On the whole, the results confirmed the *Studien*'s argument about the decline of the contemporary family's authority. They also implied the increased atomization of man in mass society, for, as Miss Komarovsky wrote, "the unemployed man and his wife have no social life outside the family. The extent of the social isolation of the family is truly striking." [86] Still, her interpretation of the implications of these changes was less gloomy than those of subsequent Institut studies in the forties. Miss Komarovsky articulated her own viewpoint more than that of Horkheimer and the other central Institut figures when she wrote: "Even a partial breakdown of parental authority in the family as an effect of the depression might tend to increase the readiness of coming generations to accept social change." [87] The longer the Institut remained in America, the more it became convinced that the opposite was true. Whether or not they or Miss Komarovsky will be proved right in the long run, the crisis in familial relations, more recently popularized as the "generation gap," was to become an increasing object of scholarly study and popular concern. Here, as in so many other instances, the Frankfurt School anticipated later issues of widespread interest.

Before we discuss the empirical work in the forties supporting the Institut's growing pessimism, which we shall do in Chapter 7, other Institut treatments of authority that had a less empirical perspective should be mentioned. Particularly suggestive were the analyses of cultural phenomena by Adorno, Benjamin, and Lowenthal, which appeared in the *Zeitschrift* in the thirties. Of the three, Lowenthal's approach was most closely related to the *Studien*, partly because he was involved with its preparation, while the others were not. Although echoes of its conclusions appear in Benjamin's and Adorno's articles — for example, in Adorno's discussion of Wagner[88] — the aesthetic theories that informed their work are sufficiently idiosyncratic to deserve separate treatment, which they will receive in a subsequent chapter. Lowenthal's work, on the other hand, was rooted in a more straightforward sociology of literature, which allowed him to discern traces of many of the patterns of authority explored in the *Studien*.

From 1928 until 1931 Lowenthal had been engaged in a lengthy study of nineteenth-century German narrative literature, which was entitled *Narrative Art and Society: The Social Problematic in the German Literature of the Nineteenth Century.*[89] Levin Schücking's writings on the sociology of taste, the criticism of Georg Brandes, and most importantly Georg Lukács's *The Theory of the Novel* were among the few models Lowenthal chose to emulate. Included in the study were essays on Goethe, the Romantics, Young Germany (especially Gutzkow), Eduard Möricke, Gustav Freytag, Friedrich Spielhagen, Conrad Ferdinand Meyer, and Gottfried Keller. Close textual critiques alternated with analyses of the psychological and sociological influences on the various authors. Although Lowenthal avoided a reductionist approach, he did attempt to situate the literature in its historical context. Thus, for example, the Young Germans were interpreted as the first real representatives of bourgeois class-consciousness, fighting as they did for the intellectual equivalent of the *Zollverein* with its lack of restrictions on competition.[90] In opposition to their Romantic predecessors, they wrote works in which men were securely at home in their world, a trend that would intensify in the novels of the mid-century realists and culminate in Freytag's *Debit and Credit*, the "most unidealistic and unromantic book of the nineteenth century." [91]

Lowenthal, however, considered the work unfinished, and with the pressure of his new duties as managing editor of the *Zeitschrift*, he was unable to prepare it for immediate publication. Instead, several selections from it were included in subsequent collections.[92] The opening essay, a study of the methodology he had used, was published in the initial issue of the *Zeitschrift.*[93] In it he outlined the tasks of a sociologist of literature.

In so doing, he attempted to walk a thin line between the literary criticism of orthodox Marxists such as Franz Mehring and the idealistic alternative most recently posed by the New Criticism. Although the critic, so he argued, must not reduce art to a simple reflex of social trends, he may legitimately see in art the indirect reflection of a society. To treat works of art as isolated, extra-social phenomena would be to understand them poetically, not critically. Historical analysis, on the other hand, must be enriched by a Diltheyan *Verstehen* (understanding) of the artist's purpose, although qualified by a materialist situating of the artist in his socio-economic milieu. At the same time, a valid literary criticism must be open to the psychology of the artist as a mediating factor between the society and the finished work of art. Here psychoanalysis, despite its relatively rudimentary state, had something to offer.[94] Employing as examples such writers as Balzac, Zola, Stendhal, and Gutzkow, Lowenthal then attempted to demonstrate the usefulness of his method in analyzing literary form, recurrent motifs, and actual thematic content. The article ended with the mention of yet another area for a materialist critic to investigate: the social effect of literary works. Lowenthal's general theme, as might be expected, was that a sociology of literature must itself be part of a general critical theory of the social totality.

In a series of articles in subsequent *Zeitschrift* issues, Lowenthal put his ideas into practice. As with much of the work of other Institut members, these demonstrated the integrated quality of the Frankfurt School's thought. The first of his critiques dealt with the heroic view of history in Conrad Ferdinand Meyer's fiction.[95] Here many of the themes developed the following year in Marcuse's article "The Struggle against Liberalism in the Totalitarian View of the State" were demonstrated in a different context. History in Meyer's novellas, Lowenthal argued, was reduced to the stage of heroic deeds. Like his Swiss compatriot, the historian Jacob Burckhardt, Meyer sought heroes in the past as anticipations of the great men of the present. In addition, nature in Meyer's work served as the continuation of history by other means; it too was the backdrop for heroic actions. Although stressing individualism, Meyer's stories lacked a developed psychological sense. His heroes were ultimately ineffable; the milieu in which they operated appeared mythical and irrational. What resulted was an implicit ideology of the strong man not unrelated to the Bismarck cult, which flourished at the same time and which Meyer in fact supported in his expository writings.

Lowenthal continued by arguing that despite the patrician elements in Meyer's background, he was closer in some ways to the mentality of the National Liberal industrial magnates. In fact, the patrician-bourgeois mixture in his writings mirrored the actual alliance of the German ruling classes in the Second Reich. "In Germany," Lowenthal wrote, "there was never an actual liberalism as the expression of the class-consciousness of a leading class, but rather a union of large agrarians, businessmen, and the military originating in certain economic and political conditions and extraordinarily susceptible to a heroic irrationalism." [96] In short, what Lowenthal attempted to do was to unmask a historical philosophy based on the rule of great men, which corresponded to a certain phase in Germany's development.

If history had been mythicized in Meyer's work, it was even more severely distorted in the cultural phenomenon that Lowenthal next treated: the reception of Dostoyevsky in Germany before the First

World War.[97] By examining the some eight hundred pieces of critical literature on Dostoyevsky in German, Lowenthal attempted what was really a pioneer study of readers' reactions.[98] In later years, he would admit that the methodology was still relatively crude:

> Had I known at the time about advanced methods of opinion research and projective psychology, I would probably have never designed this study, for it attempts to accomplish the same ends as these methodologies in a primordial fashion. It assumes that the works of a writer serve as projective devices for the display, through widely published commentaries, of hidden traits and tendencies typical for broad strata of a population. In other words, it studies readers' reactions indirectly through the medium of printed material, which is inferred to represent typical group reactions.[99]

However primitive the method, the results tended to confirm the Institut's analysis of authoritarianism. Whereas Meyer's readership had consisted primarily of moderately prosperous members of the middle class, Dostoyevsky, on the other hand, was most widely read by the less successful petite bourgeoisie. His appeal to this most confused and frightened segment of the German population, Lowenthal argued, was derived largely from the consolation his works offered them. In addition, the mythicizing of his personal life contributed to the general acceptance of personal suffering as ennobling and inevitable. *Völkisch* theorists such as Arthur Moeller van den Bruck were particularly drawn to the spiritual reconciliation advocated in his work, to its nationalist transcendence of class conflict and ideology of universal love. Dostoyevsky himself contributed to this reading of his novels by his failure to develop a belief in the possibility of earthly happiness, which was also reflected in his hostility towards political and social radicalism. The emphasis on love and pity that he substituted for political activism was not unlike the *völkisch* distortion of matriarchal theory, leading once again to passivity and dependence.

Unlike Meyer, however, Dostoyevsky did offer a sensitive exposition of internal psychological reality. But paradoxically, this proved one of his major attractions at a time of indecision in German history, between the rising and declining periods of bourgeois power. As his work was interpreted in prewar Germany, *Innerlichkeit* (inwardness) replaced social interaction as the crucial focus of cultural life. Fascination with the disturbed and criminal mentalities that Dostoyevsky so skillfully portrayed expressed a genuine interest in alienation, but one that was ideologically distorted by its blindness to the social origins of this condition.[100] In general, then, so Lowenthal argued, the enormous popularity of Dostoyevsky's novels in certain sectors of the German populace betokened an increasing flight from a harsh reality and the growing acceptance of irrational authority. It was thus not surprising that after the war Dostoyevsky was linked to Kierkegaard as a prophet of social resignation.

There were, however, exceptions to the ideological implications of the literature of the late bourgeois period; certain authors, Lowenthal recognized, were able to pierce through the facade of false reconciliation promised by bourgeois culture to expose the less attractive reality beneath. One such writer was the subject of his next *Zeitschrift* study, Henrik Ibsen.[101] To Lowenthal, Ibsen was both a true liberal and one of the most spirited critics of the late liberal era. Although not writing self-conscious "social drama," Ibsen probed the decline of liberalism where it was seemingly most invulnerable: in the sphere of private life and the family. By portraying so vividly the unattainable promise of individual self-realization in an age of destructive competition, Ibsen exploded the liberal myth of personal happiness. "Competition," Lowenthal wrote, "turns out to be not only a struggle for social and economic success among various individuals; it is also an inner struggle in which the individual must drastically curtail certain sides of his own being, his personality, in order to realize his personal ambitions." [102]

Furthermore, by depicting the decline of the family, Ibsen exposed the social penetration of the private sphere through the specialization of roles. "The position of husband, wife, friend, father, or mother," Lowenthal wrote, "is seen as a form of existence at odds with the prerogatives of the individual himself as well as with those of the other members of the family." [103] The families in Ibsen's plays corroborated the conclusions the *Studien* had reached about the decreasing function of the family as a preserve of human interaction: the only truly human relationships in the plays seemed to occur at the moment of a character's death, when society's bonds were finally transcended. In place of the optimism that characterized art in an earlier bourgeois era, Ibsen's dramas radiated despair and disillusionment. To Lowenthal, Ibsen offered no way out: "Two parallel themes run throughout Ibsen's works: the one shows an effort to live up to established social values and ideals only to meet with defeat, and the other shows the defeat of those who reject these values and have nothing to put in their place." [104]

The one exception, Lowenthal admitted, might be seen in Ibsen's female characterizations. Here, he argued, were echoes of the matriarchal alternative Fromm had discussed in the *Zeitschrift*. "The clash between the self-seeking world of men and the love and humanity represented by women is crucial in Ibsen's dramas." [105] Female egotism as it was depicted by Ibsen expressed a legitimate demand for material happiness, unlike the empty idealism of many of his male characters. Yet the reality of feminine existence in the late nineteenth century, which Ibsen's plays also showed, betrayed the principles his female characters espoused. Their negation of the prevailing reality remained entirely without consequence.

The same, Lowenthal pointed out, might be said of another of the metaphors of protest frequently found in late nineteenth- and early twentieth-century literature: nature as a superior alternative to society. In perhaps his most insightful essay, Lowenthal turned to the distortion of this counterimage in the novels of the Norwegian Knut Hamsun.[106] When in 1934 Lowenthal first argued that Hamsun's works contained only a pseudonegation of the status quo, he was met with skepticism by other members of the Institut.[107] *Hunger*, *Pan*, *The Growth of the Soil*, and other of Hamsun's works were understood as genuine protests against the alienation and emptiness of modern life. Lowenthal, however, had the satisfaction of having his counterargument "proved" a few years later when Hamsun joined Quisling's collaborators in Norway. This explicit confirmation of the trends Lowenthal had discerned under the surface of Hamsun's novels was one of the most unambiguous successes of the Institut's program.

It was, in fact, in his treatment of nature that Lowenthal had seen anticipations of Hamsun's authoritarianism. In later years, Horkheimer and Adorno would call for a reconciliation of man and nature, but, as we shall see, in a way very different from that depicted in Hamsun's novels. Unlike the romantic idea of nature, most cogently expressed in Rousseau's work, Hamsun's no longer had a critical, progressive edge. In his novels, man was not reconciled with nature; rather, he surrendered to its power and mystery. The traditional liberal goal of mastering nature (which Horkheimer and Adorno were to question in *Dialectic of the Enlightenment*, but which Lowenthal did not criticize here) was abandoned in favor of passive capitulation. "To Hamsun," Lowenthal wrote, "nature means peace, but a peace which has lost its spontaneity and its will to know and to control. It is a peace based on submission to every arbitrary power, a pantheism which offers an escape from the gloomy framework of history. Nature comes to mean the solace of the unchangeable and the all-pervasive." [108] The characteristically Kantian pride in human autonomy was replaced by the acceptance of natural brutality. In Hamsun's work, sentimentality and ruthlessness were combined in a way typical of Nazism (Goering, for example, was the head of the German version of the ASPCA). The timeless, repetitive rhythms of nature replaced the possibility of human *praxis,* a phenomenon the Institut was later to call "mimesis." "The social counterpart to the law of natural rhythm," Lowenthal wrote, "was a blind discipline." [109] In all of this, he concluded, there was ample evidence of the sado-masochistic character type Fromm had described in the *Studien.*

Further manifestations of Hamsun's authoritarianism included his hero-worship, his glorification of the peasant and traditional life, and his reduction of women to their reproductive and sexual functions alone. All these symptoms, it should be added, were to be found in German *völkisch* literature as well,[110] along with the denigration of urban life and rabid anti-intellectualism of Hamsun's work. As early as 1890 and *Hunger*, Hamsun had shown that vulgarization of *Lebensphilosophie* to which Horkheimer had so often alluded in the *Zeitschrift.* What began as a protest had clearly been turned into a defense of the status quo. As in the reception of Dostoyevsky in Germany, consolation for misery was the message of Hamsun's novels, but a consolation that "turns against those consoled," who "must accept life as it is, and that means the existing relations of domination and subordination, of command and serve." [111] In Hamsun, the exhaustion of European liberalism was complete, the capitulation to totalitarianism blatantly manifest. In the last part of his essay, omitted from the version in *Literature and the Image of Man*, Lowenthal discussed the reception of Hamsun's work in Europe after the war. Whereas before that time he had been criticized for his resignation by socialist commentators and even a few bourgeois ones, after it he was universally hailed. Both *Die Neue Zeit* and Arthur Rosenberg's Nazi bible, *The Myth of the Twentieth Century*, sang his praises after 1918, evidence of the growing paralysis of authoritarian behavior.

As we have noted previously, the Institut's main concern in the thirties was the exposure, analysis, and combatting of the fascist threat. Although set within the context of the more general investigation of authoritarianism discussed in this chapter, the Institut's efforts were primarily focused on the German variant its members had experienced at first hand. Italian fascism, it should be noted parenthetically, was practically ignored in the *Zeitschrift* and the *Studien.* Although Paolo Treves occasionally reviewed Italian books from Milan, no Italian emigré scholar ever wrote for Institut publications, evidence of the lack of communication between the two refugee communities. The Institut's preoccupation was clearly with Nazism as the most significant and frightening manifestation of the collapse of Western civilization. The richness and variety of its contributions to the analysis of Nazism require a separate discussion, which is the task of the following chapter.

V

The Institut's Analysis of Nazism

> State capitalism is the authoritarian state of the present . . . a new breathing space for domination.
> — MAX HORKHEIMER

> The very term "state capitalism" is a *contradictio in adiecto.*
> — FRANZ NEUMANN

"We were all possessed, so to speak, of the idea we must beat Hitler and fascism, and this brought us all together. We all felt we had a mission. That included all the secretaries and all coming to the Institut and working there. This mission really gave us a feeling of loyalty and belonging together." [1] So Alice Maier, Horkheimer's secretary in New York, described the Institut's overriding concern in the late thirties and early forties. Common purpose, however, did not necessarily mean complete analytical agreement, as we shall see in the present chapter. The continuing influx of refugees from Europe into the Institut's affairs brought with it new and sometimes conflicting perspectives. In some cases, such as that of Adorno, who became a full-time member in 1938, older trends in the Institut's work were reinforced. Adorno's approach to fascism rested on the same psycho-social assumptions that had informed the *Studien über Autorität und Familie.* Theoretically, he was very close to Horkheimer, as we have seen in Chapter 2. With other new entrants into Institut life, however, this uniformity of approach was no longer the case. The three additions who were most important were Franz Neumann, Otto Kirchheimer, and Arkadij R. L. Gurland. A fourth, Paul Massing, had little direct impact on the debate, although his place in Institut affairs after 1941 was an important one in other respects. The presence of these men in New York contributed to an enrichment of the Institut's investigations of Nazism, but also led to a subtle challenge to the basic premises of Critical Theory.

Of the three, Neumann was the most influential, largely through the impact of his now classic study of Nazism, *Behemoth*,[2] a book, as we shall see, in many ways at odds with the work of the older members of the Frankfurt School. Neumann came to the Institut in 1936 on the recommendation of Harold Laski, one of the Institut's sponsors in London and Neumann's teacher at the London School of Economics. He was not, however, totally unknown to the Institut, having met Lowenthal in Frankfurt in 1918, where they were both instrumental in the founding of the Student Socialist Society. London, his initial place of exile, had proved uncongenial, despite Laski's efforts to help him become established; as Neumann later wrote, English "society was too homogeneous and too solid, her opportunities (particularly under conditions of unemployment) too narrow, her politics not too agreeable. One could, so I felt, never quite become an Englishman."[3] America, however, offered a more hospitable welcome, and Neumann chose to spend the rest of his life on this side of the Atlantic.

Before the emigration, his life had been that of a political activist as well as a scholar. Neumann was of the same generation as the Institut's inner circle around Horkheimer. He was born in 1900 into an assimilated Jewish family in the town of Kattowitz near the Polish border. Like Marcuse, he first became politically involved in the Soldiers' Councils at the end of the war. During the Weimar period he became increasingly committed to the moderate Marxism of the Social Democratic Party, although he was to the left of its leadership, whose policies he often disputed. His political activities were of sufficient magnitude to lead to his arrest in April, 1933; escape to London followed after a month of imprisonment.[4]

Neumann's academic background differed from most of the Institut's other members. His university training at Breslau, Leipzig, Rostock, and Frankfurt was predominantly legal rather than philosophical. In Frankfurt he studied with the distinguished jurist Hugo Sinzheimer, whose other students included such future refugees as Hans Morgenthau and Ernst Fraenkel. In the half decade before the collapse of Weimar he lived in Berlin, where he gave legal advice to the SPD and one of its affiliated unions, and wrote for a number of scholarly and political journals.[5] At the same time he taught at the famed Deutsche Hochschule für Politik (German College of Politics), which sent other scholars such as Arnold Wolfers, Hans Simon, Ernst Jaeckh, and Sigmund Neumann (no relation) to American universities after 1933. Neumann also maintained a legal practice in Berlin, which on occasion brought him before the Federal Supreme Labor Court. As might be expected, his expertise in German law proved useless in England. And so, under Laski's guidance, he set out to retrain himself in political science. In 1936, the year he joined the Institut, Neumann was granted a doctorate by the London School of Economics.

Coming to political theory from his legal background, Neumann had a different perspective from Horkheimer and the other members of the Institut's inner circle. His Marxism, so they always felt, was less dialectical and more mechanistic than Critical Theory. Neumann was also far less concerned with the psychological dimension of social reality than Horkheimer, Fromm, or Adorno, which also served to distance his work from theirs. In short, although it is clear that Neumann possessed an analytically probing mind, which the others recognized, he was generally considered closer in many respects to Grossmann and Wittfogel, despite his distaste for their Stalinism.

Neumann's first contribution to the *Zeitschrift* in 1937 reflected his legal interests.[6] In it, he traced the changing function of legal theory in bourgeois society, with particular emphasis on developments in the twentieth century. He focused, among other things, on the vaunted liberal notion of equality before an impersonal law, which, he contended, served as an ideological cover for the rule of the bourgeoisie and an aid in the operation of a free-enterprise system dependent on legal calculability. The so-called rule of law, Neumann suggested, contained a deception, in its refusal to admit that behind the laws were always men, or more precisely, certain social groups.[7]

At the same time, however, he pointed to the positive side of liberal theory, with its guarantee of at least a minimum of legal equality. "Equality before the law is, to be sure, 'formal,' i.e., negative [the distinction between positive and negative freedom made in the previous chapter will be recalled]. But Hegel, who clearly perceived the purely formal-negative nature of liberty, has already warned of the consequences of discarding it." [8] In so reasoning, Neumann paralleled the arguments of Horkheimer and Marcuse on the place of formal logic: although inadequate in itself, formalism provided a vital safeguard, which substantive rationality, whether legal or logical, ignored at its peril. Formalism, in short, was a genuine moment of the dialectical totality, which ought not to be simply negated.

Neumann then turned to an analysis of the function of legal formalism, with special emphasis on the notion of the generality of the law, in Weimar and after. Generality, he pointed out, had enjoyed a recent resurgence of support among legal theorists after a brief eclipse around the turn of the century. Only now, its function was very different from what it had been in the heyday of liberalism in the nineteenth century. The source of the change had been economic: "The postulate that the state should rule only by general laws becomes absurd in the economic sphere, if the legislator is dealing not with equally strong competitors but with monopolies that reverse the principle of the free market." [9] In other words, generality no longer served the same equalizing function as before. Its obsolescence was in fact recognized by Weimar's authoritarian successor, which had replaced it with an arbitrary, nonegalitarian decisionism. Fascist legal theory, to be sure, claimed to have introduced "institutionalism," which replaced the legal individual with institutions or corporations. But, Neumann argued, this was an ideological facade for decisionism, because the institution was "divorced from the context of power relationships, without which it is unintelligible." [10]

Thus, Neumann concluded, law in the fascist countries was illegitimate, because it lacked the generality of liberal, positivist law without being grounded in the rational foundations of natural law.[11] Furthermore, he implied, the trend in nonfascist countries was in the same direction: "Under monopolistic capitalism private property in the means of production is preserved, but general law and contract disappear and are replaced by individual measures on the part of the sovereign." [12] In other words, political existentialism, which Marcuse had discussed in an earlier *Zeitschrift* piece,[13] had permeated the fascist legal sphere and threatened to do the same in all other societies dominated by monopoly capitalism.

In his next essay in the *Zeitschrift*[14] Neumann indicated the legal alternative he favored. Here he was in agreement with the other members of the Institut: reason ought to be the source of law as well as the ground of all social relations. All the doctrines of natural law that Neumann examined in his article were rooted, he claimed, in a concept of man as a rational being. Neumann expressed his agreement with Hegel, who had attacked the previous forms of natural law but not the notion of rational law itself. "We must not be driven," he wrote, showing Horkheimer's influence, "to the extreme of positivism, pragmatism, and perhaps still further to a nihilistic relativism. . . . The truth of a doctrine will depend upon the extent to which it embodies concrete liberty and human dignity, upon its ability to provide for the fullest development of all human potentialities. It is thus in the historic development and the concrete setting of the natural law doctrines that their truth must be determined." [15]

All varieties of natural law, he continued, are rooted in the belief that the principles of law can be somehow derived from the lawfulness of nature, a lawfulness in which man himself shares. They are thus incompatible with a radically historicist politics such as Aristotle's, which defines man solely in terms of his socio-political existence. There must be a doctrine of man's underlying nature, Neumann argued, in a way that showed some divergence from Critical Theory's "negative anthropology." There of course had been many different notions of human nature, ranging from the optimism of Locke, Hooker, and the anarchists to the pessimism of Epicurus, Spinoza, and Hobbes. In contrast to both extremes Neumann expressed sympathy with what he called agnosticism, which characterized man in the state of nature as neither good nor bad. Here he singled out Rousseau as the most articulate spokesman of this position: "[Rousseau's] agnostic view believes that only in civil society can man's original rights merge with those of his fellow citizens into one collective right." [16] Natural law theories, if based on an optimistic view of man's innate nature, logically lead to anarchism; if pessimistic, they imply absolutism. The agnostic view, on the other hand, can lead to a democratic state in which "the sovereign power then ceases to be sovereign, is no longer an external power confronting the subjects. It is rather society itself which governs and administers itself." [17]

In short, of all the theories of natural law — and Neumann discussed several others, such as the Thomist and the constitutionalist — he found most congenial the one that corresponded to the isonomy of positive freedom, implying the identity of rulers and ruled. Accordingly, he rejected the argument that political power and state authority were inherently wicked, at least in the period before the perfect identity of particular and universal interests had been achieved.[18] Here he agreed with the general assumption of Critical Theory that the one authority, legal as well as political, that men should follow was that of reason. And accordingly, because natural law theories were rooted in a normative rationality, they were necessarily critical of prevailing legal conditions.

The source of Neumann's distance from Horkheimer and the other members was not in this conclusion, but rather in the legalistic approach he used to derive it. It also arose from his psychologically spare characterization of man as already endowed with reason, which ignored all the findings of the *Studien* concerning the sway of irrational forces over modern man's behavior. Still, in many ways, Neumann's essays on legal theory in the *Zeitschrift* demonstrated the influence of his discussions in the Institut and of Horkheimer's editorial suggestions. The real quarrel came with the publication of *Behemoth* in 1942.

Before embarking on a discussion of this formidable work, the two other new Institut members who contributed to the analysis of Nazism should be introduced. In fact, in many places *Behemoth* reveals the influence of their collaboration. Of the two, Otto Kirchheimer[19] was the more active participant in Institut affairs. In many ways his background was similar to Neumann's. Five years his junior, Kirchheimer was born in 1905 in Heilbronn, also of Jewish parentage. From 1924 to 1928 he studied law and politics at Münster, Cologne, Berlin, and Bonn. His teachers included Max Scheler, Rudolf Smend, Hermann Heller, and perhaps most importantly, Carl Schmitt. Kirchheimer's doctoral dissertation at Bonn was a contrast of the socialist and Bolshevik concepts of the state, strongly influenced by Schmitt's decisionism and his notion of the "emergency situation." [20] During the waning years of Weimar, Kirchheimer, like Neumann and Gurland, participated in SPD affairs, lecturing in trade-union schools and writing for such journals as *Die Gesellschaft*.

The most trenchant of his writings during this period was an analysis of the Weimar constitution, *Weimar — And What Then?*,[21] which combined insights from both Marx and Schmitt. During the late twenties Kirchheimer expressed little sympathy for the reformist wing of the Social Democratic Party, but was equally reluctant to embrace the Jacobin notion of the party advocated by the Leninists further to his left. Like Schmitt, he argued that true democracy could exist only on the basis of a unified people, free of social contradictions. Where he broke with his former teacher, however, was in rejecting the idea that the racial nation was such a homogeneous community. To Kirchheimer, as a Marxist, true unity was reserved for the classless society of the future.

In the period before the Nazi take-over of power, Kirchheimer, like the members of the Institut then in Frankfurt, preserved a guarded hope that the proletariat might still fulfill its historical role. In 1932 he argued against the importance of mass culture as a sufficient explanation of the working class's reluctance to realize its revolutionary potential. Here, of course, he was more optimistic than his future colleagues: "However one may evaluate this process Ortega y Gassett has called *The Revolt of the Masses*, it seems clear that the condition which is interpreted either as self-limitation or as submission of the masses, depending on one's ideological attitude, belongs to the past." [22] In fact, Kirchheimer's optimism led him to argue that the corporate-institutional state that Schmitt had lauded for transcending social antagonisms was in fact sharpening them. Because of his faith in the revolutionary potential of the workers, Kirchheimer was able to argue that the SPD ought not to support the presidential government of Brüning, despite the arguments to the contrary of more moderate Socialists.[23] To Kirchheimer, the authoritarian "state above the parties" was less an obstacle to fascism than a prelude.[24] The way to prevent Weimar's collapse to the right was to accelerate its potential to the left.

In 1933, of course, his optimism proved faulty and Kirchheimer, like so many others, was forced to flee. In Paris, his first way-station, he was able to join the Institut's branch in 1934 as a research associate. During his stay in the French capital, he began writing for French legal journals[25] and worked on a critique of the Third Reich, which was published in Germany pseudonymously and under the ostensible auspices of the then Councillor of State Carl Schmitt.[26] In 1937 he resettled in New York as a research associate at the Institut's central office.

In New York Kirchheimer was assigned the completion of the work George Rusche had begun in 1931 on the relationship between penal practices and social trends. The result, *Punishment and Social Structure*, published in 1939, was the first of the Institut's major works to appear in English.[27] Rusche had completed the first part dealing with the period before 1900; Kirchheimer picked up where he left off, writing a final chapter on fascism and, with Moses I. Finkelstein's help, translating the manuscript into English. The basic premise of the study was that "punishment must be understood as a social phenomenon freed from both its juristic concept and its social ends. . . . Every system of production tends to discover punishments which correspond to its productive relationships." [28] In examining such modes of punishment as imprisonment, fines, solitary confinement, deportation, and forced labor, Rusche and Kirchheimer were able to demonstrate a rough correlation between such variables as the labor market and the circulation of money on the one hand and specific penal forms on the other. In his chapter on changes under twentieth-century authoritarian regimes, Kirchheimer pointed to the general collapse of legality in the period of monopoly capitalism, which Neumann had noted and which Kirchheimer himself was to explore in a subsequent *Zeitschrift* essay.[29] "The separation of law from morality," he wrote, "as an axiom in the period of competitive capitalism, has been replaced by a moral conviction derived immediately from the racial conscience." [30] The result, he argued, was a much harsher penal policy, characterized by the reintroduction of capital punishment and the decreased use of fines. Statistics in Germany, as well as in France and England, however, demonstrated no connection between such penal measures and the crime rate. Only social change, he concluded, could lead to a decrease in the rate of criminal offenses.

Kirchheimer's contribution to the Institut's analysis of Nazism came in a series of articles he wrote for the *Zeitschrift* and for its successor in late 1939, *Studies in Philosophy and Social Science.* Before turning to these, which we shall do when discussing *Behemoth* later in the present chapter, we must complete the account of the Institut's new members. Some attention must also be paid to the work of the older Institut figures, whose analyses of Nazism contrasted in certain respects with Neumann's and Kirchheimer's. The third new entrant who wrote extensively on Nazism was Arkadij R. L. Gurland. Gurland's association with the Institut, however, was shorter than Neumann's or Kirchheimer's, lasting from 1940 to 1945, and his influence was correspondingly less. Born in 1904 in Moscow, the son of an engineer, Gurland went to gymnasia in Moscow and Sebastopol before coming to Germany in 1922. There he studied economics, philosophy, and sociology at Berlin and Leipzig, writing his doctoral dissertation at the latter university on the concept of dictatorship in the materialist theory of history.[31] In the late twenties Gurland became active in the SPD, contributing to affiliated publications such as *Der Klassenkampf (The Class Struggle)*, which was to the left of the party leadership.

Many of the positions Gurland took at the time were similar to those advocated independently by the Institut. For example, he strongly attacked Karl Kautsky's mechanistic materialism, in favor of a Marxism that recognized its roots in Hegelian dialectics.[32] He also chided the Communist Party for its subservience to Moscow and its unwillingness to jeopardize its party structure to make a revolution.[33] Like Kirchheimer and Neumann, he was a member of the SPD's left wing, imploring its membership to engage in active *praxis* instead of waiting for capitalism to collapse from the weight of its own contradictions. And like both of them, he was driven into exile by the events of 1933. In Paris his career in political journalism was difficult to sustain, and Gurland began to retrain himself as a student of Nazi economics. By the time he came to New York and the Institut in 1940, he was writing almost exclusively on that subject. Despite his earlier interest in philosophy, Gurland did not contribute anything theoretical to Institut publications. His work for the *Zeitschrift* showed more of an affinity for the approach of his former colleagues in the SPD than for that of Critical Theory.

If Neumann, Kirchheimer, and Gurland brought with them ideas somewhat unlike those nurtured in Frankfurt and matured in New York by the Institut's inner circle, they were not the first in the Institut's history to differ with Horkheimer's approach. We have already discussed Wittfogel's more orthodox Marxism and the diminution of his association with the Institut. Henryk Grossmann, the last member of the Grünberg generation of Institut members to remain on its staff, was also a more orthodox Marxist critic of Critical Theory.[34] After several years in London and Paris, Grossmann emigrated to New York in 1937, but his connection with the others on Morningside Heights became increasingly tenuous during the next decade. In fact, the last significant contribution he made to the *Zeitschrift* was his long critique of Borkenau's *The Transition from the Feudal to the Bourgeois World View*, which appeared in 1934. Except for occasional reviews, thereafter his work ceased being published by the Institut. During the late thirties he worked at home rather than in the Institut's building on 117th Street. The termination of the *Zeitschrift* during the war prevented the publication of his study of Marx's relationship to the classical economists,[35] which he had spent much of his time preparing with the major objective of stressing the severity of Marx's repudiation of their work. In the forties several of his pieces appeared in non-Institut journals.[36]

Clearly Grossmann's most productive period had been in the decade before 1933, which culminated with his treatise on the collapse of capitalism. The disruption of European intellectual life brought about by the Nazis helped prevent it from receiving the attention it might have earned at a less turbulent time. Thereafter, the dislocation of Grossmann's personal life added to the waning of his productivity. In America Grossmann led a lonely and isolated existence, having left a wife and children behind in Europe. In New York he had no official connection with Columbia or any other university and scarcely more than a formal one with the Institut. There is also evidence to show that in the early forties his intellectual differences with other Institut members were supplemented by strains in personal relationships.[37] Grossmann's continued support for Stalinist Russia did little to endear him to the others.[38] In addition, according to Alice Maier,[39] he began to fear that his former countrymen, the Poles, were intent on hurting him. Ill health brought on by a stroke compounded his general unhappiness. Finally, after the war he decided to try to resettle in Europe. Unlike some of the other Institut members who returned to Frankfurt, Grossmann went to Leipzig, where the East German government offered him a chair in 1949. The Institut helped him ship his belongings, but by then his bitterness had led to a complete break. Thus only indirectly, through Mrs. Maier, did word reach them of his disappointment with Leipzig in the short time before his death at the age of sixty-nine in November, 1950.

Grossmann's ideological inflexibility prevented him from having much impact on the Institut's analysis of Nazism, or on much else in its work for that matter. It would, however, be a very great mistake to assume that the Institut's analysis of the crisis of modern society completely lacked an economic dimension. Almost every issue of the *Zeitschrift* had an article on an economic problem. Gerhard Meyer analyzed the emergency measures of the Western democracies and their relation to a truly planned economy.[40] Kurt Mandelbaum wrote from London on technological employment and the theory of economic planning.[41] Critiques of non-Marxist economic models were made by "Erich Baumann" and "Paul Sering" (a pseudonym for Richard Löwenthal).[42] Joseph Soudek, who helped Pollock with administrative matters in New York, contributed occasional reviews. Even Felix Weil returned to write a few essays on related matters.[43] Further discussions of the relationship between economics and technology were added by Marcuse and Gurland.[44] In short, although the Institut often castigated vulgar Marxists for their economic determinism, it still acknowledged Marx's insight into the crucial role of the economy in capitalist society.

It would, on the other hand, be an error to argue that these economic analyses were really integrated into the heart of Critical Theory. Horkheimer and Adorno, however broad the scope of their interests and knowledge, were never really serious students of economics, Marxist or otherwise. In fact, Horkheimer's attempts to discuss economic theory were greeted with considerable skepticism by the more orthodox Marxists in the Institut.[45] Even the non-Marxist economists like Gerhard Meyer remember how uneasy the relationship was between the Institut's leaders and the economic analysts.[46] There seems to have been some residue of the long-standing German philosophers' distaste for the more mundane world of getting and spending.

Where Critical Theory broke new ground was in its argument that the role of the economy had changed significantly in the twentieth century. In fact, the debate within the Institut over the nature of fascism centered largely on the character of that change. *Behemoth* shared many of the same assumptions about the nature of monopoly capitalism with orthodox Marxists such as Grossmann. The older members of the Institut's inner circle, on the other hand, followed the lead of its associate director, Friedrich Pollock, who, despite his administrative duties, found time to devote to scholarly pursuits.

The centerpiece of Pollock's work was his theory of state capitalism, with which he described the prevailing trends of modern societies. In large measure, the theory was an extrapolation of his earlier analysis of the Soviet economic experiment.[47] Pollock, it will be recalled, did not feel that Russia had succeeded in introducing a truly *socialist* planned economy. In fact, one of the reasons for the Institut's relative silence on Soviet affairs was its belief that the Russian economy, despite its unique qualities, was a variant of state capitalism. As early as the first issue of the *Zeitschrift* in 1932, Pollock had discussed the prospects for achieving a stabilized capitalist economy despite the Depression.[48] The conclusions he drew were directly opposed to those of crisis theorists such as Grossmann, who predicted the demise of the system within a relatively short period of time. Pollock pointed instead to the growing use of economic planning by government direction as a means to contain capitalist contradictions indefinitely. He also discussed such additional factors as the deliberate encouragement of technological innovation and the effects of an increasing defense sector, which contributed to capitalism's staying power.

In 1941 Pollock extended his observations about the durability of the system into a general theory of state capitalism.[49] Liberal laissez-faire economics, he argued, had been superseded by monopoly capitalism. This in turn had been replaced by a qualitatively new form of capitalism, characterized by governmental direction. Although the authoritarian regimes of Europe had been the first to introduce extensive controls, the Western democracies, including the United States, were likely to follow. Unlike both earlier stages, state capitalism suspended the free market in favor of price and wage control. It also pursued the rationalization of the economy as a deliberate policy, assumed control over investments for political purposes, and restricted consumer-oriented commodity production.

What perhaps distinguished it most strongly from earlier capitalist phases, Pollock argued, was its subordination of individual or group profits to the needs of the general plan. Social relations consisted no longer of the interaction of employer and employee, or producer and consumer through the mediation of the market. Instead, individuals confronted one another as commander and commanded. Although not completely lost, "the profit motive," Pollock argued, had been "superseded by the power motive." [50] One reflection of this, he continued in a way reminiscent of James Burnham,[51] was the loss of control by stockholders over management. The traditional capitalists were becoming little more than *rentiers* living off diminished profits.

The general prognosis for collapse that emerged from Pollock's analysis was bleak. Forced full employment through public works was being used by state capitalism to forestall Marx's predicted pauperization of the proletariat. Problems of distribution were solved by administered prices and predefined needs. Overaccumulation, which

Grossmann had especially stressed, would be solved by the continued expansion of the military sector of the economy. In short, a new system of directed capitalism now existed, and was likely to endure for some time.

Pollock's pessimism was, however, cautiously tempered by certain qualifications. The contradictions of capitalism — class struggle, falling profit rate, and so forth — were not truly resolved, as they were to be in a socialist society. Moreover, the state, which had seized control of the economy, was itself directed by a mixed ruling group of bureaucrats, military leaders, party functionaries, and big businessmen (the same components as in Neumann's analysis). Conflict among them, although currently minimized, was by no means an impossibility. Other sources of possible instability in the system included the natural limits on resources and skills and the friction that might arise between popular demands for an increased living standard and the needs of a perpetual war economy. Still, the general trend that Pollock saw was in the direction of the proliferation and strengthening of state-capitalist economies. Pollock finished his article by posing several questions about the viability of a democratic as opposed to an authoritarian state capitalism, questions whose answers he said could be given only by history.

In his next essay in the *Studies in Philosophy and Social Science*, entitled "Is National Socialism a New Order?," Pollock focused on the Nazi variant of state capitalism. In opposition to Gurland and Neumann, he argued that almost all the essential characteristics of private property had been destroyed by the Nazis. No longer was investment for maximum profits an inalienable prerogative of big business. Although Nazi planning was still haphazard, the government had introduced a deliberate, and generally successful, policy of full employment, capital rather than consumer production, price control, and relative economic autarky. The individual's position in Nazi society, Pollock continued, was now dependent on his status in the social hierarchy rather than on his entrepreneurial skill or private property.[52] In general, technical rationality had replaced legal formalism as the guiding principle of the society.

In short, Pollock answered the question posed in his title affirmatively. That Nazism was a truly "new order," he argued, drawing on the Institut's studies of authority and family, was shown by its deliberate attempt to hasten the disintegration of the traditional family,[53] which had been a bulwark of bourgeois society. The old capitalist order, even in its monopolistic stage, had been an exchange economy; its successor was what the Nazi economic theorist Willi Neuling had called a "command economy."[54] The Nazis had thus achieved the "primacy of politics" over the economy.[55] Unless they lost the war, Pollock concluded with characteristic pessimism, their system was not likely to collapse from within.

In stressing the politicization of the economy, Pollock was very much in the mainstream of Critical Theory. If the Frankfurt School refused to develop a discrete political theory, as we have argued in Chapter 4, it equally rejected a purely economic approach to social theory. In his article "Philosophy and Critical Theory," which appeared alongside an essay by Marcuse with the same name, Horkheimer had made it clear that he considered domination by the economy a purely historical phenomenon. It would be a mistake, he argued, to judge the future society according to its economic form. Moreover, "this is true for the period of transition in which politics gains a new independence in relation to the economy."[56] The fetishization of the economy was left to more orthodox Marxists, such as Grossmann. Economic relations were always understood as representing relations among men in all their complexity, although admittedly they were the reified form in which capitalist men tended to relate to one another. The profit motive, Pollock stressed, had always been a variant of the power motive.[57] Today, however, the mediation the market had provided was disappearing. Domination was becoming more blatant in the "command economy" of the authoritarian state-capitalist systems. In so reasoning, it should be noted, Pollock was still in the Marxist tradition, in the sense that Marx had always understood economics as "political economy." Inherent in all of Marx's economic writings, even *Capital,* was the underlying assumption that economic relations were basically human interactions, which in capitalism were variations on what Hegel had called the "master-slave" relationship.[58]

Thus, in creating his model of state capitalism, Pollock was speaking for Horkheimer, and probably Lowenthal and Adorno as well. (Marcuse, who was personally much closer to Neumann, adopted a position nearer to Neumann's in *Reason and Revolution*, where he wrote: "The most powerful industrial groups tended to assume direct political control in order to organize monopolistic production, to destroy the socialist opposition, and to resume imperialist expansion.")[59] To Horkheimer, however, state capitalism was "the authoritarian state of the present . . . a new breathing space for domination."[60] In all his work during the late thirties and early forties, Horkheimer stressed the end of the liberal mediations, economic, political, and legal, that had previously forestalled the realization of the domination implicit in capitalism (which he was later to expand into the entire Western "enlightenment" tradition). As he wrote in his preface to a special volume of the *Studies in Philosophy and Social Science* devoted to the transition from liberalism to authoritarianism, "With the advent of fascism, dualisms typical of the liberalistic era, such as individual and society, private and public life, law and morals, economy and politics, have not been transcended but obscured." [61] The essence of modern society had been revealed as domination by "gangsters." [62] Racket protection, Horkheimer argued, using one of Benjamin's favorite categories, was the "ur-phenomenon" of modern domination. The notion of rackets, it should be added parenthetically, was also prominent in Kirchheimer's analysis of Nazism.[63]

In the service of domination, Horkheimer argued, the ruling groups employed a technological rationality, which, as he often noted, was a betrayal of reason's true essence. Connecting this indirectly with one of his philosophical *bêtes noires,* he wrote: "Fascists have learned something from pragmatism. Even their sentences no longer have meaning, only a purpose." [64] In "Authoritarian State" he developed a critique of technological rationality, which applied as well to its socialist practitioners, anticipating many of the arguments he was to develop with Adorno in *Dialectic of the Enlightenment.* The locus of his analysis of fascism had thus shifted away from the orthodox Marxist concept of the last stage of monopoly capitalism to a more general analysis of technology. This was related to the critique of Marx's own overemphasis on the process of production and his fetishization of labor, which we encountered in Chapter 2 when examining the foundations of Critical Theory. When in "The Jews and Europe" Horkheimer wrote that "he who does not wish to speak of capitalism, should also be silent about fascism," [65] it should be understood that he meant state capitalism, not its liberal or monopoly predecessors.

In fact, Horkheimer's distaste for the technological rationalization of advanced capitalism led him to express grave doubts about a socialist movement that saw itself as its inevitable successor. Engels and others like him, Horkheimer argued,[66] who equated the socialization of the means of production with the end of domination, were the true utopians. In fact, the naive expectation of freedom as the result of such a socialization anticipated the authoritarian state of the present. The perverse alliance of Lasalle and Bismarck was a symbolic expression of this fact. True freedom, Horkheimer argued, could be achieved only by breaking out of the technological straitjacket that state capitalism had forged and that socialism, at least as embodied in the Soviet Union, had perpetuated. Appropriately included in a volume of essays devoted to the memory of Walter Benjamin, who shared the belief that the realization of freedom could only come from a rupture in the continuum of history,[67] "Authoritarian State" expressed the most radical strains in Critical Theory. In one of his most important statements, Horkheimer wrote:

Dialectics is not identical with development. Two antagonistic moments, the take-over of state control and the liberation from it, are contained together in the concept of social revolution. [Social revolution] brings about what will happen without spontaneity: the socialization of the means of production, the planned direction of production, and the domination of nature in general. And it brings about what without active resistance and constantly renewed struggle for freedom will never appear: the end of exploitation. Such a goal [social revolution] is no longer the acceleration of progress, but rather the jumping out of progress [*der Sprung aus dem Fortschritt heraus*].[68]

In 1942, when this was written, Horkheimer did not yet despair that such "active resistance" might yet be forthcoming. Here he remained somewhat more optimistic than Pollock. "The eternal system of authoritarian states," he could write, "though terribly threatening, is no more real than the eternal harmony of the market economy. As the exchange of equivalence was still a shell of inequality, so the fascist plan is already open theft. . . . The possibility is not less than the despair." [69] The cement of fascism, he argued, was not merely the psychic compliance of the authoritarian personality, although this was very important. It was also based on the constant and unremitting application of terror and coercion.[70] The various components of the ruling class were themselves united only in their common fear of the masses, without which they would dissolve into a band of squabbling gangsters.* [71]

Moreover, Horkheimer argued, the material conditions for the realization of freedom had finally been achieved. Like Marcuse, who developed this idea in his article on technology in the *Studies in Philosophy and Social Science*, he maintained that the end of scarcity, as well as new forms of domination, might possibly result from the

* As Brecht's play *The Resistible Rise of Arturo Ui* shows, many refugees saw the Nazis as gangsters, at least metaphorically. Not all did, however. Hannah Arendt, for example, in *The Origins of Totalitarianism* (New York, 1958), wrote: "The totalitarian form of government has very little to do with lust for power or even the desire for a power-generating machine. . . . Totalitarian government, all appearances not withstanding, is not rule by a clique or a gang. . . . Isolation of atomized individuals provides not only the mass basis for totalitarian rule, but is carried through to the very top of the whole structure" (p. 407). Miss Arendt singled out *Behemoth* for criticism on this score in an accompanying footnote. Later, in the aphorism "Massengesellschaft" in *Dialectic of the Enlightenment*, Horkheimer and Adorno also abandoned the gangster comparison and argued that the fascist leaders were basically the same as the masses they led. In Chaplin's *The Great Dictator*, they pointed out, the dictator and the barber were the same man.

spread of the technological ethos. In fact, the break with the past for which he called was now dependent solely on the wills of men. In the most direct expression of what might be called a "Luxemburgist" or syndicalist strain in Critical Theory, he wrote: "The modalities of the new society are first to be found in the course of its transformation. The theoretical conception, the council system, which according to its pioneers is supposed to show the way to the new society, arises from *praxis*. It goes back to 1871, 1905, and other events. The revolution has a tradition on whose continuation theory is dependent." [72] Thus, instead of a Leninist transitional dictatorship, Horkheimer seemed to support the direct seizure of control by the people. The choice was clear, he wrote: "a retreat into barbarism or the beginning of history." [73]

Yet despite the hortatory note of "Authoritarian State," it was becoming increasingly apparent to Horkheimer that the chances for barbarism were greater. In the same article he expressed for perhaps the first time the argument that the life of the mind was becoming the last refuge of revolutionary *praxis*, an argument that was to appear with increasing frequency in the subsequent work of the Frankfurt School. "Thought itself," he wrote, "is already a sign of resistance, of the effort to allow oneself no longer to be deceived." [74] Once "barbarism," or at least its fascist embodiment, had been defeated, without leading to the "beginning of history" that had seemed its only alternative, Critical Theory began to question the possibility of *praxis* itself in the modern world.

To discuss this development in any detail now, however, would be to leave our central concern, the Institut's treatment of Nazism. As mentioned earlier, Neumann, Kirchheimer, and Gurland brought with them different viewpoints from those of Horkheimer, Pollock, and many of the older Institut figures on such questions as the nature of the Nazi economy. Of the three, Kirchheimer was perhaps closest in spirit to Critical Theory, despite the more positivistic bent of his mind and the legalistic basis of his education.[75] His first article in the *Studies in Philosophy and Social Science* after the publication of *Punishment and Social Structure* showed a continued interest in criminology.[76] In analyzing criminal law in Nazi Germany, Kirchheimer distinguished between two phases in the development of legal theory after 1933: the authoritarian and the racist. In the former, which lasted only briefly after the seizure of power, Roland Freisler's volitional notion of law prevailed, stressing the subjective motivations of defendants rather than their objective acts. It was soon superseded by the antinormative, antigeneralist "concrete" legal theory of the so-called Kiel School of "phenomenological" law.[77] Here the judge's intuition of the "essential" nature of the defendant replaced the judgment of his actual actions. Crimes committed by omission were extended; the "social feelings of the people" as revealed through the pronouncements of their leaders and the rulings of the judicial bureaucracy influenced judicial decisions, even to the point of retroactive legislation. Departmentalization of jurisdictions — the SS, the labor service, the party, for example, all had separate legal hierarchies — replaced the unified system of criminal law that had prevailed before 1933. In short, the judiciary had been transformed into a dependent administrative bureaucracy increasingly responsive to the ideological demands of the state.

One of the major contentions of the phenomenological school, and of Nazi political theory in general, was that it had brought together the spheres of law and morality, which had been separated in liberal jurisprudence. In a subsequent essay Kirchheimer sought to express the ideological nature of this claim by revealing the underlying character of Nazi law. Of the old pillars of liberal law, private property and liberty of contract, Kirchheimer argued that the former, although still in existence, was "heavily mortgaged to the political machine,[78] while the latter had been rendered practically meaningless. In one sense then, Nazi legal doctrine had bridged the old liberal gulf between the private and public realms, but only at the cost of the liquidation of the former. The Nazi claims of a "concrete" policy had been realized in certain areas, such as anti-Semitic legislation and pro-populationist measures (for example, reducing sanctions against illegitimate births and supporting larger families). But in most other areas, such as agriculture, where the ideology of "blood and soil" had been sacrificed to the demands of modernization, this was not the case. In fact, the basic thrust of Nazi law was in the direction of that technological rationality that Horkheimer had emphasized. "Rationality here," Kirchheimer wrote, "does not mean that there are universally applicable rules the consequences of which could be calculated by those whom they affect. Rationality here means only that the whole apparatus of law and law-enforcing is made exclusively serviceable to those who rule." [79] Still, Kirchheimer did not go as far as Pollock in describing the new order as postprivate capitalism: in Kirchheimer's words,

> The concentration of economic power which characterizes the social and political development of the Nazi regime crystallizes in the tendency toward preserving the institution of private property both in industrial and agricultural production, whilst abolishing the correlative to private property, the

freedom of contract. In the contract's place the administrative sanction now has become the *alter ego* of property itself.[80]

Yet Kirchheimer, more than Neumann or Gurland, felt that the power of the state, or at least the ruling clique around Hitler, was basically unchallenged. In a broader discussion in the *Studies in Philosophy and Social Science* of the political changes that had occurred under the Nazis he offered his reasons.[81] He distinguished three phases of political compromise in recent Western European history. In the liberal era, a "complex of working agreements among parliamentary representatives and between them and the government" prevailed.[82] The influence of money in politics was particularly strong. Around 1910, however, the elements in the compromise began to shift as the era of mass democracy came of age. Voluntary organizations of capital and labor were the major participants in the struggle for power, with the central banks acting as mediators between the economic and the political spheres. Monopolies replaced individuals in both politics and economics. In the third period, which began with the rise of fascism, the influence of economic factors had declined drastically. The fascist governments were too strong to be toppled by an investors' strike or other manifestations of private economic pressure. Although monopolies obviously still existed in such areas as labor (government-controlled), industry (still private), and the so-called Food Estate (also private), the government had seized the whip hand. In fact, the Nazi party was now involved in creating a competitive economic apparatus of its own, which helped increase its bureaucratization. But this meant a betrayal of earlier Nazi promises: "The party proved no support for the independent middle classes in their struggle for survival, but, instead, actually hastened their final decline more than any other single factor in modern German history." [83]

The new structure of political compromise that resulted from all this was now dependent on the Führer and his clique. With money no longer a real expression of social power, "leadership" had become the arbiter of intergroup conflicts. These were relatively frictionless only because of the expansive nature of fascist imperialism, which permitted a division of the spoils among all the competing elements of the ruling coalition. "It is this interdependence between the unquestionable authority of the ruling group and the program of expansion which offers the characteristic phenomenon of the compromise structure of the fascist order, directs its further course, and decides its ultimate fate." [84]

The imperialist dynamic of Nazism also played a key role in the analyses of Gurland and Neumann. In his first article for the *Studies in Philosophy and Social Science*,[85] Gurland focused on the importance of economic expansion as a means to prevent conflict within the Nazi system. Although admitting that the government sector had grown significantly, he opposed Pollock's argument about the drastic reduction of big business's power. The government, he asserted, represented the antimonopolistic resentment of the petite bourgeoisie, but without really challenging the prerogatives of the entrenched business interests. In fact, the discontented *Mittelstand* (white collar workers, small business owners, and petty bureaucrats) had always wanted less the destruction of big business than a sense of participation in its prosperity. With imperialist expansion, this yearning had been fulfilled to the benefit of both the government and big business. In opposition to Pollock, Gurland stated that "expansion guarantees the realization of the profit motive and the profit motive stimulates expansion." [86]

Although Gurland agreed that technological rationalization had been advanced under the Nazis, he did not feel that this spelled the end of private capitalism. In fact, the bureaucratization and centralization of the economy had started within and among private corporations well before the Nazis took power. These private conglomerates, Gurland argued, were still much more powerful than such Nazi competitors as the Hermann Goering Steel Works. The technological innovations that Pollock had stressed were more the work of these concerns, especially in the chemical industry, than of the government. Moreover, although managerial growth had certainly taken place, this too did not mean the transformation of capitalism, for "those who control the means of production are the actual capitalists whatever they may be called." [87] The managers still derived their income from profits (although not from dividends, as had the traditional stockholders). In short, the system as Gurland understood it was still monopoly capitalist, although based on the condominium of political bureaucracy and economic managers united in their pursuit of imperialist expansion.

Gurland's unwillingness to discount the perseverance of monopoly capitalism was also shared by Neumann, to whose *Behemoth* we can now finally turn. Ultimately to become a classic, although suffering a relative eclipse during the Cold War, *Behemoth* was a work of enormous and painstaking scholarship, all the more remarkable for Neumann's distance from his sources. In several areas, such as the history of the German labor movement, Neumann was able to draw on his own personal experience before 1933. All of this was recognized by Horkheimer and the other members of the Institut's inner circle, but Neumann's conclusions and the methodology that he had used to derive them were sufficiently foreign to Critical Theory to prevent the inner circle from considering *Behemoth* a real expression of the Institut's views.[88]

There were, to be sure, some similarities between his approach and theirs. Neumann, for example, minimized the independent importance of anti-Semitism and racism in general,[89] as had Horkheimer in all his writings from *Dämmerung* until the war. He went so far as to call the German people "the least anti-Semitic of all," [90] a belief curiously shared by the other Institut members.* Neumann also agreed that fascism lacked a true political theory because of its irrationalism, whereas a "political theory cannot be nonrational." [92] And finally, he felt that the system would not inevitably collapse from within without conscious political *praxis:* "The flaws and breaks in the system and even the military defeat of Germany will not lead to an automatic collapse of the regime. It can only be overthrown by conscious political action of the oppressed masses, which will utilize the breaks in the system." [93]

Yet the differences were on the whole more significant. Neumann's general disdain for psychology has already been mentioned on several occasions. Like the left-wing historian Eckart Kehr, whose influence on Neumann was considerable,[94] he felt that psychoanalysis was little more than a bourgeois ideology. *Behemoth* did contain a short section on the psychology of charisma, but it ignored the Institut's earlier work on the authoritarian personality entirely. There was scarcely anything in *Behemoth*'s more than six hundred pages (including an appendix added in 1944) to suggest that Neumann accepted Fromm's notion of the sado-masochistic character type. Furthermore, in his analysis of the failure of the working class during Weimar,[95] Neumann ignored Fromm's study of the ambivalent mentality of the German proletariat.

More central still was his disagreement with Pollock's notion of state capitalism. To Neumann, "The very term 'state capitalism' is a

* When I mentioned Neumann's remark to Lowenthal, he said that many of the Institut's members thought the Germans less anti-Semitic than the Americans they had come to know after emigrating to this country. The discrimination to which they referred was social, which was practically unknown in Weimar, rather than political. All the Institut members with whom I spoke stressed how completely assimilated they had felt in Germany before being forced to leave. This attitude towards the amount of anti-Semitism in Germany was echoed in the 1939 prospectus the Institut prepared on the general problem, in the *Studies.* Today the following statement, which was included in the prospectus, sounds more than a bit naive: "While frank disgust for the anti-Semitism of the government is revealed among the German masses, the promises of anti-Semitism are eagerly swallowed where fascist governments have never been attempted." [91]

contradictio in adiecto." Quoting Hilferding, he continued, "Once the state has become the sole owner of the means of production it makes it impossible for a capitalist economy to function, it destroys that mechanism which keeps the very processes of economic circulation in active existence." [96] That the "primacy of politics" and the managerial revolution had not yet been achieved Neumann set out to prove by examining the German economy empirically. In doing so, he also made it clear that he did not share Pollock's general gloom about the invulnerability of the system: "The present writer does not accept this profoundly pessimistic view. He believes that the antagonisms of capitalism are operating in Germany on a higher and, therefore, a more dangerous level, even if these antagonisms are covered by a bureaucratic apparatus and by the ideology of the people's community." [97]

The evidence he first cited was the testimony of the Nazi leaders themselves, none of which seemed to indicate a deliberate policy of state control.[98] Neumann then presented considerable data concerning the increased cartelization and rationalization of big business that had taken place during Weimar. This process, he contended, had created an unstable situation in which the economy was becoming more rigid, more susceptible to cyclical changes, and vulnerable to pressures from the discontented masses. As a result, the state had to intervene to break the increasingly explosive deadlock. Its choice was clear: "Shall the state crush monopolistic possessions, shall it restrict them for the sake of the masses, or shall interference be used to strengthen the monopolistic position, to aid in the complete incorporation of all business activities into the network of industrial organizations?" [99] To Neumann, the answer was obvious: the Nazis had taken the latter course, despite their propaganda to the contrary. Still, Neumann's analysis was more complicated than the orthodox Marxist position, classically expressed by George Dimitrov at the seventh World Congress of the Comintern, that fascism was "the open, terrorist dictatorship of the most reactionary, most chauvinistic, and most imperialist elements of finance capital." [100] To Neumann, "The German economy of today has two broad and striking characteristics. It is a monopolistic economy — *and* a command economy. It is a private capitalistic economy, regimented by the totalitarian state. We suggest as a name best to describe it, 'Totalitarian Monopoly Capitalism.' " [101]

This was demonstrated, he continued, in such ways as compulsory cartelization legislation. The rulers and benefactors of the new monopolies, he argued, were not the new managers, but in most cases the old private entrepreneurial individuals or families. The Nazis, he pointed out, had refrained from nationalizing most industries; "on the contrary, there is a definite trend away from nationalization." [102] Even the construction of the party's alternative economic structure did not spell the end of capitalism. "On the contrary, it appears as an affirmation of the living force of capitalistic society. For it proves that even in a one-party state, which boasts of the supremacy of politics over economics, political power without economic power, without a solid place in industrial production, is precarious." [103] In short, although a command economy was in the process of being created, it was by no means replacing the old monopolistic capitalism. In fact, Neumann argued, agreeing with Gurland, the two could survive side by side as long as imperialist expansion permitted the satisfaction of the claims of the various groups in the ruling elite.

That Neumann distinguished among groups within this elite — big business, the party, the military, and the bureaucracy — showed that he was not positing a simplistic view of fascism as solely the creature of the monopolies. "This does not mean," he wrote, "that National Socialism is merely a subservient tool of German industry, but it does mean that with regard to imperialistic expansion, industry and party have identical aims." [104] Still, unlike the analyses of Pollock and Horkheimer, Neumann's was rooted in more traditional Marxist categories. Pollock had written of the power motive. In reply, Neumann remarked: "We believe that we have shown that it is the profit motive that holds the machinery together. But in a monopolistic system profits cannot be made and retained without totalitarian political power, and that is the distinctive feature of National Socialism." [105] The new order that Pollock had described was really not so new after all.

Nor were such theorists as the New School's Emil Lederer, an old Institut foe, correct in calling Nazi Germany an amorphous mass society without class differentiation. In fact, the Nazis' atomization of the masses had stopped short of the self-atomization of the elite. If anything, Neumann argued, "the essence of National Socialist social policy consists in the acceptance and strengthening of the prevailing class character of German society." [106] Where Neumann did agree a change had occurred was in the class solidarity of the lower and lower middle classes. The Naxis had introduced a new hierarchy based more on status than on traditional class, thus reversing Sir Henry Maine's classic formula about the transition from status to class.[107] This had been accomplished by a deliberate attempt to atomize the masses, a process whose ramifications Neumann explored in analyses of propaganda, terror, labor and wage policy, and Nazi law (based largely on his and Kirchheimer's earlier articles in the *Zeitschrift* and the *Studies*).

Neumann's more orthodox class analysis prevented him from seeing domination in technological terms, as the group around Horkheimer was beginning to do. Like Gurland, he felt that the rationalization and centralization of the economy were not incompatible with private capitalism. In fact, the technological revolution had "originated within the very mechanism of capitalistic production, refuting the belief of those who hold that capitalism has lost its dynamic." [108] Yet Neumann felt it possible that the tension between the logic of technological rationalization and the demands of profit-maximization might increase in the long run. "We believe," he wrote, "that the antagonism between the engineer, by whom we understand all technicians and foremen, and totalitarian monopoly capitalism is one of the decisive flaws in the regime." [109]

Still, the major burden of Neumann's argument was that, contrary to Pollock, Nazism was a continuation of monopoly capitalism, albeit by other means. *Behemoth*, however, had a secondary thesis as well, which corresponded somewhat more closely to some of the notions of the Institut's inner circle. This argument was reflected in the book's title, which referred to Hobbes's study of the chaos of the English civil war of the seventeenth century. To Neumann, "National Socialism is — or [is] tending to become — a non-state, a chaos, a rule of lawlessness and anarchy." [110] Not only was "state capitalism" a misnomer, but the existence of a state in any traditional sense was itself questionable. Instead, domination was becoming more nakedly unmediated without the buffer, however imperfect, provided by the liberal state.

In other words, Neumann, like Horkheimer and the others, felt that the semi-humane mediations of the past were rapidly being eroded in the authoritarian states. Where they disagreed was in their descriptions of the nature of the unmediated domination. To Neumann, it was still along the lines of capitalist over exploited worker, without the state acting to lessen the viciousness of the class conflict. He could therefore still write, "there exists objectively a profound antagonism between the two classes. Whether or not it will explode we do not know." [111] To Horkheimer, on the other hand, the domination was becoming increasingly psychosocial, without the buffering of the capitalist market. Following Pollock, he asserted that the state was the main perpetrator of the domination, which also included the deliberate application of terror and coercion. In time, however, the role of the state would cease to be very great in his analysis, as domination became a kind of pervasive condition in the society as a whole. Here Horkheimer's arguments concerning the increasing role of the technological ethos played a crucial part. As we shall see when examining the later work of the Frankfurt School, especially as related to its analysis of American society, domination in what Marcuse was to popularize as "one-dimensional" society seemed to exist without the conscious direction of dominators, whether economic or political. As a result, it appeared more sinister and invulnerable, and the chances for effective action to negate it even more remote.

In summary, then, it can be said that the Institut employed two general approaches in its analysis of Nazism. One, associated with Neumann, Gurland, and Kirchheimer, focused on changes in legal, political, and economic institutions, with only a passing glance at social psychology or mass culture. Its basic assumptions were those of a more orthodox Marxism, stressing the centrality of monopoly capitalism, although with considerable refinement. The other major approach, followed by the group around Horkheimer, saw Nazism as the most extreme example of a general trend towards irrational domination in the West. Although agreeing that this had occurred as an outgrowth of advanced capitalism, it no longer considered the economic substructure the crucial locus of the social totality. Instead, it paid increased attention to technological rationalization as an institutional force and instrumental rationality as a cultural imperative. In so doing, it explored with far greater interest than Neumann or the others of his persuasion the psychosocial mechanisms of obedience and sources of violence. By pointing to the various ways in which advanced capitalism had avoided the fulfillment of Marx's predictions of its collapse, it revealed a more profound skepticism about the possibilities for change, which was to increase in the years to come.

Because the Horkheimer-Pollock approach had gone beyond the orthodox Marxist concentration on the economy, it was able more easily to be applied to American social phenomena after the war. The economy of the United States, after all, might be characterized as monopoly capitalist, but its society had proved resistant to fascism just the same. The postwar transformation of Neumann and those in his camp into uneasy liberals can perhaps be partly attributed to their acknowledgment of this reality. The group around Horkheimer, on the other hand, shared a pessimism about the future of the proletarian revolution, but did not become liberals in the same sense as Neumann, Kirchheimer, and Gurland. In Marcuse's case, as we shall see, radicalism was intensified. In Horkheimer's and

Adorno's, the caution was far greater, but the basic analysis never became truly liberal or pluralist in its assumptions. To speak of postwar developments now, however, is to anticipate our narrative. This cannot be done until the Institut's refocusing of its attention on America is discussed in our next chapters.

Before turning to the Institut's analysis of American society, its history during the war must be brought up to date. With the expansion of fascism's power in Europe and America's entry into the war there came a general reorganization of the Institut's institutional structure and a reevaluation of its goals. The French branch, the sole remaining Institut outpost in Europe at the outbreak of the war, was closed with the occupation of Paris in 1940. During the thirties, the Paris office had not only been a liaison with the Institut's publishers and a source of data for the *Studien über Autorität und Familie*, but also a link with the French academic and cultural community. Walter Benjamin was not the only contributor of articles to the *Zeitschrift* living in Paris. Other pieces were written by Celestin Bouglé, Raymond Aron, Alexandre Koyré, Jeanne Duprat, Paul Honigsheim, Maxime Leroy, Bernard Groethuysen, and A. Demangeon. In 1938 Bouglé was one of two distinguished European scholars to deliver a series of public lectures at the Institut's New York branch (Morris Ginsberg was the other).

Now the link was broken. In addition, the Librairie Félix Alcan could no longer continue to print the *Zeitschrift.* Instead, the Institut decided to publish in America the third section of the 1939 volume, which appeared in the summer of 1940. This necessitated a reversal of the Institut's long-standing unwillingness to write in English. As Horkheimer explained in his foreword to the rechristened *Studies in Philosophy and Social Science*:

> Philosophy, art, and science have lost their home in most of Europe. England is now fighting desperately against the domination of the totalitarian states. America, especially the United States, is the only continent in which the continuation of scientific life is possible. Within the framework of this country's democratic institutions, culture still enjoys the freedom without which, we believe, it is unable to exist. In publishing our journal in its new form we wish to give this belief its concrete expression.[112]

Publishing in America, however, was more expensive than it had been in Europe, and the Institut's funds were not what they once were. In the late thirties its capital endowment had suffered a setback of some seriousness. Unsuccessful investments in a bear market, a disastrous real estate transaction in upstate New York, and the distribution of considerable sums of money to other refugees on the Institut's enlarged staff resulted in a limitation of its financial options. Thus, by 1941, when the Institut transferred the last of its capital from Switzerland and Holland to America, where it was administered by the Kurt Gerlach Memorial Foundation, the Hermann Weil Memorial Foundation, and the Social Studies Association,[113] the amount it brought was not sufficient to permit the continuation of all the Institut's programs. One of the first casualties was the *Studies in Philosophy and Social Science,* which was initially changed into a yearbook and then, in March, 1942, with the third issue of volume nine (officially 1941), discontinued for the duration of the war. It was never to reappear in its original form, thus ending a journal of remarkable distinction and accomplishment. With hindsight, it might well be argued that the brief decade of its existence was the Institut's true *Blütezeit,* its period of greatest creativity.

The Institut's financial problems also necessitated a reduction of its staff, which had been swelled by the influx of new refugees from Europe. Some of the Institut's associates — Karl Landauer, Andries Sternheim, and, most prominently, Walter Benjamin — had resisted its pleas to emigrate until it was too late. In many other cases, however, escape proved successful. By the war, new "research associates," who were often very peripherally associated with the Institut, included Karl Wilhelm Kapp (economics), I. Graebner (anti-Semitism), Fritz Karsen (education),[114] Olga Lang (Sinology), Wilhelm Mackauer (history), Alois Schardt (art), Joseph Soudek (economics), Edgar Zilsel (sociology), Paul Lazarsfeld (sociology), Maximilian Beck (philosophy), Kurt Pinthus (literature), and Hans Fried (sociology). Many of them, in addition to other recipients of Institut grants such as Joseph Maier, Alice Maier's husband, could no longer be retained on the Institut's reduced budget.

The same problem existed among the senior members of the staff. By 1939, as we have seen, Fromm had left to pursue his private practice, Gumperz was involved with his activities as a stockbroker, and Wittfogel had found new sources of income. Adorno was employed part-time by Lazarsfeld's Radio Research Project at Princeton and later at Columbia, which was a source of research and secretarial assistance for Lowenthal as well. Government consultation was also a means of supplementing income while doing useful work. Neumann was the first to go to Washington to aid in the war effort. In 1942 he joined the Board of Economic Warfare as its chief consultant and then, soon after, the Office of Strategic Services, as the deputy chief of the Research and Analysis Branch's Central European section. Neumann's departure from the Institut, which proved permanent, was hastened by personal as well as theoretical differences with older Institut figures,[115] as was the case with others such as Fromm and Wittfogel. Horkheimer was displeased with the summary way in which Pollock's arguments were treated in *Behemoth.* Furthermore, there was an apparent rivalry between them over the selection of a professor at Columbia from among the Institut's members. The older figures from the Frankfurt period were distressed by the prospect that Neumann, with his divergent opinions, would be representing the Institut on the regular Columbia faculty. In fact, after the war Neumann was offered such a position, which he accepted, but by that time the Institut had decided to allow its connection with Columbia to lapse.

Other Institut members spent a considerable part of their time in Washington during the war. Kirchheimer also joined the OSS, as did Marcuse after completing *Reason and Revolution*, his last extensive publication for more than a decade. Here they were members of a remarkable community of intellectuals, which included such distinguished scholars as Hajo Holborn, Norman O. Brown, Carl Schorske, H. Stuart Hughes, Leonard Krieger, Crane Brinton, and Franklin Ford. Marcuse had briefly served with the Office of War Information before joining the OSS. The OWI was also the focus of Lowenthal's governmental work after 1943. Although he continued to spend some time in the Institut's New York office, he served for a time as an OWI section chief. Pollock was an occasional consultant to the Department of Justice's antitrust division and to the Board of Economic Warfare. Gurland, although remaining for the most part in New York, found time to collaborate with Kirchheimer and Neumann on a study, *The Fate of Small Business in Nazi Germany*,[116] for a special Senate subcommittee led by Claude Pepper.

Despite the reduction of the Institut's budget and the partial dispersion of its staff, the effort to continue its scientific work did not flag. But for the first time, supplementary grants were necessary to make its projects feasible. These were not always forthcoming. In February, 1941, a prospectus for an analysis of the "Cultural Aspects of National Socialism,"[117] under the joint direction of Horkheimer and Eugene N. Anderson of American University in Washington, was announced. The projected responsibilities for individual sections were as follows: Pollock was to study bureaucracy; Lowenthal, literature and mass culture; Horkheimer, anti-Christianity; Neumann, the ideological permeation of labor and the new middle classes; Marcuse, the war and the postwar generation; and Adorno, art, and music. Grossmann was described as "an adviser for economic history, statistics, and economics for all sections where such problems may enter."[118] But the project could not be started for lack of a foundation cosponsor. Nor was money available for the continuation of the *Studies in Philosophy and Social Science* as a yearbook. In fact, only with the support of the American Jewish Committee and the Jewish Labor Committee, acquired in October of 1943, could the Institut devote its collective energies to a large and costly project. The series, *Studies in Prejudice*, that resulted will be the subject of Chapter 7.

In one instance, the Institut's financial recovery allowed it to reverse the trend towards the reduction of its staff. Paul Massing, who had joined as a research associate in 1941, became one of the Institut's more important contributors in the next few years. He was not, however, a total newcomer to Institut affairs, having started his dissertation under Grünberg in 1927.[119] Yet in one way Massing was a unique addition. Unlike most other important figures in the Institut's history, he was of gentile origin, a factor that he was later to feel prevented his full acceptance by the Institut's inner circle. In the twenties Massing had been a close friend of Karl Wittfogel for both personal and political reasons. Like Wittfogel, he was one of the several Communist Party members associated with the Institut before the emigration, having joined the Party in 1927. And like his older friend — Massing was born in a small village near Koblenz in 1902, six years after Wittfogel — he was put into a concentration camp for his politics when Hitler took power. Both men were liberated at approximately the same time and both left Germany in 1934. Each wrote of his experiences in the concentration camp in pseudonymously published novels: Wittfogel's, written under the name Klaus Hinrichs, was called *Staatliches Konzentrationslager VII*; Massing's was entitled *Schutzhäftling 880* and was published under the name Karl Billinger, which he had whimsically chosen as a combination of John Dillinger, the master criminal, and Richard Billinger, a German poet jailed by the Nazis.[120] Accompanied by a pro-Soviet introduction by Lincoln Steffens, Massing's novel was translated as *Fatherland* in 1935. Its publication in English cost him dearly by delaying his naturalization until the late 1940's.

Another parallel between the two men was their growing disenchantment with communism. Wittfogel had left the Party as a dues-paying member by the time he departed the Continent for England in 1934, eight months before his emigration to America. His final break with his Communist past, however, did not come until the summer of 1939, after his experiences in China in the middle thirties.[121] Massing's apostasy was considerably more dramatic. Although he had made a brief trip to the United States after his liberation from the camp, he and his wife, Hede, returned to Europe to work for the Party. In 1937 he was summoned to Moscow to discuss his affairs with his superiors. By this time the purge trials were at their height, and like many others, Massing was becoming disenchanted with Stalinist practice. Although discouraged by his wife, he decided to go to the Soviet Union, as he remembers it, out of a sense of honor to announce his break with communism. What began as a two-week visit ended as an eight-month nightmare with no certainty of survival.[122] Finally, in 1938, Massing was permitted to leave both Moscow and the Party, but his involvement with communism was not yet entirely over. After returning, he began a comparison of Hitler's foreign policy with the intentions announced in *Mein Kampf*, in the hope of putting together a marketable book. *Hitler Is No Fool*, as it was finally called, was published in 1940 by Modern Age, at that time secretly controlled by Communist editors. "Karl Billinger's" contention that the war in the west was merely a preliminary for a drive eastward went against the new party line after the Nazi-Soviet Pact. Consequently, the book was suppressed by its own publishers and copies already printed were recovered if at all possible.

The loss of Massing's book was paralleled by the loss of his friendship with Wittfogel, although for precisely the opposite reasons. As noted earlier, Wittfogel began to shift rightward after his return from China. His third wife, Esther Goldfrank, was herself conservative and seems to have influenced the intensity of Wittfogel's change. In addition to leaving the Party, he began to distrust anyone who had ever been connected with it in any way. Massing fell into this category, and his relations with Wittfogel progressively deteriorated. The final break came in 1948, so Massing recalls, over his refusal to support unreservedly the allegations of Ruth Fischer in her *Stalinist Germany*. In Wittfogel's account, their falling out had more personal reasons.[123] What is clear is that Massing, no longer a member of the Party but unwilling to share Wittfogel's rabid anticommunism, had reached a political position not dissimilar to that of the Institut's leadership. By 1941, when he joined its ranks, his political career was clearly over. In fact, his contribution in the forties showed little effect of the Marxism he had so actively espoused at an earlier date. In this he mirrored the Institut's gradual withdrawal from an aggressively Marxist stance, some of whose effects we have seen in this chapter. In fact, a number of factors during the war and the immediate postwar years contributed to this change in the Frankfurt School's attitude towards Marxism. These will become readily apparent in our subsequent discussions of its work in the forties.

Perhaps the most important change in the Institut's history during the war resulted from Horkheimer's health. Because of a mild heart condition, his doctors advised him to leave New York for a more temperate climate. As a result, Horkheimer, accompanied by Adorno, who came largely out of personal loyalty,[124] moved to Pacific Palisades near Santa Monica, California, in early 1941. Without Horkheimer's personal stimulus, the Institut's New York office lost some of its vitality. Lowenthal and Pollock remained as its directors, and Marcuse, Kirchheimer, Gurland, Massing, and Felix Weil continued to do work there. Still, the volume of research, for all the reasons mentioned above, generally declined during the war. In June, 1944, the building on 117th Street was turned over to the U.S. Navy for training courses, and the Institut was relocated in smaller quarters in Low Memorial Library and in another building on Morningside Heights. Clearly, the Institut's Columbia period was drawing to a close when it distributed an account of its achievements in 1944 entitled "Ten Years on Morningside Heights." [125]

In moving westward to California, Horkheimer and Adorno gave symbolic confirmation of the Institut's increased distance from its European origins. In February, 1940, while still in New York, Horkheimer, Pollock, Marcuse, and Lowenthal had taken out naturalization papers. By the end of the war almost all the Institut members had become American citizens. The end of the *Zeitschrift* meant the beginning of a new English-speaking audience for the Institut. Starting with *Punishment and Social Structure* in 1939, all the Institut's published work appeared in its adopted language. In the forties the *Studies in Prejudice* picked up where the *Studien über Autorität und Familie* had left off, but now the focus was on American forms of authoritarianism.

With the shift in subject matter came a subtle change in the center of the Institut's work. Authoritarianism in America appeared in different guises from its European counterparts. Instead of terror or coercion, more gentle forms of enforced conformism had been developed. Perhaps the most effective of these were to be found in the cultural field. American mass culture thus became one of the central concerns of the Frankfurt School in the forties. To understand its work, we must now return to our long delayed discussion of the Institut's analyses of cultural phenomena. We have already treated Lowenthal's contribution to those analyses. In the next chapter we shall turn to the extensive and penetrating work of Adorno and Benjamin in the context of the Institut's treatment of what Horkheimer called "affirmative culture." [126]

VI

Aesthetic Theory and the Critique of Mass Culture

There is no document of civilization which is not at the same time a document of barbarism.

— WALTER BENJAMIN

It is not that chewing gum undermines metaphysics but that it *is* metaphysics — this is what must be made clear.

— MAX HORKHEIMER

Mass culture is psychoanalysis in reverse.

— LEO LOWENTHAL

Marxist aesthetic criticism, as George Steiner has argued,[1] has traditionally proceeded along two separate lines. The first, derived primarily from the writings of Lenin and codified by Zhdanov at the first Soviet Writers' Congress in 1934, finds merit only in those works displaying unabashed political partisanship. Lenin's demand for *Tendenzliteratur* (partisan literature), conceived in combat with aesthetic formalism around the turn of the century, ultimately culminated in the sterile orthodoxy of Stalinist socialist realism. The second strain, which Steiner among many others considers more fruitful, follows the lead of Engels, who valued art less by the political intentions of its creator than by its inherent social significance. The objective social content of a work, Engels maintained, might well be contrary to the avowed desires of the artist and might express more than his class origins. This second approach has been pursued by the non-Soviet bloc critics Michel Crouzet once called para-Marxists. Among the most prominent of these were, at varying times in their careers, Jean-Paul Sartre and Lucien Goldmann in France, Edmund Wilson and Sidney Finkelstein in America, and members of the Frankfurt School in Germany.

To Steiner, as to other commentators, Georg Lukács presents a complex case, with characteristics placing him in both camps. Lukács, certainly the most gifted critic who remained within the Soviet orbit, sought to bridge the gap between the Leninist and the "Engelian" positions. In developing Engels's now famous dichotomy between realism and naturalism — the former, exemplified in the works of Shakespeare, Goethe, and Balzac, reconciling objective world and subjective imagination organically; the latter, best illustrated in Zola's writings, mechanically reflecting the artist's unassimilated phenomenal environment — Lukács pursued an important distinction neglected by orthodox Zhdanovists. Zola, despite his sympathy for the oppressed, so Lukács maintained, is artistically inferior to the royalist Balzac, whose artistic imagination allowed him to portray the historical totality with greater fidelity. Similar considerations led to Lukács's unexpected praise in *The Historical Novel* for the works of Sir Walter Scott.[2]

And yet, Lukács, the man who repudiated his own *History and Class Consciousness* because of criticisms by the Party hierarchy, never truly freed himself from the Leninist straitjacket. This was apparent in a number of ways. One of the better known is his practically unrelieved hostility to artistic modernism of all kinds.[3] To such writers as Proust, Joyce, and Kafka, Lukács turned a deaf ear, because of their alleged formalism and subjectivity. Much of twentieth-century art Lukács associated with the alleged irrationalism in the writings of Dostoyevsky, Nietzsche, and Kierkegaard.[4] Along with this attitude went a rather conservative preference for the masterpieces of bourgeois culture and a less than critical deference for the products of socialist realism. This latter aspect of his work was perhaps due to an overly optimistic appreciation of the reconciliation of contradictions already achieved in socialist countries.[5] Still another manifestation of his adherence to Leninist standards appeared in his relative indifference to the effects on art of technological innovation; class conflict remained the sole motor of history underlying his criticism. For all the insights contained in the vast corpus of his critical works, Lukács's compromise with political authority and his almost temperamental insensitivity to modernist art prevented his achieving the kind of critical flexibility that Western para-Marxists, such as those connected with Frankfurt School, were able to attain.

Having said this, however, it must be acknowledged that much of what the para-Marxists wrote would not have been the same without certain of Lukács's writings. *History and Class Consciousness*, whatever its author may have thought of it later, was a seminal work for them, as Benjamin, for one, was to admit.[6] As Adorno also acknowledged in a much later piece on Lukács whose tone was generally critical, it was the first study to focus on the crucial problem of reification, the key to a Marxist or neo-Marxist analysis of culture.[7]

Moreover, the Frankfurt School, like other para-Marxists, shared the "Engelian" distinction between realism and naturalism that Lukács did so much to develop, although they tended to agree more with his definition of the latter than of the former.[8] Whatever the disagreements that separated them in subsequent years — and they were serious — the Institut and Lukács spoke to similar questions from within a common tradition.

The objective of this chapter is the presentation of those elements that made the Frankfurt School's aesthetic criticism different from both its traditional bourgeois and its orthodox Marxist competitors. Special attention will be paid to the contributions of Adorno and Benjamin, with side glances at Horkheimer, Marcuse, and Lowenthal, whose discussions of mass culture will be considered as well. The chapter will end with a treatment of the way in which the Institut integrated its critique of art with its more general analysis of modern society.

From the very beginning, of course, the post-Grünberg generation of Institut members had been interested in aesthetic and cultural phenomena. Hans Cornelius, the major academic influence on a number of Institut figures, had been an artist *manqué* and had written extensively in the philosophy of art.[9] Horkheimer's excursions into fiction, which continued into the forties,[10] have already been mentioned, as have Adorno's more substantial musical pursuits. Adorno's study of Kierkegaard, in which aesthetics played a central role, has also been discussed, as have Wittfogel's plays and aesthetic criticism. And finally, we have paid attention to Lowenthal's numerous essays in the *Zeitschrift* on literary matters.

What remains to be done is a more complete presentation of the other components of the Institut's extensive analysis of cultural subjects, particularly the work of Adorno and Benjamin. The difficulties in such a task are formidable. The antisystematic impulse of Critical Theory was extended to the cultural criticism it fostered. The result makes summary a difficult, if not impossible, project. In addition, the form in which the criticism appeared was an essential part of its total effect. The unique texture of an Adorno or a Benjamin essay and the studied intricacy of their prose styles defy translation,[11] not to mention reduction to their fundamentals. Their mode of reasoning was rarely inductive or deductive, a reflection of their insistence that every sentence must be mediated through the totality of the essay in order to be understood fully. Reading a piece by Adorno or Benjamin brings to mind a comment the filmmaker Jean-Luc Godard is once said to have made when asked if his films had a beginning, a middle, and an end. "Yes," he replied, "but not necessarily in that order." The principle that Adorno attributed to the symbolists also informed their work: "Defiance of society includes defiance of its language." [12] The difficulties that resulted for the average reader were thus less the product of caprice or inarticulateness than a direct challenge to the reader to respond with commensurate seriousness. Adorno himself indicated his purpose indirectly when he wrote of Schönberg's music: "It requires the listener spontaneously to compose its inner movement and demands of him not mere contemplation but *praxis*." [13] Other artists, such as Kafka,[14] whose work Adorno particularly praised, seem to be guided by the same consideration.

Benjamin's concern for language and style was no less great. In fact, as Adorno once suggested,[15] Benjamin saw himself as the vehicle for the expression of objective cultural tendencies, a belief that made the mode of expression particularly crucial. One manifestation of this was his hope to exclude all subjective elements from his work by writing an essay consisting solely of quotations from other sources.[16] Although this never came to pass, Benjamin strove to give his words a richness and resonance that normal prose lacked. His interest in the Talmud and the Cabala may have led him to the conviction that multiple levels of meaning exist in every sentence.[17] If Benjamin's style differed from that of other Institut members, it was a product of his searching for the most concrete mode of expression possible. Because his thought was more analogical than theirs, he was less inclined to use traditional philosophical jargon, which he dismissed as the language of procurers.[18] In fact, Benjamin and Horkheimer exchanged letters in which their different appreciations of the value of philosophical language came to the surface.[19] Neither convinced the other, and Benjamin's style remained closer to the evocative prose of artistic literature than to the denotative language of theoretical philosophy. This, in addition to the fragmentary condition of much of his later work, the recent disputes over the authenticity of some of his texts, and the distance he always maintained from Critical Theory, makes an assessment of his contribution to the Institut's work especially difficult.

Still, with these qualifications in mind, the general outlines of the Frankfurt School's approach to aesthetics, shared by Adorno and, to some extent, by Benjamin, can be discerned. If, as we have seen earlier, the Institut refused to fetishize economics or politics, it was equally reluctant to treat culture as a realm apart in society. Occasionally, this seemed to mean an almost reductionist analysis of art to a reflection of social trends, as when the Institut in one of its official histories wrote: "We interpret [art] as a kind of code language for processes taking place within society, which must be deciphered by means of critical analysis."[20] Although generally less direct, the Institut was certainly at the opposite pole from the tradition of *Geisteswissenschaften* (cultural sciences) in Germany, which tended to treat intellectual history in a social vacuum. Members of the Institut never tired of attacking the opposition between culture as a superior sphere of human endeavor and material existence as a lesser aspect of man's condition. The interrelationship between culture and society was such that the former never fully succeeded in transcending the inadequacies of the latter. Thus, Adorno praised Spengler for demonstrating "the way culture itself, as form and order, is in complicity with blind domination."[21] And Benjamin stated baldly that "there is no document of civilization which is not at the same time a document of barbarism."[22]

Equally foreign to the Institut's thinking was the evaluation of artistic phenomena as merely expressions of individual creativity. Horkheimer, it will be recalled, wrote his *Habilitationsschrift* on Kant's *Critique of Judgment.* Almost two decades later, he returned to Kant's argument that an element of common humanity, of shared hope for the potential of mankind, informed every aesthetic act.[23] The supra-individual subject was not, however, abstractly transcendental, as Kant had believed, but was historical instead.[24] The artistic subject was in a sense social as well as individual. Works of art thus expressed objective social tendencies unintended by their creators. The artist's alleged creative freedom was in some ways illusory. "Like artists' lives," Adorno wrote in his essay on Valéry and Proust, "their works appear 'free' only when seen from the outside. The work is neither a reflection of the soul nor the embodiment of a Platonic Idea. It is not pure Being but rather a 'force-field' between subject and object."[25]

Thus, to the Frankfurt School, the aesthetic rationale of expressionism, which was particularly popular in the Germany of their youth, was ultimately false. In an article written on Kafka during the forties, Adorno returned to an argument he had used earlier in his critique of Kierkegaard: "Absolute subjectivity is also subjectless. . . . The more the I of expressionism is thrown back upon itself, the more like the excluded world of things it becomes. . . . Pure subjectivity, being of necessity estranged from itself as well and having become a thing, assumes the dimensions of objectivity which expresses itself through its own estrangement."[26] Although the spontaneity of subjective creativity was a necessary element in genuine art, it could realize itself only through objectification. And objectification inevitably meant working with materials already filtered through the existing social matrix. This in turn meant the necessity of at least some reification. In his critique of Aldous Huxley, Adorno wrote that "humanity includes reification as well as its opposite, not merely as the condition from which liberation is possible, but also positively, as the form in which, however brittle and inadequate it may be, subjective impulses are realized, but only by being objectified." [27] Adorno's use of reification as a synonym for objectification in this passage indicates his pessimism about the total de-reification of life. Here his stress on nonidentity, which we have examined earlier, was especially evident. The complete reconciliation of subjective imagination and objective materials might be approached in great works of art, but never fully achieved. Thus, even when discussing such artists as Valéry, Proust, George, and Hoffmanstahl,[28] for whom he had great respect, Adorno chose to discuss them in dialectical pairs in order to transcend the inherent insufficiency of individual accomplishments.

If artistic creativity was limited by social factors, so too was the subjective appreciation of art. The liberal notion of individual "taste," so Adorno and Lowenthal frequently pointed out,[29] had been fully undermined by the gradual liquidation of the autonomous subject in modern society. The implications of this development were crucial for an understanding of mass culture, in which the manipulation of preferences was almost complete. As we have already seen in Chapter 4 when discussing Lowenthal's essay on Dostoyevsky's readership in prewar Germany, the Institut saw the changes in the reception of art as a valid field for its investigation.

What distinguished the Frankfurt School's sociology of art from its more orthodox Marxist progenitors', however, was its refusal to reduce cultural phenomena to an ideological reflex of class interests. In Adorno's words, "the task of criticism must be not so much to search for the particular interest-groups to which cultural phenomena are to be assigned, but rather to decipher the general social tendencies which are expressed in these phenomena and through which the most powerful interests realize themselves. Cultural criticism must become social physiognomy." [30] In fact, one of the sources of disagreement between Adorno and Benjamin was the latter's tendency to seek more specific correspondences between social groups and cultural phenomena.[31]

Critical Theory's stress on dialectics and negation prevented its analyses of art from becoming simple exercises in decoding class references, although this was not totally absent from the Institut's work. Not only was art the expression and reflection of existing social tendencies, but also — and here is where the Institut diverged most sharply from Leninist criticism, and from Lukács as well — genuine art acted as the last preserve of human yearnings for that "other" society beyond the present one. "Art," Horkheimer wrote, "since it became autonomous, has preserved the utopia that evaporated from religion." [32] Kant's notion of the disinterestedness of beauty was therefore wrong: true art was an expression of man's legitimate interest in his future happiness. Art, to use a phrase of Stendhal's that the Institut was especially fond of quoting, gave "*une promesse de bonheur.*" [33] Thus, although false in one sense, the claims of culture to transcend society were true in another.

All culture was not a bourgeois swindle, as vulgar Marxists seemed at times to think.[34] All art was not simply false consciousness or ideology. A dialectical, or "immanent," critique of art, Adorno argued, "takes seriously the principle that it is not ideology in itself which is untrue but rather its pretension to correspond to reality." [35] One way in which art might offer a "true" foretaste of the future society was in its harmonious reconciliation of form and content, function and expression, subjective and objective elements. Certain artists, such as Beethoven or Goethe, were capable of achieving at least moments of such fulfillment in their work, although "the utopia of art transcends individual works." [36] In fact, in accordance with Critical Theory's distrust of any positive representation of the reconciliation of contradictions, the harmonies it most admired always contained a recognition that a solely aesthetic reconciliation was insufficient: "A successful work, according to immanent criticism, is not one which resolves objective contradictions in a spurious harmony, but one which expresses the idea of harmony negatively by embodying the contradictions, pure and uncompromised, in its innermost structure." [37] In other words, until social contradictions were reconciled in reality, the utopian harmony of art must always maintain an element of protest. "Art," Adorno wrote, "and so-called classical art no less than its more anarchical expressions, always was, and is, a force of protest of the humane against the pressure of domineering institutions, religious and otherwise, no less than it reflects their objective substance." [38] In short, the aesthetic sphere was inevitably political as well, a realization, as Marcuse pointed out,[39] that was most clearly expressed in Schiller's *Letters on the Aesthetic Education of Man.*

Not all that passed for art, however, contained this negative moment. In fact, at the heart of the Institut's critique of mass culture was its belief that the "*promesse de bonheur,*" the vision of the other society, had been systematically eradicated from what was increasingly an "affirmative culture." * How seriously the Frankfurt School took this development we shall see later in this chapter. What is necessary to note now in our more general discussion of the Institut's approach to culture is that even in its moments of greatest pessimism about the elimination of negativity, a dialectical qualification usually appeared. (This might also be said about Marcuse's later popularization of this analysis in *One-Dimensional Man*, although here the qualifications were few and far between). A good example of this reluctance to close off the possibility of negativity appeared in Adorno's article on Thorstein Veblen, which appeared in the *Studies in Philosophy and Social Science* in 1941. Veblen's notion of "conspicuous consumption," which might be considered an integral part of any mass culture analysis, was attacked by Adorno for its undialectical shallowness. "The happiness that man actually finds," he wrote, "cannot be separated from conspicuous consumption. There is no happiness which does not promise to fulfill a socially constituted desire, but there is also none which does not promise something qualitatively different in this fulfillment." [40] In other words, even the distorted desire for status recognition contained a critical element in its demand, first of all, for real happiness, and secondly in its recognition that such a condition necessarily included a social component. Consumption, however conspicuous, still meant a protest against the asceticism the Frankfurt School so disliked.

Among the salient characteristics of "affirmative culture" was such an ascetic moment. As we saw when discussing the nature of the Institut's materialism, the demand for happiness was a fundamental element in Critical Theory. What Adorno later said of Benjamin might well serve as a description of the Frankfurt School as a whole: "Everything that Benjamin said or wrote sounded as if thought, instead of rejecting the promises of fairy tales and children's books with its usual disgraceful 'maturity,' took them so literally that real fulfillment itself was now within sight of knowledge. In his philosophical topography, renunciation is totally repudiated." [41] Furthermore, the Institut's notion of true happiness went well beyond its equation with economic well-being, which characterized the limited thinking of many orthodox Marxists. In fact, the very separation of culture

* "By affirmative culture," Marcuse wrote, "is meant that culture of the bourgeois epoch which led in the course of its own development to the segregation from civilization of the mental and spiritual world as an independent realm of value that is also considered superior to civilization. Its decisive characteristic is the assertion of a universally obligatory, eternally better, and more valuable world that must be unconditionally affirmed: a world essentially different from the factual world of the daily struggle for existence, yet realizable by every individual for himself 'from within,' without any transformation of the state of fact" (*Negations*, p. 95).

from material contentment was one of the clues that the Institut saw as betraying orthodox Marxism's inability to transcend affirmative culture. The dichotomy of substructure and superstructure, however accurate it may have been in describing a certain moment in bourgeois history, ought not be eternalized. In the society of the future, the two spheres would be integrated in a healthy way. As Marcuse argued in his discussion of hedonism, the continued separation of production and consumption was part of an unfree society.[42]

This integration, however, was still a utopian hope. In the present, the greatest threat came from cultural tendencies that implied the premature reconciliation of contradictions at the level of popular consciousness. Vulgar Marxism's sociological reductionism was itself a manifestation of this trend. As in Critical Theory in general, the Frankfurt School's aesthetic criticism maintained a determined stress on the importance of mediation[43] and nonidentity. Because Adorno, like others in the Institut, denied the existence of philosophical first principles, he always interpreted even the most reified artifacts of affirmative culture as something more than derivative reflections of a more fundamental reality. "The less the dialectical method can today presuppose the Hegelian identity of subject and object, the more it is obliged to be mindful of the duality of the moments." [44] An example of Adorno's consistent reliance on dialectical antireductionism came in his treatment of one of the fundamental Marxist categories, the fetishism of commodities (by which Marx meant the process of estranging commodities from their human origins, thereby making them into mysterious, opaque, alien objects rather than the transparent embodiment of social relations). Here he disagreed with Benjamin, to whom he wrote on August 2, 1935, that "the fetish character of commodities is not a fact of consciousness, but dialectic in the eminent sense that it produces consciousness." In other words, it was a social and not merely a psychological reality. To talk of the commodity form *an sich* (in itself), as Benjamin seemed to be doing, was to give it a metaphysical rather than a historical sense.[45] Elsewhere, in his essay on Veblen, Adorno argued in a similar fashion: "Commodity fetishes are not merely the projection of opaque human relations into the world of things. They are also the chimerical deities which originate in the primacy of the exchange process but nevertheless represent something not entirely absorbed in it." [46] In criticizing other cultural critics such as Lukács or Veblen, Adorno was always careful to single out any traces of reductionism he detected in their work. One frequent manifestation of such reductionism was the dismissal of appearances as totally insubstantial, a fallacy that he also noted in philosophical phenomenology. "As the reflction of truth," he wrote, "appearances are dialectical; to reject all appearance is to fall completely under its sway, since truth is abandoned with the rubble without which it cannot appear." [47]

Adorno's sensitivity to dialectical mediation was most clearly demonstrated in the studies of music to which he devoted a major portion of his intellectual energy throughout his life. To Adorno, polyphonic music, the least representational of aesthetic modes,[48] was perhaps best suited for the expression of that imageless "other" that Critical Theory refused to define positively. In addition, the complexities of its mediations — composer, performer, instrument, technical reproduction — made music a particularly rich field for the play of his dialectical imagination. Originating in the rhythms and rituals of everyday life, music had long since transcended its purely functional role. It was thus both tied to material conditions and above them, responsive to changes in social realities and yet more than merely their reflection.

As early as the 1920's and his years in Vienna,[49] Adorno began to explore all facets of musical expression: the history of classical composition, the current production of avant-garde music, the reproduction and reception of musical forms, and the composition and psychosocial function of popular music.[50] In the first two issues of the *Zeitschrift* in 1932, he outlined the principles underlying his approach to music.[51] From the beginning, Adorno made it clear that he was no ordinary musicologist. Music, he argued, contained social contradictions in its own structure, although its relation to social reality was problematical. As was the case with all cultural phenomena, it was neither fully reflective nor fully autonomous. Still, in the current era, its autonomy was severely threatened. Most music displayed the characteristics of a commodity, dominated more by exchange than by use value. The real dichotomy, Adorno contended, was not between "light" and "serious" music — he was never a defender of traditional cultural standards for their own sake — but rather between music that was market-oriented and music that was not. If at the present time the latter tended to be incomprehensible to most listeners, this did not mean that it was objectively reactionary. Music, like theory, must go beyond the prevailing consciousness of the masses.[52]

In the first installment of his essay, Adorno concentrated on the primary trends of contemporary composition. His major focus was on the opposition between the music of Schönberg and that of Stravinsky. Understood more as the embodiment of certain aesthetic principles than as personalities, these were the two composers who were to play the central roles in his later work on the *Philosophy of*

Modern Music.[53] As might be expected, Adorno's sympathies lay with the man in whose school he had been tutored in Vienna. Schönberg's development of the possibilities of atonality, Adorno argued, expressed a refusal to compromise with the unresolved dissonances of contemporary society. The content of his early expressionist period pointed away from false reconciliations. With the unselfconsciousness of the true artist, Schönberg allowed his own unconscious impulses to express their contradictions. Since, however, atonality sought to avoid tonality at all costs, it led away from pure arbitrariness into a new order based on the twelve-tone row, which prohibited the repetition of any one note until all twelve had been sounded. In so progressing, Schönberg had objectified his subjective impulses in a way that put him in touch with the classical tradition. The articulation of the new twelve-tone order was a dialectical product of his earlier music, not a short-circuited imposition of order from without. By withdrawing into the logic of the music itself, Schönberg was able to protect himself somewhat from the external pressure of social forces.

In turning to a musical form in which alienation and contradictions were overcome, however, it might be argued that Schönberg had reconciled himself to the perpetuation of alienation in the social sphere. On the deepest level, the ideal of the fulfilled work of art, taken from classical art, might not be compatible with the means he chose to realize it. The creation of a "pure" music, like Karl Kraus's notion of a "pure" speech, might be ultimately unattainable.[54] But Schönberg's striving to attain it presented a constant standard against which the reality of bourgeois society could be measured.

In later years, it might be added parenthetically, Adorno's estimation of the negative, critical element in Schönberg's type of music was to decline, especially after the twelve-tone row became a more rigid imperative of composition to his followers. "It is not the method itself that is false," he wrote in 1952, "— no one can compose any longer who has not sensed with his own ears the gravitational pull towards twelve-tone technique — but rather its hypostatization. . . . To be true to Schönberg is to warn against all twelve-tone schools." [55] In the thirties, however, Adorno identified Schönberg with all that was progressive in modern music.

The opposite was the case with Stravinsky, the composer to whose works he turned after a brief treatment of Schönberg's disciples, Berg and Webern. To Adorno, Stravinsky represented an antipsychological, neoclassical "objectivism," which ignored the alienation and contradictions of modern society and returned to prebourgeois tonal forms such as the dance. Unlike the romantics, who used the past as a negation of the present, the objectivists belonged with the purveyors of *völkisch* culture, who undialectically adopted old forms to current needs. Although the mediating connection was difficult to illustrate satisfactorily, Adorno went so far as to suggest that objectivism was in a sense the correlate of fascism. Its use of neoprimitive rhythms corresponded to the shocks of unintegrated *Erlebnis* (experience) fostered by fascist society. The irrationality of the objectivists' principles of composition — the composer's "taste" rather than the immanent dialectic of the music was decisive — suggested the arbitrary control of the fascist Führer.[56] Stravinsky might be attacked by the fascists for his "destructiveness," but whether they knew it or not, his music expressed their ideology.

Perhaps more "reactionary" still was the music of one of Frankfurt's most celebrated sons, Paul Hindemith. Hindemith's naiveté, "healthy humor," [57] and anti-ironic style further extended the ideological thrust of objectivist music. The despair occasionally expressed by Stravinsky in such works as *L'Histoire du Soldat* was fully absent from Hindemith's work, which resembled the false facades of *Neue Sachlichkeit* architecture and the illusory community of *völkisch* propagandists. Similarly, certain proletarian music, such as that composed by Hanns Eisler, suffered from the same problem, despite its agitprop value. Socialist realism in music, as in all art, was almost as reactionary, Adorno intimated, as neoclassical objectivism. Both constructed premature harmonies, ignoring the persistence of social contradictions in a way that Schönberg did not. What resulted was a kind of *Gebrauchsmusik* (utilitarian music), which was dependent on a model of technological rationality and thus served less to enlighten than to divert. Only occasionally, as in the music of Kurt Weill, was *Gebrauchsmusik* turned in a critical direction. Adorno praised Weill's fragmentary montage style, which employed shocks in a different way from Stravinsky, as the most progressive and critical popular music of the day.

In the second part of his article, in the next issue of the *Zeitschrift*, Adorno turned from an analysis of composition to the historical dialectic of reproduction, the mediating link between producer and consumer. Here he distinguished between precapitalist music, in which a continuum of production, reproduction, and improvisation existed, and music in the capitalist era, in which such a relationship did not exist. In the latter, the composition was like an isolated commodity separated from the performer, whose interpretive flexibility was highly circumscribed. In the nineteenth century there had been "irrational" performers whose individualism corresponded to the persistence of areas of subjectivity in liberal society. In the twentieth century, however, with the rise of monopoly capitalism, their counterparts were really trapped by the tyranny of the text. Here once again Adorno mentioned Stravinsky's imposition of his own "taste" on the performer, although he was also afraid that Schönberg's music could not avoid similar problems when it was performed.[58]

In the rationalized, administered world of the present, the public still yearned for the "soul" of the nineteenth-century artist. The organic was glorified over the mechanical, personality over anonymity, and inwardness over emptiness. Objectivism attempted to capture these traits in its composition, but without success, because, for reasons Adorno did not explain, they should be the attributes more of reproduction than of production itself. Efforts to redress this situation, Adorno argued, were failures: the "soulful" conductor with his imperious gesture of command was a poor substitute for genuine spontaneity. In fact, he represented the musical equivalent of the authoritarian dictator.

Adorno next turned to the popularity of certain musical forms and their significance in a historical context. Opera, he argued, had lost its appeal with the upper middle classes, although the petite bourgeoisie was still attracted to its repressive elements. Instead, the upper middle classes increasingly patronized concerts, which provided a false sense of subjective inwardness and suggested a phony reconciliation of property and education.[59] The search for true inwardness, however, was no longer realizable in modern society. Richard Strauss was the last meaningful "bourgeois" composer, but even in his music, as Ernst Bloch once pointed out, all negation had been lost. As he used them, chromaticism and dissonance had lost their critical power and become emblems of world economic mobility.[60]

What followed after Strauss, with the exception of avant-garde atonal music, was *Kunstgewerbe*, art as commodity alone. Light music, which once used to mock the aristocracy, now served to reconcile man to his fate. Folk music was no longer alive, because the spontaneous *Volk* had been consumed in a process that left popular music, like all popular culture, the creature of manipulation and imposition from above. Adorno ended the article by remarking on the ideological function of various forms of popular music, a foretaste of the project he set himself in his next few *Zeitschrift* essays.

The first of these, "On Jazz,"[61] was written primarily during his stay in England. It was published pseudonymously under the name "Hektor Rottweiler," because Adorno still made occasional trips back to Germany. Much of its content came from conversations Adorno had had with the jazz expert at the Frankfurt conservatory,

Mátyás Seiber, before 1933.[62] Adorno himself had yet to visit America and thus had not experienced jazz at first hand. This distance from his subject allowed his dialectical imagination full sway. It also produced an essay with occasionally outrageous assertions, made in an uncompromising manner designed less to persuade than to overwhelm. Other members of the Institut were themselves unwilling to agree entirely with Adorno's conclusions.[63]

"I remember clearly," Adorno admitted later, "that I was horrified when I read the word 'jazz' for the first time. It is plausible that [my negative association] came from the German word *Hatz* (a pack of hounds), which evoked bloodhounds chasing after something slower." [64] Whatever the initial verbal association, jazz remained for Adorno a source of continued horror. He began his article by emphatically rejecting any kind of purely aesthetic analysis of jazz in favor of psychosocial critique. Here the verdict was uncompromisingly unfavorable. Jazz, he wrote, "does not transcend alienation, it strengthens it. Jazz is commodity in the strictest sense." [65] All of jazz's claims to express liberation Adorno scornfully rejected. Its primary social function, he contended, was to lessen the distance between the alienated individual and his affirmative culture, but in the repressive manner of *völkisch* ideology. It thus served to reverse what Brecht had called the *Verfremdungseffekt* (estrangement effect) of true art in the modern era. At the same time, jazz gave a false sense of returning to nature, whereas in fact it was totally a product of social artifice. Furthermore, jazz was pseudo-democratic in its substitution of collective for individual fantasies. It was likewise pseudo-individualistic, all alleged improvisation being repetitions of certain basic forms. The "hot" varieties of jazz represented only an illusory sexual emancipation. If anything, the sexual message of jazz was castration, combining the promise of liberation with its ascetic denial.

Moreover, its ideological function was confirmed in the myth of its Negro origins. In fact, Adorno argued, "the skin of the Negro as well as the silver of the saxophone was a coloristic effect." [66] If the Negro contributed anything to jazz, it was less his rebellious reaction to slavery than his half-resentful, half-compliant submission to it. In a later essay on the same subject, Adorno made the point even clearer: "However little doubt there can be regarding the African elements in jazz, it is no less certain that everything unruly in it was from the very beginning integrated into a strict scheme, that its rebellious gestures are accompanied by the tendency to blind obeisance, much like the sado-masochistic type described by analytic psychology." [67]

In denigrating the black contribution to jazz, it might be argued that Adorno displayed a characteristic European ethnocentrism. Indeed, there was a provincial streak in his make-up that came out most clearly in his lack of interest in non-Western musical forms. Hans Mayer, who had known Adorno since 1934, once remarked on this quality of his personality: "Adorno, as far as I see, never took a trip out of the simple desire to see. Europe sufficed for him entirely. No India or China, no Third World, not the people's democracies and not the workers' movement. Even in his needs for life experience, he remained a citizen — and sovereign — of a small state." [68] Still, what also must be remembered is that the jazz he was most concerned with was the commercial variety churned out by Tin Pan Alley, not the less popular variety rooted in black culture itself. Much of his apparent insensitivity came from his failure to make the appropriate distinction between the two.

From a purely musical point of view, jazz, Adorno argued, was also completely bankrupt. Its beat and syncopation were derived from the military march, which suggested its implicit relation to authoritarianism, despite its being banned in Germany. Cool jazz was similar to the musical impressionism of Debussy and Delius, but watered down and conventionalized. Its subjective element was derived from salon music, but it had long since lost any spontaneity. In fact, any attempts to reintroduce elements of true spontaneity were quickly absorbed into its reified system. "The pseudo-vocalization of jazz," Adorno wrote in yet another treatment of the subject, "corresponds to the elimination of the piano, the 'private' middle-class instrument in the era of the phonograph and radio." [69] The piano, we scarcely need to add, was Adorno's own instrument and his bias in its favor obvious.

More significant still, jazz tended to spatialize rather than temporalize musical movement. Here Adorno was pointing to one of the key characteristics of mass culture as the Institut understood it: the substitution of mythic repetition for historical development. "In jazz, one substitutes the immobility of an ever-identical movement for time." [70] The decline of temporality was connected implicitly with the liquidation of the autonomous individual. As Kant had argued, temporal development was a crucial attribute of individuality. Further evidence of the destruction of the individual subject in jazz, Adorno asserted in a supplement to the article he wrote in 1937,[71] was its being used more often as dance or background music rather than being listened to directly. This meant that it did not require, in a Kantian sense, a synthetic unity of apperception. The listener, instead of being forced to engage in a kind of *praxis,* as was the case with Schönberg's atonal music, was reduced to masochistic passivity.

If there was a negative moment in jazz — and Adorno was reluctant, despite his dialectical intentions, to admit there was — it existed in its potentially ambiguous sexual *(Zwischengeschlechtlicher)*[72] implications. Anticipating Marcuse's later praise of polymorphous perversity, Adorno wrote that the suppression of the genital-centric subject, although possibly suggesting regression to sadism or homosexuality, might also provide a foretaste of the social order beyond patriarchal authoritarianism. The saxophone, the most characteristic jazz instrument, gave intimations of this sexual liberation because it was a metal instrument played like a woodwind.[73] But in almost every other respect, jazz represented a capitulation before the powers of the status quo.

This evaluation of jazz, it might be added, did not change after Adorno's emigration to America. In 1953 he wrote another essay, "Perennial Fashion — Jazz,"[74] which was as hostile as ever. And just a short time before his death he discussed the original "Hektor Rottweiler" piece as having been too optimistic in its estimation of jazz's spontaneous character.[75] What Adorno thought of popular music and its connection to the student protest movement in the 1960's is difficult to know, as to my knowledge he never discussed it in print. The likelihood is that, unlike Marcuse,[76] he was impressed more by its pseudo-liberating aspects than by its genuine ones.

After "On Jazz" was published in the *Zeitschrift*, Adorno did not have to wait long before sampling American popular culture at first hand. His time at Oxford, where he wrote on Husserl and began studies of Beethoven and Wagner (only the second of which was ever completed), was drawing to a close. Returning to Germany, it grew increasingly clear, had become practically impossible. Moreover, Horkheimer and his colleagues in New York were anxious to draw him across the Atlantic. In the mid-thirties his gravitation towards the Institut had grown to the extent that Horkheimer was able to write jubilantly to Lowenthal on July 13, 1936, that Adorno now "really belongs to us." The Institut's reduced budget, however, made a direct invitation to become a full member difficult. Still, with Horkheimer's prodding, Adorno made his first visit to New York in June, 1937.[77] His impressions were generally favorable, and he decided to come if the opportunity arose. He did not have long to wait, as Paul Lazarsfeld's Princeton Office of Radio Research, located at that time in Newark, offered him a half-time position as the head of its music study in February, 1938.[78]

Adorno's tenure with the Office of Radio Research was an uneasy one, primarily for methodological reasons that we shall discuss in the following chapter. In addition, he faced all the problems of adjustment that had plagued the other Institut members when they emigrated a few years earlier. In March, Lazarsfeld wrote of his first impressions of the new arrival in a memorandum to two of his colleagues at the project, Hadley Cantril and Frank Stanton:

> He looks exactly as you would imagine a very absent-minded German professor, and he behaves so foreign that I feel like a member of the Mayflower Society. When you start to talk with him, however, he has an enormous amount of interesting ideas. As every newcomer, he tried to reform everything, but if you listen to him, most of what he says makes sense.[79]

In subsequent years, Adorno's refusal to make himself over as an American remained firm, and his critical distance from American culture did not diminish substantially.

Despite this, or perhaps because of it, his scholarly production continued to be prodigious. His first piece written in America, "On the Fetish Character of Music and the Regression of Hearing," appeared in the *Zeitschrift* in 1938.[80] Continuing his generally critical evaluation of contemporary music, the article served as a rebuttal of the more optimistic analysis of the social significance of another mode of popular culture, the film, which Benjamin had contributed to an earlier issue[81] and to which we shall return shortly. Once again, Adorno attacked the false harmony of much contemporary music. Instead, he argued for a new asceticism, which would imply the *promesse de bonheur* in its very denial of the fraudulent happiness of affirmative art. And also as before, he stressed the end of true subjectivity in society and in the art it produced. "The liquidation of the individual," he wrote, "is the particular signature of the new musical situation."[82]

What was new in the article was his exploration of the concepts of fetishism and the "regression" of hearing. Totality, as we have already noted, was one of the central categories of the Frankfurt School's social theory. To the Institut, one of the fundamental characteristics of a nonideological theory was its responsiveness to the interrelationships of past history, present realities, and future potentialities, with all the attendant mediations and contradictions. Concentrating on only one aspect of these — as for example, the positivists did by hypostatizing present "facts" as the only reality — was to make a fetish of one part of the whole. Fetishization, however, was not only a methodological failing. As Marx had demonstrated, it was even more fundamentally an element of alienated capitalist culture, a culture in which men blindly venerated their own products as reified objects. Fetishization, Adorno argued in the Marxian manner, was not merely a psychological category; it was an economic one as well, rooted in the commodity character of a society dominated by exchange rather than use value.[83]

Because music had been invaded by the capitalist ethos, its fetishization was almost total. On one level, that of production, it appeared in the inordinate focus on arrangements rather than composition, in the frequent introduction of coloristic effects, and in the nostalgic resurrection of outdated musical styles for their evocative value. On another, the reception of the music, it manifested itself in the stress on "stars," in both classical (for example, Toscanini) and popular music; in the cult of instruments such as Stradivarius and Amati violins; in the importance of being at the "right" concert rather than going to hear the music itself; and in the empty ecstasy of the jazz enthusiast who listens for the sake of listening alone. To verify fetishization, however, by normal social scientific techniques was impossible — here was the crux of his conflict with Lazarsfeld. Questionnaires or interviews were inadequate because the opinions of the listeners themselves were unreliable. Not only were they incapable of overcoming the conformity of cultural norms, but even more fundamentally, their ability to hear had itself degenerated. It had regressed, not physiologically, but psychologically. The regression was not to an earlier musical era, but rather to an infantile state in which the listener was docile and afraid of anything new, a state similar to the passive dependency Fromm had described in his article "The Feeling of Impotency." Like children who demand only food they have enjoyed in the past, the listener whose hearing had regressed could respond only to a repetition of what he had heard before. Like children who respond to bright colors, he was fascinated by the use of colorative devices that gave the impression of excitement and individuality.

The regressed listener, Adorno argued, was not confined to any one class.[84] If there was a social moment expressed in his condition, it was that of the meaningless leisure of the unemployed. Although at present depoliticized and passive, his masochistic self-abnegation might develop into destructive rage turned outwards. The frustrated sexuality of the frantic jitterbugger expressed this pent-up hostility. Adorno was not optimistic however, about the constructive purposes to which this repressed anger might be put. He was also far less sanguine than Benjamin about the revolutionary potential of popular art, at least in its present affirmative form. "The collective powers also liquidate unsalvageable individuality in music," he wrote, "but only individuals are still capable of representing consciously and negatively the concerns of collectivity."[85] Adorno, as might be expected, saw his role and that of other members of the Institut in this light. His tenure with the Princeton Radio Research Project, although complicated by his methodological differences with the more empirically oriented Lazarsfeld, was by no means unproductive. With the "editorial assistance" of George Simpson,[86] he wrote a total of four papers for the project. The first, "A Social Critique of Radio Music," was delivered in 1940, although not published until 1945.[87] Here Adorno built on the work done by another former student of Schönberg, Ernst Krĕnek, with whom he had been friends since their Viennese days.

Krĕnek had already contributed a study of radio music to the *Zeitschrift* in 1938.[88] Its conclusions were based on a survey of sixty-seven stations in eleven countries. Most stations, he noted, played very little modern, atonal music of the kind he wrote himself. His explanation was that the central function of radio, the transmission of information, had permeated its musical broadcasts as well. Moreover, the information it conveyed through its music was the need to conform. Music, he argued, had been reduced by the radio to an ornament of everyday life. Furthermore, by being a reproductive medium of the second order, after the actual performance itself, radio brought about a crucial change in the aesthetic experience of the listener. In simulating the sense of attending the concert in the flesh, radio could preserve the *nunc* or "nowness" of a performance but not its *hic* or "hereness." In so doing, it destroyed one of the crucial features of what Benjamin had called the "aura" of a work of art, its ritual, cultish nimbus. Instead of experiencing the music with its "auratic" qualities intact, the radio listener heard it in a depersonalized, collective, objectivized form, which robbed it of its negative function.

Adorno's own study of radio music agreed with Krĕnek's conclusions. He began his paper by stating certain basic axioms: the commodity character of modern society; the trend towards monopoly in all sectors of the society, including communications; society's reaction to any threats to its preservation by a tightening of its conformist elements; and the existence of social antagonisms in the cultural sphere.[89] What followed from these premises was similar enough to the analysis of Krĕnek's paper and Adorno's own work, described above, not to require recapitulation here. His three subsequent essays with the Radio Research Project were devoted to explorations of popular music, the NBC "Music Appreciation Hour," and the radio symphony.[90]

The first of these, "On Popular Music," was published in a special issue of the *Studies in Philosophy and Social Science* concentrating on mass communications, done in collaboration with the Radio Research Project.[91] The essay continued the hostile appraisal of jazz that Adorno had begun while still in Europe. Standardization and pseudo-individuality were among the salient traits of popular music in Adorno's eyes. Recognition of the familiar was the essence of mass listening, serving more as an end in itself than as a means to more intelligent appreciation. Once a certain formula was successful, the industry promoted and plugged the same thing over and over again. The result was to make music into a kind of social cement operating through distraction, displaced wish-fulfillment, and the intensification of passivity. However, as in the case of jazz, Adorno felt there might still be an isolated element of negation in popular music. Here he saw it potentially existing in the spiteful resentment of passivity that the pseudo-activity of jitterbugging implied. The energy thus expressed, he contended in a way reminiscent of Nietzsche's analysis of the ascetic priest, at least expressed a vestige of unextinguished will. "To become transformed into an insect," he wrote, playing on the name of the dance, "man needs that energy which might possibly achieve his transformation into a man." [92]

Adorno's third study for Lazarsfeld was a content analysis of the NBC "Music Appreciation Hour," showing how it spread false musical knowledge. Of greater interest than this project, which was never published and was soon outdated, was his final contribution to the Office of Radio Research, an analysis of the radio symphony.[93] Like Krěnek, he argued that the "presence" of the music was lost to the radio listener, and with it, a part of music's "auratic" spell. Also lost was the actual volume of the performance and the sense of community created by being a member of a live audience. By isolating the individual, the radio served to destroy the symphonic "space," which, like that of a cathedral, surrounded the listener at a real concert. It also served to return the listener to serial time rather than immersing him in the "suspension of time-consciousness" [94] that characterized great symphonies like Beethoven's. (What Adorno meant by this suspension was different from the repetitive timelessness of affirmative culture. Normal time was indeed suspended by great works of art, but in its place was a type of coherent development, which was a foretaste of the temporal order of the "other" society. Benjamin was especially fond of distinguishing between "homogeneous, empty" time and time "filled by the presence of the now.") [95] Serial time corresponded to the breakdown of true individuality, which, as we have seen, meant meaningful development and relatedness to the totality. To Adorno, "the tendency towards atomized listening" was "perhaps the most universal of [the] present day's musical consciousness." [96] Deprived of its unity as an aesthetic totality, the symphony degenerated into a series of reified quotations, snatches of melody taken out of their context, without any negative resonance at all.

In a second section of the original manuscript Adorno continued his critique of the deleterious effects of radio by pointing to its stimulus to standardization. Although relating this to the permeation of the exchange ethic of capitalism, he also saw a connection with technical rationality itself, in a way similar to Horkheimer's analysis of trends in the authoritarian state. "Its basic standardization," he wrote, "is certain to prevail in some way or other under noncapitalist forms of production. Technical standardization leads to centralized administration." [97] Once again, he gave clear evidence of his distance from the Leninist strain in Marxist aesthetic criticism, with its general indifference to technological innovation. Published in shortened form in the 1941 volume of *Radio Research*, the essay met with considerable opposition from American commentators. And in later years Adorno was to admit that one of his arguments had been made obsolete: "that the radio symphony was not a symphony at all, a thesis derived from the technologically produced alterations in sound . . . which have since been overcome by the techniques of high fidelity and stereophonics." [98] In general, however, it can fairly be said that Adorno's musical criticism found an unsympathetic audience in this country, which was only partly a function of its being written primarily in German.

Moving to Los Angeles in 1941 meant an end to Adorno's fitful collaboration with Lazarsfeld. It also led to a redirection of his attention away from the consumption and reception of music back to its production. To discuss in detail the complexities of his work in this area beyond what has already been done, let alone to analyze it critically, would be beyond my ability. Still, certain points relating it to the Institut's other work can be made.

In New York, Adorno had put the finishing touches on his study of Wagner, parts of which had appeared in the *Zeitschrift* in 1939.[99] Publication of the completed manuscript was delayed until his return to Germany in the 1950's. Many of the categories he used, however, demonstrated how close in spirit the work was to other examples of Institut thinking in the thirties. For example, Adorno used Fromm's notion of the "social character" to integrate Wagner's anti-Semitism, antibourgeois posturing, and pseudo-rebelliousness with certain strains in his music. Here he introduced such terms as "conductor-composer" and the "gestural type" of composition to illuminate the social content of the music. Another new concept was "phantasmagoria," which indicated Wagner's tendency to mask the social-psychological genesis of his music by making it appear to be derived from "natural" sources, a deception characteristic of much authoritarian thought, as we have seen in Marcuse's and Lowenthal's work. This was a characteristic of Wagner's ideology that Adorno connected with the mythical elements in his music dramas, elements that sought to interpret the unconscious while at the same time dissolving reality into it. Adorno also discussed the *Ring* in terms of the betrayal of the revolutionary by the "rebel," once again using concepts developed by Fromm in his theoretical essay in the *Studien über Autorität und Familie*. In the last fragment that appeared in the *Zeitschrift*, Adorno analyzed the pessimism and nihilism Wagner had adopted from Schopenhauer. Here he admitted that a certain measure of utopian protest was contained in Wagner's vision, in the way in which his dialectical approach always, or almost always, perceived a subdued strain of negation in even the most affirmative cultural products.

Although unpublished, the Wagner manuscript circulated among Adorno's friends in the exile community in the Los Angeles area. While New York was clearly the center of resettlement for most refugees, a number of exiles had emigrated to California, some of them drawn to Hollywood and the work it offered in the movie industry. Among the more celebrated were Heinrich Mann, Alfred Polgar, Bertolt Brecht, Alfred Döblin, and William Dieterle. After their arrival in 1941, Horkheimer and Adorno were quickly accepted into the exile community.[100] One of the most illustrious of their number was Thomas Mann, about whom Horkheimer had written not entirely with favor in an earlier year. Mann's celebrated irony, Horkheimer had argued in 1938,[101] had passive implications, and his support for Weimar was ill conceived. Still, he recognized that Mann's repudiation of the Nazis had moved him in a more progressive direction and predicted an increasingly radical future for him.

By the time of their arrival in California, previous disagreements had been muted, and Mann became close friends with the two fellow emigrés. During the forties Mann occasionally participated in Institut-sponsored seminars and lent his name to an Institut study of the help German gentiles had given to persecuted Jews, which was conducted in 1943 primarily through a survey in the *Aufbau*, the leading emigré newspaper.[102] Increasingly occupied with an attempt to render the Nazi experience and its origins in a fictional form, Mann hit on the device of using the life and works of a composer as the symbolic equivalent of Germany's cultural decline. Not unexpectedly, he was attracted to Adorno, with his unique background in both music and philosophy, as a source of information. The first example of Adorno's work that came to his attention was the manuscript on Wagner. Mann recognized it as an "extremely shrewd treatise . . . which never entirely passes over to the negative side . . . and has a certain kinship with my own essay, 'Sufferings and Greatness of Richard Wagner.'" [103]

Adorno's subsequent work made an even greater impression on Mann when Adorno gave it to him in July, 1943. The first half of what was later called *Philosophy of Modern Music* was an essay on Schönberg, developing some of the themes Adorno had first discussed in the *Zeitschrift* in 1932. By the forties, Adorno, as we have mentioned earlier, had grown more critical of the changes in his former idol's music, especially his acceptance of his pupils' hypostatization of the twelve-tone system. According to Mann, Schönberg, who at that time was also living in southern California, "sensed the critical note within his disciple's respect," [104] making relations between them strained. Mann, on the other hand, was very enthusiastic about what he read and set about incorporating it into the novel he was then engaged in writing.

In his later discussion of that novel, *Doctor Faustus*, Mann expressed his gratitude for Adorno's help: "The analysis of the row system and the criticism of it that is translated into dialogue in chapter XXII of Faustus is entirely based on Adorno's essay. So are certain remarks on the tonal language of the later Beethoven, such as occur early in the book in Kretschmar's sputterings: the uncanny relationship that death establishes between genius and convention." [105] Throughout the writing of the work, Mann returned to Adorno for advice. In October, 1943, Mann heard Adorno play "the entire Sonata Opus 111 [of Beethoven] in a highly instructive fashion." The effect on him was profound. "I had never been more attentive," he remembered. "I rose early the following morning and for the next three days immersed myself in a thoroughgoing revision and extension of the lecture, which became a significant enrichment and embellishment of the chapter and indeed of the whole book. Into the poetic little illustrative phrases I wrote for the arietta theme I slipped Adorno's patronymic, Wiesengrund (Meadowland), by way of showing my gratitude." [106] In December, 1945, Mann wrote Adorno a ten-page letter apologizing for his "scrupulously unscrupulous" [107] borrowings from his work, and asked for still more advice, which was quickly forthcoming. When the novel was finally published in 1947, Adorno received a copy inscribed by Mann to his "privy councillor." [108] Mann's relations with Schönberg, it might be noted in passing, were seriously undermined by the composer's accusation that his ideas had been stolen without attribution; Mann added an explanation to all subsequent editions of the novel.[109] *Philosophy of Modern Music* itself appeared the following year, with a section on Stravinsky written during the war to balance the Schönberg chapters. Later, Adorno was to call the entire work a long excursus on *Dialectic of the Enlightenment*, which we shall examine in Chapter 8.

In the forties Adorno also collaborated with another refugee in California, the composer Hanns Eisler, on a book dealing with music in the film. However, because of Adorno's reluctance to be associated with the more politically involved Eisler, his name was not on the title page when the book was published in 1947.[110] He also found the time in California to write essays on Huxley, Kafka, and cultural criticism in general, which were included in a volume called *Prismen* published in Germany after his return. In the summer of 1948, immediately following the completion of *Philosophy of Modern Music*, he turned his attention to music in the Soviet bloc. The result was a highly critical essay entitled "Gegängelte Musik,"[111] (*gängeln* roughly means being fettered or led around by the nose), in which he attacked the promotion of "healthy" art by advocates of socialist realism.

In addition to his work on cultural matters, Adorno maintained his theoretical interests leading to *Dialectic of the Enlightenment* and his book of aphorisms, *Minima Moralia*;[112] he also spent time trying to employ American empirical techniques in his work on *The Authoritarian Personality* and in a study of an American demagogue.[113] Adorno returned to Germany with Horkheimer in 1949, but his work in California had not yet ended. In the winter of 1952–1953 he came back for a few months, primarily to retain his American citizenship. Through connections made while working on *The Authoritarian Personality*, he secured a position as director of the scientific branch of the Hacker Foundation in Beverly Hills. Here his two final works on American mass culture were composed. The first was a study, written with Bernice T. Eiduson, of the new mass communications medium, television, for which they performed content analyses of scripts with the aim of uncovering the latent messages of the shows.[114] The second was a longer and in some ways more original study of the *Los Angeles Times*' astrology column.[115] Adorno had already written several pages on the occult in *Minima Moralia*.[116] With the additional work of *The Authoritarian Personality* behind him, he was able to broaden his critique considerably.

In "The Stars Down to Earth," as the study was called, Adorno treated astrology as a "secondary" superstition, in the sense that it affected secondary groups like classes rather than primary ones like the family. Thus, although Adorno used psychoanalytical insights, with the help of Dr. Frederick Hacker, a trained analyst, they were not directed primarily at individuals but rather at groups. Or more precisely, they were used to explore the psychosocial layer between individual psyches and allegedly individual consciousnesses. The Freud Adorno was most interested in here was the Freud of *Group Psychology and the Analysis of the Ego.*[117] As a result, the study showed the convergence of the Institut's critique of mass culture with its analysis of authoritarianism, which will be examined in the next chapter. Astrology, Adorno concluded, was an "ideology of dependence" [118] answering many of the irrational needs of types of people who were "high scorers" on *The Authoritarian Personality*'s "F Scale."

Adorno's California years were thus enormously productive. In his essay on Huxley he had written: "It is made unmistakably clear to the intellectual from abroad that he will have to eradicate himself as an autonomous being if he hopes to achieve anything or be accepted as an employee of the super-trust into which life has condensed." [119] Adorno never sought, nor did he receive, that acceptance, but his achievement was, if anything, strengthened by his remaining stubbornly on the outside. Instead of succumbing to the demands of the American cultural "super-trust," he was able to write, as the Institut almost always had done, for a constituency more ideal than real — the exception being the Institut's work on authoritarianism. And ironically, after his return to Germany, an audience was to materialize large enough to make Adorno into one of the major European intellectual figures of his time.

A strong sense of the pressures of American cultural life played as great a role in the life of Walter Benjamin, to whose contribution to the Institut's history we can now turn. Throughout the thirties Benjamin resisted the Institut's entreaties to join its other members in New York.[120] In January, 1938, at what was to be their last meeting, Benjamin turned down Adorno's urgent plea by saying, "there are still positions in Europe to defend." [121] By the time these positions had been overrun and remaining in Paris was no longer possible — the Gestapo seized Benjamin's apartment in the summer of 1940 — emigration to America had become increasingly difficult. German refugees who had escaped to France at an earlier date were in danger of being returned to the Nazis by the Vichy government. Benjamin was put into an internment camp at Nevers in anticipation of such a move. The Institut began then to do all it could on his behalf. Maurice Halbwachs and Georges Scelle intervened to have him released from the camp.[122] A certain number of emergency visas to the United States were available, and, primarily through Pollock's efforts, one was obtained for the reluctant refugee. Benjamin was less successful, however, in securing an exit visa from France. Although an obstacle, this did not present an insurmountable problem, as a generally unguarded road over the Pyrenees to the Spanish border at Port Bou was considered a safe alternative. Benjamin, in ill health at the time because of a heart condition, was one of a party of refugees who set out for the frontier on September 26, 1940. In his baggage were fifteen tablets of a morphia compound, which, so he told Arthur Koestler in Marseilles a few days earlier, "were enough to kill a horse." [123] By chance, the Spanish government had closed its border just before their arrival. Tired by the trip, distraught over the prospect of returning to Gestapo seizure, and still unenthusiastic about his future in America, Benjamin swallowed the pills during the night. Refusing to have his stomach pumped the next morning, he died in agony, a few months past his forty-eighth birthday. On the next day, the Spanish border guards, shaken by his suicide, allowed the rest of the party to pass through to safety. As a grim footnote to the story, Koestler, hearing the news, took some of the same pills, which Benjamin had given him in Marseilles. "But," he wrote later, "Benjamin apparently had a better stomach, for I vomited the stuff out." [124]

What Benjamin's emigration to New York would have meant to the Institut, or to American intellectual life for that matter, will of course never be known. How well he would have integrated his talents with those of the other Institut members can only be conjectured. Horkheimer and Adorno had hoped to win him over more closely to Critical Theory, having previously tried to do so from afar, but whether or not he would have continued to resist is a matter for speculation alone. What can be said with certainty is that the Institut was sorely disappointed and upset by his premature death. In subsequent years it sought to secure for him the recognition and acclaim he had been denied in life. The first manifestation of this was a memorial volume circulated in a limited, mimeographed edition (because of the Institut's financial problems) in 1942. It contained essays by Adorno, Horkheimer, and Benjamin himself.[125] After the Institut returned to Germany, Adorno, with the help of Benjamin's old friend Gershom Scholem, published editions of his writings and letters, which have sparked widespread interest in Benjamin's work in the last decade. Whatever his critics may have said about Adorno's interpretation of his friend's ideas, and its repercussions on the picture of Benjamin he fostered, they could not deny that only through his efforts, in collaboration with Scholem, did Benjamin become a figure of controversy at all.

What Adorno never denied was that Benjamin's perspective, combining theological and materialist elements in a unique way, was all his own. To explore it adequately would require another study, one moreover that Rolf Tiedemann has already written[126] and that therefore need not be attempted now. In fact, merely to sift through the controversy that has surrounded Benjamin's name in the past decade would be a task of considerable proportions.[127] What will be attempted here instead is a discussion of Benjamin's specific relations with the Institut and his contribution to its work, especially its analysis of mass culture.

Benjamin was born in 1892 in Berlin, and grew up, like most of the other Institut members, in a family of well-to-do assimilated Jews. His father was an antiquarian and art dealer from whom he inherited a collector's fascination with books and the artifacts of the past.[128] Relations with his family, however, were never easy. Although he would return to his childhood again and again in his work,[129] it was apparently a period of great sadness for him.[130] Like many other disaffected bourgeois German adolescents, he joined Gustav Wyneken's Youth Movement before the war, becoming a member of its most radical wing, which was composed largely of Jewish students.[131] During the period of his affiliation, he rose to the presidency of the Berlin Free Student Association and was a frequent contributor to Wyneken's *Der Anfang*, under the pseudonym "Ardor." During the war, however, his interest in another escape from the oppressiveness of bourgeois life crowded out the Youth Movement. Zionism became the dominant passion of his life for the next few years. His interest in it was strengthened by the close friendship he began with Gershom Scholem in 1915, who also awoke his curiosity in Jewish theology and mysticism. Benjamin's wife Dora, whom he married in 1917, was herself the daughter of a prominent Zionist, Leon Kellner. Benjamin's commitment to Zionism, however, was never undiluted. In 1922 he resisted Scholem's entreaties to accompany him to Palestine, although later letters indicate his continued interest in such a move.[132] With the collapse of his marriage in the twenties — divorce came in 1930 — what was perhaps another stimulus to the maintenance of his Zionism disappeared.[133]

Yet the impact of his Jewish studies under Scholem's influence remained strong through the rest of his life, although after 1922 — the year of Scholem's departure and the failure of a projected literary review with a religious perspective, to be called *Angelus Novus* — it was never as central as before. We have already discussed the influence of certain Jewish strains on the Institut's work: the unwillingness to name or describe the "other" at the heart of Critical Theory, and Fromm's interest in a philosophical anthropology similar to that of Martin Buber and his colleagues in the Frankfurt Lehrhaus. The influence of Jewish thought and custom on Benjamin was somewhat different. Benjamin's keenest interest was in the Cabala, the most arcane of Jewish mystical works; here his friendship with Scholem was crucial. When Max Rychner, the editor of the *Schweizer Rundschau*, asked Benjamin about the particularly abstruse introduction to his book on baroque tragedy, *The Origin of German Tragedy*, Benjamin referred him to the Cabala.[134] What appealed to Benjamin about it was the exegetical skill needed to probe its levels of meaning. In a letter to Rychner written in 1931, well after Benjamin had become interested in Marxism, he could still comment, "I have never been able to do research and think in a way other than, if I may so put it, in a theological sense — namely, in accordance with the Talmudic teaching of the forty-nine levels of meaning in every passage in the Torah." [135] As has often been noted,[136] Benjamin's examination of cultural phenomena resembled that of a biblical scholar probing a sacred text. In his hope of writing a book consisting solely of quotations, Benjamin expressed a quasi-religious desire to become the transparent mouthpiece of a higher reality. His theory of language was similarly rooted in the assumption of a central reality, which could be revealed, albeit incompletely, by the power of exegesis.[137]

If Benjamin responded to the revelatory elements in Judaism, he was equally sensitive to its redemptive strains. The messianic current in Jewish thought, which was appropriated in a secularized form by Marxism, ran through his writings from beginning to end. One of the last essays he wrote, the posthumously published "Theses on the Philosophy of History," made this very evident. It was here that Benjamin most clearly articulated his distinction between homogeneous, empty time and the messianic *Jetztzeit* (the fulfilled time of the present)[138] that the revolution was supposed to usher in. It was also here that he made clear his life-long commitment to a theological mode of thinking, in the parable that opened the "Theses":

> A puppet in Turkish attire and with a hookah in its mouth sat before a chessboard placed on a large table. . . . Actually, a little hunchback who was an expert chess player sat inside and guided the puppet's hand by means of strings. One can imagine a philosophical counterpart to this device. The puppet called "historical materialism" is to win all the time. It can easily be a match for anyone if it enlists the services of theology, which today, as we know, is wizened and has to keep out of sight.[139]

It should be added that the Institut, far from encouraging the theological elements in Benjamin's thought, as some of its critics have implied, sought to influence him in a more secular direction. The general reaction to the "Theses" within the Institut was not especially favorable.[140] Adorno's correspondence also shows his disapproval of the Jewish residues in Benjamin's thought.[141]

On the other hand, the Institut was not entirely enthusiastic about the brand of Marxism Benjamin adopted in the mid-twenties. Unlike the others, Benjamin came to dialectical materialism following its heroic period in the immediate postwar years,[142] although his curiosity had doubtless been aroused as early as 1918, when he became friends with Ernst Bloch in Bern.[143] Lukács's early work served as another bridge to Marx, especially *History and Class Consciousness* and *The Theory of the Novel.*[144] Personal acquaintances also played a key role. In 1924, on holiday in Capri, Benjamin met the Russian director and actress Asja Lacis, who was traveling with a company performing Brecht's *Edward II.* Possibly, Benjamin, whose marriage to Dora Keliner was in trouble, fell in love with Miss Lacis. In any case, she introduced him to her circle of Marxist friends and helped arrange a trip to Moscow for him in the winter of 1926–1927. In the Soviet capital he met Mayakovsky and Byeli and made arrangements to write an article on Goethe for the Soviet Encyclopedia, which was never actually completed. And then in 1929 Asja Lacis introduced him to the man who was to play the most important role in his Marxist development, Bertolt Brecht.

Brecht's relationship with Benjamin has been one of the major sources of recent controversy. Scholem and Adorno both considered Brecht's influence more destructive than beneficial.[145] Rolf Tiedemann, Adorno's student, asserted that the relationship ought to be understood less in intellectual than in psychological terms, because of Benjamin's fear of Brecht.[146] Especially baleful, they all agreed, was Benjamin's acceptance of Brecht's crude, even vulgar, materialism. Almost as unfortunate, at least in Adorno's eyes, was Benjamin's adoption of his friend's overly optimistic attitude towards the revolutionary potential of popular art and technological innovation. Personal distrust of Brecht doubtless contributed to their dislike of his hold over Benjamin. The Frankfurt School, it should be noted, never saw eye to eye with Brecht on political matters, despite their respect for his literary achievements. The sentiment was returned in kind. Well after Benjamin's death, when Brecht had moved to California, he, Horkheimer, and Adorno saw each other socially; but as his diary demonstrates,[147] the old animosities continued unabated. To Brecht, the Institut consisted of "Tui-intellectuals," who prostituted themselves for American foundation support. (His proposed novel, set in the fictitious Chinese kingdom of the Tuis, was never actually completed.) They in turn considered him a petit-bourgeois *poseur* and an apologist for Stalinism.

To Benjamin, on the other hand, Brecht was far more attractive. "My agreeing with Brecht's production," he wrote in 1933, "represents one of the most important and most reinforced points in my entire position." [148] Hannah Arendt, who knew Benjamin in Paris in the thirties, has commented that the attraction lay in Brecht's "crude thinking," [149] the very rejection of dialectical subtleties that Adorno so loathed. Benjamin, she continued, saw in Brecht's unmediated materialism "not so much a referral to practice as to reality, and to him this reality manifested itself most directly in the proverbs and idioms of everyday language." [150] Miss Arendt was not alone in pointing to the fascination Brecht held for Benjamin. Other detractors of the Institut further to the left went so far as to accuse Adorno and Scholem of deliberately minimizing Brecht's importance for their own purposes.[151] This seems not to be the case, however, for Tiedemann, who is usually identified with the Adorno-Scholem camp, edited a collection of Benjamin's articles and reviews of Brecht in 1966.[152] That they considered the relationship harmful no one denies. And in fact it might be argued that Benjamin, for all his admiration, shared some wariness about the friendship, which manifested itself in his refusal to leave Paris permanently to join Brecht in his Svendborg, Denmark, exile.[153] Brecht, on the other hand, seems to have remained devoted until Benjamin's death. In fact, he wrote two moving poems on that subject in 1940.[154]

The undialectical note that Adorno detected in Benjamin's acceptance of Brecht's more vulgar materialism was perhaps a product of the difference between Benjamin's intellectual background and that of the other Institut members. Benjamin's university training had taken place in Berlin, Freiburg, and Bern, where, during the war, he received his degree with a thesis on the German romantics.[155] The most important philosophical influence on his thinking had been neo-Kantian. Near the end of his life, he wrote to Adorno that Heinrich Rickert had been his most influential teacher.[156] From the beginning, however, it seems that Benjamin was dissatisfied with Kant's agnostic dualism, with its distinction between noumena and phenomena. In an early essay he wrote: "It is the task of the coming theory of knowledge to find the sphere of total neutrality in relation to the concepts of object and subject; in other words, to ascertain the autonomous, original sphere in which this concept in no way signified the relationship between two metaphysical entities." [157] In so arguing, of course, he was on ground familiar to Horkheimer, Marcuse, and Adorno. Where he differed, however, was in the comparatively minor impact of Hegel on his thinking. In general, he sought to free himself from the burden of philosophical jargon, which he dismissed as the chatter of pimps *(Zuhältersprache)*.[158] On this score, as their correspondence reveals, he and Horkheimer were at odds.[159]

Another source of friction between Benjamin and at least Adorno was his relative indifference to music, especially as a potentially critical medium. According to Adorno,[160] he had developed an animosity to music in his youth, which was never entirely overcome. In an important essay, "The Author as Producer," [161] written when Brecht's influence was at its height, Benjamin suggested that words must be added to music to give it any political content. The model he chose was the collaboration between Brecht and Hanns Eisler on *The Measures Taken.* There is little indication in his work that he shared Adorno's taste for the more demanding forms of modern music or his belief in the importance of music's nonrepresentational quality.

Moreover, Benjamin's thinking was always more analogical than Horkheimer's or Adorno's, more concerned with the universal implicit in the particular. For all Critical Theory's interest in the interplay of totality and moment, it is unlikely that Horkheimer and the others would have accepted without qualification Benjamin's assertion that "a historical materialist approaches a historical subject only where he encounters it as a monad." [162] Their mode of thinking was always more explanatory than his, more concerned with uncovering the discontinuities and mediations among various social phenomena. To Benjamin, the importance of nonidentity was not as great as his colleagues argued. And as a result, he was not as concerned with the salvation of subjectivity as they were. His "dialectics at a standstill" [163] was far more static and direct than Critical Theory. Still, Adorno took pains to avoid lumping him together with the phenomenologists, whose lack of dialectical irony he often scored:

> To interpret his lack of system and of a closed theoretical foundation as sufficient reason to align him with the representatives of 'intuition,' eidetic or otherwise . . . is to overlook what is best in him. It is not his glance as such which lays claim to the unmediated possession of the absolute; rather his manner of seeing, the entire perspective is altered. The technique of enlargement brings the rigid in motion and the dynamic to rest.[164]

If Benjamin's unique perspective distanced him from Critical Theory, it also served to undermine his chances for a successful academic career. His critical study of Goethe's *Elective Affinities*, written in 1924–1925, appeared under the sponsorship of Hugo von Hofmannsthal.[165] But the work explicitly criticized the ideology of the then powerful circle around Stefan George, which resulted in his being ostracized from the scholarly world into which their influence extended.[166] Later attempts to gain his *Habilitation* at the University of Frankfurt were equally fruitless. The work he submitted as his credentials was a study of German baroque drama in which he sought to "rescue" the category of allegory. It proved, however, too obscure for his examiners, among whom were the head of the literature faculty, Franz Schultz, and the university's expert on aesthetics, the same Hans Cornelius who had been the teacher of several Institut members.[167] Although ultimately published in 1928, *The Origin of German Tragedy* failed to earn Benjamin a place in the academic hierarchy. With this defeat went his father's refusal to continue supporting him, and Benjamin was forced to eke out an existence as a private critic and occasional translator of writers like Proust.[168] In the twenties and early thirties he wrote for such journals as the *Literarische Welt* and such newspapers as the *Frankfurter Zeitung*. He also did reviews for a Frankfurt radio station directed by his friend Ernst Schoen.[169] Although his work was often of the highest quality — his evocative memories of childhood, later published as *Berlin Childhood Around 1900*,[170] were serialized in the *Frankfurter Zeitung* — it received relatively little notice.

The Nazi take-over meant the end of the few sources of income Benjamin had in Germany. After attempts to write pseudonymously as "Detlef Holz" and "C. Conrad" proved unsuccessful, he accepted the necessity of emigration. Paris, a city in which he had felt comfortable on previous visits, became his chosen refuge. In many ways, the modern city was one of the central foci of his work,[171] and Paris was the European metropolis *par excellence*. As early as 1927 he had begun writing a major analysis of bourgeois culture, an *Urgeschichte* (prehistory) of the nineteenth century, which used Paris as its central metaphor. Entitled the *Passagenarbeit* (a reference to the *Passagen*, or arcades, of Paris), it was to occupy Benjamin for the remainder of his life. Although extending to thousands of pages, only parts of it were ever actually completed to his satisfaction.

The Institut's role in the development of this project has been another source of controversy. Benjamin's main support in Paris after the end of 1935 was the Institut's stipend. Other projects, such as the collection of letters he published as "Detlef Holz" in Switzerland,[172] might have brought in some income, but, as his own correspondence indicates, not very much. Benjamin had been acquainted with Adorno since 1923, when they had met in Frankfurt.[173] In 1934, after

Benjamin's flight from Germany, Adorno persuaded Horkheimer to accept some of his work for the *Zeitschrift.* His first essay, a study of the social position of current French writers, appeared in the first issue of that year.[174] It was soon followed by a survey of linguistic sociology, in which Benjamin revealed his life-long interest in language and its broader implications. Shortly thereafter, Horkheimer extended an invitation to Benjamin to join the Institut in America. Although Benjamin had written in April, 1935, that "there is nothing so urgent to me as connecting my work as tightly and productively with the Institut as possible," [175] he declined the offer. At the end of the year, however, he was made a research associate of the Institut's Paris branch and began to receive a regular stipend, which, although never very much, allowed him to say that it "brought about an immediate unburdening." [176]

Because of Benjamin's admitted financial dependency on the Institut, it has been argued by the *Alternative* circle that his work was changed in fundamental ways, even censored, by his editors in New York. Without going into the textual questions in all their complexity, it does seem accurate to say that on occasion the wording of Benjamin's essays was altered in a less radical direction. A clear example of this was his article "The Work of Art in the Era of Mechanical Reproduction," which ended in Benjamin's original text with the words: "This is the situation of politics which Fascism is rendering aesthetic. Communism responds by politicizing art." These are the words that also appear in the English translation, in *Illuminations* (page 244). In the *Zeitschrift*, however, the printed version replaced "Fascism" with "the totalitarian doctrine" and "Communism" with "the constructive forces of mankind" (page 66). On the same page, the original "imperialistic warfare" was changed to "modern warfare." [177]

These changes, however, were usually made in correspondence with Benjamin and not after he had submitted finished versions to the New York branch of the Institut. What is crucial to understand is that they were not done specifically to bring Benjamin into line with a dogmatic Critical Theory, but were rather a reflection of the Aesopian language the *Zeitschrift* frequently used, to protect itself from political harassment. The accusations of other refugees at the New School, Adorno's later reluctance to be associated with Hanns Eisler, the subtle change in the English translation of the title of Grossmann's book have all been previously mentioned. It is abundantly clear that the Institut felt insecure in America and wished to do as little as possible to jeopardize its position. Well before the actual emigration, Horkheimer had written in *Dämmerung*: "Sooner or later, the right of exile for political refugees will be abolished in practice. . . . The right of exile will disappear from the common interests of the international capitalist class, as soon as it no longer concerns emigrés from Russia or *völkisch* terrorists." [178] Having already been forced to flee one continent, he and his colleagues were not anxious to court a similar fate.

This fear comes out clearly in the Lowenthal-Horkheimer correspondence. For example, on July 30, 1939, Lowenthal wrote to Horkheimer of a new deportation law being considered in the Senate, with a very broad scope. Accordingly, he advised Horkheimer to add "European" before "liberalism" in the article he was preparing. Later, on July 30 and August 4, 1940, he mentioned police visits to the Institut, which, although routine, seemed ominous enough to report. And even as late as July 26, 1944, when the Institut was studying anti-Semitism in American labor, Horkheimer could still worry about the reaction of American right-wingers to "a bunch of foreign-born intellectuals sticking their noses into the private affairs of American workers." This feeling of insecurity, in combination with the Institut's traditional desire to remain a "scientific" rather than a political institution, resulted in its striking the more inflammatory passages from Benjamin's texts.

On the other hand, what is equally clear is that the *Zeitschrift* did print certain of Benjamin's essays with which Horkheimer and Adorno were not in complete agreement — his "The Work of Art in the Era of Mechanical Reproduction" and "Eduard Fuchs, the Collector and Historian," [179] which were in some ways too radical for their taste. How much the published versions were altered, however, is uncertain.[180] One part of Benjamin's work, an important section of the *Passagenarbeit*, was turned down completely, primarily, it would seem, because of Adorno's reservations. In 1936 Benjamin had been very impressed with the little-known cosmological speculations of Auguste Blanqui, the nineteenth-century French revolutionary, which appeared in a book by Blanqui called *L'Éternité par les astres.*[181] Blanqui's mechanical view of nature seemed to Benjamin to be related to his social order, which was dominated by a kind of eternal return. What Benjamin attempted to do in his essay, which was entitled "The Paris of the Second Empire in Baudelaire," was to develop the hidden relationship between Blanqui and the poet who was the central figure of Benjamin's entire work, Baudelaire. The essay was planned as the second part of a tripartite study, a more focused version of the *Passagenarbeit*, and one tentatively called *Paris, the Capital of the Nineteenth Century.* The first part was to be a discussion of Baudelaire as allegorist; the second, the section just discussed, was to be its antithesis, a social interpretation of the poet; the third part was to synthesize the first two by analyzing the commodity as poetic object.[182]

On his first reading of the draft of "The Paris of the Second Empire in Baudelaire," Adorno was critical. Vacationing in Hornberg in the Black Forest, in the summer of 1935 — Adorno occasionally returned to Germany after the Nazis took over — he wrote Benjamin a long letter outlining his objections.[183] His most general criticism was of Benjamin's allegedly undialectical use of such categories as the fetishism of commodities. As noted earlier, Adorno saw some reification as a necessary element in all human objectifications. Accordingly, he argued against Benjamin's equation of the commodity with the "archaic" as such.

Tied to this criticism was Adorno's dissatisfaction with Benjamin's use of "dialectical images" *(dialektische Bilder),* which were objective crystallizations of the historical process. In his letter, Adorno argued that as they were conceived by Benjamin, they reflected social reality too closely. Instead, he contended, "dialectical images are models not of social products, but rather objective constellations in which the social condition represents itself. Consequently, the dialectical image can never be expected to be an ideological or in general a social 'product.' "[184] Moreover, to reduce the dialectical images to a kind of Jungian collective unconscious, as Benjamin on occasion seemed to be doing, was to ignore the continued importance of the individual. "When I reject the use of the collective unconscious," Adorno explained,

> it is of course not to allow the "bourgeois individual" to stand as the actual substratum. It is to make the social function of the intérieur [a term, it will be recalled, he used in his study of Kierkegaard] transparent and to uncover its inclusiveness as illusion. But as illusion not in opposition to a hypostatized collective conscious, but the real social process itself. The "individual" is thus a dialectical instrument of passage *[Durchgangsinstrument]* which should not be mythicized away, but can only be sublated *[aufgehoben]*.[185]

In a subsequent letter to Benjamin in November, Adorno expressed his continued disappointment with the progress of the essay on Baudelaire and Paris.[186] Here he spelled out his objections to Benjamin's theological and philological approach as undialectical. "One can express it thus," he wrote. "The theological motive to name things by their names tends to be transformed into the astounding presentation of simple facticity. If one wants to speak drastically, one could say the work has settled in a crossroads between magic and positivism. This spot is bewitched. Only theory can break the spell: your own merciless, good, speculative theory." [187] As a result of his reservations, Adorno advised against accepting the essay, which Lowenthal had advocated printing in part, because it "represents you not in the way this work must represent you." [188]

Chastened, but not willing to give in entirely, Benjamin wrote back in his own defense.[189] His major argument was in favor of the philological approach employed in the essay:

> The appearance of closed facticity, which adheres to philological investigation and casts a spell on the researcher, will disappear to the extent that the object will be constructed in historical perspective. The base lines of this construction converge in our own historical experience. Therefore the object constructs itself as a monad. In the monad, everything which is mythically fixed in the text will come alive. . . . If you think back on my other work, you will find that the critique of the philogical position is an old affair with me — and innately identical with that of the myth.[190]

Adorno, however, remained unconvinced of the dialectical merit of the essay, and it was never published by the Institut.[191] In the correspondence that followed, both men continued to debate the progress of Benjamin's "prehistory" of the nineteenth century. Finally, in the first issue of the 1939 *Zeitschrift*, the section of *Paris, the Capital of the Nineteenth Century* that Benjamin had intended as its "thesis," "On Certain Motifs in Baudelaire," was published. In this essay Benjamin broached many of the basic themes of the entire study, several of which we have mentioned earlier. One of these was his distinction between two types of experiences: integrated *Erfahrungen* and atomistic *Erlebnisse.* Drawing on insights from Proust, Bergson, and Freud, Benjamin argued for the place of tradition in genuine experience: "Experience is indeed a matter of tradition, in collective existence as well as private life. It is less the product of facts firmly anchored in memory than of a convergence in memory of accumulated and frequently unconscious data." [192] Adorno also stressed the relevance of tradition, which he saw alive, it will be recalled, in Schönberg's music, despite its obvious novelty. Both he and Benjamin saw an erosion of true experience *[Erfahrungen]* as characteristic of modern life. One example that Benjamin gave — the replacement of coherent narration by dissociated information as the dominant mode of communication — was also used by Ernst Krĕnek in his essay on radio music. Another, the increase of traumatic shocks as stimuli in modern life,[193] also found an echo in the Institut's various psychosocial studies. A third, the role of the crowd in

Baudelaire's work, was a frequent motif in the Institut's work on mass culture. Benjamin, it should be noted, was somewhat critical of Baudelaire's understanding of the crowd: "Baudelaire saw fit to equate the man of the crowd . . . with the *flâneur.* It is hard to accept this view. The man of the crowd is no *flâneur.*" [194]

Benjamin's fascination with the *flâneur,* the idler who strolled leisurely through the arcades of Paris, has encouraged the commentators who stress the static element in his work.[195] Even more striking support for this position was the interest Benjamin's essay showed in Baudelaire's attempt to preserve the *correspondances* which art revealed. "What Baudelaire meant by *correspondances,*" Benjamin explained somewhat cryptically,

> may be described as an experience which seeks to establish itself in crisis-proof form. This is possible only within the realm of the ritual. If it transcends this realm, it presents itself as the beautiful. In the beautiful the ritual value of art appears. The *correspondances* are the data of remembrance — not historical data, but the data of prehistory.[196]

Elsewhere, Benjamin revealed a similar fascination with what Goethe had called *Urphänomene,* the eternal forms that persist throughout history.[197] In all of this, the theological roots of his thought would seem apparent.

Yet what also must be understood is the historical moment in his thinking, which was strengthened by his brush with Marxism. In the same essay on Baudelaire, Benjamin took Bergson to task for removing death from his notion of endured time, using an argument similar to Horkheimer's in his own essay on Bergson:[198] "The *durée* from which death has been eliminated has the miserable endlessness of a scroll. Tradition is eliminated from it. It is the quintessence of a passing moment *[Erlebnis]* that struts about in the borrowed garb of experience." [199] Moreover, as Tiedemann has pointed out,[200] the *Urphänomene* were transferred from nature in Goethe to history in Benjamin. The *Passagenarbeit* was to be a "prehistory" of the nineteenth century, not all human history. Even Benjamin's fondness for Karl Kraus's saying that "Origin is the goal," which he quotes in the "Theses on the Philosophy of History," [201] should not necessarily be understood as meaning a desire to return to a Platonic or Goethean Ur-form. Origin *(Ursprung)* can also mean newness.[202] And to Benjamin, one of the primary aspects of myth was its repetitive, uncreative sameness; the *Immergleiche* (always the same) was one of the salient characteristics of that mythic sensibility produced by alienated capitalist society.

To be fair to those who stress the static component in Benjamin's thinking, it should be added that much of what he wrote betrayed a kind of nostalgia for that ritual value he associated with the *correspondances.*[203] This was evident at the end of "On Certain Motifs in Baudelaire," where he touched on the "crisis of artistic reproduction,"[204] but it was even more obvious in his earlier essay in the *Zeitschrift*, "The Work of Art in the Era of Mechanical Reproduction." It was here that he developed his notion of the "aura," which was so frequently used in the Institut's cultural analyses. As mentioned earlier, the aura was the unique nimbus that surrounded an original work of art. It was the special sense of *hic et nunc,* (here and now) giving authenticity to the work. It also existed, Benjamin suggested, in nature, where it was "the unique phenomenon of a distance, however close it may be."[205] In art as well, this quality of unapproachability was an essential element in a work's aura, not unconnected with the ritual, magical context out of which art originally came. It was this unique aura of a genuine work of art that could not be preserved once the art was reproduced — clearly, Benjamin was referring more to the plastic arts than to music or drama, although, as we have seen in Adorno's and Křenek's discussions of radio, music might also have an aura.

Whatever the prehistoric, ritual quality attached to the aura, Benjamin also acknowledged its historical element, which went beyond the *correspondances.* "The authenticity of a thing," he contended, "is the essence of all that is transmissible from its beginning, ranging from its substantive duration to its testimony to the history which it has experienced."[206] And later in the same essay: "The uniqueness of a work of art is inseparable from its being imbedded in the fabric of tradition."[207] Thus the end of "auratic" art in the era of mass reproduction meant not merely the loss of the artistic *correspondances,* but also the end of *Erfahrung* (experience rooted in tradition). It was this aspect of the cultural crisis of modern society with which Benjamin's colleagues at the Institut were in agreement. They also tended to accept the conclusion he drew from the loss of aura: "The instant the criterion of authenticity ceases to be applicable to artistic production, the total function of art is reversed. Instead of being based on ritual, it begins to be based on another practice — politics."[208] With the advent of mechanical reproduction, the cult value of an art work was replaced by its exhibition value. The best example of this, Benjamin asserted, was the film.

Where the other members of the Institut, especially Adorno, disagreed with Benjamin was in assessing the repercussions of this change. First of all, they had always considered art to have a political function: the presentation of a foretaste of the "other" society denied by present conditions. What they now feared was that mass art had a new political function diametrically opposed to its traditionally "negative" one; art in the age of mechanical reproduction served to reconcile the mass audience to the status quo. Here Benjamin disagreed. For, while mourning the loss of the aura, he paradoxically held out hope for the progressive potential of politicized, collectivized art. Here once again he followed the lead of Brecht, who was still optimistic about the revolutionary function of the film, despite his personally disappointing experiences with the film industry.[209] In Benjamin's words:

> Mechanical reproduction of art changes the reaction of the masses toward art. The reactionary attitude toward a Picasso painting changes into the progressive reaction toward a Chaplin movie. The progressive reaction is characterized by the direct, intimate fusion of visual and emotional enjoyment with the orientation of the expert. . . . With regard to the screen, the critical and the receptive attitudes of the public coincide.[210]

Moreover, whereas Adorno always demanded concentration on the part of the viewer or listener — we have already mentioned his stress on the *praxis* of genuine aesthetic reception — Benjamin was more sympathetic to the positive implications of distraction: "The tasks which face the human apparatus of perception at the turning points of history cannot be solved . . . by contemplation alone. They are mastered gradually by habit. . . . The ability to master certain tasks in a state of distraction proves that their solution has become a matter of habit."[211] It was on this assumption that Benjamin could end his article by calling for the Communist politicization of art as a response to what he called the fascist "aestheticization of politics."[212]

Adorno, as we have seen, was far less sanguine, and responded to Benjamin in his article "On the Fetish Character of Music and the Regression of Hearing." Benjamin tried to patch things up by writing: "In my work I sought to articulate the positive moments as clearly as you brought the negative to the fore. I consequently see a strength of your work where a weakness of mine lay."[213] He then suggested that sound films were undermining the revolutionary potential of the cinema and proposed to Adorno a collaborative study of their effects. This, however, was never to occur, because of Benjamin's death. The Institut's subsequent work on mass culture, in the forties, to which we now turn, lacked the optimistic thrust of his analysis. The spirit of that work was far closer to that expressed in the now famous remark Benjamin made in an earlier period (and which was used much later to end Marcuse's *One-Dimensional Man*): "It is only for the sake of those without hope that hope is given to us."[214]

In the forties, a number of Institut members devoted their time to investigating American popular culture. In 1941 the *Studies in Philosophy and Social Science* put out a special issue on mass communications, in cooperation with Lazarsfeld's Office of Radio Research, now at Columbia. Horkheimer began, with "Notes on Institute Activities," which contained the most concise restatement of the principles of Critical Theory to appear in English. Lazarsfeld contributed a comparison of "Administrative and Critical Communications Research," which stressed their compatible features. Articles followed by Herta Herzog, Harold Lasswell, William Dieterle, Charles A. Siepmann, and Adorno.[215] In the next issue, the last of the *Studies* to appear, Horkheimer used Mortimer Adler's *Art and Prudence* as an occasion for a general denunciation of mass culture,[216] many of whose points we have already incorporated into our treatment of the Institut's work in this area.

The member of the Institut who became most extensively engaged in the analysis of mass culture was Leo Lowenthal. As early as 1929 Lowenthal had written regular drama criticism and articles on aesthetic problems for the *Volksbühne*, in both Berlin and Frankfurt. Although his early articles in the *Zeitschrift* were primarily on literary figures such as Ibsen and Meyer, he was also interested in the popular reception of high culture, as illustrated by his essay on Dostoyevsky's public in prewar Germany. In the forties he turned his attention to more direct examples of popular art. With the help of Lazarsfeld's project, which supplied him with secretarial and office assistance, he conducted analyses of news commentators and news programs in Philadelphia, which remained in manuscript form. He also made a content analysis of popular biographies in Germany after World War I, which was published many years later in a *Festschrift* for Marcuse.[217] His similar treatment of biographies in American magazines appeared in Lazarsfeld's *Radio Research: 1942–1943*.[218] Lowenthal also contributed to the discussions that led to the essay on the *Kulturindustrie* (Culture Industry) in *Dialectic of the Enlightenment.* In fact, throughout the forties and during the period after his connection with the Institut was severed, Lowenthal continued his exploration of mass culture, the culmination of which was his collection of essays published in 1961, *Literature, Popular Culture, and Society.*

Fragments of the correspondence between Horkheimer and Lowenthal after the former had moved to California are worth dwelling on here for the light they cast on the Institut's conception of mass culture. On February 3, 1942, Lowenthal wrote of his forthcoming essay on magazine biographies:

While, on the one hand, historical information for the masses becomes a cobweb of lies and of ridiculous accumulation of the most insignificant facts and figures, the same masses show by their very occupation with these people and with their ways of "consumption" a longing for a life of innocence. From my whole inner life I can deduct more and more how hateful the whole idea of production in the sense of permanent changes, transformations, incessant treatment of man and nature by machines and organizations must become to the unconscious and even conscious life of the majority. In a certain sense, the German biographies which I have studied in former years and the American material belong quite closely together. The first one falsifies history by an enchanting net of profound metaphysical and metapsychological phantasmagories; the second one is just the reverse and instead of taking history serious, it takes it funny *[sic]*. But: they both represent distorted utopias of a concept of man to which we stand in an affirmative way, namely, they both imply the unconditional importance of the real, living, and existing individual: dignity, happiness.

Several months later, Horkheimer mentioned the essay in one of his letters to Lowenthal. On June 2 he wrote, referring to his own work on *Dialectic of the Enlightenment*:

I was particularly delighted by the paragraphs on "repetition." This category will play a most decisive role in the whole book. What you call the lack of rebellion against the eternal repetition in life and art points to the bad resignation of modern man, which is, so to speak, the main topic between your lines and which will become one of the basic concepts of our book. . . . We cannot blame people that they are more interested in the sphere of privacy and consumption rather than [in] production. This trait contains a Utopian element; in Utopia production does not play a decisive part. It is the land of milk and honey. I think it is of deep significance that art and poetry have always shown an affinity to consumption.

On October 14 Horkheimer spent a large part of his letter to Lowenthal discussing the article:

You lay too much stress on activity vs. passivity, sphere of production vs. sphere of consumption. You say that the life of the reader is scheduled and governed by what he gets, not by what he does. The truth is, however, that doing and getting [have] become identical in this society. The mechanisms which govern man in his leisure time are absolutely the same [as] those which govern him when he works. I would go as far as to say that still today the key for the understanding of the behavior patterns in the sphere of consumption is the situation of man in industry, his schedule in the factory, the organization of office and working place. Consumption tends to vanish today, or should I say, eating, drinking, looking, loving, sleeping become "consumption," for consumption already means that man has become a machine outside as well as inside of the workshop?

You will remember those terrible scenes in the movies when some years of a hero's life are pictured in a series of shots which take about one or two minutes, just to show how he grew up or old, how a war started and passed by, a[nd] s[o] o[n]. This trimming of an existence into some futile moments which can be characterized schematically symbolizes the dissolution of humanity into elements of administration. Mass culture in its different branches reflects the fact that the human being is cheated out of his own entity which Bergson so justly called "durée." This is true for the heroes of biographies as well as for the masses. . . . The countertrend in mass culture is represented in escape from it. Since man's wakeful state today is regulated in all details, the real escape is sleep or madness, or at least some kind of shortcoming and weakness. The protest against the movies is not found so much in bitter critiques but in the fact that people go in and sleep or make love to each other.

And finally, Lowenthal responded to Horkheimer's arguments in his return letter on October 22:

Your remark about the montage of a life story in the moving picture is especially revealing for me, because it throws more light on my observation of the isolated and piecemeal sequence of hardship and breaks of childhood and adult life. All this seems to be also tied up with the concept of lovelessness, because the criterion of love is continuity and this is just the phenomenon which is never admitted. Mass culture is a total conspiracy against love as well as against sex. I think that you have hit the nail on the head by your observation that the spectators are continuously betrayed and robbed of real pleasure by sadistic tricks. This sadism has the special function to prevent psychologically and physiologically "Vorlust." Take, for example, the ballet scene in "Holiday Inn," one of the newest pictures, where a couple starts dancing a minuet, but as soon as this minuet develops to a more amorous situation and one could very well imagine that the dancing partners will end by kissing each other, the sweet and melodious music is suddenly stopped and replaced by jazz which almost verbally castrates the dancers. This fits very well together with the elucidating remarks which Teddie [Adorno] once wrote about the connection of castration and jazz.

A number of characteristics of the Institut's critique of mass culture are evident in the interchange. More than once, for example, is its concern for genuine happiness evident. Unlike more conservative critics of popular culture, the Frankfurt School refused to defend high culture as an end in itself apart from material concerns. Like Nietzsche, whose seminal contribution to the analysis of mass culture the Institut often acknowledged, Horkheimer and his colleagues saw a subterranean connection between the notion of transcendent culture, which pretended to be above material life, and psychological asceticism. They consistently attacked such commentators as Aldous Huxley for the puritanical streak in their protest against mass culture.[219] With equal fervor they denounced the nostalgic yearnings of elitist critics such as Jose Ortega y Gasset. "The right to nostalgia, to transcendental knowledge, to a dangerous life cannot be validated," Horkheimer wrote. "The struggle against mass culture can consist only in pointing out its connection with the persistence of social injustice." [220] As Marcuse argued in 1937, the segregation of cultural life from its material base served to reconcile man to the inequalities implicit in the latter; idealist, bourgeois culture was in this sense "affirmative."

What the letters also show is how strongly the Institut, for all its Marxist tendencies, valued tradition. As we have already seen, Adorno spoke of the traditional component in Schönberg's seemingly revolutionary music, and Benjamin considered tradition to be a part of an art work's aura. In his letter of October 22 Lowenthal referred to continuity as the "criterion of love," an observation that followed on the heels of Horkheimer's assertion in the previous letter that mass culture deprived man of his *durée.* What should be understood, however, is that by tradition, the Institut meant something very different from the continuation of "progress," as it was understood by Enlightenment thought. This was clear in the essay "Authoritarian State," which we examined in the previous chapter, as well as in the *Dialectic of the Enlightenment*, to which we shall come presently. Tradition referred to the type of integrated experience the Institut members called *Erfahrung*, which was being destroyed by so-called "progress."

Yet another thing the letters demonstrate is the effect of personal experiences on the Frankfurt School's analysis. That such a connection existed, Critical Theory would not have denied. As Horkheimer wrote in his letter on Freud, "the greater a work, the more it is rooted in the concrete historical situation." [221] As refugees from Central Europe, who had been tutored in all that its rich cultural heritage had to offer, they were inevitably ill at ease in the less rarified atmosphere of their new environment. On occasion, this alienation meant an unresponsiveness to the spontaneous elements in American popular culture — Adorno's unremitting hostility to jazz, for example, suffers from a certain a priori insensitivity. But at the same time, it provided an invaluable critical distance from the culture, which prevented the Institut from equating mass culture with true democracy. The category of "repressive desublimation," [222] which Marcuse was to develop years later to characterize the pseudo-liberation of modern culture, existed in embryo in the personal experience of the Institut's members. Having known an alternative cultural milieu, they were unwilling to trade in its *promesse de bonheur* for the debased coin provided by the culture industry.

As Adorno later explained,[223] the phrase "culture industry" was chosen by Horkheimer and himself in *Dialectic of the Enlightenment* because of its antipopulist connotations. The Frankfurt School disliked mass culture, not because it was democratic, but precisely because it was not. The notion of "popular" culture, they argued, was ideological; the culture industry administered a nonspontaneous, reified, phony culture rather than the real thing. The old distinction between high and low culture had all but vanished in the "stylized barbarism" [224] of mass culture. Even the most "negative" examples of classical art had been absorbed into what Marcuse was later to call its "one-dimensional" facade. Tragedy, which once meant protest, now meant consolation. The subliminal message of almost all that passed for art was conformity and resignation.

As in so many other areas, the Institut believed that liberal platitudes about the preservation of the autonomous individual had been rendered obsolete by social change. Kant had defined art formalistically as "purposiveness without purpose," but in the modern world it had become "purposelessness for purposes," purposes dictated by the market.[225] Even the excuse of popular art as diversion, which Benjamin had supported, Adorno and Horkheimer thought suspect: leisure was the continuation of labor by other means. The only laughter permitted by the culture industry was the derisiveness of *Schadenfreude*, laughing at the misfortunes of others. Suppression replaced sublimation, desire was aroused only to be denied; mass culture, in short, followed the ritual of Tantalus.[226]

Increasingly, the Institut came to feel that the culture industry enslaved men in far more subtle and effective ways than the crude methods of domination practiced in earlier eras. The false harmony of particular and universal was in some ways more sinister than the clash of social contradictions, because of its ability to lull its victims into passive acceptance. With the decline of mediating forces in the society — here the Institut drew on its earlier studies of the lessening role of the family in the process of socialization — the chances for the development of negative resistance were seriously diminished.

Moreover, the spread of technology served the culture industry in America just as it helped tighten the control of authoritarian governments in Europe. Radio, Horkheimer and Adorno argued, was to fascism as the printing press had been to the Reformation.

In short, all the celebrated pessimism of Marcuse's *One-Dimensional Man* was anticipated in the essay on the culture industry in *Dialectic of the Enlightenment*. The only hint of negation preserved in mass culture Horkheimer and Adorno allowed was in corporeal rather than intellectual art: for example, the circus performer, whose fully reified body promised to break through the commodity character of mass art by carrying objectification to its extreme, thereby exposing what had hitherto been veiled.[227] Aside from this, the Institut feared the closing-off of all possibilities for a transformed future, short of that "explosion in the continuum of history" that the essays in the Benjamin memorial volume had still been able to cite as a possibility.

In many ways, the Institut's critique of mass culture and its related analysis of the American authoritarian potential had the greatest impact on American intellectual life of all the work it did in this country.[228] One obvious reason was that, unlike the theoretical essays of the thirties, much of it was written in English. But more important, it came at a time when Americans themselves had begun to fear the realization of those dire prophecies that foreign visitors since Tocqueville had made about the effects of mass democracy.[229] Before the Second World War, sociologists like Robert Park and his pupil at the University of Chicago, Herbert Blumer, had been engaged in rudimentary studies of mass society, but generally in isolation and with more hopeful conclusions. By the mid-forties, however, the interest in this type of analysis had grown both within and outside the academic community. Clement Greenberg and Dwight MacDonald, the latter through his influential journal, *Politics*, began to disseminate a critique of mass culture among a wider public. Sociologists like David Riesman increased scholarly awareness of the same issues.[230] Richard Hoggart did the same for English-speaking readers across the Atlantic.[231] For the first time, popular culture was attacked from a radical rather than a conservative direction. Here the Institut's influence, and that of former members such as Fromm, played a significant role in adding substance and depth to the attack, and it was frequently acknowledged.

What was crucial in the radical critique was its implicit political overtones. It would be a mistake to interpret the Institut's shifting of focus from base to superstructure as an abandonment of its commitment to the ideals of its earlier period. The decline of traditional, "negative" culture was not a matter for intellectuals alone. Mass culture was the seed-bed of political totalitarianism. The mediating mechanisms between culture and politics were best understood, so Horkheimer and those around him felt, in psychosocial terms. Their studies of popular culture were thus connected with the investigations of the authoritarian potential in America that they conducted in the forties. These investigations were cast primarily as psychological analyses, although always based on the broader assumptions of Critical Theory. Because these theoretical premises were rarely understood by American commentators, however, the "Studies in Prejudice" were often taken as strictly psychological. As we shall see in our next chapter, this was not the case. As Adorno had explained to Benjamin in 1935, the bourgeois individual was only a dialectical *Durchgangsinstrument* (instrument of transition); the totality remained the central reality. If in its studies of mass culture and psychological authoritarianism the Institut seemed to fall back on the embattled individual, it was only because the utopian alternative they sought was preserved nowhere else but in the "damaged lives" [232] of cultural outsiders.

VII

The Empirical Work of the Institut in the 1940's

> The central theme of the work is a relatively new concept — the rise of an "anthropological" species we call the authoritarian type of man.
>
> — Max Horkheimer

The war years brought a serious reevaluation of the Institut's goals and a gradual redefinition of its institutional structure. Horkheimer's circulatory illness, which necessitated the move to California, and the increased involvement of other Institut members in government service meant that the type of connection with Columbia enjoyed by the Institut since 1934 was no longer possible. Moreover, a new internal factor within the university's sociology department spelled potential trouble for the future. The struggle for control between the department's more speculative wing, led by Robert MacIver, and its empirically oriented counterpart around Robert Lynd had been resolved largely in favor of the latter. Or at least so Lowenthal reported to Horkheimer by letter on January 23, 1942. Thus, not surprisingly, Horkheimer was willing to permit the loosening of the Institut's ties with Columbia brought by the war and his illness. In fact, as early as May, 1941, before the resolution of the Lynd-MacIver conflict, he had expressed to Lowenthal ambivalence about the consequences of the sustained relationship with Columbia.[1] The leadership of the Institut, despite its awareness of the need to maintain an institutional identity, was always concerned about the possible sclerosis that over-institutionalization might bring.

Still, with the end of the war, an attempt was made to keep the Institut on Morningside Heights. Horkheimer's illness had become less of an immediate worry, allowing him to come back to New York in 1944 and 1945 for extended periods of time. Although certain Institut members, such as Marcuse, chose to remain with the government, others were eager to return to a full academic life. Within Columbia hopes were still alive to retain the Institut in some capacity. Ironically, the major effort to revive the Institut's connection came from within the ranks of the empirical sociologists. Paul Lazarsfeld, who had transformed his Office of Radio Research into a newly constituted Bureau of Applied Social Research,[2] suggested the integration of the Institut into his bureau. Despite the failure of his collaboration with Adorno before the war, Lazarsfeld was optimistic about the interaction of Critical Theory with his own brand of "administrative research." [3] In a series of letters to other members of the department, such as Theodore Abel and Robert Merton, Lazarsfeld extolled the Institut's accomplishments. On February 5, 1946, he wrote to Abel that the department had done an injustice to the Institut, but not because of the former's own shortsightedness:

> the whole mess is due to the idiocy of the Institute group. I told them for years that publishing in German will finally destroy them. But they had the fixed idea that their contribution to America will be greater if they preserve in this country the last island of German culture. This is especially true of their *Zeitschrift*. I have asked Lowenthal, its former editor, to make a brief content analysis of the ten volumes which have appeared in this country. Everyone will be surprised how much of value is buried there.[4]

As a solution, he proposed the affiliation of the Institut's empirical wing with the Bureau of Applied Social Research. Lowenthal, Massing, and Marcuse were to have full-time memberships; Pollock and Neumann, part-time. Horkheimer, because of his health, and Adorno were expected to remain in California in what presumably would be the Institut's speculative rump. Lazarsfeld left the door open for at least Horkheimer's return if his condition improved. Although the sociology department acted on Lazarsfeld's recommendation and extended an invitation to the Institut, it was ultimately declined, Horkheimer citing his health as the reason.[5] Of all the Institut members, only Neumann chose to return to Columbia after the immediate postwar period.

One probable reason for the Institut's decision to refuse the offer was the improvement of its financial position. As mentioned earlier, in 1938 unsuccessful financial investments combined with the extended use of capital for the support of new refugees had seriously depleted the Institut's resources. During the next few years, foundation sponsorship for a projected study of German culture proved unavailable, and the *Studies in Philosophy and Social Science* were discontinued, primarily for financial reasons. The situation was critical enough for Horkheimer to speculate in a letter to Lowenthal on the possible dissolution of the Institut if no sponsor were found. A grant must be obtained, Horkheimer wrote, "otherwise the work for which we live and which, I suppose, is your aim as well as mine — not only the work but our lives as scholars with specific tasks and responsibilities — and not only our intellectual lives but the material basis of our lives — will be destroyed."[6] During the summer of 1942, however, a contact had been made with the American Jewish Committee, and in October of the same year Horkheimer had a successful interview with John Slawson, the AJC's executive vice-president. As early as 1939 the Institut had prepared a prospectus for a study of anti-Semitism, which was printed in the penultimate issue of its journal.[7] Not unexpectedly, the AJC expressed an interest in the project, with the hope of preventing in America what was already happening in Europe. The result was a grant of considerable size, which helped to keep the Institut together as well as to finance the most exhaustive study of prejudice ever attempted. In May, 1944, a two-day conference on prejudice was held in New York, at which an ambitious research program was outlined for the future. At the same time, the AJC established a Department of Scientific Research, with Horkheimer at its head. It was here that the *Studies in Prejudice*, which were to employ a variety of methodological approaches to the study of social bias, were officially launched. Thus began the Institut's most extensive and sustained concentration on empirical research.

What ought not to be forgotten, however, was that at the same time, Horkheimer and Adorno were engaged in serious speculative work, which produced a number of important new statements of Critical Theory. Foremost among these were their joint effort in *Dialectic of the Enlightenment*, Horkheimer's *Eclipse of Reason*, and Adorno's *Minima Moralia*. These will be the subject of the next chapter, which will deal with the Institut's changing theoretical perspective in its last decade in America. At times, however, some of their new ideas will play a role in our present discussion of the empirical work, and we shall also refer on a number of occasions to the analysis of the Institut's critique of mass culture in the last chapter.

Before embarking on a detailed analysis of the *Studies in Prejudice*, certain basic attitudes of the Institut towards the proper role of empirical research should once again be made clear. From the first, it will be recalled, the Frankfurt School was critical of the reductionist tendencies implicit in inductively oriented, empirical social science. In the exploration of social phenomena, it placed theory prior to the gathering of "facts," just as in politics it put theory before *praxis*. At the same time, of course, it was never satisfied with the cavalier dismissal of all empirical research, including the quantification of results, which characterized certain of the more obscurantist German sociological schools. As Fromm's study of German workers and the *Studien über Autorität und Familie* demonstrated, it was anxious to use empirical methods for the enrichment, modification, and support (although never quite verification) of its speculative hypotheses. Although the Institut admitted the primitive level of its techniques before the emigration, it looked forward to their growing sophistication with time. Thus it willingly sponsored such studies as Mirra Komarovsky's analysis of *The Unemployed Man and His Family*, and sought to apply American techniques to the study of mass culture.

The difficulties, however, often proved greater than expected, as Adorno's experience with the Office of Radio Research demonstrated. His ideas about the changes in music-listening patterns, which were described in the previous chapter, proved untranslatable into testable hypotheses. The reasons, so Adorno felt, were not merely technical. Three decades later, he wrote:

> It appeared to me, and I am still persuaded today, that in the cultural sphere what is regarded by the psychology of perception as a mere "stimulus" is, in fact, qualitatively determined, a matter of "objective spirit" and knowable in its objectivity. I oppose stating and measuring effects without relating them to these "stimuli," i.e., the objective content to which the consumers in the cultural industry, the radio listeners, react. . . . To proceed from the subjects' reactions, as if they were a primary and final source of sociological knowledge, seemed to me thoroughly superficial and misguided.[8]

What caused Adorno particular distress was the unmediated way in which cultural phenomena were transformed by his new American colleagues into quantitative data. The very equation of culture with measurable quantities seemed to him a prime example of the reification characteristic of mass culture. "When I was confronted with the demand to 'measure culture,' " he later recalled, "I reflected that culture might be precisely that condition that excludes a mentality capable of measuring it." [9] This was an assumption that made his collaboration with Lazarsfeld, whose "administrative research" was grounded in the rigorous use of quantitative methods, unlikely to succeed from the start. By the summer of 1939 this was clear to both men.

Lazarsfeld wrote a five-page letter to Adorno voicing his extreme disappointment with the outcome of their association.[10] Its tone was pointed, even harsh at times. Clearly Lazarsfeld felt the time for euphemism was past. Referring to one of Adorno's memoranda, he wrote:

> You pride yourself in attacking other people because they are neurotic and fetishists, but it doesn't occur to you how open you are yourself to such attacks. . . . Don't you think that [it] is a perfect fetishism the way you use Latin words all through the text? . . . I implored you repeatedly to use more responsible language and you evidently were psychologically unable to follow my advice.

At other points in the letter, Lazarsfeld went beyond personal criticism to attack Adorno's "grave deficiencies of elementary logical procedure." He also accused Adorno of both arrogance and naiveté when it came to his remarks on verification techniques: "Your disrespect for possibilities alternative to your own ideas becomes even more disquieting when your text leads to the suspicion that you don't even know how an empirical check upon a hypothetical assumption is to be made." And finally, he expressed extreme dismay at the stylistic deficiencies in Adorno's texts, which were all the more disturbing in view of Adorno's frequently asserted concern for the importance of correct language.

Lazarsfeld's last paragraph deserves full quotation, not only for the light it casts on this specific instance of a conflict between two strong-willed, highly intelligent scholars with differing views, but also for the insight it provides into the complex character of one of the men who played a central role in the Institut's history. Few men who knew Adorno doubted his intellectual brilliance and imaginative powers; fewer still — and here Horkheimer was the major exception — found him an easy collaborator. "It was not a pleasant task to write this letter," Lazarsfeld concluded,

> and I would not have spent two solid working days in working it out if I didn't feel that it is vital for our project to make you think yourself about the whole situation. You and I agree upon the superiority of some parts of your intellectual work but you think because you are basically right somewhere you are right everywhere. Whereas I think that because you are right somewhere you overlook the fact that you are terrible in other respects, and the final reader will think that because you are outrageous in some part of your work where he can easily catch you, you are impossible altogether. So I am sure that what I have done in this letter will be finally beneficial for yourself. . . . Let me assure you once more of my unwavering respect, friendship, and loyalty.

When the Rockefeller Foundation reviewed its grant for the Radio Research Project in the fall of 1939, the music project was omitted from its budget. Later, in a more mellow frame of mind, Lazarsfeld ruminated on the failure of his collaboration with Adorno.[11] The success of *The Authoritarian Personality* had demonstrated that Critical Theory and quantification were not as irreconcilable as the music project had made it seem. "I have an uneasy feeling," Lazarsfeld generously wrote, "that my duties in the various divisions of the Princeton project may have prevented me from devoting the necessary time and attention to achieve the purpose for which I engaged Adorno originally." [12]

Whatever the real reasons, the music project was unsuccessful, while *The Authoritarian Personality* became a classic of social science immediately after its completion. The explanation for this change cannot be sought solely in Adorno's own development — he was only one of a large number of coworkers on the second project — but with time, he did gain valuable methodological experience that caused a modification of his initial hostility to American techniques. Thus, for example, his stress on grasping the "objective spirit" rather than measuring subjective reactions to it had diminished by the end of the decade. As we shall see, the "objective" dimension of prejudice was by no means ignored, but it was never fully integrated into the subjective analyses of his and the Institut's work on the problem. Culture might not be measurable, but it seemed as if bias more easily could be.

Adorno, of course, was not the only one who gained methodological experience in the early forties. The New York branch of the Institut, although reducing its activities during the war, did not cease to function. After the closing of the *Studies in Philosophy and Social Science*, several of its members began to spend more time with empirical work. One of their projects was an inquiry into the pattern of help extended by German gentiles to Jewish victims of Hitler. With the prestigious cosponsorship of Thomas Mann, data was collected by such means as advertisements in the *Aufbau*, the leading German-language refugee newspaper. Although never published, the study did show that Catholics and conservatives had given more assistance than Protestants and liberals. According to Paul Massing, this conclusion was later used by Horkheimer to support his argument that conservatives were often better preservers of critical ideals than liberals.[13]

Far more ambitious was a massive study of the degree of anti-Semitism within American labor, which the Institut began to organize in 1943 and carried out in the following two years. At about the same time as the American Jewish Committee had extended its offer of support, the Jewish Labor Committee, chaired by Adolph Held, made a grant of somewhat more modest proportions available for research into its own special area of interest. The JLC had created a Committee to Combat Anti-Semitism with Charles S. Zimmerman as its head and was anxious to begin with a scientific analysis of the problem. Its contacts with the AFL, the CIO, and various nonaffiliated unions facilitated the collection of data, which was carried on in New York, California, and Detroit.

The amount of data accumulated was, in fact, so overwhelming that the Institut had difficulty in organizing it for publication. A four-volume, 1300-page report was made to the JLC in 1944, but subsequent efforts to whittle it down to publishable size failed. Gurland, Massing, Lowenthal, Pollock, and Weil had been involved in the original collection and analysis of the material. Added help from Herta Herzog of the Bureau of Applied Social Research was obtained for the quantification of the data, and Adorno wrote frequent memoranda, methodological and substantive, throughout its progress. The problems of organization and editing, however, remained insurmountable. After allowing the study to lie fallow for several years, renewed efforts were made in 1949. Paul Lazarsfeld and Allen Barton were recruited to write a methodological introduction. By 1953, the Free Press of Glencoe announced its forthcoming publication with a description of the contents, which were predominantly devoted to a qualitative analysis of anti-Semitic belief patterns. But disagreements within the Institut about the value of presenting a study made almost a decade earlier persisted,[14] with the final result that the book never went to press.

Because of the publication of the *Studies in Prejudice* in the interim, the findings of the labor project now seemed redundant. Its goal was therefore changed, as Adorno wrote in one of his memoranda; it was now "to find out how to study anti-Semitism, not to obtain final results." [15] But here once again, the methodological achievements of the various volumes in the *Studies in Prejudice* overshadowed the more primitive techniques the earlier report had developed. Moreover, another reason for the Institut's general reluctance to publish the work had an effect. As Pollock remembers it,[16] the conclusions of the study were so damaging to American labor that the Institut, with its characteristic caution, was hesitant about broadcasting its findings. As early as July, 1944, as mentioned earlier, Horkheimer had worried about the reaction of American domestic opinion to "a bunch of foreign-born intellectuals sticking their noses into the private affairs of American workers." [17] More than half the workers surveyed had shown anti-Semitic bias of one sort or another,[18] but in 1953 the Institut's leadership wished to tone this down. Moreover, the attempts to shorten the manuscript had resulted in certain oversimplifications. Massing wrote to Lowenthal of his indignation at the changes:

> I most seriously object to these "Conclusions." These pages show the transformation the study has undergone from a socio-political to a purely psychological one. In the present version, there cannot be any such old-fashioned remarks as to "danger signals," need for education, and any reference to "American Labor" is outright ludicrous. The American labor that appears in part I of the present study is anti-Semitic.

The revisions of the first part of the study, he charged, had ruined it: "It reads like a mediocre high-school attempt, operates with two or three broad psychological concepts which are ridden to death, is repetitive to the *n*th degree . . ." [19] Apparently, Barton, who with Lazarsfeld was to write the methodological introduction, felt the same way.[20] For all these reasons, Horkheimer ultimately decided to withdraw the book from publication.

Still, the goal expressed by Adorno in his memorandum was in fact attained to a significant extent. What the Institut learned most clearly was the necessity of approaching anti-Semitism as indirectly as possible. Sample populations in factories on both coasts and in the Midwest were examined in basically the same way. Instead of distributing questionnaires or conducting direct interviews, "screened" interviews were developed, in which the objective of the project was concealed as much as possible. This meant that 270 workers in the factories were selected as agents of the project. They were instructed to memorize a prepared set of questions which they used to probe the reactions of workers when anti-Semitic or related incidents occurred. A total of 566 interviews were conducted and the results broken down by such categories as ethnic background, union or nonunion membership, AFL or CIO. Much of the material gathered in this way and some of the questions were later used in the interviews for *The Authoritarian Personality.*[21] Moreover, the conceptual structuring of the findings contributed to the refinement of the typologies developed in the later work. Thus, although in one sense stillborn, the project proved an important testing ground for the Institut's more ambitious work for the AJC.

Before turning to the specific studies that were a part of the *Studies in Prejudice*, certain comments about their relation to the Institut's general outlook should be made. On the surface, it appears as if the *Studies* were a radical departure from some of the basic tenets of the Critical Theory. In certain ways this was true. The caution we have seen displayed in America by the Institut on a number of occasions was unmistakably apparent in its empirical work in the forties. For example, the opposite of the "authoritarian personality" was no longer the "revolutionary," as it had been in the *Studien über Autorität und Familie*, it was now the "democratic" instead. The values expressed by the various authors connected with the *Studies*, especially those foreign to the Institut's ways of thinking, were invariably liberal and New Deal rather than Marxist or radical. Education for tolerance, rather than *praxis* for revolutionary change, was the ostensible goal of the research, which aroused the scorn of more orthodox Marxists like Brecht.[22] "Our aim is not merely to describe prejudice," Horkheimer and Samuel Flowerman wrote in the Introduction to the *Studies*, "but to explain it in order to help in its eradication. That is the challenge we would meet. Eradication means reeducation, scientifically planned on the basis of understanding scientifically arrived at. And education in a strict sense is by its nature personal and psychological." [23] Nowhere in any of the volumes did the critique of tolerance for its own sake, which had first appeared in Fromm's work on Freud and was later repeated by Adorno and Marcuse, make an appearance.

But perhaps what seemed most characteristic of the change in emphasis was an unwonted stress on psychological rather than sociological explanations of prejudice, a choice deliberately made in connection with the pedagogical goals of the project.[24] This was so pronounced that two of *The Authoritarian Personality*'s most serious critics, Herbert H. Hyman and Paul B. Sheatsley, could argue that its authors "take the irrationality out of the social order and impute it to the respondent, and by means of this substitution it is decided that prejudiced respondents derive their judgments in an irrational way." [25] If this were true, then Critical Theory had certainly gone a long way towards abandoning its original position. Further evidence of the dilution of its radical component could be found in the type of psychological analysis actually used in the various studies. Although the basic perspective was Freudian, a certain measure of ego psychology was added to the analytic framework, the same ego psychology of Hartmann and Kris whose conformist implications Adorno criticized elsewhere.[26] Similarly, the use made in *The Authoritarian Personality* of a character typology seemed at first glance to contradict Adorno's critique of Fromm's typology.[27] By describing integrated character types, he and his colleagues appeared to be abandoning that insistence on nonidentity that was one of the central tenets of Critical Theory. Adorno, to be sure, attempted to answer this criticism in advance by defending the use of a typology on historical grounds:

> The reason for the persistent plausibility of the typological approach, however, is not a static biological one, but just the opposite: dynamic and social. . . . The marks of social repression are left within the individual soul. . . . Individualism, opposed to human pigeonholing, may ultimately become a mere ideological veil in a society which actually *is* inhuman. . . . In other words, the critique of typology should not neglect the fact that large numbers of people are no longer, or rather never were, "individuals" in the sense of traditional nineteenth-century philosophy.[28]

This, however, might explain the use of a typology to explain reified personalities, but not those who still retained some authentic subjectivity. These, presumably, would be the more tolerant, but Adorno used a typology to describe them as well.

In general, however, the situation was considerably more complicated than a cursory reading of the *Studies in Prejudice* suggested. First of all, the Institut's Marxist origins, although altered in a manner that will be examined in the next chapter, were not obliterated entirely. Evidence of their persistence appeared in a number of ways outside the work itself. Occasionally, for example, an Institut member would make a remark that showed how reluctant he was to take sides in the incipient Cold War. Thus, in 1946, Horkheimer could write, in terms that would later appear naive, that "at present the only country where there does not seem to be any kind of anti-Semitism is Russia. This has a very obvious reason. Not only has Russia passed laws against anti-Semitism, but it really enforces them; and the penalties are very severe." [29] At about the same time, he defined for Lowenthal "the task of theory in this historical period" in a way that made clear his priorities:

> Deserving as it may be to point out the horrors of German or Russian despotism, the effort of conceptual thinking has, in my opinion, still to be concerned with the social development in industrialized society as a whole. To conceive the horror is as horrible as to see the night. The horror in the human world should be understood as the verdict against specific forms of social self-preservation. Today the world has become too much of a totality as to justify the isolation of one power block so as to oppose it to the rest of civilization as good or bad, or better or worse. Such a procedure is justified in practical respects but not when it comes to theoretical thinking. Here, I must say the principle of the lesser evil is even more dangerous than in politics.[30]

In short, although the Institut refused to provide excuses for Stalinism — by no means a new development in its history — it also refused to join the chorus of apostate former Marxists in excoriating the "God that failed." Its critique extended to "industrialized society as a whole," which certainly included the United States.

More important from a methodological point of view, the psychological emphasis of the *Studies in Prejudice* did not represent as much of a break with Critical Theory as some of its critics on the left assumed. In fact, frequent reminders ran throughout the volumes, especially those sections written by Adorno, that prejudice had to be understood on its most basic level as a social rather than an individual problem. For example, in his discussion of personalization in politics, he wrote: "Ever more anonymous and opaque social processes make it increasingly difficult to integrate the limited sphere of one's personal life experience with objective social dynamics. Social alienation is hidden by a surface phenomenon in which the very opposite is being stressed: personalization of political attitudes and habits offers compensation for the dehumanization of the social sphere, which is at the bottom of most of today's grievances." [31] Despite Hyman and Sheatsley's contention, the Frankfurt School continued to see the social order as inherently irrational. Thus, at no time was the sufficiency of a psychological approach suggested. What was problematical, however, and what caused so much confusion was the proper roles of sociology and psychology in analyzing the phenomenon of prejudice. Although never spelled out explicitly in the *Studies*, the Institut, if not its collaborators, did have a strong opinion on the correct relationship between the two levels of interpretation. Fromm, it will be recalled, had been criticized for what the Institut considered the premature reconciliation of psychology and sociology in his work in the forties. In doing so, Adorno and the others argued, Fromm had smoothed over the vestiges of nonidentity that Freud's intransigent "biologism" had preserved. Thus, in the same way in which the Institut challenged the unity of theory and *praxis* on the one hand, and the unity of theory and empirical verification on the other, it discounted the possibility of unifying sociology and psychology in one grand theory. This was made clear in one of the memoranda Adorno wrote for the Labor Project in 1944, in which he suggested certain methodological axioms to be included in the final report:

a) We do not call the influence of socio-economic factors psychological since they are more or less on a rational level. They are motivating ideas rather than compulsory psychological forces.

b) The term psychological should be reserved for those traits which are *prima facie* irrational. This dichotomy means that we do not approve of a socio-psychological approach à la Fromm, but rather think in terms of rational and irrational motivations which are essentially to be kept apart.

c) This means, methodologically, that our psychological analyses lead us the deeper into a social sense the more they abstain from any reference to obvious and rational socio-economic factors. We will rediscover the social element at the very bottom of the psychological categories, though not by prematurely bringing into play economic and sociological surface causations where we have to deal with the unconscious, which is related to society in a much more indirect and complicated way.[32]

Although the rather simplistic equation of rational with socio-economic and irrational with psychological was never really operative in the Institut's analyses, the dichotomy between the two methodological approaches in general was.

Accordingly, the Institut did articulate a more sociological interpretation of the problem of anti-Semitism and prejudice, which treated them as part of the "objective spirit" rather than merely as individual, subjective delusions. One of the sections of *Dialectic of the Enlightenment* was entitled "Elements of Anti-Semitism." Unfortunately, it appeared only in German, which contributed to the unbalanced understanding in America of the Institut's work on prejudice. Although a full appreciation of the essay will be possible only after a discussion of the general argument of the book in which it appears, which must wait until the next chapter, certain of its points should be mentioned now to provide a foil for the treatment of the more psychological work that follows.

In "Elements of Anti-Semitism," Horkheimer and Adorno went beyond the reactions of anti-Semites to a discussion of the function of the Jew himself in Western civilization. Like Marx in his essays on the Jewish question,[33] they rejected the liberal assumption that Jews were different from other men only in their religion. Jewishness, they argued, was also a socio-economic category, although one that had been forced on the Jews in the past and perpetuated today largely out of irrational needs. "Bourgeois anti-Semitism," they wrote, "has a specific economic basis — the veiling of domination in production." [34] Anti-Semitism was in one sense the self-hatred of the bourgeoisie projected onto the Jews, who in fact were relatively impotent, confined as they were mostly to the sphere of distribution, rather than participating in production. Because of the continuation of the contradictions of capitalism, the Jews, or a group like them, were a necessary outlet for repressed frustrations and aggressions. Thus, the liberal hope for assimilation was a fraud, because of its assumption that mankind was a potential unity under prevailing socio-economic conditions. Liberalism, Horkheimer and Adorno pointed out, had promised happiness without power to both the Jews and the masses. But the masses, denied both happiness and power, turned their fury on the Jews, out of the mistaken belief that what had been withheld from them had been given to the Jews.

This part of their analysis was within the Marxist tradition, but Horkheimer and Adorno also went beyond Marx in a number of ways. First, in their discussion of the "objective spirit" of anti-Semitism they employed psychological categories, such as paranoia and projection, in an epistemological and sociological context. They argued, for example, that paranoia was not simply a delusion. In its denial of the merely given, its mediation of immediacy, paranoia transcended a naive positivist understanding of the world.[35] Thus, all true thought contained what might be called a moment of paranoia. In fact, in projecting its internal fears and desires onto an external object, paranoid thought expressed a distorted protest against the suppression of the reconciliation between particular and universal, a suppression that bourgeois society perpetuated behind its facade of universality.

Yet, of course, Horkheimer and Adorno did not deny the distortion in the protest. Paranoia was fundamentally a delusion, a "shadow of knowledge." [36] True knowledge, they contended, meant the ability to distinguish between intellectual and emotional projections. Paranoia was really the system of the half-educated, who go beyond immediacy only to reduce reality to a reified formula. Incapable of enduring the dichotomy between inner and outer life, appearance and essence, individual fate and social reality, the paranoid achieves harmony at the cost of his own autonomy. In late capitalism, they argued, this condition had been generalized. Collective projections such as anti-Semitism took the place of individual ones, with the result that the system of the half-educated became the objective spirit.[37] Finally, under fascism, the autonomous ego was destroyed entirely by the domination of collective projections. The totality of the paranoid's delusory system corresponded to the totalitarianism of fascist society.

Horkheimer and Adorno also went beyond Marx in suggesting that anti-Semitism had certain archaic roots, which extended back further than capitalism and liberalism. This meant more than religious origins, although they did devote considerable attention in their essay to the Christian contribution to anti-Semitism. The roots they had in mind extended back into the dim prehistory of Western man. In an unpublished paper written in 1940 [38] Adorno had proposed one of his more speculative hypotheses, half historical, half meta-historical. The pre-Diaspora Jews, he argued, had been a nomadic, wandering people, "the secret gypsies of history." [39] The abandonment of this mode of life in favor of a sedentary existence, which had come with the development of agriculture, had been achieved at a terrible price. The Western concepts of work and repression were intertwined with the postnomadic attachment of man to the soil. A subterranean memory of the wandering Jew, however, persisted in Western culture. This image of the Jew, Adorno held, "represents a condition of mankind which did not know labor, and all later attacks against the parasitic, consumptive character of the Jews are simply rationalizations." [40] In other words, the Jew embodied the dream of gratification without toil, a dream whose frustration resulted in the displacement of fury onto those who seemed to have realized its promise.

In a letter to Lowenthal in 1944 [41] Horkheimer made a similar point with special reference to the curious intertwining of Jewish and German destinies. Here the historical reference was not to the Jew as pre-Diaspora wanderer, but rather as post-Exilic dweller in alien lands. "If both Germans and Jews show a militant sort of patriotism," he suggested,

> the patriotism of the Jews is characterized by a longing for the soil which was lost, while the Germans want to win soil which they never possessed. The unconscious is alike insofar as they dream of getting the fruits of the earth without laboring it themselves. The land of milk and honey is represented in the German soul by the nostalgia of the South.

In its final formulation in "Elements of Anti-Semitism," this general idea was brought up to date. The Jews were hated, Horkheimer and Adorno argued, because they were secretly envied. Having lost even their economic function as middlemen, they seemed to embody such enviable qualities as wealth without work, luck without power, a home without boundaries, and religion without a myth.[42]

On the one hand, then, the Jews represented a covert challenge to the work ethic and instrumental rationality, which had been important elements in the Enlightenment logos. They were in a peculiar way an embodiment of the reaction of nature to the domination implicit in the Enlightenment program, which, as we shall see in the next chapter, was one of the major themes of *Dialectic of the Enlightenment.* In this, they were the *Gegenrasse*[43] of the Nazis, whose pseudo-naturalism was a distorted reflection, even partly an imitation, of the Jews' seeming embodiment of unrepressed nature. *Gegenrasse* meant a kind of misbegotten, inferior race in Nazi ideology. Here Horkheimer and Adorno used it ironically, to mean the reflection of the Nazi's own perverted qualities.

On the other hand, the Jews were also identified with the Enlightenment and its liberal, rationalist traditions. As Horkheimer had argued in "The Jews and Europe," the emancipation of the Jews had been intimately connected to the emergence of bourgeois society. Accordingly, with the decline of that society in the twentieth century, the position of the Jews had been rendered extremely vulnerable. The identification was more than merely external or fortuitous. Despite the image of the "natural" Jew mentioned above, Jews through the centuries had contributed significantly to the "disenchantment of the world" and the manipulation of nature that it implied. In a letter to Lowenthal in July, 1946, Horkheimer wrote of the role Jews had played in one aspect of this process, the instrumentalization of language:

> The root of fascist agitation is the fact that there is something rotten in language itself. The rottenness I have in mind is . . . a phenomenon which is expressed in Jewish religion by the verdict against trying to call God by His name and by the story of the Tower of Babel. The corruption of language seems also to be expressed in the legend of the Expulsion from Paradise, where all the creatures had been named by Adam. We must beware of the idea that the fascist use of language is something radically new in our society. . . . The distrust of the peasant against the city-dweller with his mastery of language was partly justified. This distrust is an element of anti-Semitism itself, and the Jew who manipulates language so easily is not free from guilt in the prehistory of what you explain as the fascist handling of language. Here, too, the Jew is the pioneer of capitalism.[44]

In short, the dilemma of the Jew was that he was identified both with the Enlightenment and with its opposite. His true emancipation as a man could only come when domination — that of capitalism, and more fundamentally, of the Enlightenment in its most instrumental and manipulative forms — was itself ended. Only when reconciliation, which ironically was the highest value of the Jewish faith,[45] was realized in the social sphere could anti-Semitism truly end. Partial solutions such as Zionism[46] and assimilation were destined to fail.

Finally, Horkheimer and Adorno took little comfort in the "defeat" of anti-Semitism brought by the victory of the Allies over Hitler. Overt antagonism to the Jews might have been successfully extirpated, but its underlying cause had been preserved in what might be called a "ticket mentality," which threatened to destroy all vestiges of individuality in Western culture. "Anti-Semitic psychology," they wrote, "has largely been replaced by a mere "yes" to the fascist ticket, to the list of slogans of quarrelsome heavy industry."[47] Implicitly, of course, this applied to all advanced industrial societies in the West, including the United States. As Horkheimer had written to Lowenthal, in theoretical speculation "the principle of the lesser evil is even more dangerous than in politics." Hitler's conquerors might have eliminated the more obvious effects of anti-Semitism, but they had done little to destroy its root causes. *Dialectic of the Enlightenment*, as we shall see in the next chapter, was in large measure a phenomenology of the alternative displacements that stemmed from those causes.

This then was the general analysis of the objective dimension of anti-Semitism that informed the Institut's thinking while it conducted its empirical probes of the subjective side of the problem. It was expressed, however, only in German or in private correspondence. As a result, one side of Adorno's methodological division was lost to public view, leaving in its place what seemed to some like psychological reductionism and the abandonment of Critical Theory's stress on the totality. Years later Adorno would refer the curious reader to "Elements of Anti-Semitism," [48] but at the time the *Studies in Prejudice* appeared few readers had known enough to anticipate this advice. This was one of the disadvantages resulting from the Institut's wariness about betraying its more radical side to the American audience.

What also must be kept in mind, of course, is that from the beginning the series as a whole, including the work on which the Institut had worked most extensively, *The Authoritarian Personality*, was a collaborative effort. Non-Institut members tended to be psychoanalytically trained, but in most cases unfamiliar with the larger perspective of Critical Theory. Thus, although Horkheimer was general director of the project, he could not exert the guiding influence he had been able to exercise within the Institut in the past. This was even more the case after his health forced him back to California and Samuel Flowerman replaced him as director in 1946. The Lowenthal-Horkheimer correspondence contains ample evidence that relations with officials of the AJC, especially near the end of the project, were anything but smooth. Personal frictions played a role, but theoretical disagreements certainly existed as well.

The *Studies* as they were originally conceived at the New York conference in 1944 were to consist of two types of research. The first was to be more limited and deal with specific problems facing educational agencies. The second was to be broader in scope and its questions more comprehensive. Both short- and long-range studies were to be conducted with interdisciplinary methods. When the *Studies* were finally published at the end of the decade, however, their form was somewhat different. Three of the five volumes dealt with prejudice as a basically subjective phenomenon: *Dynamics of Prejudice: A Psychological and Sociological Study of Veterans*, by Bruno Bettelheim and Morris Janowitz;[49] *Anti-Semitism and Emotional Disorder: A Psychoanalytic Interpretation*, by Nathan W. Ackerman and Marie Jahoda;[50] and *The Authoritarian Personality*, by T. W. Adorno, Else Frenkel-Brunswik, Daniel J. Levinson, and R. Nevitt Sanford. The fourth, *Prophets of Deceit*, by Leo Lowenthal and Norbert Guterman,[51] analyzed the techniques of the demagogue. The last, Paul Massing's *Rehearsal for Destruction*,[52] presented a straightforward historical account of anti-Semitism in Germany.

Although of the three subjectively oriented studies, *The Authoritarian Personality* is most germane to our analysis of the Institut's empirical work, brief comment should be made about the other two volumes. The most strictly psychoanalytic of these was the Ackerman-Jahoda study. Ackerman was himself a practicing analyst associated with the Psychoanalytic Clinic for Training and Research at Columbia. His professional orientation was Freudian, although ego psychology served to modify his orthodoxy. Before the founding of the AJC's Department of Scientific Research, he had approached John Slawson about the possibility of doing a Freudian study of anti-Semitism. When the *Studies* were launched, his suggestion provided the basis for one of its projects. His collaborator, Marie Jahoda, came to work with him primarily through an indirect connection with the Institut. She had been Paul Lazarsfeld's colleague, coauthor of *The Unemployed of Marienthal*,[53] and, for a time, his wife, in Vienna before the war. After an eight-year exile in England, she emigrated to America in 1945 and became a research associate with the AJC. Although trained as a social psychologist, she had been personally analyzed and was familiar with Freudian theory.

Collection of data for the study began at the end of 1945. Twenty-five analysts, primarily from the New York area, were asked to volunteer material from their clinical practices. Patterns revealed in the forty case studies that were ultimately contributed were then summarized, without any attempt at quantification. Considerable caution was also displayed in relating specific emotional disorders to types of prejudice. In fact, few generalizable conclusions emerged from the study, although its descriptive content was often highly suggestive.

At no time did sociological considerations enter into the discussion.

Also rooted in Freudian theory, the second study of the subjective dimension of social bias, *Dynamics of Prejudice*, went beyond the Ackerman-Jahoda book in its willingness to introduce statistical analysis and sociological insights. Bruno Bettelheim, not yet the author of the works that would make him one of America's most celebrated psychologists,[54] had emigrated from Vienna in 1939. At the time of his work for the AJC he was on the faculty of the University of Chicago as assistant, then associate professor of educational psychology. His collaborator, Morris Janowitz, was a sociologist at the same university with a special interest in political sociology.

The conclusions of *Dynamics in Prejudice* were based on interviews that lasted four to seven hours administered to one hundred fifty male veterans in Chicago. Veterans were chosen because their counterparts in Europe after the First World War had shown themselves to be highly susceptible to the attractions of fascism. Bettelheim and Janowitz hoped to see whether or not similar conditions of faulty reintegration into society prevailed in America after World War Two. They explored such psychological hypotheses as the projection of past frustrations and anxieties about the future onto outgroups because of inadequate ego strength. They also attempted to uncover relationships between ethnic intolerance and the individual's social dynamics, and sought correlations between anti-Jewish and anti-Negro sentiments. What they did not hope to uncover, however, was a general syndrome of the intolerant personality, which was the primary goal of their counterparts at Berkeley.

Among the conclusions reached by Bettelheim and Janowitz were the following. Tolerance tended to correlate positively with such variables as ego strength and acceptance of external authority (acceptance, it should be noted, was said to differ from submission, but whatever the term, this was a conclusion very much at odds with that reached in *The Authoritarian Personality*). A relationship between bias against Jews and bias against blacks did exist, although alienated superego traits tended to be projected on Jews (for example, Jews control the country), while alienated id characteristics were projected on blacks (for example, blacks were dirty and sexually licentious). This last finding, it might be added parenthetically, was very different from what had existed in Europe, where Jews were the objects of both types of projections.

Correlations between intolerance and socio-economic conditions, including familial relations, were less easy to establish. One conclusion that did emerge was that rapid social mobility, especially when in a downward direction, often correlated positively with prejudice.

The key determinant, however, was less the objective experience of the individual than his subjective feelings of deprivation. The demands made by sudden social change were most inadequately handled in those cases where childhood experiences had hindered the development of a strong ego. Thus, "the weaker the personality, the stronger becomes the influence of the social field." [55] This was a conclusion, it will be recalled, which was close to the one reached in the *Studien über Autorität und Familie*, with the difference that in the earlier study, the decline of the family was seen as the source of the weaker ego, a decline that was placed in the larger context of the liquidation of mediating factors in advanced capitalist society. Bettelheim and Janowitz refrained from speculations on this more cosmic level. Similarly, the recommendations that appeared at the end of *Dynamics of Prejudice* were well within a liberal framework. They included better parental training to create more integrated personalities; the strengthening of the legal system, which was understood as the basic symbol of external social control; and increased preschool training for tolerance.

As Bettelheim and Janowitz were themselves later to note,[56] their work differed from that of the group in Berkeley in a number of other ways. Most significantly, *Dynamics of Prejudice* found intolerance most prevalent among those who resisted society and rejected its values, the reverse of the correlation between prejudice and conformity discovered by the California researchers. The difference, as Nathan Glazer was to point out,[57] was perhaps due to the disparity in population samples of the two projects. The Chicago study tested predominantly lower-class and lower-middle class subjects, whereas the Berkeley project confined itself to the middle class. The implication of this difference, of course, was that *Dynamics of Prejudice* lacked the implicit critique of the social totality that informed *The Authoritarian Personality*.

As might be expected, *Prophets of Deceit*, in whose writing Leo Lowenthal had a central role, was much closer to the traditions of Critical Theory. Content analysis, the basic technique he and Norbert Guterman used, had been applied to literature and popular biographies in his earlier work for the Institut. The historical frame of reference of the study, so its authors explained,[58] was the analysis of earlier agitators, such as Cola di Rienzi, Savonarola, and Robespierre, in Horkheimer's "Egoism and the Movement for Emancipation." Moreover, the basic assumption of the work — that manipulation rather than free choice was the rule in modern society — had served to underlie the Institut's work on mass culture. As was the case with most of the Frankfurt School's earlier work, it sought to go beyond appearances and unmask the "objective" content of the phenomenon it studied. Thus Lowenthal and Guterman could write that "the agitator should be studied in the light of his *potential* effectiveness within the context of present-day society and its dynamics, rather than in terms of his immediate effectiveness." [59] This meant that more than the individual susceptibility to demagoguery was at issue; latent trends within the society as a whole were important as well.

In writing a phenomenology of political agitation, Lowenthal and Guterman had earlier, unpublished studies by Massing of Joseph E. McWilliams, by Adorno of Martin Luther Thomas, and by Lowenthal himself of George Allison Phelps to build on. They also benefited from the work being done simultaneously by the other authors of the *Studies* on subjective elements of prejudice. Whereas the other studies focused on the responses of the persons most accessible to demagogic propaganda, *Prophets of Deceit* examined the various devices used to evoke those responses. The language of the agitator, its authors held, had to be deciphered by a kind of psychological Morse code.[60] As was to be expected, the major source of the code was psychoanalysis, which also served as the basis for a more theoretical analysis of fascist propaganda by Adorno in an article written two years later.[61]

Lowenthal and Guterman also introduced the work of another refugee, Erik Erikson, to supplement Freud's seminal insights. Erikson's study "Hitler's Imagery and German Youth" [62] had argued that Hitler was the embodiment of the rebellious big brother as well as an authoritarian father figure. This facilitated the paradoxical search for and rejection of authority that characterized fascism. Erikson's perception of the confused rebelliousness of the fascist personality corresponded nicely to the "rebel" as developed by Fromm in the *Studien.* Furthermore, his remark that the German father suffered from an "essential lack of true inner authority — that authority which results from an integration of cultural ideal and educational method" [63] — fitted well with the *Studien*'s observation about the breakdown of familial solidarity. On the surface, however, Erikson's view of the German family seemed to contradict the argument about the family structure best suited for the cultivation of authoritarian potential that appeared in *The Authoritarian Personality*, at least as some commentators understood it.[64]

Before discussing whether or not such a contradiction did in fact exist, the origins and methodology of the project that produced the most important volume in the *Studies in Prejudice* should be made clear. As in much of the work done by the Institut, Horkheimer's guiding influence was strong.[65] Because he took no part in the actual writing of the book, however, his name did not appear among the coauthors. In 1944 Horkheimer had made contact with a group of social psychologists at Berkeley that included R. Nevitt Sanford, Daniel Levinson, and Else Frenkel-Brunswik.[66] His initial interest in their work had been aroused by a study of pessimism directed by Sanford.[67] The basic irrationality of the pessimism that was studied suggested that an underlying personality trait or constellation of traits was at its root. This, of course, was the direction the Institut's earlier findings had taken as well. Thus, with the grant from the AJC just acquired, Horkheimer was able to suggest a working relationship between the Institut and the social scientists around Sanford, who called themselves the Berkeley Public Opinion Study Group. His proposal was accepted, and work on what was to become *The Authoritarian Personality* began in the following year.

Adorno and Sanford were selected as codirectors of the project, with Levinson and Mrs. Frenkel-Brunswik as chief associates. Although all four senior members of the staff cooperated on the various parts of the project, their major responsibilities were divided.[68] Sanford was most concerned with research techniques and the two case studies, which were presented in full detail. Adorno was responsible for setting the data in a more general sociological framework, with special emphasis on the ideological content of the interviews. Mrs. Frenkel-Brunswik worked on some of the personality variables and was charged with the categorization and quantification of the interview material. And finally, Levinson was primarily responsible for the project's scales, for the psychological interpretation of the interview data and the projective questions, and for the overall statistical methods.

Pollock, who by the end of the war had moved out to the West Coast, was selected to organize a secondary research team in Los Angeles, which included C. F. Brown and Carol Creedon. Lowenthal, although busy with his own research, contributed to the content analysis in Adorno's chapters in the final version of the project's findings. In addition, individual monographic studies were contributed by various members of the Berkeley Public Opinion Study Group: Betty Aron on the Thematic Apperception Test, Maria Hertz Levinson on psychiatric clinic patients, and William R. Morrow on prison inmates.

The basic objective of all the research was the exploration of a "new anthropological type," [69] the authoritarian personality. As postulated, its characteristics resembled those of the sado-masochistic character type constructed by Fromm in the *Studien.* Similarities also existed with the so-called J-type developed by the Nazi psychologist E. R. Jaensch in 1938,[70] although the sympathies of the authors were of course very different from his. Jaensch's J-type was defined by its unwavering rigidity. Its opposite he called the S-type, for synaesthesia, the capacity to confuse senses, which he equated with the effete, vacillating uncertainty of the democratic mentality. There was also a striking resemblance to the portrait of an anti-Semite drawn by Jean-Paul Sartre in his *Anti-Semite and Jew*, a book that appeared after *The Authoritarian Personality* was well under way.[71] Wilhelm Reich and Abraham Maslow were also acknowledged predecessors in the construction of the syndrome.[72] As it was finally understood, the authoritarian character, in Horkheimer's words, had the following qualities:

> a mechanical surrender to conventional values; blind submission to authority together with blind hatred of all opponents and outsiders; anti-introspectiveness; rigid stereotyped thinking; a penchant for superstition; vilification, half-moralistic and half-cynical, of human nature; projectivity.[73]

That such a type did in fact exist was not the issue in question. As Adorno later admitted:

> we never regarded the theory simply as a set of hypotheses but as in some sense standing on its own feet, and therefore did not intend to prove or disprove the theory through our findings but only to derive from it concrete questions for investigation, which must then be judged on their own merit and demonstrate certain prevalent socio-psychological structures.[74]

Thus, despite its use of American empirical and statistical techniques, the Institut had not truly abandoned the methodology of Critical Theory. In general it remained faithful to the tenets of that methodology as outlined in "Traditional and Critical Theory," although with the important change that *praxis* was no longer stressed as the testing grounds for the theory. The Institut's critique of the hypothesis-verification-conclusion model of social research, however, was still in effect. Induction, as normally understood, was not acceptable. As Horkheimer wrote in the *Studies in Philosophy and Social Science* in 1941:

> Categories have to be formed through a process of induction that is the reverse of the traditional inductive method, which verified its hypotheses by collecting individual experiences until they attained the weight of universal laws. Induction in social theory, per contra, should seek the universal within

the particular, not above or beyond it, and, instead of moving from one particular to another and then to the heights of abstraction, should delve deeper and deeper into the particular and discover the universal law therein.[75]

Accordingly, *The Authoritarian Personality* saw its individual interviews as extremely important complements to its statistical surveys. Its highly detailed reproductions of two of those interviews — one with a highly prejudiced respondent named Mack, the other with a low scorer on the scales called Larry — were meant less as examples of abstract types than as monad-like particulars embodying universals. In a sense, they were really not very different from Weberian "ideal types," with their stress on individuality and disdain for abstract laws.

With the expertise of the group around Sanford to draw on, however, statistical refinements were introduced into the project that went well beyond anything the Institut had done in the past. As in the *Studien* and in Sanford's work on pessimism, the basic assumption was the existence of different personality levels, both manifest and latent. The goal of the project was the exposure of the underlying psychological dynamics corresponding to the surface expression of a prejudiced ideology or indicating a potential for its adoption in the future. Public opinion questionnaires based on the conscious articulation of beliefs were dismissed as inadequate for two reasons. First, they failed to reveal a coherent syndrome of opinion, and second, they were incapable of probing the psychological predispositions that might correspond to the syndrome.[76] Perhaps the primary methodological objective of the project was to develop a relatively simple device to test the existence of the underlying psychological structure or structures fostering authoritarian beliefs and possibly authoritarian behavior.

The research began with the distribution of questionnaires containing factual questions, opinion-attitude scales, and projective, open-answer questions to a group of seven hundred college students. A number of the questions had been used before in the *Studien* and in the labor project. The opinion-attitude scales were designed to uncover quantitative estimates of anti-Semitism (the A-S Scale), ethnocentrism (the E Scale), and political and economic conservatism (the PEC Scale). With practice the scales were refined, so that specific items on each one became reliable indicators of a more general configuration of opinions: "The procedure was to bring together in a scale items which, by hypothesis and by clinical experience, could be regarded as 'giveaways' of trends which lay relatively deep within the personality, and which constituted a *disposition* to express spontaneously (on a suitable occasion), or to be influenced by, fascist ideas." [77]

Ultimately the subject population numbered 2099 and was composed of a number of groups. Almost all those questioned, however, were white, native-born, gentile, middle-class Americans. To clarify the statistical data that resulted from the questionnaires, clinical interviews and Thematic Apperception Tests were administered to a selected number of those who fell in the highest and lowest quarters of the curve. The interviews lasted for one and a half hours and were divided into an ideological and a clinical-genetic section. As in the labor project, the interviewees were not informed of precisely what they were being questioned about. Under Mrs. Frenkel-Brunswik's direction, a scoring manual with ninety categories and subcategories was devised to help the nine interviewers decipher the results. Both "underlying" and "manifest" questions were put to the forty men and forty women chosen for the interviews. The TAT's were given to approximately the same subjects. In both cases, quantification of the results was attempted.

During the course of the research, the various techniques were both "expanded" and "contracted":

> Expansion was exemplified in the attempt to bring more and more aspects of antidemocratic ideology into the developing picture and in the attempt to explore enough aspects of the potentially antidemocratic personality so that there was some grasp of the totality. Contraction took place continuously in the quantitative procedures as increasing theoretical clarity permitted a boiling down so that the same crucial relationships could be demonstrated with briefer techniques.[78]

The scaling procedures that were used had been developed by Rensis Likert in 1932, as a modification of an earlier technique created by L. L. Thurstone.[79] In both cases, varying degrees of agreement or disagreement with the question were allowed on a scale ranging from plus-three to minus-three. A neutral zero was excluded from the possible responses. Refinement of the scale consisted of weeding out items that failed to correlate with the general score or that lacked clear discriminatory power. If the Likert scale had a major disadvantage, it was the possibility that different patterns of response might produce the same final score.[80] The interviews were designed in part to overcome this potential problem by revealing the specific configurations of belief in individual cases.

The most valuable methodological achievement of the project was the condensation of the three original attitudinal scales into one set of questions capable of measuring authoritarian potential on the latent psychological level. The new measuring device was the celebrated "F Scale."[81] The content analyses of the various agitators' devices, previous experience with the empirical work of the *Studien über Autorität und Familie*, and the studies in New York of anti-Semitism in labor all contributed to its construction. It sought to test nine basic personality variables:

CONVENTIONALISM. Rigid adherence to conventional, middle-class values.

AUTHORITARIAN SUBMISSION. Submissive, uncritical attitude towards idealized moral authorities of the ingroup.

AUTHORITARIAN AGGRESSION. Tendency to be on the lookout for, and to condemn, reject, and punish, people who violate conventional values.

ANTI-INTRACEPTION. Opposition to the subjective, the imaginative, the tender-minded.

SUPERSTITION AND STEREOTYPY. The belief in mystical determinants of the individual's fate; the disposition to think in rigid categories.

POWER AND "TOUGHNESS." Preoccupation with the dominance-submission, strong-weak, leader-follower dimension; identification with power figures; overemphasis upon the conventionalized attributes of the ego; exaggerated assertion of strength and toughness.

DESTRUCTIVENESS AND CYNICISM. Generalized hostility, vilification of the human.

PROJECTIVITY. The disposition to believe that wild and dangerous things go on in the world; the projection outwards of unconscious emotional impulses.

SEX. Exaggerated concern with sexual "goings-on."[82]

A certain number of questions were designed to reveal as indirectly as possible the subject's position on each variable. At no time were any minority groups mentioned explicitly. With increased testing, the correlation between the F Scale and the E Scale reached approximately .75, which was considered a sign of success. More questionable, however, was the .57 correlation between the F and the PEC Scales. To explain this failure, a distinction was introduced between genuine and pseudo-conservatives, only the latter being truly authoritarian personalities. No attempt was made (or at least reported in the final results) to correlate the F with the A–S Scale. More specific correlations within the subgroups of the sample population showed considerable consistency among all the different groups. And as we have seen, the clinical interviews were used to substantiate the findings of the scale. Examinations of their results seemed to support the F Scale's accuracy.

In subsequent years, however, the success of the F Scale as an indicator of authoritarian potential was the subject of a lively controversy. The most exhaustive critique of its effectiveness was made by Hyman and Sheatsley in a volume devoted solely to the impact of the study.[83] In general, they were very critical, and in a number of cases their criticisms were telling. Paul Lazarsfeld, on the other hand, whose skepticism concerning the unqualified application of Critical Theory to empirical problems was clearly shown in his collaboration with Adorno, was far more positive. The F Scale's individual indicators, he wrote in 1959, play both "an expressive role in regard to the underlying trait and a predictive role in regard to the originating observation which the trait is supposed to explain." [84] Roger Brown, a more severe critic of the project, ended his analysis by admitting that "there is a substantial residue possibility that the chief conclusion of the questionnaire work is correct." [85]

Critical assessment of the interpretation of the interview material proved to be equally mixed. The interviewers began with specific questions in mind in six general areas — vocation, income, religion, clinical data, politics, and minorities and "race" — and continued to probe indirectly until they thought the questions had been answered. Certain critics objected to the fact that the interviewers were "too knowledgeable" [86] because of their advance information on the scores of the individual respondents on the scales. Other criticism dealt with the coding of the results. Despite the scoring manual prepared by Mrs. Frenkel-Brunswik, the coders' interpretative leeway remained considerable. On occasion, it was argued,[87] certain circular reasoning seemed to creep into their interpretations. For example, rigidity was equated with an intolerance of ambiguity, while intolerance was itself explained by rigidity. Other attacks were directed against the choice of high and low scorers rather than middle groups for the interviews, a procedure, so it was argued, that was designed to support the data rather than seek a representative cross section of the sample population.[88]

Criticisms, as might be expected, were not confined to methodology alone. The substantive conclusions of the project came in for their share as well. Paul Kecskemeti, for example, challenged the implicit assumption that prejudice in general, and anti-Semitism in particular, foreshadowed a total overthrow of the democratic system. This "catastrophic perspective," he argued, was far too alarmist.[89]

More specific questions were raised by others about the genetic explanations of authoritarianism. Unfortunately, all the data about the childhood origins of the personality types under examination came from adult memories rather than the actual observation of children. Mrs. Frenkel-Brunswik addressed herself to this problem in a subsequent study, which was regrettably not completed before her premature death in 1958.[90] As revealed in the available interview data, authoritarian characters were most likely to be nurtured in a home in which discipline was strict but often arbitrary. Parental values were frequently very conventional, rigid, and externalized. As a result, it was likely that those values remained ego-alien to the child as well, which prevented the development of an integrated personality. Resentment at parental harshness was often displaced onto others, while the outward image of the father and mother proved to be highly idealized. The "stern and distant"[91] father frequently reported in interviews of the high scorers on the F Scale often seemed to promote passivity in the child combined with repressed aggressiveness and hostility. These were qualities, it will be recalled, evident in the sado-masochistic type developed from Fromm in the *Studien über Autorität und Familie.* By contrast, the parents of the low scorers were remembered as less conformist, less status-anxious, and less arbitrarily demanding. Instead, they were more ambivalent, emotionally demonstrative, and affectionate. Accordingly, the image their children had of them was less idealized and more realistic. And perhaps most important, ego-alienation of moral norms was less pronounced, indicating the likelihood of a more integrated personality.

One of the questions raised by subsequent commentators was the compatibility of this view of the authoritarian family with the Institut's assertion, so often made elsewhere, that the family had declined in modern society. Leon Bramson was the most insistent critic on this point, calling the argument about the decline (which he mistakenly attributed to Marcuse's *Eros and Civilization* alone without seeing its antecedents in the *Studien*) "directly contradictory to the work of the early Fromm and the Berkeley group."[92] As Bramson saw them, these studies seemed to indicate the continued strength of the authoritarian family. On a closer examination, however, it can be seen that the two interpretations were by no means as irreconcilable as Bramson believed.

First, as mentioned before, the Institut was impressed with Erikson's picture of the German family, in which the father lacked true inner authority. The pseudo-revolt of what Fromm had called the "rebel" was in fact a search for a new authority, produced in part by the absence of a positive authority model at home. This was a syndrome that *The Authoritarian Personality* certainly acknowledged, giving it a prominent place in Adorno's analysis of "high" character types.

Even in those cases where identification with a seemingly strong father rather than rebellion against him was the rule — admittedly the most frequent syndrome — the contrast with the earlier analysis in the *Studien* was not that marked. In fact, in describing the "authoritarian syndrome" [93] Adorno referred the reader to Fromm's sado-masochistic character and employed Freud's ideas about the Oedipus complex to explain its origins.[94] In cases where Oedipal conflicts were poorly resolved in childhood, aggression against the father was transformed into masochistic obedience and displaced sadistic hostility. What connected this purely psychological explanation to the more sociological perspective of the *Studien* was Horkheimer's theory that "external social repression is concomitant with the internal repression of impulses. In order to achieve 'internalization' of social control, which never gives as much to the individual as it takes, the latter's attitude towards authority and its psychological agency, the superego, assumes an irrational aspect." [95] This was a syndrome, Adorno concluded, that was highly prevalent among the lower middle classes in Europe and might be expected "among people whose actual status differs from that to which they actually aspire" [96] in America. In short, the classic authoritarian syndrome did not mean simple identification with a strong patriarchal figure, but implied instead considerable ambivalence and conflict about the relationship. External repression, when intensified, served to activate the latent tensions in the poorly resolved Oedipal situation.

Adorno outlined other syndromes that expressed ways in which this ambivalence might be acted out. These included "surface resentment," the "crank," and the "manipulative type." Another syndrome found among high scorers was the "conventional," which most closely approximated a conflict-free internalization of parental and social norms. It was this latter type that seemed most congenial to a patriarchal family structure in which paternal authority was still relatively intact.

The authoritarian family that emerged from the interview data was itself a reflection of growing external pressures. Anxious about its status, rigidly adhering to values it no longer held spontaneously, the authoritarian family was obviously overcompensating for the hollowness at its core. The authority it tried so frantically to protect was in fact no longer rational. As Horkheimer argued in an essay written in 1949,[97] the more the economic and social functions of the family were liquidated, the more desperately it stressed its outmoded, conventional forms. Even the mother, whose warmth and protectiveness had once served as a buffer against the arbitrary harshness of the patriarchal world — Fromm's strictures on matriarchalism were echoed here — was no longer capable of functioning in the same way. "The 'Mom'," Horkheimer wrote, "is the death mask of the mother." [98] "By contrast," *The Authoritarian Personality* revealed, "the family of the typical low-scoring man seems to be centered about a mother whose primary function is to give love rather than to dominate, and who is not weak or submissive." [99]

It was no surprise, then, that the authoritarian personality usually felt no pity, a motherly quality. The Nazis' undermining of the family, despite their propaganda to the contrary, was no accident. The authoritarian family did not produce authoritarian children solely because of what it did — provide a model for arbitrary domination — but equally for what it could not do — protect the individual against the claims made on his socialization by extra-familial agencies. Thus, although *The Authoritarian Personality* concentrated on the intra-familial origins of the "new anthropological type," the implications of its analysis pointed outward to the society at large. The Institut's earlier emphasis on the decline of the family, Bramson to the contrary notwithstanding, was preserved in the portrait of the authoritarian family it drew in its later work.

Perhaps some of the confusion about this question was a product of terminological ambiguity. As a number of commentators have pointed out,[100] there is an important distinction that should be drawn between authoritarianism and totalitarianism. Wilhelminian and Nazi Germany, for example, were fundamentally dissimilar in their patterns of obedience. What *The Authoritarian Personality* was really studying was the character type of a totalitarian rather than an authoritarian society. Thus, it should have been no surprise to learn that this new syndrome was fostered by a familial crisis in which traditional paternal authority was under fire. Much of the difficulty — and perhaps some of it was conceptual as well as linguistic — might have been avoided if this distinction had been clearly articulated.

Another, perhaps more substantial criticism of the study was made by Edward Shils and echoed by a number of others.[101] The political bias of the project's directors, they argued, colored its findings. Why, they asked, was authoritarianism associated with fascism alone and not communism? Why was the F Scale not the "C Scale," or at least the "A Scale?" Why was political and economic conservatism seen as connected with authoritarianism, while the demand for state socialism was not? In short, why was the old left-right distinction upheld, when the real opposition was between liberal democracy and totalitarianism of both extremes?

The great irony of this attack lay in the fact that the Institut had abandoned many of its more radical ideas in its work for the AJC. As we have seen, the fundamental assumptions underlying the *Studies in Prejudice* were liberal and democratic. Even so hostile a critic of the work as Paul Kecskemeti could write: "the authors' own liberalism is plainly conservative insofar as the American constitutional tradition is concerned." [102] Toleration had never been an end in itself for the Frankfurt School, and yet the nonauthoritarian personality, insofar as it was defined, was posited as a person with a nondogmatic tolerance for diversity. What the Institut always feared was the fetishization of tolerance as an end rather than a means. A good, although indirect, example of this can be found in Bettelheim and Janowitz's *Social Change and Prejudice*, where the nonconformist, antiauthoritarian character valued by the Berkeley research team was criticized in the following way: "If some nonconformists display a high level of tolerance, it may be the result of a reaction formation or displacement of hostility generated by unsatisfactory relations with authority. It is not farfetched to call these persons false tolerants, for while they may be tolerant of minorities, they often are intolerant of accepted ways of social life." [103]

Nor had political democracy in its representative form been the Institut's final goal. Yet *The Authoritarian Personality* gave little evidence of the traditional Marxist critique of "bourgeois democracy," which had informed the Institut's earlier work. There was a further irony in Shils's claim that the old left-right dichotomy had been outmoded. As we have already noted, Horkheimer stressed the necessity of unmasking domination in any political form, whether fascist, ostensibly socialist, or otherwise. From its first years in Frankfurt the Institut had been skeptical about the Soviet experiment. With time, skepticism had turned to outright disillusionment. As Pollock had argued, the Soviet Union was no more than a state capitalist system with little to distinguish itself from similar systems in the West. The key difference with Shils and other American thinkers was that the Institut refused to contrast totalitarianism to an individualist, libertarian, nonideological pluralism as a polar opposite. As we have seen in looking at its treatment of mass culture in the West, the Institut saw domination working in new and subtle ways to destroy the vestiges of true individuality behind a facade of diversity. *Dialectic of the Enlightenment* extended its gloomy analysis of current trends to all modernized societies. Thus, in a way, the Frankfurt School agreed that the left-right dichotomy, at least as it was embodied in actual political structures, was no longer relevant. Where it did disagree, of course, was on the level of theory, where its sympathies remained basically the same as before.

The Authoritarian Personality gave little direct evidence of this pessimism. It refrained from offering any conclusions about the prevalence of authoritarianism within the society as a whole by extrapolating from its limited sample. It did not even go as far as the unpublished labor project in presenting percentages of high and low scorers within its sample population. Instead, it merely presented a descriptive typology of authoritarian and nonauthoritarian characters, without suggesting anything about their respective frequency. On occasion, though, it did offer hints about the extent of authoritarian personalities in its sample. Thus, for example, Adorno wrote that "it is one of the unpleasant results of our studies, which has to be faced squarely, that this process of social acceptance of pseudo-conservatism has gone a long way — that it has secured an indubitable mass basis." [104] On the whole, however, it held to the view that "the majority of the population are not extreme but, in our terminology, 'middle.' " [105]

Shils's critique of latent political bias was perhaps more on the mark when it turned to the study's implicit assumption that conservatism and authoritarianism were somehow related. The unreliability of the PEC Scale to correlate significantly with the F Scale had led to an attempt to distinguish between genuine and pseudo-conservatives. The former were defined as people, "whatever the merits of [their] political views," who were "seriously concerned with fostering what is most vital in the American democratic tradition." [106] The latter were only outward conservatives, whose underlying personalities marked them as potential candidates for fascism. Although this distinction was designed to overcome the simple equation of right-wing ideology and authoritarian personality structure, the association lingered subconsciously, because there were no comparable efforts to develop a typology of pseudo-liberalism or radical authoritarianism. In fact, there was no real attempt to distinguish among nonconservative ideologies. The prototype liberal, who "actively seeks progressive social change, who can be militantly critical (though not necessarily totally rejective) of the present status quo, who opposes or deemphasizes numerous conservative values and beliefs . . . and who would diminish the power of business by increasing the power of labor and the economic functions of government," [107] was seen as the primary foil of the genuine or pseudo-conservative. How problematical this characterization was became evident in the next generation, when New Deal liberalism itself came under strong attack as an ideology oriented towards the status quo.

If *The Authoritarian Personality* did attempt to account for authoritarianism of the left, it did so by constructing a vaguely defined category of "rigid low scorers." [108] In later years, Adorno would refer to this subtype as an answer to such critics as Shils.[109] On closer observation, however, this proved a less than satisfactory response. Whereas in the case of the PEC Scale, the discrepancy between conscious opinions and subconscious personality structure could be used to explain the inadequate correlation with the F Scale, there could be no such discrepancy in the F Scale itself, because it had been designed explicitly to measure trends in the subconscious personality. Thus to say that low scorers were rigid was tantamount to saying that the scale had failed to measure their rigidity, "stereotypy," and conformity, which were key features of the high-scoring syndrome. It would be to negate the very purpose of the project, which was to develop a device to measure the existence of authoritarian potential beneath the level of conscious ideology. Clearly, more work had to be done on authoritarianism of the left, and, in fact, in the next few years it was carried out by other researchers in America.[110]

Other difficulties in the methodology and conclusions of *The Authoritarian Personality* might be mentioned, but to dwell on them unduly would be to miss the tremendous achievement of the work as a whole. As Adorno himself was later to admit, "if *The Authoritarian Personality* made a contribution, this is not to be sought in the absolute validity of the positive insights, even less in statistics, but above all in the posing of the issues, which were motivated by a genuine social concern and related to a theory that had not previously been translated into quantitative investigations of this sort." [111] Although nearly a thousand pages in length, the final volume was understood by its authors as only a "pilot study." If this indeed was the real purpose, then there can be no doubt of its success. One of the early reviewers of all the volumes in the *Studies in Prejudice* was right in calling them "an epoch-making event in social science." [112] In the years that followed, an enormous flood of research resulted from the stimulus they, and in particular the Berkeley study, provided.[113]

As a postscript, it might be added that the impact was not confined to America alone. When the Institut returned to Germany in the early fifties, it brought with it the social scientific techniques it had acquired in New York and California. Its first collaborative effort after the reestablishment of the Institut was a study of group interaction published under Pollock's name in 1955, whose basic purpose was the introduction of American methodology to a German audience.[114] In fact, even Adorno found himself in the unwonted position of promoting empirical techniques to counteract the traditional German hostility to anything smacking of Anglo-Saxon positivism. In a conference of sociologists held in Cologne in 1952, Adorno argued that sociology must no longer be considered as a *Geisteswissenschaft* (a cultural science), because the world, dominated as it was by reification, could scarcely be understood as "meaningful." "The much abused inhumanity of empirical methods," he told his audience, "is always more human than the humanization of the inhuman." [115] Accordingly, the methods of administrative research should be used, albeit within a critical framework, to explore social phenomena. Although theory could not be proved or disproved by empirical verification — this was a tenet of Critical Theory he was not prepared to abandon — when translated into research questions, theoretical ideas could be immensely enriched. Thus, for example, psychoanalysis had been significantly improved by its translation into empirical questions, although of course its initial formulation had been anything but inductive.

By the end of the 1950's, however, the Institut's attitude towards empiricism had undergone a serious reversal of emphasis.[116] Bringing American methods to the attention of German social scientists had succeeded too well. And so, once again, the Frankfurt School's sensitivity to the reductionist abuse of an empirical methodology came to the fore. In the next decade, to jump out of our chronological framework for a moment, German sociology was split into warring camps of dialectical and empirical methodologists, whose polemical interchanges evoked comparisons with the great *Methodenstreit* (methodological dispute) of the Wilhelminian era.[117] Although the Institut and such allies as Jürgen Habermas at the University of Frankfurt were the major exponents of the dialectical position, they were careful to avoid the wholesale repudiation of the techniques that the Institut had mastered with such effect in America.

How to integrate those techniques with a truly critical approach stressing the primacy of theory was the real problem. As we have seen, this was more than merely a methodological dilemma; it reflected real divisions and contradictions within the society as a whole. The success of the *Studies in Prejudice*, it might be argued, had resulted in part from an avoidance of the issue. The analyses of anti-Semitism in *The Authoritarian Personality* and in "Elements of Anti-Semitism" — the one dealing with the subjective dimension, the other more with its objective side — were never really reconciled. In fact, one reason why the Berkeley project succeeded while Adorno's collaboration with Lazarsfeld was a failure was that the former did not concern itself with the "objective spirit" of modern society in the way in which the latter did. When the Frankfurt School did speculate on those objective trends, its prognosis was bleak indeed. How much so we shall see in the next chapter, which is devoted to the theoretical work of the Institut in its last decade in America.

VIII

Toward a Philosophy of History: The Critique of the Enlightenment

> If by enlightenment and intellectual progress we mean the freeing of man from superstitious belief in evil forces, in demons and fairies, in blind fate — in short, the emancipation from fear — then denunciation of what is currently called reason is the greatest service reason can render.
>
> — MAX HORKHEIMER

The problem of discontinuity was perhaps the central internal dilemma for Critical Theory in the 1940's. The Institut, it will be recalled, had been launched with the intention of synthesizing a broad spectrum of disciplines. Its founders had also hoped to integrate speculation and empirical research. And finally, they had sought to overcome the academic isolation of traditional theory from its practical implications without at the same time reducing speculative thought to a utilitarian tool of polemical interests. In short, although criticizing the adequacy of orthodox Marxism, they had not rejected its ambitious project: the ultimate unity of critical theory and revolutionary practice. By the 1940's, however, the Frankfurt School began to have serious doubts about the feasibility of these syntheses. Its interests remained interdisciplinary, but the mediations between its theory and both empirical research and political *praxis* grew increasingly problematical.

As noted in the previous chapter, the *Studies in Prejudice*, even those parts most heavily influenced by members of the Institut, often departed from the tenets of Critical Theory as they had been articulated in the *Zeitschrift*. Most obviously, the analysis of anti-Semitism in *The Authoritarian Personality* differed significantly from its counterpart in *Dialectic of the Enlightenment*. Although attributable in part to the role of non-Institut scholars in the Berkeley project, the discrepancies were also a reflection of more fundamental developments in the theory itself. So too were new uncertainties in the Institut's attitude towards political activism. One of the essential characteristics of Critical Theory from its inception had been a refusal to consider Marxism a closed body of received truths. As the concrete social reality changed, so too, Horkheimer and his colleagues argued, must the theoretical constructions generated to make sense of it. Accordingly, with the end of the war and the defeat of fascism, a new social reality had emerged, which required a new theoretical response. This was the task that presented itself to the Frankfurt School in its last decade in America. By examining the changes that its members made in their theoretical work, we can better understand the sources of the discontinuities that later observers would find so troubling.

Our discussion will proceed as follows. We will begin by exploring the basic change in Critical Theory, a new emphasis on the underlying relationship between man and nature. The first part of our presentation will center on the Frankfurt School's critique of what it considered to be the prevailing relationship throughout most of Western history. This will be followed by a discussion of the alternative that it proposed, including its more problematical elements. We will then turn to the connections between that alternative and the Institut's continued stress on rationality and philosophical thought in general. And finally, we will focus on the implications of the change in the theory for the Institut's attitude towards *praxis,* subjectivity, and utopianism.

Although the articulation of the new elements in Critical Theory did not occur until the late forties, Horkheimer had recognized the need to rethink certain of the Frankfurt School's basic ideas in the years before the war. One of the sources of his willingness to leave New York was impatience with his institutional responsibilities, which prevented the assimilation and interpretation of the immense amount of work done by the Institut in the years after his assumption of the directorship. As early as 1938, he expressed his eagerness to begin work on a book on the dialectic of the Enlightenment.[1] The circulatory disorder that made it necessary for him to leave New York also made it possible to cast aside his administrative duties and begin the long-awaited theoretical summation. With Adorno his most frequent companion in California, their thinking merged even closer than before. While only one of their theoretical statements in the forties, *Dialectic of the Enlightenment*, bore both their names, the other two, *Eclipse of Reason* and *Minima Moralia*, were strongly affected by the collaboration.

Unlike his friend, however, Horkheimer was never a prolific writer and now seems to have had even greater difficulty. On January 20, 1942, he wrote to Lowenthal that "philosophical argument, which has lost its basis with the abolition of the sphere of circulation, now seems to me impossible." Although he was perhaps distinguishing between traditional philosophy and Critical Theory here, the latter was becoming increasingly arduous as well. "I am getting into my work again," he wrote Lowenthal on November 27, "and it has never been as difficult as now. I feel that this undertaking is almost too great for my forces and in my letter to P[ollock] today, I reminded him of the fact that even Husserl needed about ten years for his *Logische Untersuchungen* and even about thirteen years until the publication of his '*Ideen*' . . ." On February 2 of the following year, he continued in the same vein, adding a moving expression of his sense of isolation:

> Philosophy is overwhelmingly complicated, and the procedure depressingly slow. The idea that you are, and always will be, aware of our raison d'être at least as clearly as myself has always meant more than encouragement: it strengthened in me that feeling of solidarity which is the very basis of what I am doing—beyond the three or four of us there are certainly other hearts and brains that feel similarly to ours, but we cannot see them, and perhaps they are prevented from expressing themselves.

Horkheimer's concern about the isolation of his thought was in fact justified. The theoretical work that he finally did publish in the late forties had a minimal impact in comparison with that of the *Studies in Prejudice. Dialectic of the Enlightenment*, written during the war, was not published until 1947, and then in German by a Dutch publishing house.[2] The *Eclipse of Reason*, which Oxford published in the same year, although accessible to the English-speaking public, was received with little critical fanfare[3] and less commercial success. Only in the 1960's, when the *Dialectic* became an underground classic in Germany — it was widely circulated in a pirated version until its official republication in 1970 — and the *Eclipse* was translated into German as a part of Horkheimer's *Kritik der instrumentellen Vernunft*,[4] did they achieve the audience they deserved. Adorno's *Minima Moralia*, also never translated into English, had no impact whatsoever in America.

The critical shift in the Frankfurt School's perspective, which these works expressed, was a product of their last decade in the United States, and thus makes a fitting conclusion to our study of the Institut's American experience. Although it would be unfair to say that after their return to Germany, Horkheimer and Adorno did little but work out the implications of these books — this would be especially misleading for Adorno, who continued to write at his characteristically furious pace — there is an element of truth in such an observation. *Dialectic of the Enlightenment*, *Eclipse of Reason*, and *Minima Moralia* presented so radical and sweeping a critique of Western society and thought that anything that followed could be only in the nature of a further clarification. Even Marcuse's later work in America, which is outside the purview of this study, did not really represent the breaking of new ground, although the nuances were often different. As we have seen on several occasions, many of the arguments he developed in *Eros and Civilization*, *One-Dimensional Man*, and his lesser works were contained in an embryonic form in his and others' articles in the *Zeitschrift*. Still others appeared in the works of his colleagues now under consideration.

In calling Horkheimer's and Adorno's critique "radical," the word should be understood in its etymological sense of going to the roots of the problem. This is especially important to grasp in view of the Frankfurt School's growing distrust of what passed for "radical" politics in later years. Paradoxically, as the theory became more radical, the Institut found itself decreasingly capable of finding a connection to radical *praxis*. The desperate hopes of Horkheimer's wartime essay on the "Authoritarian State" soon gave way to a deepening gloom about the chances for meaningful change. Disillusioned with the Soviet Union, no longer even marginally sanguine about the working classes of the West, appalled by the integrative power of mass culture, the Frankfurt School traveled the last leg of its long march away from orthodox Marxism.

The clearest expression of this change was the Institut's replacement of class conflict, that foundation stone of any truly Marxist theory, with a new motor of history. The focus was now on the larger conflict between man and nature both without and within, a conflict whose origins went back to before capitalism and whose continuation, indeed intensification, appeared likely after capitalism would end. Signs of the new emphasis had appeared in the debate over fascism among Institut members during the war. To Horkheimer, Pollock, Adorno, and Lowenthal, domination was taking increasingly direct, noneconomic forms. The capitalist mode of exploitation was now seen in a larger context as the specific, historical form of domination characteristic of the bourgeois era of Western history. State capitalism and the authoritarian state spelled the end, or at least the radical transformation, of that epoch. Domination, they argued, was now more direct and virulent without the mediations characteristic of bourgeois society. It was in a sense the revenge of nature for the cruelty and exploitation that Western man had visited upon it for generations.

With hindsight, it is possible to see intimations of this theme in numerous places in the Institut's earlier work,[5] although in a secondary role. Adorno had employed it in his study of Kierkegaard [6] as well as in certain of his pre-Institut writings on music.[7] Several of the aphorisms in *Dämmerung*[8] had attacked cruelty to animals and the ascetic premises of the work ethic in a way that anticipated the *Dialectic.* Lowenthal had mentioned the liberal notion of the domination of nature while criticizing Knut Hamsun's distorted protest against it.[9] Fromm's discussion of matriarchal culture contained explicit misgivings about the domination over women in patriarchal society, which was facilitated by the equation of womanhood with natural irrationality.[10]

Perhaps most clearly, this motif surfaced in Horkheimer's *Habilitationsschrift, The Origins of the Bourgeois Philosophy of History.*[11] Here, in fact, Horkheimer directly related the Renaissance view of science and technology to political domination. The new conception of the natural world as a field for human manipulation and control, he argued, corresponded to a similar notion of man himself as an object of domination. The clearest exponent of this view in his eyes was Machiavelli, whose political instrumentalism was used in the service of the rising bourgeois state. Underlying Machiavelli's politics, Horkheimer maintained, was the undialectical separation of man from nature and the hypostatization of the distinction. In fact, he argued against Machiavelli, "nature" was dependent on man in two ways: civilization changes it and man's concept of what it is itself changes. Thus history and nature were not irreconcilably opposed.

They were, however, not entirely identical. Hobbes and later Enlightenment thinkers had assimilated man to nature in a manner that made man into an object, just as nature had been objectified in the new science. In their eyes, both man and nature were no more than machines. As a result, the assumption that nature repeated itself eternally was projected onto man, whose historical capacity for development, so closely bound to his subjectivity, was denied. For all its progressive intentions, this "scientific" view of man implied the eternal return of the present.

This was not the case, however, with the figure Horkheimer had chosen to end his study of early modern philosophies of history: Giambattista Vico. Vico's attack on Cartesian metaphysics and the growing idolatry of mathematics set him apart from his contemporaries. So too did his insight that man could know history better than the natural world because man was history's maker. Vico had also transcended the limitations of the Enlightenment interpretation of the origins of myths, which he saw less as priestly tricks than as the projection of human needs onto nature. In so arguing, Vico had anticipated the later Marxist view of ideology. Thus, despite his cyclical theory of the rise and fall of civilizations, which was similar to Machiavelli's, he was unique in seeing that human activity was the key to understanding historical development. Vico had understood that *praxis* and the domination of nature were not the same. Although he separated man and nature, he did so in a way that avoided placing one above the other. By insisting on the subjectivity of man, he preserved the potentiality of the subjectivity of nature.

In his subsequent writings Horkheimer spent little time with Vico, but the critique of the Enlightenment made by the Italian theorist was one he continued to share. In his essays in the *Zeitschrift* he frequently castigated the legacy of Cartesian dualism in Western thought. The stress on nonidentity in Critical Theory never meant the absolute separation of subject and object. Such a separation, the Frankfurt School held, was connected to the needs of the rising capitalist order. "Since Descartes," Horkheimer wrote in "Reason and Self-Preservation," "bourgeois philosophy has been a single attempt to make knowledge serve the dominant means of production, broken through only by Hegel and his kind." [12] Before the war, this type of connection between substructure and superstructure was a frequent feature of the Frankfurt School's work. But even then, the precise relationship was never made clear.[13] This was especially difficult to do because at different times, materialist rationalists like Hobbes, empiricists like Hume; and idealists like Kant were all seen to serve the capitalist system in one way or another. By the mid-forties, the traditional Marxist theory of ideology was even more tenuously applied in the Institut's work. As we have already noted, the chapter on anti-Semitism in the *Dialectic* discussed its precapitalist, archaic roots in a way that Marx would have rejected. In fact, the notion of the Enlightenment underwent a basic change in the forties. Instead of being the cultural correlate of the ascending bourgeoisie, it was expanded to include the entire spectrum of Western thought. "Enlightenment here is identical with bourgeois thought, nay, thought in general, since there is no other thought properly speaking than in cities," Horkheimer wrote Lowenthal in 1942.[14] In *Eclipse of Reason* he went so far as to say that "this mentality of man as the master [which was the essence of the Enlightenment view] can be traced back to the first chapters of Genesis." [15]

Thus, although Horkheimer and Adorno still used language reminiscent of Marxism — such terms as the "exchange principle" [16] played a key role in their analysis — they no longer sought answers to cultural questions in the material substructure of society. In fact, their analysis of the exchange principle as a key to understanding Western society was as reminiscent of Nietzsche's discussion in the *Genealogy of Morals*[17] as of Marx's in *Capital.*

Moreover, not only did the Frankfurt School leave the vestiges of an orthodox Marxist theory of ideology behind, it also implicitly put Marx in the Enlightenment tradition.[18] Marx's overemphasis on the centrality of labor as man's mode of self-realization, which Horkheimer had questioned as early as *Dämmerung*, was the primary reason for this argument. Implicit in the reduction of man to an *animal laborans,*[19] he charged, was the reification of nature as a field for human exploitation. If Marx had his way, the entire world would be turned into a "giant workhouse." [20] In fact, the repressive technological nightmares perpetrated by his self-proclaimed followers in the twentieth century could not be entirely dissociated from the inherent logic of Marx's own work.

Marx of course was by no means the major target of the *Dialectic.* Horkheimer and Adorno were far more ambitious. The entire Enlightenment tradition, that process of allegedly liberating demystification that Max Weber had called *die Entzauberung der Welt* (the disenchantment of the world), was their real target. Here they followed Lukács's lead in *History and Class Consciousness*, where Weber's notion of rationalization was given a greater critical edge by being connected to the concept of reification.[21] Horkheimer had in fact always been an interested reader of Weber. In "Reason and Self-Preservation" he adopted the basic analysis of Weber's *Protestant Ethic and the Spirit of Capitalism* for his own purposes. "Protestantism," he wrote, "was the strongest force in the extension of cold, rational individuality. . . . In the place of work for the sake of salvation appeared work for work's sake, profit for profit's sake; the entire world became simply material. . . . From Leonardo to Henry Ford, there was no other path than through religious introversion." [22] Calvin's theological irrationalism, he charged, contained "the cunning of technocratic reason." [23]

Yet whereas Weber faced the process with stoic resignation, the Frankfurt School still held out the hope for a break in the continuum of history. This was more apparent in the early years of the forties — once again "Authoritarian State" should be mentioned as its highwater mark — but it was not totally absent after the war. Perhaps the major source of this guarded optimism was the residual belief in the ultimate validity of *Vernunft* that remained in Critical Theory. *Vernunft*, as noted earlier, meant the reconciliation of contradictions, including the one that split man and nature. Despite their distrust of absolute identity theories, Horkheimer and his colleagues stressed the importance of "objective reason" as an antidote to the one-sided ascendency of instrumentalized "subjective reason." "The two concepts of reason," Horkheimer wrote,[24] "do not represent two separate and independent ways of the mind, although their opposition expresses antinomy. The task of philosophy is not stubbornly to play the one against the other, but to foster a mutual critique and thus, if possible, to prepare in the intellectual realm the reconciliation of the two in reality."

This was a hope that Weber, with his neo-Kantian skepticism about the irreconcilability of practical and theoretical reason, could not hold. Although recognizing the replacement of what he called "substantive" reason by its formal counterpart, Weber was unable to entertain the possibility of its restoration. The "rationalization" of the modern world was meant solely in a nonsubstantive sense. Weber, unlike some of his more romantic contemporaries, did not hope to turn the clock back, but it was clear that he greeted the world's disenchantment with little enthusiasm.

Nor, of course, did the Frankfurt School. In fact, they were anxious to point out how little the world had really become "rational." Reason, as the title of Horkheimer's book indicated, was very much in eclipse. In fact, the Enlightenment, for all its claims to have surpassed mythopoeic confusion by the introduction of rational analysis, had itself fallen a victim to a new myth. This was one of the major themes of the *Dialectic.* At the root of the Enlightenment's program of domination, Horkheimer and Adorno charged, was a secularized version of the religious belief that God controlled the world. As a result, the human subject confronted the natural object as an inferior, external other. At least primitive animism, for all its lack of self-consciousness, had expressed an awareness of the interpenetration of the two spheres. This was totally lost in Enlightenment thought, where the world was seen as composed of lifeless, fungible atoms: "Animism had spiritualized objects; industrialism objectified spirits." [25]

Conceptual thinking, at least in the Hegelian sense, had preserved the primitive sensitivity to the mediations between subject and object. The German word *Begriff* (concept) was connected with the verb *greifen* (to grasp). Thus, *Begriffe* were concepts that had a complete grasp of their content, including negative as well as positive moments. In fact, one of the major distinctions between men and animals was the ability of the former to think conceptually, while the latter could not go beyond immediate sense perceptions. Man's sense of selfhood, of identity through time, was the product of his conceptual powers, which embraced potentiality as well as actuality. The major epistemological tendency of the Enlightenment, however, was the replacement of concepts by formulae, which failed to go beyond nondialectical immediacy. "Concepts in the face of the Enlightenment," Horkheimer and Adorno wrote, "are like *rentiers* in the face of industrial trusts: neither can feel themselves secure." [26] Moreover, the Enlightenment's overemphasis on logical formalism and its assumption that all true thought tended towards the condition of mathematics meant that the static repetition of mythic time had been retained, thwarting the dynamic possibility of historical development.

What was especially disastrous was the effect of the Enlightenment domination of nature on the interactions of men. In developing this argument, Horkheimer and Adorno continued the train of thought expressed in Marcuse's article, "The Struggle Against Liberalism in the Totalitarian View of the State." [27] Totalitarianism was less the repudiation of liberalism and the values of the Enlightenment than the working out of their inherent dynamic. The exchange principle underlying the Enlightenment notion of nature as fungible atoms was paralleled in the increasing atomization of modern man, a process that culminated in the repressive equality of totalitarianism. The instrumental manipulation of nature by man led inevitably to the concomitant relationship among men. The unbridgeable distance between subject and object in the Enlightenment world view corresponded to the relative status of rulers and ruled in the modern authoritarian states. The objectification of the world had produced a similar effect in human relations. As Marx noted, although restricting it to an effect of capitalism, the dead past had come to rule over the living present.

All of these changes were reflected in the most basic of cultural creations, language. As noted earlier, Walter Benjamin had always been keenly interested in the theological dimensions of speech.[28] At the root of his theory of language was the belief that the world was created by the Word of God. To Benjamin, "In the beginning was the Word" meant that God's act of creation consisted in part of the bestowing of names. These names were of course perfectly expressive of their objects. However, man, created as he was in God's image, also had the unique gift of name-giving. But his names and God's were not the same. As a result, there developed a chasm between name and thing, and the absolute adequacy of divine speech was lost. To Benjamin, formal logic was the barrier that separated the language of Paradise from its human counterpart. Man tended to overname things by abstractions and generalizations. It was in fact "the task of the translator to release in his own language that pure language which is under the spell of another, to liberate the language imprisoned in a work in his re-creation of that work." [29] Similarly, the function of the cultural critic was the recovery of the lost dimension of God's speech by hermeneutically decoding man's various inferior approximations.

Benjamin's quest for a pure language had its roots, as we have noted before, in his immersion in Jewish mysticism. It perhaps also reflected the influence of French symbolist poetry, which he knew well. In Benjamin's essay on translation, Mallarmé was quoted as saying that "the diversity of idioms on earth prevents everybody from uttering the words which otherwise, at one single stroke, would materialize as truth." [30] And finally, as some commentators have argued,[31] the subterranean residue of Swabian Pietism on the German idealist tradition may have had an effect on his linguistic theories. Whatever the origins, it is important to understand that Benjamin was far more interested in words than in sentence structure as the divine text, a fact that makes it hard to call him a "structuralist *avant la lettre,*" [32] as he has sometimes been labeled.

Adorno and Horkheimer, although eschewing the consciously theological underpinnings of Benjamin's theory of language, did accept the notion that "pure" speech had been corrupted.[33] "Philosophy," Horkheimer wrote in *Eclipse of Reason*, "is the conscious effort to knit all our knowledge and insight into a linguistic structure in which all things are called by their right names." [34] The concept of truth in every genuine philosophy, he continued, is "the adequation of name and things." [35] Once again, the reconciliation theme of *Vernunft* was at the root of Critical Theory's utopian impulse.

By stressing it in their works in the forties, however, Horkheimer and Adorno were not abandoning that refusal to name or describe the "other," which as we have seen was one of the central premises of Critical Theory from the start. In fact, their reluctance to do so was consistent with the Jewish taboo against uttering the sacred. Jews do not call God by his right name because to do so would be premature; the messianic age has not yet arrived. Similarly, the Frankfurt School's unwillingness to outline a utopian vision reflected its members' conviction that true reconciliation could never be achieved by philosophy alone. As Marx had argued, the "realm of freedom" could not be envisaged by men who were still unfree. Until social conditions drastically altered, philosophy had a limited role to play: "inasmuch as subject and object, word and thing, cannot be integrated under present conditions, we are driven by the principle of negation to attempt to salvage relative truths from the wreckage of false ultimates." [36] Adorno, in fact, had taken Benjamin to task for his theological attempt to call things by their right names, as a combination of magic and positivism.[37] In the chapter on the culture industry in the *Dialectic*, he and Horkheimer used the same combination of apparent opposites to describe the ideological, instrumental language produced by mass culture.[38] Negation rather than the premature search for resolutions was the real refuge of truth.

In fact, the greatest failing of the Enlightenment mentality was not its inability to create social conditions in which name and thing might be legitimately united, but rather its systematic elimination of negation from language. This was the reason why its substitution of formulae for concepts was ultimately so destructive. The philosophy of the Enlightenment was overwhelmingly nominalist rather than realist; in Benjamin's sense, it recognized only the speech of man, ignoring God's. Man was the sole name-giver, a role commensurate with his domination of nature. Language thus became, to use Marcuse's later term, one-dimensional.[39] Incapable of expressing negation, it could no longer voice the protest of the oppressed. Instead of revealing meanings, speech had become nothing more than a tool of the dominant forces in society.

Anticipations of this decline of language were evident in the cultural document Horkheimer and Adorno chose to study in their first of two excursuses in the *Dialectic*, Homer's *Odyssey*. The trick Odysseus played on Cyclops by calling himself "No-man" was also a denial of his identity, which to the primitive, pre-Enlightened mind of the giant was the same as his name. Ultimately, however, the trick was on Odysseus, since Western man had in fact lost his identity, as language capable of conceptualization and negation had been replaced by language capable only of acting as an instrument of the status quo.

In other ways as well, Homer's epic — or more correctly, half mythic epic, half rational proto-novel — had anticipated the major themes of the Enlightenment. One example was the realization that self-denial and renunciation were the price of subjective rationality. As we have noted in Chapter 2 when discussing Horkheimer's "Egoism and the Movement for Emancipation," Marcuse's "On Hedonism," and other examples of the Institut's earlier work, asceticism in all of its forms was a frequent target of criticism. In the *Dialectic* the critique was extended: "the history of civilization is the history of the introversions of sacrifice; in other words, the history of renunciation."[40] In fact, that initial denial of man's oneness with nature was at the root of all the subsequent inadequacies of civilization. The *Odyssey* abounded in clear examples of the inherent relationship between self-renunciation and self-preservation in Western thought: Odysseus's refusal to eat Lotus or the cattle of Hyperion, his sleeping with Circe only after extracting an oath from her not to transform him into a pig, his tying himself to the mast of his ship to avoid seduction by the song of the Sirens.

This last episode was especially pregnant with symbolic meaning for Horkheimer and Adorno.[41] The ears of Odysseus's sailors were stopped with wax to prevent their hearing the Sirens. Like modern laborers, they repressed gratification in order to continue their toil. Odysseus, on the other hand, was not a worker and thus could hear the song, but under conditions that precluded his response to its temptation. For the privileged, culture still remained "*une promesse de bonheur*" without the possibility of fulfillment. Here Odysseus experienced that separation of the ideal from the material sphere that was characteristic of what the Institut called "affirmative culture."

Even more fundamentally, Odysseus's version of rationality was an ominous adumbration of things to come. In struggling against the mythic domination of fate, he was forced to deny his oneness with the totality. By necessity, he had to develop a particularist, subjective rationality to insure his self-preservation. Like Robinson Crusoe, he was an atomized, isolated individual living by his wits in the face of a hostile environment. His rationality was thus based on trickery and instrumentality. To Horkheimer and Adorno, Odysseus was the prototype of that paragon of Enlightenment values, modern "economic man." His treacherous journey anticipated the bourgeois ideology of risk as the moral justification of profits. Even his marriage to Penelope involved the exchange principle — her fidelity and the renunciation of her suitors during his absence in exchange for his return.

Still, despite the important prefigurations of the Enlightenment in Homer's epic, it also contained a strong element of homesickness, of the desire for reconciliation. The home to which Odysseus sought to return, however, was still alienated from nature, whereas true homesickness was justified, as Novalis had known, only when "home" meant nature. In the next excursus in the *Dialectic*, "Juliette, or Enlightenment and Morals," Horkheimer and Adorno examined distorted "returns" to nature, which ran like an undercurrent through the Enlightenment. Here return often meant the revenge of brutalized nature, a phenomenon that culminated in the barbarism of the twentieth century. The Institut's earlier work on fascist pseudo-naturalism — Lowenthal's incisive essay on Knut Hamsun in particular — provided a backdrop for the discussion.

Once again, Horkheimer and Adorno stressed the continuity between bourgeois liberalism, in this case symbolized by Kant, and totalitarianism, here prefigured by de Sade and, to some extent, Nietzsche. Kant's effort to ground ethics solely in practical rationality, they argued, was ultimately a failure. The Enlightenment's treatment of nature, and by extension of men, as objects was fundamentally in accord with the extreme formalism of the categorical imperative, despite Kant's injunction to consider men as ends rather than means. Carried to its logical extreme, calculating, instrumental, formal rationality led to the horrors of twentieth-century barbarism. De Sade was one of the way-stations along the route. His *Histoire de Juliette* was the model of functional rationality — no organ left idle, no orifice unplugged. "Juliette makes science her credo. . . . She operates with semantics and logical syntax like the most modern positivism; but unlike the employees of the most recent administration who direct their linguistic criticism predominantly against thought and philosophy, she is a daughter of the Enlightenment struggle against religion." [42] De Sade's other works, such as the *One Hundred Twenty Days of Sodom*, were the cynical, reverse image of Kant's architectonic system. Others, like *Justine*, were the Homeric epic with the last vestiges of mythology removed. In so ruthlessly separating the spiritual from the corporeal side of love, de Sade was merely working out the implications of Cartesian dualism. Moreover, implicit in his cruel subjugation of women was the characteristic Enlightenment mastery of nature.[43] Women, reduced to their biological function alone, were robbed of subjectivity. The Church's cult of the Virgin, which was a partial concession to matriarchal warmth and reconciliation, was ultimately a failure. The witch trials of the early modern period were far more symbolic of the Enlightenment's implicit attitude towards women, despite its outward support for their emancipation. De Sade's blatant brutality was merely the most obvious example of what was a far more pervasive phenomenon. In fact, the Enlightenment's sadism towards the "weaker sex" anticipated the later destruction of the Jews — both women and Jews were identified with nature as objects of domination.

Nietzsche's will-to-power, no less than Kant's categorical imperative, foreshadowed this development by positing man's independence from external forces. His anthropocentric hubris was also at the root of Kant's notion of "maturity," which was one of the prime goals of the Enlightenment as Kant understood it. Man as the measure of all things inherently meant man as the master of nature. It was the overemphasis on man's autonomy that paradoxically led to man's submission, as the fate of nature became man's own. Fascism, in fact, used the rebellion of suppressed nature against human domination for the sinister purposes of that very domination.[44] Mastery in one direction might well turn in the opposite direction; the true "return" to nature was very different from fascist pseudo-naturalism.

In de-emphasizing the total autonomy of man, it might be added parenthetically, Horkheimer and Adorno were being faithful to that refusal to define a positive anthropology which characterized Critical Theory from the beginning. Such a project, they seemed to be saying, implied an acceptance of man's centrality, which in turn denigrated the natural world. Critical Theory, for all its insistence on a standard against which the irrationalities of the world might be measured, was not really a radical humanism at heart.[45] Horkheimer's interest in religion, which surfaced in later years, was thus not as fundamental a departure from the premises of his earlier work as might appear at first glance.

In the remainder of *Dialectic of the Enlightenment*, Horkheimer and Adorno considered the working out of the Enlightenment ethos in the culture industry and in modern anti-Semitism, both of which have been discussed in previous chapters. At the end of the book they included a number of aphorisms, on subjects as disparate as the underground history of the body and the theory of ghosts. Throughout, as we have had occasion to note several times, the tone was pessimistic and the prognosis bleak. The alienation of man from nature so central to the current crisis of Western civilization seemed an almost irreversible trend. In an aphorism devoted to the philosophy of history, Horkheimer and Adorno explicitly rejected the optimistic premises of Christianity, Hegelian idealism, and historical materialism. Hope for better conditions, if not entirely illusory, rested less in the guarantee of their attainment than in the determinate negation of the existing. There was, however, no distinct *praxis* suggested by reason that might help in the struggle.[46]

In fact, the Frankfurt School increasingly treated any attempt to realize the promises of philosophy as instrumentalization. In an aphorism on propaganda, Horkheimer and Adorno excoriated the instrumental use of philosophy and language to bring about social change. In *Eclipse of Reason* Horkheimer made a similar point: "Is activism, then, especially political activism, the sole means of fulfillment, as just defined? I hesitate to say so. The age needs no added stimulus to action. Philosophy must not be turned into propaganda, even for the best possible purpose." [47]

As a result, programmatic advice for methods to change society was not very evident in any of the Frankfurt School's work in the forties. (Not that it had been before, but at least the call to *praxis* was a frequent element in the Institut's earlier work.) Reconciliation with nature was the obvious goal, but what this meant precisely was never fully spelled out. What it clearly did not mean, of course, was the submission of man to hypostatized natural forces. The Frankfurt School did not wish to revive Engels's crude dialectic of nature. Nor did its members want to succumb to the right-wing version of the apotheosis of nature, which Lowenthal had so devastatingly unmasked in his essay on Knut Hamsun. And finally, they sought to distinguish themselves from those all-too-frequent critiques of the Enlightenment running through German intellectual history, which were often little more than a nostalgic yearning for an idealized "state of nature."

Nature, Horkheimer and Adorno made clear, was in itself neither good nor bad. Moreover, a complete reconciliation with nature in the sense of total identity could only mean a regression to a state of unmediated stasis. Critical Theory continued to stress nonidentity in a way that precluded the reduction of subject to object and vice versa. It was on this point that its creators differed with Benjamin and Ernst Bloch, whose philosophy of hope spoke of the resurrection of a natural subject in a manner that seemed to obliterate the distinction between subject and object.[48] Not in the unity of object and perception, Horkheimer and Adorno argued in their discussion of projection, but in the reflective opposition between them was the utopia of reconciliation preserved.[49] Elsewhere, they made it clear that it was the *memory* of nature, rather than nature itself, that was the enemy of domination.[50]

Memory, in fact, played a key role in the Frankfurt School's understanding of the crisis of modern civilization. Here the Freudian component of Critical Theory came to the fore.[51] One of the greatest costs of progress, Horkheimer and Adorno wrote in one of their aphorisms, was the repression of the pain and suffering caused by the mastery of nature. Nature was to be understood not merely as something external to man, but also as an internal reality. "All reification," they pointed out, "is a forgetting." [52] As noted earlier, the search for a liberated future in the integrated recapture of the past had been one of the major themes of Walter Benjamin's work. His theory of experience and concern for the memorabilia of childhood [53] were reflections of this interest. In fact, it was in a letter to Benjamin written in 1940 that Adorno first used the phrase "All reification is a forgetting." [54] The stimulus was Benjamin's *Zeitschrift* article on Baudelaire, in which he discussed *Erfahrung* (integrated experience) and the Proustian *mémoire involontaire* (involuntary memory).

The process of emancipation was understood in part as the development of self-consciousness and the resurrection of the lost past. Here of course the Hegelian roots of Critical Theory were apparent. To Hegel, the process of history was the journey of the spirit becoming conscious of its alienated objectifications. Where Horkheimer and Adorno departed from Hegel was in their refusal, first, to hypostatize subjectivity as a transcendent reality above individuals, and, second, to treat it as the sole source of objective reality. The Frankfurt School never reverted to the idealist notion of the world as the creation of consciousness. As Adorno noted in his letter of February 29, 1940, to Benjamin, some forgetting is inevitable, and by extension, some reification. The complete identity of the reflecting subject and the object of his reflection was impossible.[55]

As was to be expected, the Frankfurt School distrusted the anthropocentric impulse it perceived at the core of the idealists' stress on consciousness, even when that consciousness was theoretically "objective." In 1945, Horkheimer returned to Columbia to give a series of lectures on the subject matter of his books. In one of them,[56] he accused classical German philosophy of wanting to overcome the dualism between man and God, a desire that led to the inclusion of the demonic in its systems. This produced theodicies like Leibniz's and Hegel's with their quietistic implications. In all of the classical philosophers' work, the idea of grace was absent, an indication of their inherent hubris. To avoid this, the Frankfurt School implied, the autonomous integrity of the natural object had to be preserved, although not to the extent of ignoring its mediated interaction with the human subject. What Marx had called the "humanization of nature" and the "naturalization of man" [57] was necessary, but not at the cost of obliterating their inherent differences.

What should be understood, of course, is that the Institut's stress in the forties was heavier on the need for reconciliation than on the necessity to maintain the distinctions. Implicit in their program was the ultimate bridging of the gap between natural and social sciences that Dilthey and his followers had done so much to establish in the late nineteenth century. This was a dichotomy, it might be added, that had worked its way into Marxist theory by the 1920's.[58] Lukács had accepted it in his fight against the reduction of Marxism to a natural science by Engels, Kautsky, and their followers in the Second International. The young Marcuse, in his days before joining the Institut, had stressed the unbridgeable distance between history and nature. "The boundary between historicity and nonhistoricity," he wrote in 1930, "is an ontological boundary." [59] Even Horkheimer, in his favorable contrast of Vico to Descartes, had supported the view that the study of man and the study of nature were not precisely the same.

Although never explicitly repudiating this view, the Frankfurt School in the forties did call it into question by attacking the permanence of the distinction between man and nature. This did not mean, of course, a return to a "scientific" view of history — this was left to later Marxists like Louis Althusser[60] and his followers — but it did imply a modification of the strict dichotomy between *Geisteswissenschaften* (cultural sciences) and *Naturwissenschaften* (natural sciences). Talking about the need for a reconciliation of man and nature, albeit one that did not imply identity, jibed poorly with a belief in the "ontological boundary" between historicity and nonhistoricity. However, precisely what this would mean for a future science of man was never fully spelled out in the Institut's writings.

Equally problematical was the psychological level on which the reconciliation was to take place. Here the Frankfurt School introduced a new term into its vocabulary: mimesis. To be sure, imitation as an explanation of social behavior had been a perennial favorite of certain social theorists. Durkheim, for example, had devoted an entire chapter of his *Suicide* to demolishing such predecessors as Gabriel Tarde for their use of mimesis.[61] Freud in his *Group Psychology and the Analysis of the Ego* also discussed Tarde's work, but subsumed imitation under the more general category of "suggestion," which Le Bon had employed.[62] The use to which it was put by these theorists, however, was primarily as an explanation for certain types of group behavior, especially mass or crowd behavior. The Institut also used mimesis for this purpose, but it developed the concept in another context as well.

In 1941, in the Institut's prospectus for a project on anti-Semitism, the importance of childhood mimesis was introduced, to refute Nazi theories of hereditary racial characteristics.[63] In his later lectures at Columbia and in *Eclipse of Reason*, Horkheimer expanded on this initial suggestion. Imitation, he argued, was one of the primary means of learning during early childhood. Subsequent socialization, however, taught the child to forego imitation in favor of rational, goal-directed behavior. A phylogenetic correlate of this ontogenetic pattern was one of the central patterns of the Enlightenment. Western "civilization" began with mimesis, but ultimately transcended it. "Conscious adaptation and eventually domination replace the various forms of mimesis. The progress of science is the theoretical manifestation of this change: the formula supplants the image, the calculating machine the ritual dances. To adapt oneself means to make oneself like the world of objects for the sake of self-preservation."[64] Mimesis, however, was not fully overcome in Western civilization. "If the final renunciation of the mimetic impulse," Horkheimer warned,

> does not promise to lead to the fulfillment of man's potentialities, this impulse will always lie in wait, ready to break out as a destructive force. That is, if there is no other norm than the status quo, if all the hope of happiness that reason can offer is that it preserves the existing as it is and even increases its pressure, the mimetic impulse is never really overcome. Men revert to it in a regressive and distorted form.[65]

Modern persecutors often mimic the pathetic gestures of their victims; demagogues frequently appear like caricatures of their targets.[66] Even the less virulent forms of mass culture express a certain sadistic element in their repetition of the status quo, an observation made by Adorno in his study of jazz.

Mimesis, however, was not in itself a source of evil. On the contrary, Horkheimer implied, it was healthy when it meant the imitation of the life-affirming aspects of nature, that is, maternal warmth and protection. It was the task of philosophy, he suggested in one of his Columbia lectures,[67] to reawaken the memory of childhood mimesis, which had been obscured by later socialization. The decline of the family must therefore be reversed, or at least the child's imitative impulse, which had become fixated on extra-familial agencies, must be restored to its original object in the family. This goal, it might be added, was closely connected with the unity of word and thing experienced in pure language. As Horkheimer argued, "Language reflects the longings of the oppressed and the plight of nature; it releases the mimetic impulse. The transformation of this impulse into the universal medium of language rather than into destructive action means that potentially nihilistic energies work for reconciliation."[68] Ontogenetically, this condition existed in the consciousness of the two-year-old child to whom all nouns, in a sense, were proper nouns.

If the goal was the restitution of this stage of human development, or at least certain of its better characteristics, what would happen to the ego, which was developed, according to Freud, at a later date? In their speculative works in the forties, Horkheimer and Adorno assumed a very different tone when discussing the ego from that evident in the *Studies in Prejudice*. Now, instead of stressing the need for an integrated ego to combat the projections of ego-alien traits onto minority scapegoats, they connected the development of the ego with the domination of nature. In *Eclipse of Reason*, Horkheimer contended:

> As the principle of the self endeavoring to win in the fight against nature in general, against other people in particular, and against its own impulses, the ego is felt to be related to the functions of domination, command, and organization. . . . Its dominance is patent in the patriarchal epoch. . . . The history of Western civilization could be written in terms of the growth of the ego as the underling subliminates, that is, internalizes, the commands of his master who has preceded him in self-discipline. . . . At no time has the notion of the ego shed the blemishes of its origin in the system of social domination.[69]

Moreover, the struggle of the subjectively rational ego against nature, both external and internal, had been completely counterproductive in the end. "The moral is plain," Horkheimer concluded; "the apotheosis of the ego and the principle of self-preservation as such culminate in the utter insecurity of the individual, in his complete negation." [70]

Here the ego was meant partly in philosophical terms — the *ego cogito* from Descartes to Husserl had been a target of the Institut from the beginning[71] — but it clearly had psychological significance as well. Marcuse's later concept of the "performance principle" as the specific reality principle of Western society was rooted in this earlier critique of the ego as tool of domination. In *Eros and Civilization*, however, he attempted to outline the contours of a new reality principle, whereas Horkheimer and Adorno were content to undermine the traditional ego without offering a fully worked out alternative, an omission that would worry later Frankfurt School adherents like Jürgen Habermas.[72]

Despite the potentially primitivist implications of their arguments, Horkheimer and Adorno were careful to reject anything implying a return to natural simplicity. Nostalgia, as we have seen, was castigated when it appeared among conservative cultural critics; similarly, nostalgia for the lost youth of mankind was not really the Frankfurt School's dominant sentiment. This was clearly demonstrated in Horkheimer's complicated discussion of the relationship between reason and nature in *Eclipse of Reason.* As we have frequently observed, the Institut was highly critical of what passed for reason in the modern world. Instrumental, subjective, manipulative reason, its members argued, was the handmaiden of technological domination. Without rational goals, all interaction was eventually reduced to power relationships. The disenchantment of the world had gone too far, and reason itself had been gutted of its original content.

In so arguing, of course, Horkheimer and his colleagues were by no means alone. In fact, they were at one with a wide variety of thinkers with whom they were rarely in agreement on other issues. As Fritz Ringer has shown, the academic "mandarins" of the Weimar years were obsessed with the rationalization of the world and its consequences.[73] Max Scheler, for example, had criticized the rational domination of nature as early as 1926.[74] Similar sentiments flowed from the pen of another antagonist, Martin Heidegger, whose early influence on Marcuse has often been cited as responsible for the antitechnological bias allegedly to be found in his former student's work.[75] In the forties, conservative writers from totally different traditions also launched heated attacks against instrumental rationality and its effects. Michael Oakeshott's influential essay "Rationalism in Politics"[76] appeared in the same year as *Dialectic of the Enlightenment* and *Eclipse of Reason.*

What distanced the Frankfurt School from some of these writers was, as we have seen, its members' insistence on the varieties of reason, one of which might avoid the clash with nature. What distinguished their view from others was their refusal to accept the possibility that this type of substantive reason might be immediately realized in social terms. Nonantagonistic reason was always a hope, but one whose existence, albeit through negation of the status quo, prevented the uncritical apotheosis of nature. In *Eclipse of Reason* Horkheimer devoted a chapter to a demonstration of the intimate relationship that existed between alleged "returns" to nature and instrumental rationality. Here the argument was similar to that developed in the discussion of de Sade in the *Dialectic.* To Horkheimer,

> the revolt of natural man — in the sense of the backward strata of the population — against the growth of rationality has actually furthered the formalization of reason, and has served to fetter rather than to free nature. In this light, we might describe fascism as a satanic synthesis of reason and nature — the very opposite of that reconciliation of the two poles that philosophy has always dreamed of.[77]

Symptomatic of the connection between the revolt of nature and domination was Darwinism, at least in its social guise. To Horkheimer, Social Darwinism had reversed the potential for reconciliation inherent in Darwin's initial insight into man's oneness with nature. Instead, "the concept of the survival of the fittest was merely the translation of the concepts of formalized reason into the vernacular of natural history." [78] Not surprisingly, he pointed to pragmatism, one of his consistent *bêtes noires*, as an offshoot of Darwinism.[79] Benjamin in his article on Eduard Fuchs had already established the relationship between Darwinian evolutionism and the shallow optimism of Bernsteinian socialists.[80] This type of reconciliation of reason and nature, which really reduced the former to an organ of the latter, was no solution. Regression to pre-Enlightenment "naturalism" was an obvious fallacy with sinister results. "The sole way of assisting nature," Horkheimer suggested, "is to unshackle its seeming opposite, independent thought." [81]

"Independent thought," of course, did not mean a return to pre-Marxist notions of totally autonomous speculation. In *Eclipse of Reason* Horkheimer explicitly rejected attempts to revive earlier metaphysical systems. Neo-Thomism, which in the late forties was enjoying an upsurge of interest, served as the major target of his attack. The neo-Thomist search for absolute dogmas he dismissed as an attempt to overcome relativism by fiat. Its advocates' desire to make Aquinas's teachings relevant in the modern world he ridiculed as conformist and affirmative. To Horkheimer, neo-Thomism was fundamentally akin to pragmatism in its neglect of negation. "The failure of Thomism," he charged, "lies in its ready acquiescence to pragmatic aims rather than in its lack of practicability. When a doctrine hypostatizes an isolated principle that excludes negation, it is paradoxically predisposing itself to conformism." [82] The innate defect of Thomism, as of all positivist systems, "lies in its making truth and goodness identical with reality." [83]

Another popular attempt at "independent thought" that appeared after the war was the existentialist movement. Well before its faddish success, the Institut had been antagonistic towards thinkers who would later be considered its leading spokesmen. Adorno's critique of Kierkegaard was the most extensive attack, but Horkheimer had written unsympathetically of Jaspers,[84] and Marcuse, after joining the Institut, had come to criticize Heidegger's work,[85] as well as the political existentialism of Carl Schmitt.[86] After the war, the most important statement of the movement was Sartre's *Being and Nothingness.* When it came to Horkheimer's attention in 1946, he wrote to Lowenthal:

After having a good taste of Sartre I am deeply convinced that it is our duty to have our book published as soon as possible. Despite my inner resistance, I have read a great part of Sartre. . . . This is a new kind of philosophical mass literature. . . . From a philosophical point of view, the most amazing phenomenon is indeed the naive reification of dialectical concepts. . . . The dialectical finesse and complexity of thought has been turned into a glittering machinery of metal. Words like "l'être en soi" and "l'être pour soi" function as kinds of pistons. The fetishistic handling of categories appears even in the form of printing, with its enervating and intolerable use of italics. All the concepts are *termini technici* in the literal sense of the word.[87]

In *Eclipse of Reason*, however, no mention of existentialism was made. The task of demolition was left to Marcuse in the only article he published during his tenure with the State Department after the war.[88] Marcuse's assessment of *Being and Nothingness* was scarcely less critical than Horkheimer's. In several ways, his arguments anticipated Sartre's own self-criticism of later years.[89] To Marcuse, Sartre had erroneously made absurdity into an ontological rather than a historical condition. As a result, he fell back into an idealistic internalization of freedom as something opposed to the outside, heteronomous world. Despite his avowed revolutionary intentions, his politics and his philosophy were totally at odds. By locating freedom in the *pour-soi* (being-for-itself, a version of Hegel's *für-sich*) and denying that the *pour-soi* could become *en-soi* (being-in-itself, or *an-sich*), Sartre severed subjectivity from objectivity in a way that denied reconciliation even as a utopian possibility. Moreover, by overemphasizing the freedom of the subject and ignoring the constraints produced by his historical condition, Sartre had become an unwitting apologist for the status quo. Arguing as Sartre did that men chose their fate, even if it was a horrible one, was monstrous:

If philosophy, by virtue of its existential-ontological concepts of man or freedom, is capable of demonstrating that the persecuted Jew and the victim of the executioner are and remain absolutely free and masters of a self-responsible choice, then these philosophical concepts have declined to the level of a mere ideology which offers itself as a most handy justification for the persecutors and executioners.[90]

To Marcuse, the entire project of an "existentialist" philosophy without an a priori idea of essence was impossible. This Sartre's own work demonstrated against its intentions: the *pour-soi*, with its perfect freedom, was a normative description of man in his generic state, not in his empirical condition. By absorbing negation into this affirmative view of human nature, Sartre had lost the dialectical tension of essentialist philosophies. In fact, his concept of the *pour-soi* as constant action and self-creation had a specifically affirmative function in bourgeois society. "Beyond the nihilistic language of existentialism," Marcuse charged, "lurks the ideology of free competition, free initiative, and equal opportunity." [91] Sartre's subject, which resembled Stirner's anarchistic ego, was very much in the Enlightenment tradition of the domination of nature.[92]

The only element of *Being and Nothingness* to which Marcuse gave grudging approval was Sartre's discussion of sexuality. As Paul Robinson has pointed out,[93] Marcuse's interest in this question was a way-station to his later involvement with Freud. It also referred to arguments he had made a decade before in the *Zeitschrift.*[94] What struck Marcuse in Sartre's treatment of sexuality was the "negation of the negation" implicit in sexual desire, which when carried to an extreme negated the activity of the *pour-soi.* In sexuality, the body tended to become a completely reified, passive object controlled solely by the pleasure principle rather than by the dominant reality principle. As early as 1937 Marcuse had written:

> when the body has completely become an object, a beautiful thing, it can foreshadow a new happiness. In suffering the most extreme reification man triumphs over reification. The artistry of the beautiful body, its effortless agility and relaxation, which can be displayed today only in the circus, vaudeville, and burlesque, herald the joy to which men will attain in being liberated from the ideal, once mankind, having become a true subject, succeeds in the mastery of matter.[95]

Although no longer talking in terms of the "mastery of matter," Marcuse continued to feel that the passive freedom of total sexual reification negated the existentialist reduction of freedom to the activity of the aggressive *pour-soi.* This, in fact, offered greater insight into the potential transformation of society than Sartre's clumsy attempts to derive a radical politics from his philosophy.[96] The negation of the *pour-soi* — which seemed to operate according to what Marcuse would later call "the performance principle" [97] — suggested a kind of reconciliation with nature, although it was of course only a partial step in that direction. Complete reification meant the negation not only of the dominating aspects of the ego, but also its nondominating ones as well. This was a reality that concerned Horkheimer and Adorno in their own treatment of the reification of the body in *Dialectic of the Enlightenment.*[98]

It might be argued that the Frankfurt School's most pressing fear in the postwar era was the obliteration of just those elements of subjectivity. As we have seen in looking at the Institut's treatment of mass culture and its empirical work on authoritarian personalities, the existence of genuine individuality was declining at an alarming rate. The Institut did not, of course, wish to revive the old bourgeois individual with his dominating ego, but it did feel that in some ways his replacement by manipulated mass men meant a loss of freedom. As Adorno had written to Benjamin,[99] the "individual" was a *Durchgangsinstrument*, an instrument of passage, which could not be mythicized away, but had to be preserved in a higher synthesis instead. The bourgeois individual, defined as he was in opposition to the totality, was not fully free. As we have noted on previous occasions, the goal of positive freedom implicitly upheld by the Frankfurt School was grounded in the unification of particular and universal interests. But, on the other hand, negative freedom was a moment in that dialectical totality. The bourgeois subject was thus both free and unfree at the same time. In the forced identity of mass man with the social totality, however, there was no freedom at all. At least earlier bourgeois society had contained tangible contradictions that preserved negations of its dominant tendencies. Egoism, it will be recalled, had been defended by Horkheimer for its recognition of the moment of individual happiness preserved in the genuine reconciliation of contradictions. Marcuse had made similar arguments in his qualified defense of hedonistic philosophies.

Now it appeared that the very existence of contradictions, or at least the consciousness of their existence, was in jeopardy, even though capitalism had not been superseded by socialism.[100] In what Marcuse was later to make famous as "one-dimensional" society, the redeeming power of negation was almost totally absent. What was left in its place was a cruel parody of the dream of positive freedom. The Enlightenment, which had sought to liberate man, had ironically served to enslave him with far more effective means than ever before. Without a clear mandate for action, the only course open to those who could still escape the numbing power of the culture industry was to preserve and cultivate the vestiges of negation that still remained. "Philosophical theory itself cannot bring it about that either the barbarizing tendency or the humanistic outlook should prevail in the future," Horkheimer warned. "However, by doing justice to those images and ideas that at given times dominated reality in the role of absolutes — e.g., the idea of the individual as it dominated the bourgeois era — and that have been relegated in the course of history, philosophy can function as a corrective of history, so to speak." [101]

This was the task that Adorno set himself in his most personal and idiosyncratic book, *Minima Moralia*, which was written in bits and pieces throughout the forties and published in 1951. Its fragmented, aphoristic style was no accident: to Adorno negation and the truth it precariously preserved could be expressed only in tentative, incomplete ways. Here Critical Theory's fundamental distrust of systematizing was carried to its extreme. The location of philosophical insight was no longer to be found in abstract, coherent, architectonic systems, as in Hegel's day, but rather in subjective, private reflection. In his introduction, Adorno emphasized how far he thought philosophy had come since Hegel, who in his more generous moments had tolerated aphorisms as "conversation." [102] Hegel, consistently attacking the *für-sich sein* of subjectivity as inadequate, had made one major error. He had hypostatized the bourgeois individual and civil society of his day as irreducible realities. This permitted him to pay as much attention as he did to the totality. Since his time, however, their vulnerability had been amply demonstrated. By the mid-twentieth century the forces of the social totality were so great that subjectivity, bourgeois or otherwise, was in mortal danger. "In the face of totalitarian unity," Adorno wrote, "which cries out for the elimination of differences directly as meaning *[welche die Ausmerzung der Differenz unmittelbar als Sinn ausschreit]*, something of the liberating social forces may even have converged in the sphere of the individual. Critical Theory lingers there without a bad conscience." [103] In short, as Adorno wrote in one of his most often quoted epigrams, *Das Ganze ist das Unwahre*,[104] "the whole is the untrue."

Accordingly, the bulk of *Minima Moralia* consisted of oblique distillations of Adorno's own experiences, reflections, as he put it in the book's subtitle, of a "damaged life." As in all of the Frankfurt School's work, traditional philosophical pigeonholes such as epistemology or ethics were transcended. "Intelligence," Adorno wrote elsewhere at about the same time, "is a moral category. The separation of feeling from understanding, which makes it possible for the moron to speak freely and blissfully, hypostatizes the historically created separation of men according to function." [105] Philosophy therefore must return to its original intention: "the teaching of the correct life." [106] Under present conditions, however, it must remain a "melancholy science," rather than a "joyful" one, as Nietzsche had hoped, because of the slim chances for its success. Above all, it must disturb rather than comfort: "the splinter in your eye is the best magnifying glass." [107]

At the end of his effort, in the last aphorism of the book, Adorno showed how far he had come from a belief in the possible realization of the hope for final reconciliation. The terms he chose to use were now self-consciously theological. Philosophy can once again become responsible, he suggested, through the "effort to regard all things as the way they would represent themselves from the standpoint of salvation *[Erlösung]*. Knowledge has no other light than that which shines from salvation on the world; all others exhaust themselves in *post facto* construction and remain a part of technology." [108] Where Adorno drew back, however, was from suggesting that salvation or redemption might be actually achieved. In other words, he denied the possibility of realizing the absolute without at the same time negating the reality of the finite and contingent. Thought, he paradoxically asserted, must comprehend this impossibility for the sake of what was in fact possible: "Against the challenge which emanates from this realization, the question of the reality or unreality of salvation itself is almost immaterial." [109]

Shortly before his death, Benjamin had written that "our image of happiness is indissolubly bound up with the image of redemption. . . . Like every generation that preceded us, we have been endowed with a *weak* messianic power." [110] In *Minima Moralia* Adorno seemed to agree with the connection between redemption and happiness, but denied even a weakened messianic power to his age. Positive freedom and the genuine reconciliation it promised, he implied, were perpetually utopian hopes incapable of earthly realization. The negation of the negation, that dream of alienation returning to itself which motivated both Hegel and Marx, must remain frustrated. The dialectic, as the title of one of his subsequent books indicated, could be only negative.[111] Horkheimer's later expression of interest in Schopenhauer confirmed this turn in Critical Theory's focus. When Horkheimer wrote that "to stand up for the temporal against merciless eternity is morality in Schopenhauer's sense," [112] he was merely seconding Adorno's observation in *Minima Moralia* that the demands of the totality could not be met without the destruction of the finite and contingent.

At the same time, of course, the Frankfurt School continued to hold that utopian hopes, although never fully realizable, must be maintained. Paradoxically, only such hopes could prevent history from returning to mythology. As Horkheimer wrote to Lowenthal in 1943 about the Nazis' historical sense:

> Their concept of history boils down to the veneration of monuments. There is no such thing as history without that utopian element which, as you point out, is lacking in them. Fascism, by its very exaltation of the past, is anti-historical. The Nazis' references to history mean only that the powerful must rule and that there is no emancipation from the eternal laws which guide humanity. When they say history, they mean its very opposite: mythology.[113]

In so arguing, the Frankfurt School put itself in a long line of thinkers whose utopian visions were less blueprints for action than sources of critical distance from the gravitational pull of the prevailing reality.[114]

It was this subtle, but crucial, transformation of the Institut's theoretical intentions in the forties that was the major reason for the second discontinuity mentioned earlier. With the shifting of the Institut's emphasis away from class struggle to the conflict between man and nature, the possibility of a historical subject capable of ushering in the revolutionary age disappeared. That imperative for *praxis*, so much a part of what some might call the Institut's heroic period, was no longer an integral part of its thought. Adorno's much quoted remark made shortly before his death in 1969, that "when I made my theoretical model, I could not have guessed that people would try to realize it with Molotov cocktails," [115] was not the lament of a man who had misgauged the practical implications of his thought. It reflected instead a fundamental conclusion of the theory itself: negation could never be truly negated. By *Minima Moralia*, and perhaps before, Adorno had accepted the melancholy reality that "philosophy which once seemed outmoded is now alive because the moment of its realization has been missed." [116]

What type of *praxis* might still be pursued was by no means clear. As Horkheimer had warned in *Eclipse of Reason*, rationality provided no guidelines for political activity. The radicalizing of Critical Theory had increased its distance from what was generally accepted as radical *praxis*. Yet the Frankfurt School never really retreated into liberalism or conservatism as a compelling alternative. Preserving nonidentity and negation seemed to imply liberal pluralism, but the Institut distrusted the reality of competing groups in mass society. In other ways as well, its position was at odds with liberalism, which was very much the child of the Enlightenment. Incremental progress, technical mastery of nature, tolerance as an end in itself, all liberal faiths, were unacceptable to Horkheimer and his colleagues. So too were the irrational premises of a Burkean conservatism, despite the fact that some of its modern exponents, like Michael Oakeshott, attacked instrumental rationalism with similar fervor. Nor were the affirmative bromides of right-wing Hegelian conservatives, with their belief in the inherent rationality of the existing world, very attractive. In fact, Critical Theory was now incapable of suggesting a critical *praxis*. The inherent tension in the concept of positive freedom had become too powerful to ignore. The union of freedom as reason and as self-realizing action was split asunder. The Frankfurt School, following its initial instincts, could only choose reason, even in the muted, negative form in which it might be found in the administered nightmare of the twentieth century. Theory, Horkheimer and the others seemed to be saying, was the only form of *praxis* still open to honest men.[117]

Epilogue

In the spring of 1946, Lowenthal reported to Horkheimer some encouraging news from Germany:

> Josef Maier [a former student of the Institut and the husband of Alice Maier, then the administrative head of the New York branch] wrote in a letter to his wife that the better students and intellectuals in Germany are more interested in getting our writings than in getting food. And you know what that means. He thinks that all the universities would like to have the *Zeitschrift* if they could get it.[1]

The audience for whom the Frankfurt School had so long insisted on writing in German was beginning to materialize. Several months after Maier's letter, the Institut was approached by members of the Frankfurt community, Ministerial Advisor Klingelhöfer, University Rector Hallstein, and Dean Sauermann, with the first concrete offer to return to the city of its origin.[2]

For the time being, Horkheimer was reluctant to respond positively. The *Studies in Prejudice* were not yet completed, and the Institut's commitments in America for the next few years were great enough to postpone an immediate decision. By April, 1947, however, there were signs that Horkheimer had begun to weaken. If there was to be a study of the effects of American antiprejudice programs on Germans, he wrote Lowenthal,[3] a branch in Frankfurt could be useful. Moreover, the Institut might teach American social scientific techniques to German students, thereby combatting the overly speculative bias of traditional German academics. No mention was made at this time of moving the actual center of the Institut back. In fact, possible affiliations with universities in the Los Angeles area were being considered as late as August, 1947.[4]

In the spring of the following year Horkheimer made his first visit to Germany since his hurried departure in 1933. Invited to participate in ceremonies commemorating the hundredth anniversary of the Frankfurt Parliament, he was warmly greeted as the guest of the city and gave a series of well-received lectures at the university. The eagerness of Frankfurt officials to regain some of the city's pre-Nazi intellectual eminence by enticing the Institut back was considerable. And ultimately, their efforts proved successful. With the encouragement of American occupation officials, including High Commissioner John J. McCloy, the city was able to make an offer that Horkheimer found impossible to reject. By September he was determined to return, and wrote Klingelhöfer of his decision, which was quickly accepted. On July 13, 1949, the university chair that had been taken away sixteen years before was restored, with the slight change that it was now in sociology and philosophy rather than social philosophy. With Horkheimer, of course, came the Institut itself with its endowment and library. Its reestablishment, he would later recall,[5] was not to be understood as acceptance of a *Wiedergutmachung* (compensation) by a repentant government, for nothing could make good what Germany had done. It was meant instead as a gesture to honor those Germans who had resisted Hitler by helping the Jews.

Once back in front of German students, Horkheimer's decision was quickly confirmed. "It is amazing," he wrote Lowenthal in February, "how deep and lasting an experience [of the Institut] was created in the minds of many European intellectuals up to 1933. This experience has not been discredited through the period of the Third Reich. It is now our duty to corroborate and deepen it in the future." [6] The eagerness of the students awoke in him an appropriately enthusiastic response. "I have worked literally day and night in the past two months," he wrote in April. "The most beautiful is still the teaching. Even during the vacation, we haven't lost contact with the students." [7] Horkheimer's lecturing virtuosity — Everett Hughes, who was a visiting professor in Frankfurt during those years, remembers him as the finest German speaker he had ever heard [8] — and his personal warmth in seminars quickly won him a sizable student following. Once established, Horkheimer and those who went with him never regretted having chosen the path of resettlement so few other emigrés were to follow.

Why Horkheimer hesitated for several years before making what proved to be so successful a move is not difficult to understand. Men rarely hasten back to a place where they have suffered ostracism and persecution. In addition, the precise status of the Institut after its return was unclear for a considerable time; an attempt to obtain UNESCO sponsorship ultimately foundered in a sea of personal vendettas. Moreover, despite the highly critical tone of the Institut's writings on America, the personal experiences of its members had been generally favorable. From Nicholas Murray Butler in 1934[9] to John Slawson a decade later, the Institut had received support and encouragement from a wide variety of American sources. Like many other refugees, the members of the Frankfurt School were pleasantly surprised by the number of "men of good will" [10] they encountered in the United States. In several instances, they willingly joined governmental service during the war, out of a feeling of solidarity with America's common fight against Hitler. As a result, Horkheimer and the others felt a keen reluctance to sever their ties with the country that had been home for some fifteen years. In fact, Horkheimer agreed to remain in Germany only after being assured that he could retain his naturalized citizenship. Through special legislation sponsored by McCloy and signed into law by President Truman in July, 1952, he was granted a continuation of his American citizenship despite his return to the country of his origin.[11]

What was perhaps even more distressing than the rigors of yet another resettlement was the prospect that not all of the Institut's members would accompany him back to Germany. Of their number, only Adorno was really anxious to leave. In later years, he would explain his desire in these terms:

> The decision to return to Germany was hardly motivated by simple subjective needs, by homesickness, as little as I can deny that. There was also an objective reason. That is language. Not merely because one can never express as exactly in a new language what one means, with all the nuances and the rhythms of the train of thought, as in one's own. Rather, the German language has a special elective affinity *[Wahlverwandtschaft]* to philosophy, and, to be sure, to its speculative moment.[12]

Pollock was also willing to go, largely out of loyalty to Horkheimer and the Institut, rather than dislike for America.

This, however, was not the case with other members of the Institut's inner circle, especially when it became clear that professorships at the university could not be guaranteed. On February 8, 1946, Lowenthal had written to Horkheimer that "I find myself in a funny dialectical position. In 1938, I was the strongest advocate of all of us in advising to dissolve our organizational framework. Today I see clearer than ever the possible risks." But when it came to implementing this sentiment by actually leaving for Germany, Lowenthal was unable to commit himself. His impending marriage to an American, the psychologist Marjorie Fiske, certainly contributed to his reluctance. In 1949 he accepted a position as director of the research division of the Voice of America, thus ending a twenty-three-year tenure with the Institut. Seven years later, he joined the sociology faculty at the Berkeley campus of the University of California.

Marcuse, whose connection with the Institut had grown increasingly tenuous during the forties, chose to remain with the State Department until 1950, when he returned to Columbia as a lecturer in sociology and senior fellow at the Russian Institute. During the next two years he also did research at the Russian Research Center at Harvard, which led to his book *Soviet Marxism.*[13] In 1954 he joined the history of ideas program at Brandeis, remaining for eleven years, during which his underground reputation, based on *Eros and Civilization* and *One-Dimensional Man*, steadily grew. By the time he left Waltham, Massachusetts, for the University of California at San Diego, in 1965, he was on the verge of becoming an internationally celebrated mentor of the nascent New Left.

Otto Kirchheimer also continued to work with the government after the war, first as research analyst in the State Department's Division of Research for Europe and then, from 1950 to 1955, as chief of the division's central European branch. For the next seven years, he was on the graduate faculty of the Institut's old competitor, the New School for Social Research in New York. In 1961 he published his massive work *Political Justice.* In the following year, he joined the government department at Columbia, where he taught until his death in 1965, a few days after his sixtieth birthday. Other former Institut members also found positions at American universities: Neumann at Columbia, Gerhard Meyer at the University of Chicago, and Massing at Rutgers, where Joseph Maier and M. I. Finley also joined the faculty. Kurt Mandelbaum, changing his name to Martin, ultimately became an economist in Manchester, England. Henryk Grossman, as mentioned earlier, did return to Germany, but not with the Institut. He went instead to the Soviet Zone, where he spent several unhappy years in Leipzig until his death in 1950. Gurland also returned to Germany in 1950 to teach at the Hochschule für Politik in Berlin, then at the Technische Hochschule in Darmstadt.

Wittfogel's career at this time took an important turn, which merits some comment. In 1947 he had established the Chinese History Project sponsored by the University of Washington and Columbia, which was the final step in his extrication from the Institut. Four years later, during the growing furor over alleged Communist infiltration of governmental and scholarly institutions, he was subpoenaed to appear in front of Senator Pat McCarran's Internal Security Subcommittee of the Senate Judiciary Committee.[14] Wittfogel later asserted that he went with great reluctance and that his testimony on August 7, 1951, was his only contribution to the anti-Communist hysteria of those years.[15] The Institut was mentioned solely as the initial contact with the Institute of Pacific Relations, whose infiltration he discussed at some length. Julian Gumperz, who had been cited as a Party member in the testimony of Hede Massing five days earlier, was identified as the intermediary. The only other figure peripherally associated with the Institut whose name appeared in Wittfogel's remarks was M. I. Finley, whose subsequent decision to leave America for England was certainly influenced by the repercussions of Wittfogel's allegations. Finley's move, it might be noted parenthetically, was ultimately to prove a great success, as he was given the chair in Ancient History at Cambridge in the late 1960's.

Wittfogel also introduced a plaintive note into his testimony when he claimed that his scholarly contacts had dried up when he became an avowed anti-Communist. There certainly can be no doubt that his former colleagues at the Institut found his new position anathema, especially because of his personal disclosures about previous political allegiances. They were firmly convinced that his cooperation with the witch hunters went well beyond the one day in front of the McCarran Committee, despite his angry assertions to the contrary. Wherever the truth may lie, Wittfogel became *persona non grata* to the Frankfurt School from that time on, as he did to many other liberally minded academics in this country. Whereas Horkheimer was disappointed about the decisions of certain Institut members to remain in America, he had no regrets about Wittfogel's choice.

The Institut thus returned to Frankfurt with a much diminished staff. Its support, nonetheless, was considerable. In June, 1949, a petition was circulated to urge its reopening. The list of signatories was highly impressive, an indication of the esteem in which the Institut was held by many of its scholarly colleagues. Among the names were Gordon Allport, Raymond Aron, G. D. H. Cole, G. P. Gooch, Morris Ginsberg, Eugen Kogan, Paul Lazarsfeld, Robert Lynd, Talcott Parsons, Paul Tillich, Robert MacIver, and James T. Shotwell. "The function of the revived Frankfurt branch," the petition read in part, "would be two-fold: the planning and conduct of research projects, and perhaps more significant, the instruction of a new generation of German students in modern developments in social science." [16] Financial support came from a number of sources. The McCloy Funds supplied 236,000 Marks, half the necessary total for the reestablishment. The Gesellschaft für Sozialforschung, the guardian of the Institut's endowment, gave all that it had left, which amounted to one-third more, and the rest came from the city of Frankfurt and private donors. Felix Weil, it might be added parenthetically, was no longer able to lend his support, due to the inflation in Argentina.[17]

In August, 1950, with Adorno as assistant director — five years later, he was raised to Horkheimer's level as codirector — the Institut began work in rooms at the *Kuratorium* on the Senckenberganlage and in the salvaged remains of the bombed-out building next door, which had been the Institut's original home.[18] On November 14 of the following year, a new building was dedicated on the same street not far from the site of its predecessor. Alois Geifer, its architect, designed a spare, functional building reminiscent of the *Neue Sachlichkeit* style of Franz Röckle's earlier effort. The distinguished sociologists René König and Leopold von Wiese spoke at the opening ceremony, as did Felix Weil. Appropriately, the music that began the proceedings was by Schönberg. The "Café Max," as the Institut became colloquially known among its new students, was once again fully in operation. The new nickname was a reference not merely to Max Horkheimer, but also to the Institut's prewar reputation as the "Café Marx." The dropping of the "r" symbolized the shift away from radicalism during the Institut's American period. Significantly, among its first tasks was the translation of several of the *Studies in Prejudice* into German. Although the *Zeitschrift* was not revived, the Institut soon began to publish a series of *Frankfurter Beiträge zur Soziologie*, whose first volume was a *Festschrift* for Horkheimer on his sixtieth birthday.[19]

During the first few years back, Horkheimer was occupied largely with the reorganization of the Institut and with academic affairs at the university.[20] In 1950 he was elected dean of the philosophy department and in November of the following year, at the age of fifty-six, was chosen as university rector.[21] Werner Richter, who had been made rector of Bonn a week earlier, was the first naturalized American to become head of a German university; Horkheimer was the second. Perhaps more symbolic still, he was the first Jew to achieve that post after the war. In 1952 he was selected for another twelve-month term. When his tenure ended, he was given the Goethe Prize, the highest honor bestowed by the city of Frankfurt. Seven years later, after his retirement to Switzerland, the city made him an honorary citizen for life.

Horkheimer's ties to America, however, continued to remain strong. The Institut's branch in New York, although inactive through the next two decades, was maintained with Alice Maier as its caretaker. Horkheimer himself served as foreign consultant to the Library of Congress, for which he prepared a *Survey of the Social Sciences in Western Germany*.[22] In 1954, he returned for a short time to the United States to become a part-time faculty member of the University of Chicago, to which he periodically returned for the next five years. Adorno, however, remained in Frankfurt and never returned to America after his brief time with the Hacker Foundation in Los Angeles in 1953. When Horkheimer and Pollock retired in 1958 to the Swiss town of Montagnola, where they built adjoining homes overlooking Lake Lugano, Adorno assumed the directorship of the Institut. Both Horkheimer and Pollock continued to have an active interest in Institut affairs well into the 1960's, even after new men like Rudolf Gunzert, who headed the Institut's statistical wing, and Ludwig von Friedeburg, who directed its empirical work, began to assume more of the administrative duties. Horkheimer also wrote, although at a somewhat slower pace than before. His newer essays were included with Alfred Schmidt's translation of *Eclipse of Reason* in *Kritik der instrumentellen Vernunft*, which appeared in 1967. Efforts to persuade him to republish his essays in the *Zeitschrift*, however, met with initial failure. In June, 1965, he wrote a letter to the S. Fischer Verlag explaining his reluctance in terms of the changed circumstances under which he had written the essays; their content, he argued, might well be misunderstood today as a result.[23] But in 1968 he finally relented, and the long-awaited republication took place in two volumes called *Kritische Theorie*. Their appearance was one of the primary stimuli to the interest in the earlier period of the Institut's history among whose results is the present study.

To present more than this highly schematic synopsis of the Institut's history and that of its central member after the return to Germany is not possible now. Similarly, a serious discussion of the extensive corpus of work published by Adorno from the early fifties until his death in the summer of 1969 must await another time.[24] So too must an analysis of Marcuse's influential transmission of the Frankfurt School's work to a new American audience in the 1960's.[25] By limiting ourselves to the period before 1950, we regrettably must neglect the time of the Institut's greatest impact. We have instead chosen to concentrate on the years of its highest creativity, which were lived in exile in America.

In fact, it might be argued that one of the conditions of that creative fecundity was precisely the relative isolation of the Frankfurt School during those years. After his resettlement in the early fifties, Horkheimer was lionized by a Frankfurt community grateful for the recapture of at least one survivor of Weimar culture. He rubbed shoulders with Konrad Adenauer and made frequent appearances on radio and television, and in the press.[26] The days when he could write to Lowenthal that "beyond the three or four of us there are certainly other hearts and brains that feel similarly to ours, but we cannot see them, and perhaps they are prevented from expressing themselves" [27] were clearly over.

With recognition and public acclaim came a gradual erosion of the Institut's critical edge, which had been reinforced by its earlier outsider status. The sense of a distinct "Frankfurt School" with all the inherent rigidity that implied began to crystallize. "To be true to Schönberg," Adorno had written, "is to warn against all twelve-tone schools." [28] To be true to the original spirit of Critical Theory, the Institut's critics would argue,[29] was to be wary of the reification of the "Frankfurt School." Moreover, what further dismayed the Institut's younger, more radical adherents was the ideological repercussions of this change. The Cold War spirit that Horkheimer and the others had struggled so hard to combat in the forties began gradually to filter into their pronouncements in the fifties and sixties.[30] A widening gulf began to separate Horkheimer and Adorno from Marcuse, whose political inclinations remained firmly to the left. No public acknowledgment of the rift was made because of the personal ties that still obtained, but private disagreements were keen. When Marcuse came to prominence, it was not as the head of a major American university accompanied by the chief of state. In fact, public recognition of his connection with the Frankfurt School was itself minimal. Without an institutional tie beyond that of faculty member at a number of American universities, he was unaffected by the need to present a "responsible" face to an expectant public. To attribute Marcuse's divergence from his former colleagues solely, or even primarily, to this factor would of course be overstated, but probably it had some effect.

To point to the institutional coherence of the Frankfurt School after 1950 as important is not to imply that it had lacked such coherence throughout its history. As Edward Shils has noted,[31] one of the key factors promoting its influence, at least as compared with more isolated figures such as Karl Mannheim, was its unbroken institutional continuity for almost a half century. Horkheimer, for all his avowed dislike of the pedestrian tasks of administration, was a shrewd organizer of men and skilled securer of financial support. Pollock, the trained economist who ran the Institut's administrative affairs, was said only half in jest to be less adept at managing its funds than Horkheimer, the philosopher.[32] One former associate, Paul Lazarsfeld, himself a highly skilled "managerial scholar," [33] has acknowledged the possession of similar, although not as explicit, qualities by Horkheimer.[34] The Institut's stubborn maintenance of its collective identity through a series of successive dislocations must be attributed in large measure to Horkheimer's complex personality, intellectual power, and practical organizational instincts. "You have no idea," Pollock once remarked, "how many things in the history of the Institut and the writings of its members stem from Horkheimer. Without him, all of us would have probably developed in a different way." [35] When persuasion failed, as in the case of Fromm and Neumann, Horkheimer was willing to see the intransigent opponent eased out of Institut affairs, rather than allow a prolonged difference of opinion to persist. Paul Massing, in describing the loyalty of another member of the Institut to Horkheimer, was moved to quote lines from Schiller's *Wallenstein*, roughly translatable as "since it was not given to me to be his equal, I have decided to love him without bounds." [36] Although it would certainly be unjust to reduce the other members of the Institut's inner circle to no more than satellites around Horkheimer, his predominance was generally unchallenged. Of all his colleagues, only Adorno seemed to exert as much influence on him as he exerted in return.

What set the Institut in America apart from the Institut in its second Frankfurt incarnation was thus not its organizational coherence as such. Rather, it was the role which that organization played in the Institut's interaction with its social and intellectual milieu. In the United States, it functioned to keep Horkheimer and his colleagues insulated to a significant degree from the outside world. Financially independent, at least as far as its theoretical work was concerned, and off by itself in the building on 117th Street, the Institut could continue to produce with little external pressure or interference. Its calculated decision to write in German meant, among other things, the impossibility of a large American following. Although a number of native-born students, such as Benjamin Nelson and M. I. Finley, were trained by the Institut on Morningside Heights, no real "Frankfurt School" developed on these shores. The Institut's outsider status, despite its connections with such prestigious benefactors as Columbia University and the American Jewish Committee, was thus secure.

The costs this entailed were obvious. Although often in some contact with the regular faculty at Columbia, the Frankfurt School remained generally outside the mainstream of American academic life. This allowed it to make assumptions, such as the equation of pragmatism with positivism, that lacked complete validity. It also cut the Institut off from potential allies in the American intellectual tradition, such as George Herbert Mead.[37] And finally, it unintentionally allowed the American public to form unbalanced opinions of its work based on those samples that were published in English.

The reasons why the Institut deliberately rejected the assimilation so many other refugees eagerly sought are complex. The Institut, it should be remembered, was originally staffed by men whose political involvement, although to different degrees in different cases, was on the fringes of Weimar radicalism. Despite the party affiliation of a few of its early adherents, the Institut as a whole was free from any ties to a regular political organization. In addition, from the beginning it was self-consciously distant from the normal German academic hierarchy, despite its loose connection with Frankfurt University. And finally, although its members were usually from assimilated Jewish families — here Fromm with his more orthodox background was the primary exception — they were still Jews whose marginality in German society was never fully overcome. In short, unlike many other exiles to America, the Frankfurt School had been somewhat of an outsider group before being forced to leave Germany.

Not surprisingly, the trauma of the Nazi take-over served to reinforce the Institut's alienated status. Symbolically, at one time or another many of its members were compelled to use pseudonyms: Horkheimer was "Heinrich Regius"; Adorno, "Hektor Rottweiler"; Benjamin, "Detlef Holz" and "C. Conrad"; Wittfogel, "Klaus Hinrichs," or "Carl Peterson"; Kirchheimer, "Heinrich Seitz"; Massing, "Karl Billinger"; Borkenau, "Fritz Jungmann"; and Kurt Mandelbaum, "Kurt Baumann." More seriously, the lives of men connected in various ways with the Institut were snuffed out by the Nazis. Among those lost were Andries Sternheim, Karl Landauer, Paul Ludwig Landsberg, and indirectly, Walter Benjamin. Others such as Wittfogel and Massing had seen the insides of concentration camps, but were fortunate enough to have been liberated before the camps, or ones like them, were turned into annihilation centers. There is thus little reason to question the source of the continued uncertainty of the Institut's members about their security for a number of years after they migrated to America. And with this uncertainty came the Institut's turning inward. As late as 1946, Horkheimer could include the following quotation from Edgar Allan Poe in a letter to Lowenthal:

> In like manner, nothing can be clearer than that a *very* generous spirit — *truly* feeling what all merely profess — must inevitably find itself misconceived in every direction — its motives misinterpreted. Just as extremeness of intelligence would be thought fatuity, so excess of chivalry could not fail of being looked upon as meanness in its last degree: — and so on with other virtues. This subject is a painful one indeed. That individuals *have* so soared above the plane of their race, is scarcely to be questioned; but, in looking back through history for traces of their existence, we should pass over all bi-

ographies of "the good and the great," while we search carefully the slight records of wretches who died in prison, in Bedlam, or upon the gallows.

And then he added: "During the last years I have never read any sentences which were closer to our own thoughts than these." [38]

After the return to Frankfurt, however, all this had changed. One of the purposes motivating the decision had been the effect the Institut might have on a new generation of German students. This meant a much greater participation in the normal academic life of the university community in which it was located. Instead of developing in relative isolation, the Frankfurt School was now one of the major currents of German sociological and philosophical thought. Instead of being ignored, its theoretical work was the source of an intense dispute, whose magnitude, as previously mentioned, rivaled the *Methodenstreit* (methodological dispute) that had split German social thought half a century earlier. Without the linguistic barrier that precluded the widespread dissemination of the Institut's ideas, their stimulus was felt as never before. Even that most conservative of social sciences, the discipline of history, was influenced by Critical Theory.[39] Against the spare intellectual landscape of postwar Germany, the Frankfurt School stood out even more strikingly than it might have if conditions had been similar to those prevailing in Weimar. In short, after 1950 the Frankfurt School's institutional embodiment served as a positive mediator between the ideas of its members and the society at large. In the place of insularity, it provided a platform for the propagation of Critical Theory as it developed in its new context.

It is not our purpose to dwell on the partial reintegration of the Institut after its return to Frankfurt, but rather to emphasize the contrast that this situation presented with its isolated status during the American years. Without drawing unnecessarily direct connections between the content of Critical Theory and the experiences of its creators, it must still be noted that the Frankfurt School's stress on negation, nonidentity, and the need, in a frequently used phrase, *nicht mitzumachen* (not to join in) was consonant with those experiences.

To suggest this, however, for the purposes of debunking would be a vain exercise, for the Frankfurt School apparently drew the same conclusions. Adorno's *Minima Moralia*, with its reduction of philosophy to "reflections of a damaged life," expressed this unequivocally. The Institut never accepted Mannheim's glorification of the "free-floating intelligentsia." "The answer to Mannheim's reverence for the intelligentsia as 'free-floating,'" Adorno wrote, "is to be found not in the reactionary postulate of its 'rootedness in Being' but rather in the reminder that the very intelligentsia that pretends to float freely is fundamentally rooted in the very being that must be changed and which it merely pretends to criticize." [40]

The Institut's zealous preservation of its outsider status was rooted in the recognition that such a position was in some way a precondition for the maintenance of a truly critical posture in its theoretical work. This meant, however, autonomy not only from normal politics, academic establishments, and mass culture, but also from any social forces claiming to embody negation. Unlike more orthodox Marxists, the Frankfurt School never felt that the personal interaction of workers and intellectuals would be beneficial to either. As early as "Traditional and Critical Theory" in 1937, Horkheimer had denied the necessary connection between radical theory and the proletariat, arguing instead for an alliance with all "progressive" forces willing "to tell the truth." [41] By 1951, Adorno had ruled out the possibility of any collectivity being on the side of truth and located the residue of those progressive social forces in the critical individual. In later years, this led to a denial that student radicals or other nascent "negative" groups were legitimate social forces on the side of true change. After 1950, the Institut may have been reintegrated, but it was not with those groups with whom its members had identified in its earliest stages or with their self-styled successors. Despite their scorn for Mannheim's ideas about free-floating intellectuals, the Frankfurt School's members came increasingly to resemble his model.

To explain the Institut's work solely in terms of its members' personal experiences of estrangement would of course be insufficient. For if the Frankfurt School was alienated from its present cultural surroundings, it still had vital ties to a specific historical tradition. In 1938 Benjamin had written: "The workers of the Institut für Sozialforschung converge in a critique of bourgeois consciousness. This critique takes place not from without, but as self-criticism." [42] Despite the early enthusiasm of Horkheimer and his friends for socialism, they were incontrovertibly the sons of upper bourgeois families. In a certain sense they shared the antibourgeois sentiments of many of their middle-class contemporaries. However, instead of following the classic lineage most clearly expressed in Mann's *Buddenbrooks* — the first generation making the money, the second consolidating the social position, and the third withdrawing into aesthetic malaise — they followed a somewhat different pattern. In their cases, intellectual iconoclasm combined with a sense of social responsibility directly succeeded the acquisition of wealth. Without the intervening generation of social respectability, they were less compelled to assert their independence through rebellious life-styles than other antibourgeois sons of the bourgeoisie. Avoiding the extravagances of the expressionist generation, whose moment in history came immediately before theirs, Horkheimer and the others channeled all their critical energies into the relatively impersonal realm of social thought. Except for the loss of an early religiosity on the part of Fromm and Lowenthal, they seem to have escaped what later was to be called an identity crisis. The characteristic expressionist *Wandlung* (transformation), most clearly demonstrated in the Ernst Toller play of the same name, was not a phase through which they passed. Keeping their distance from the daily absurdities of Weimar and then American life, they were also able to avoid the bitterness and bile that characterized other left-wing intellectuals closer to these occurrences, such as Kurt Tucholsky. For outsiders, they lived in comparative comfort through all their peregrinations. Benjamin, the Institut figure whose life was most marred by misfortune, might well have expressed resentment in his writings, if it had not been for the strict dissociation of life and work that was a strange element in his makeup.[43] The others reacted to their insecurities by tightening their hold on the upper bourgeois life-style in which they had been immersed since birth.

The members of the Institut not only maintained this life-style, but also remained true to some extent to the comparable cultural values. There were, in fact, certain striking similarities between their attitudes and those of the German educated elite whose fortunes Fritz Ringer has recently traced in *The Decline of the German Mandarins*.[44] The Institut, of course, had been founded to counteract the effects of what Grünberg had called *Mandarinanstalten*.[45] However, he and Ringer defined "mandarins" very differently. To Grünberg, they were the technical intellectuals who put their skills at the service of the status quo; to Ringer, they were similar to the Chinese literati studied by Max Weber: "a social and cultural elite which owes its status primarily to educational qualifications, rather than to hereditary rights or wealth."[46] In the late nineteenth century Ringer's "mandarins" had achieved a short-lived ascendancy, during the period of equilibrium produced by the decline of the landed elite and the still unfinished rise of the industrial bourgeoisie. By approximately 1890, however, they felt themselves threatened by the impending triumph of the latter over the former, as the *Industriestaat* (industrial state) began to supplant the *Agrarstaat* (agrarian state).

As a result, they assumed an increasingly defensive and rigid posture against the rise of modernity and mass society.

In certain ways, the Frankfurt School might be assimilated to Ringer's model. Like the mandarins and unlike more orthodox socialists, they wrote works permeated more with a sense of loss and decline than with expectation and hope. They also shared the mandarins' distaste for mass society and the utilitarian, positivistic values it fostered. Similarly, they opposed the spirit of specialization that seemed to pervade modern intellectual life. "What really worried them," Ringer wrote of the mandarins in a sentence that could easily apply to the Institut, "was not the isolation of the disciplines *from each other*, but the growing separation, within the disciplines, between scholarship and a certain kind of philosophy." [47] The Frankfurt School's distrust of the Enlightenment was likewise an essential element in the mandarin defense of traditional German *Kultur*. In exile, they saw themselves as embattled *Kulturträger* (culture-bearers), a self-image the mandarins would have certainly recognized. And finally, their inherently apolitical attitude, even in the period when *praxis* was an imperative in their writings, invites comparison with the mandarins' condescending disdain for the petty squabbles of interest politics.

And yet, despite these similarities, the members of the Frankfurt School defy simple categorization as latter-day mandarins in exile. First of all, Ringer's mandarins were basically academic insiders, the leaders of the established intellectual elite. As we have noted on many occasions, the Institut sought to dissociate itself from the traditional university community, whose smugness and elitism it criticized severely. Secondly, the historical locus of their values was not precisely the same as the mandarins'. As Ringer notes, "the most important formal elements in the mandarins' scholarly heritage were the Kantian critique, the theories of Idealism, and the German historical tradition." [48] The Frankfurt School, on the other hand, was far closer in outlook to the Left Hegelians of the 1840's. Thus, unlike many of the mandarins, they refused to champion vulgar idealism as an antidote to vulgar materialism. As we have seen, Critical Theory was rooted in a dialectical overcoming of the traditional idealism-materialism dichotomy. Materialism and positivism need not be synonymous, as many of the mandarins assumed. Thirdly, the Frankfurt School's defense of older cultural values never meant the hypostatization of those values as something apart from and superior to material interests. This was the very separation that characterized what the Institut castigated as "affirmative culture." The Institut's concern for corporeal, sensual happiness was rarely shared by the mandarins, whose idealism had an ascetic side. Not surprisingly, the mandarins had no use for the psychoanalysis that Horkheimer and his colleagues wished to integrate into Critical Theory.[49]

What made the Frankfurt School's critique of modern society different was that without dismissing the mandarins' values out of hand, Horkheimer and the others demonstrated that absolutizing these values in a certain way inevitably led to their betrayal. As Adorno argued:

> If cultural criticism, even at its best with Valéry, sides with conservatism, it is because of its unconscious adherence to a notion of culture which, during the era of late capitalism, aims at a form of property which is stable and independent of stock-market fluctuations. This idea of culture asserts its distance from the system in order, as it were, to offer universal security in the middle of a universal dynamic.[50]

Finally, the Frankfurt School was distinguished from the mandarins by the refusal of its members to seek immediate panaceas to the contradictions of modern society. Instead of sentimentalizing community and "peoplehood," the Institut sought to expose the dangers inherent in such premature reconciliations. Both the Nazi *Volksgemeinschaft* (popular community) and the "one-dimensional society" of postwar America meant the elimination of subjectivity in the name of an illegitimate and ideological consensus.

In short, however much the Institut's members may have absorbed from the mandarin tradition into which they were born, the impact of their early exposure to Freud, and more important, Marx, remained strong. The role of the Institut in the history of twentieth-century Marxism, to be sure, was itself problematical. Despite its ultimate abandonment of many of the essential tenets of Marxist theory — the revolutionary potential of the working class, class struggle as the motor of history,[51] the economic substructure as the center of any social analysis — the Frankfurt School did Marxism a great service in its earlier years. By helping to preserve the integrity of Marx's libertarian impulse at a time when Stalinism was rampant, Horkheimer and his colleagues played a crucial role in the recovery of that impulse by post-Stalinist radicals in later years. By persistently questioning the philosophical assumptions of Marxist theory, they significantly raised the level of discussion within Marxist circles and helped make Marxism a legitimate object of inquiry outside them. By consistently employing historical materialism as an open-ended critique rather than a body of received truths, they helped restore vitality to what was threatening to become a sclerotic dogmatism. Willing to break new ground, the Institut made possible the fruitful interpenetration of such seemingly inconsistent systems as psychoanalysis and Marxism. Finally, by skillfully applying implicit arguments in Marx to cultural phenomena in an imaginative way, the Frankfurt School helped rescue materialist cultural criticism from the sterile literalisms of socialist realism.

Yet, in the end, the Institut presented a revision of Marxism so substantial that it forfeited the right to be included among its many offshoots. By challenging the actual or even potential existence of a historical subject capable of implementing a rational society, the Institut finally jettisoned that central premise of Marx's work, the unity of theory and *praxis*. The clashes its members had with the German New Left in the 1960's were merely the working out of this earlier transformation. Even Marcuse's "Great Refusal" would seem to many more orthodox Marxists a vague and imprecise spur to political action, no more than an "indeterminate negation" of the status quo in the anarchist tradition.[52] In 1962 Lukács voiced his and other Marxists' disdain for the Frankfurt School by dubbing it the "Grand Hotel *Abgrund* (Abyss)." [53] As Marcuse's popularity grew in later years, even his more radical variant of Critical Theory served as the target for orthodox Marxist abuse. This of course was by no means new. Felix Weil, for example, remembers an incident in 1929 in which something he did occasioned the retort of a member of the KPD's central committee: "What a pity, Felix, that you never joined the Party. Otherwise we could expel you now." [54] (These were the same words, it might be noted parenthetically, that Kurt Tucholsky heard in 1932.)[55] What was new was the increasing visibility of the Frankfurt School after 1950, which made its renegade materialism a greater threat to more conventional Marxists and, as a result, a greater object of scorn.

Equally problematical was the Institut's role in the intellectual migration whose collective impact on America was so enormous. Its efforts to aid refugees coming to America were apparently substantial, although their precise dimensions cannot be known until the Institut releases the names of those it actually supported. Through its doors passed approximately fifty younger scholars who would ultimately become American professors,[56] including such influential figures as Paul Honigsheim, Hans Gerth, and Paul Baran. Collaboration with others such as the Berkeley Public Opinion Study Group also doubtless had an effect.

Yet the intellectual impact of the Institut must be considered uneven at best. The considerable influence of its empirical studies in the forties has already been noted, as has that of its critique of mass culture. But in general its theoretical work fell on deaf ears. The Institut's effort to prevent the decline of philosophy into positivist social science was without real success. In part this was a reflection of the Institut's tendency to cast its theoretical critiques in the most extreme terms. "In psychoanalysis," Adorno had written, "only the exaggerations are true." [57] In Critical Theory, so it seemed at times, the same principle was followed. Thus, for example, the Frankfurt School's critique of American society sometimes appeared to suggest that no real distinction existed between Nazi coercion and the "culture industry." In fact, so some of its critics would charge, the Nazi experience had been so traumatic for the Institut's members that they could judge American society only in terms of its fascist potential.[58] By insulating themselves from American life to the extent that they did, the unique historical factors that made American advanced capitalism and mass society different from their European counterparts were lost to view. Totalitarianism, the Institut always insisted, was an outgrowth of liberalism, not its reverse, but in America there existed a liberal, bourgeois society that resisted the transformation. Why this was so the Institut never explored in any real depth. The similarities between Europe and America its members made painstakingly clear, the differences far less so.

To suggest this implies that the mixed success of the Institut's theoretical work in America was largely its own responsibility. The reality, however, was somewhat more complex. What must also be understood was the magnitude of the Frankfurt School's challenge to the conventional wisdom of American social thought. As I have argued elsewhere,[59] a selective pattern of acceptance can be discerned in America's reception of the Central European refugees. Although by no means without exceptions, the warmest welcomes were reserved for those new arrivals whose thinking most closely approximated the *Neue Sachlichkeit* spirit that had prevailed in Weimar's middle years. Whether in architecture with the Bauhaus, in philosophy with the Vienna Circle, or in sociology with Paul Lazarsfeld's brand of quantitative research, the ethic of sober objectivity and technological progress struck a respondent chord in American intellectual life. The Institut, despite the design of its original building, had been critical of the *Neue Sachlichkeit* from the beginning.[60] To Horkheimer and the others, it represented a stylistic correlate of the liquidation of subjectivity and the premature overcoming of contradictions in modern life. Although no longer dwelling on the style as such, they continued to castigate those who worked in its spirit. In the thirties and forties, however, they were clearly going against the current. Not until somewhat later would their strictures on the disadvantages of modernity begin to make sense to an American audience. It was decades before widespread concern for such issues as ecology, instrumental rationality, and women's liberation emerged, issues that the Frankfurt School had treated with sophistication a generation before.

Whether or not the Institut would have succeeded in becoming a major force in American intellectual life if it had remained is thus a moot point. The members who chose to stay certainly thought it would have.[61] Marcuse's sudden popularity in the 1960's, based largely on writings whose general direction was foreshadowed in the Frankfurt School's earlier work, suggests that they might well have been correct. What happened instead was that less central figures in the Institut's history, such as Fromm, Neumann, and Wittfogel, acquired impressive followings, while Horkheimer remained a generally unknown figure in postwar America.

Speculating about what might have occurred is, of course, far less the task of the historian than trying to make sense out of what actually did. The Institut was a unique element in an unparalleled event in recent Western history. It was the only interdisciplinary aggregation of scholars, working on different problems from a common theoretical base, to coalesce in modern times. Moreover, whereas dispersion usually accompanied exile, the Institut managed to remain together. It was furthermore the only collective representative of Weimar culture to survive exile and return to serve as a bridge between Germany's cultural past and its post-Nazi present. When it reestablished itself in Frankfurt, it was able not only to teach methodological techniques acquired in America, but also to restore continuity with the rich heritage Hitler had done so much to obliterate. Having helped to bring German culture to America, it then proceeded to help bring it back to Germany. With students like Jürgen Habermas, Alfred Schmidt (who has just been named Adorno's successor as the Institut's director), Oskar Negt, and Albrecht Wellmer, its continued impact promises to be significant, even if its institutional survival in the 1970's seems clouded by the deaths of several of its older leaders and by increased radical turmoil in its student ranks.

A strained metaphor suggested by Hegel's notion of the spirit returning to itself might seem appropriate here, if not for the crucial fact that the true estrangement of the Frankfurt School did not end with its geographical homecoming. The reintegration of the Institut stressed earlier was never more than a partial and incomplete process. "To write poetry after Auschwitz," Adorno wrote in one of his more bitter moments, "is barbaric."[62] To write social theory and conduct scientific research was more tolerable only if its critical, negative impulse was maintained. For, so the Frankfurt School always insisted, it was only by the refusal to celebrate the present that the possibility might be preserved of a future in which writing poetry would no longer be an act of barbarism.

Chapter References and Bibliography

Chapter References

The following abbreviations are used:

Grünbergs Archiv: *Archiv für die Geschichte des Sozialismus und der Arbeiterbewegung*
SPSS: *Studies in Philosophy and Social Science*
ZfS: *Zeitschrift für Sozialforschung*

INTRODUCTION

1. William Butler Yeats, "The Choice" (1932).

2. The failure to distinguish sufficiently between the Weimar Institut and the Frankfurt School has marred certain treatments of its history. See, for example, Peter Gay, *Weimar Culture: The Outsider as Insider* (New York, 1968), in which the Institut during Weimar is erroneously described as "left-Hegelian to the core" (p. 41).

3. Herbert Marcuse, *Negations: Essays in Critical Theory*, trans. Jeremy J. Shapiro (Boston, 1968), which contains many of the essays republished in German as *Kultur und Gesellschaft*, 2 vols. (Frankfurt, 1965).

4. Max Horkheimer, *Kritische Theorie*, ed. Alfred Schmidt, 2 vols. (Frankfurt, 1968).

5. Walter Benjamin, *Schriften*, ed. Theodor W. Adorno and Gershom Scholem, 2 vols. (Frankfurt, 1955); Theodor W. Adorno, *Prismen* (Frankfurt, 1955), published in English as *Prisms*, trans. Samuel and Shierry Weber (London, 1967); *Versuch über Wagner* (Frankfurt, 1952); and *Dissonanzen: Musik der verwalteten Welt* (Frankfurt, 1956); Leo Lowenthal, *Literature and the Image of Man* (Boston, 1957); and *Literature, Popular Culture, and Society* (Englewood Cliffs, N.J., 1961); Franz Neumann, *The Democratic and the Authoritarian State*, ed. Herbert Marcuse (New York, 1957). Other, more recent collections of the work done by Institut figures include Erich Fromm, *The Crisis of Psychoanalysis* (New York, 1970); Otto Kirchheimer, *Politics, Law, and Social Change*, ed. Frederic S. Burin and Kurt L. Shell (New York, 1969); and Leo Lowenthal, *Erzählkunst und Gesellschaft: Die Gesellschaftsproblematik in der deutschen Literature des 19. Jahrhunderts* (Neuwied and Berlin, 1971).

1. THE CREATION OF THE INSTITUT FÜR SOZIALFORSCHUNG AND ITS FIRST FRANKFURT YEARS

1. Carl Schorske, *German Social Democracy, 1905–1917* (Cambridge, Mass., 1955).

2. The biographical information about Weil comes from a series of letters from him to me during 1970–1971.

3. Felix Weil, *Sozialisierung: Versuch einer begrifflichen Grundlegung* (*Nebst einer Kritik der Sozialisierungspläne*) (Berlin-Fichtenau, 1921).

4. Letter from Weil to Paul Breines, January 10, 1971, which both parties have granted me permission to quote. Another participant at the conference, Karl August Wittfogel, has disagreed with Weil's date, saying that the E.M.A. took place after Whitsuntide in 1923. Weil discounts this by pointing to the fact that the Institut was already in operation by that date.

5. Hede Massing later became an espionage agent for the Soviet Union, but repudiated her connection in the late 1930's. She gave testimony at the Alger Hiss trial in 1948 and wrote a book about her experiences called *This Deception* (New York, 1951). Besides fascinating reminiscences of what it meant to spy for the Russians, it contains several detailed, if occasionally romanticized, portraits of various Institut figures, including Julian Gumperz, Paul Massing, and Richard Sorge. Mrs. Massing herself did some interviewing for the Institut in 1944–1945, when it was engaged in a study of anti-Semitism in American labor.

6. Letter from Weil to Breines, January 10, 1971.

7. Max Horkheimer, "Zur Antinomie der teleologischen Urteilskraft" (unpub., 1922).

8. Horkheimer's *Habilitationsschrift* was entitled *Kants Kritik der Urteilskraft als Bindeglied zwischen theoretischer und praktischer Philosophie* (Stuttgart, 1925). A description of his first lecture can be found in Madlen Lorei and Richard Kirn, *Frankfurt und die goldenen zwanziger Jahre* (Frankfurt, 1966), p. 97.

9. Ludwig Marcuse, *Mein zwanzigstes Jahrhundert* (Munich, 1960), p. 114.

10. Interview with Gerhard Meyer, Meredith, N.H., July 19, 1971.

11. These were projects suggested to Hermann Weil to help persuade him to endow the Institut (interview with Friedrich Pollock, Montagnola, Switzerland, March, 1969).

12. Letter from Weil to me, January 31, 1971.

13. *Ibid.*

14. Pollock interview, March, 1969.

15. F. W. Deakin and G. R. Storry, *The Case of Richard Sorge* (London, 1966), p. 32.

16. *Institut für Sozialforschung an der Universität Frankfurt am Main* (Frankfurt, 1925), p. 13.

17. Gustav Mayer, *Erinnerungen* (Zurich and Vienna, 1949), pp. 340–341.

18. For data on Grünberg's life, see *Österreiches Biographisches Lexicon, 1915–1950*, vol. II (Graz-Köln, 1957–1959).

19. Gustav Nenning, *Carl Grünberg und die Anfänge des Austromarxismus* (Graz, 1968), p. 94.

20. Norbert Leser, *Zwischen Reformismus und Bolshewismus: Der Austromarxismus als Theorie und Praxis* (Vienna, Frankfurt, and Zurich, 1968), p. 177.

21. Georg Lukács, "Moses Hess und die Probleme der idealistischen Dialektik," *Grünbergs Archiv* XII (1926).

22. Letter from Weil to me, June 8, 1971.

23. See, for example, Heinrich Regius, "Die neue Sachlichkeit," *Dämmerung* (Zurich, 1934), p. 216. Heinrich Regius was a pseudonym for Horkheimer, which was necessary to permit the book's distribution in Germany.

24. Carl Grünberg, "Festrede gehalten zur Einweihung des Instituts für Sozialforschung an der Universität Frankfurt a.M. am 22 Juni 1924," *Frankfurter Universitäts-Reden* XX (Frankfurt, 1924).

25. Parenthetically, it might be noted that Grünberg's use of the term was the exact opposite of the use to which Fritz Ringer put it in his *The Decline of the German Mandarins* (Cambridge, Mass., 1969).

26. Wilhelm von Humboldt, *Schriften*, selected by W. Flemmer (Munich, 1964), p. 307.

27. Grünberg, "Festrede," p. 11.

28. Friedrich Pollock, *Sombarts "Widerlegung" des Marxismus* (Leipzig, 1926), a *Beiheft* of the *Grünbergs Archiv*; Max Horkheimer, "Ein neuer Ideologie Begriff?," *Grünbergs Archiv* XV (1930).

29. Letter from Oscar H. Swede to Max Eastman, October 1, 1927, Eastman collection, Manuscripts Department, Lilly Library, Indiana University. I am indebted to Jack Diggins of the University of California, Irvine, for bringing this letter to my attention.

30. In 1930 Franz Schiller wrote a long, laudatory article entitled "Das Marx-Engels Institut in Moskau," *Grünbergs Archiv* XV.

31. This aspect of the Institut's work was continued after the emigration by Hilde Rigaudias-Weiss, who uncovered a hitherto unknown questionnaire of Marx's on the condition of French workers from 1830 to 1848 (*Les Enquêtes ouvrières en France entre 1830 et 1848*; Paris, 1936).

32. Deakin and Storry, *Richard Sorge*, p. 32.

33. Pollock interview, March, 1969, in Montagnola.

34. As late as the Institut's 1944 unpublished history, "Ten Years on Morningside Heights," Korsch was listed as a "Fellow," but this seems to have meant little. The history is in Lowenthal's personal collection.

35. Weil called him "a typical loner, incapable of working in a team" (letter to me, June 5, 1971).

36. Pollock interview, March, 1969.

37. Letter from Matthias Becker to me, June 7, 1971. Becker is Horkheimer's current guardian of the Institut's files, which are kept in Montagnola and are not yet open to the public.

38. H. Regius, *Dämmerung*, pp. 122—130.

39. *Ibid.*, p. 130.

40. Henryk Grossmann to Paul Mattick, a letter included in the appendix to Grossmann's *Marx, die klassische Nationalökonomie und das Problem der Dynamik* (Frankfurt, 1969), with an afterword by Mattick, pp. 85–86 (italics in the original).

41. Biographical information about Wittfogel comes from an interview with him in New York on June 21, 1971, and from G. L. Ulmen's soon-to-be-published biography, *Karl August Wittfogel: Toward an Understanding of His Life and Work*, which the author graciously allowed me to see before publication.

42. Karl August Wittfogel, *Die Wissenschaft der bürgerlichen Gesellschaft* (Berlin, 1922), and *Geschichte der bürgerlichen Gesellschaft* (Vienna, 1924); his first book on China was *Das erwachende China* (Vienna, 1926).

43. Helga Gallas, *Marxistische Literaturtheorie* (Neuwied and Berlin, 1971), p. 111.

44. Franz Borkenau, *Der Übergang vom feudalen zum bürgerlichen Weltbild* (Paris, 1934).

45. New York, 1964. For the comparison, see George Lichtheim, *The Concept of Ideology* (New York, 1967), p. 279. Lichtheim, during our conversation of February 16, 1969, stressed Borkenau's brilliance and claimed that he had been treated unfairly by the Institut.

46. H. Grossmann, "Die gesellschaftlichen Grundlagen der mechanistischen Philosophie," *ZfS* IV, 2 (1935).

47. Grossmann, *Österreichs Handelspolitik, 1772–1790* (Vienna, 1916).

48. Interviews with Pollock in Montagnola (March, 1969), Leo Lowenthal in Berkeley (August, 1968), and Alice Maier, the former secretary of the Institut's New York branch, in New York (May, 1969).

49. Quoted in Grossmann, *Marx, die klassische Nationalökonomie und das Problem der Dynamik*, p. 113.

50. Grossmann, *Das Akkumulations-und Zusammenbruchsgesetz des kapitalistischen Systems* (Leipzig, 1929).

51. For a recent treatment of the book, see Martin Trottman, *Zur Interpretation und Kritik der Zusammensbruchstheorie von Henryk Grossmann* (Zurich, 1956). Mattick's discussion in the afterword to *Marx, die klassische Nationalökonomie und das Problem der Dynamik* is a more sympathetic appraisal.

52. See, for example, Alfred Braunthal, "Der Zusammenbruch der Zusammenbruchstheorie," *Die Gesellschaft* VI, 10 (October, 1929). Mattick has strongly attacked this type of criticism in his *Nachwort* to *Marx, die klassische Nationalökonomie, etc.* (p. 127).

53. For a discussion of Marx's own neglect of service industries and his stress on production, see George Kline, "Some Critical Comments on Marx's Philosophy," in *Marx and the Western World*, ed. Nicholas Lobkowicz (Notre Dame, Ind., 1967). Pollock's own observations were never printed.

54. F. Pollock, *Die planwirtschaftlichen Versuche in der Sowjetunion (1917–1927)* (Leipzig, 1929).

55. D. B. Ryazanov, "Siebzig Jahre 'Zur Kritik der politischen Ökonomie,'" *Grünbergs Archiv* XV (1930).

56. For a description of his dissenting behavior at the Eleventh Party Congress in 1922, see Adam Ulam, *The Bolsheviks* (New York, 1965), pp. 544–546.

57. Regius, *Dämmerung*, pp. 152–153.

58. Rudolf Schlesinger, "Neue Sowjetrussiche Literatur zur Sozialforschung," *ZfS* VII, 1 (1938), and VIII, 1 (1939).

59. For a description of Rabbi Nobel, see Nahum Glatzer, *Franz Rosenzweig: His Life and Thought* (New York, 1953), *passim.*

60. For a description of their relationship, see Theodor W. Adorno, "Der wunderliche Realist. Über Siegfried Kracauer," *Noten zur Literatur III* (Frankfurt, 1965).

61. Siegfried Kracauer, *From Caligari to Hitler* (Princeton, 1947).

62. Adorno, *Alban Berg: Der Meister des kleinsten Übergangs* (Vienna, 1968), p. 20.

63. René Leibowitz, "Der Komponist Theodor W. Adorno," in *Zeugnisse: Theodor W. Adorno zum sechzigsten Geburtstag*, ed. Max Horkheimer (Frankfurt, 1963).

64. Arthur Koestler, *Arrow in the Blue* (New York, 1952), p. 131.

65. Adorno, *Alban Berg*, p. 37.

66. *Ibid.*

67. Adorno, *Die Transzendenz des Dinglichen und Noematischen in Husserls Phänomenologie* (Frankfurt, 1924).

68. For a discussion of Tillich's relationship with the Institut and of the interaction of his theology with Critical Theory, see the reminiscences of Horkheimer and Adorno in *Werk und Wirken Paul Tillichs: Ein Gedenkbuch* (Stuttgart, 1967).

69. Adorno, *Kierkegaard: Konstruktion des Aesthetischen* (Tübingen, 1933, rev. ed. Frankfurt, 1966).

70. See footnote on pp. 6–7 for an explanation of these terms.

71. F. Weil, "Rosa Luxemburg über die Russische Revolution," *Grünbergs Archiv* XIII (1928), and "Die Arbeiterbewegung in Argentinien," *ibid.* XI (1925).

72. Horkheimer, *Die Anfänge der bürgerlichen Geschichtsphilosophie* (Stuttgart, 1930).

73. "Die gegenwärtige Lage der Sozialphilosophie und die Aufgaben eines Instituts für Sozialforschung," *Frankfurter Universitätsreden,* XXVII (Frankfurt, 1931).

74. K. A. Wittfogel, *Wirtschaft und Gesellschaft Chinas* (Leipzig, 1931). For a recent evaluation of Wittfogel's work, see Irving Fetscher, "Asien im Lichte des Marxismus: Zu Karl Wittfogels Forschungen über die orientalischen Despotie," *Merkur,* XX, 3 (March, 1966).

75. Interview with Lowenthal, August, 1968.

76. Horkheimer, "Vorwort," *ZfS* I, 1/2 (1932).

77. Horkheimer, "Bemerkungen über Wissenschaft und Krise," *ZfS* I, 1/2 (1932).

78. Grossmann, "Die Wert-Preis-Transformation bei Marx und das Krisisproblem," *ZfS* I, 1/2 (1932).

79. Pollock, "Die gegenwärtige Lage des Kapitalismus und die Aussichten einer planwirtschaftlichen Neuordnung," *ZfS* I, 1/2 (1932).

80. Leo Lowenthal, "Zur gesellschaftlichen Lage der Literatur," and Adorno, "Zur gesellschaftlichen Lage der Musik," *ZfS* I, 1/2 (1932).

81. Horkheimer, "Geschichte und Psychologie," *ZfS* I, 1/2 (1932).

82. Erich Fromm, "Über Methode und Aufgabe einer analytischen Sozialpsychologie," *ZfS* I, 1/2 (1932).

83. *Festschrift für Carl Grünberg: Zum 70. Geburtstag* (Leipzig, 1932).

84. Herbert Marcuse, *Hegels Ontologie und die Grundlegung einer Theorie der Geschichtlichkeit* (Frankfurt, 1932).

85. Adorno, review of *Hegels Ontologie, ZfS* I, 3 (1932), p. 410.

86. For a list of professors "purged" from German universities, see *The Intellectual Migration: Europe and America, 1930–1960,* ed. Donald Fleming and Bernard Bailyn (Cambridge, Mass., 1969), p. 234.

87. Charles Beard, Celestin Bouglé, Alexander Farquharson, Henryk Grossmann, Paul Guggenheim, Maurice Halbwachs, Jean de la Harpe, Max Horkheimer, Karl Landauer, Lewis L. Lorwin, Robert S. Lynd, Robert M. MacIver, Sidney Webb (Lord Passfield), Jean Piaget, Friedrich Pollock (chairman of the board), Raymond de Saussure, Georges Scelle, Ernst Schachtel, Andries Sternheim, R. H. Tawney, and Paul Tillich.

88. Letter from Horkheimer to Lowenthal, April 17, 1934.

89. According to Paul Sweezy, "there is no doubt that Paul's intellectual development was profoundly and permanently influenced by his experiences and associations in Frankfurt" ("Paul Alexander Baran: a Personal Memoir," *Monthly Review,* XVI, 11 [March, 1965], p. 32). Baran's friendship with members of the Institut continued after he came to the United States in 1939. His untimely death in 1964 occurred in Leo Lowenthal's house in San Francisco.

90. Josef Dünner, *If I Forget Thee . . .* (Washington, D.C., 1937).

91. Horkheimer [Regius], *Dämmerung,* p. 80.

92. Not until after the war did Horkheimer come to the melancholy conclusion that Zionism had been the only way out for the Jews of Europe. See his "Über die deutschen Juden," in his *Zur Kritik der instrumentellen Vernunft* (Frankfurt, 1967), p. 309.

93. Letter from Weil to me, June 1, 1969.

94. Conversation with Wittfogel, New York, June 21, 1971.

95. Franz Neumann, *Behemoth: The Structure and Practice of National Socialism 1933–1944* (New York, rev. ed. 1944), p. 121.

96. L. Lowenthal, "Das Dämonische," in *Gabe Herrn Rabbiner Dr. Nobel zum fünfzigsten Geburtstag* (Frankfurt, 1921).

97. See, for example, Edgar Friedenberg, "Neo-Freudianism and Erich Fromm," *Commentary* XXXIV, 4 (October, 1962), or Maurice S. Friedman, *Martin Buber, the Life of Dialogue* (New York, 1960), pp. 184–185.

98. Istvan Deak, *Weimar Germany's Left-Wing Intellectuals* (Berkeley and Los Angeles, 1968), p. 29.

99. Letter from Pollock to me, March 24, 1970.

100. Pollock interview, March, 1969. Many years later, Adorno defended his name change indirectly in a memorandum he wrote for the Institut's project on anti-Semitism in labor. "The idea that the Jews should show more pride by sticking to their names is but a thin rationalization of the desire that they should come into the open so that one might recognize and persecute them the more easily" (November 3, 1944, memorandum in Paul Lazarsfeld's possession).

101. Interview with Paul Massing, New York, November 25, 1970.

102. Jürgen Habermas, "Der deutsche Idealismus der jüdischen Philosophen," *Philosophisch-politische Profile* (Frankfurt, 1971).

103. Hannah Arendt, Introduction to *Illuminations* by Walter Benjamin, trans. Harry Zohn (New York, 1968), p. 29.

104. Adolph Lowe, a childhood friend from Stuttgart, remembers Horkheimer and Pollock giving their fathers an ultimatum when they were in England: either they were to be allowed to return to Germany to begin their studies or they would emigrate. The senior Horkheimer and senior Pollock seem to have given in without much resistance (conversation with Lowe, New York, N.Y., December 28, 1971).

105. Letter from Pollock to me, July 16, 1970. Although never an intellectual like Adorno's wife, Gretel, Mrs. Horkheimer was a constant source of support until her death in the fall of 1969. When I saw them together in March of that year, at the time of their forty-third and last anniversary, I was touched by the warmth and affection they showered on each other.

106. Regius [Horkheimer], *Dämmerung*, p. 165.

107. *Ibid.*

108. Andries Sternheim, "Zum Problem der Freizeitgestaltung," *ZfS* I, 3 (1932). He also contributed a monograph on economics and the family to the Institut's collaborative project, the *Studien über Autorität und Familie* (Paris, 1936), and wrote regularly in the *Zeitschrift*'s review section.

109. George Rusche, "Arbeitsmarkt und Strafvollzug," *ZfS* II, 1 (1933).

110. Kurt Baumann, "Autarkie und Planwirtschaft," *ZfS* II, 1 (1933); Gerhard Meyer, "Neue Englische Literatur zur Planwirtschaft," *ZfS* II, 2 (1933).

111. Paul Ludwig Landsberg, "Rassenideologie und Rassenwissenschaft," *ZfS* II, 3 (1933).

112. Julian Gumperz, "Zur Soziologie des amerikanischen Parteiensystems," *ZfS* I, 3 (1932), and "Recent Social Trends in the U.S.A.," *ZfS* II, 2 (1933).

113. Grossmann, *Marx, die klassische Nationalökonomie und das Problem der Dynamik*, p. 97.

114. See Franz Neumann et al., *The Cultural Migration* (Philadelphia, 1953).

115. London, 1937.

116. This was written under the name Fritz Jungmann and called "Autorität und Sexualmoral in der freien bürgerlichen Jugendbewegung," in *Studien über Autorität und Familie* (Paris, 1936).

117. Paul Honigsheim, "Reminiscences of the Durkheim School," *Emile Durkheim, 1858–1917*, ed. Kurt H. Wolff (Columbus, Ohio, 1960), pp. 313–314.

118. J. Gumperz, *Pattern for World Revolution*, with Robert Rindl, under the dual pseudonym "Ypsilon" (Chicago and New York, 1947).

119. Interview with Horkheimer, March, 1969, in Montagnola.

120. See Fleming and Bailyn, *The Intellectual Migration*; Laura Fermi, *Illustrious Immigrants* (Chicago, 1968); *The Legacy of the German Refugee Intellectuals* (*Salmagundi*, 10/11 [Fall, 1969–Winter, 1970]); and Helge Pross, *Die deutsche akademische Emigration nach den Vereinigten Staaten 1933–1941* (Berlin, 1955).

121. The well-known classicist M. I. Finley, a translator and editorial assistant at the Institut in the thirties, has stressed the New School's antipathy to the Institut's Marxism (interview in Berkeley, January 31, 1972).

122. For a full listing of the seminars and public lectures given by the Institut from 1936 to 1938, see *International Institute of Social Research: A Report on Its History, Aims, and Activities 1933–1938* (New York, 1938), pp. 35–36.

123. Horkheimer [Regius], *Dämmerung*, p. 8.

2. THE GENESIS OF CRITICAL THEORY

1. See George Lichtheim, *The Origins of Socialism* (New York, 1969), and *Marxism: An Historical and Critical Study* (New York and London, 1961); Shlomo Avineri, *The Social and Political Thought of Karl Marx* (Cambridge, 1968); and Karl Löwith, *From Hegel to Nietzsche* (New York, 1964), for discussions of the Left Hegelians.

2. See Herbert Marcuse, *Reason and Revolution*, rev. ed. (New York, 1960), and Jürgen Habermas, *Knowledge and Human Interests*, trans. Jeremy J. Shapiro (Boston, 1971), for an understanding of the transition from negative to positive social theory.

3. In his *Marxismus und Philosophie* (Frankfurt, 1966), whose title essay was originally printed in *Grünbergs Archiv* in 1923, Korsch discussed the connection between the reformist politics of the Second International and the mechanistic, nondialectical materialism it equated with Marxism.

4. See H. Stuart Hughes, *Consciousness and Society* (New York, 1958), pp. 161–229, for a discussion of Dilthey, Croce, and Sorel. Lukács was strongly influenced by the Sorelian attitudes of Ervin Szabo, the spiritual teacher of the Hungarian Social Democrats' left opposition. See Lukács's 1967 preface to *History and Class Consciousness*, trans. Rodney Livingstone (Cambridge, Mass., 1971), p. x.

5. For a discussion of their impact, see Furio Cerutti, "Hegel, Lukács, Korsch. Zum dialektischen Selbstverständnis des kritischen Marxismus," in *Aktualität und Folgen der Philosophie Hegels*, ed. Oskar Negt (Frankfurt, 1970).

6. *International Institute of Social Research: Report on Its History and Activities, 1933–1938* (New York, 1938), p. 28.

7. See for example, Max Horkheimer, "Schopenhauer Today," in *The Critical Spirit: Essays in Honor of Herbert Marcuse*, ed. Kurt H. Wolff and Barrington Moore, Jr. (Boston, 1967).

8. Conversation with Horkheimer, March, 1969, in Montagnola.

9. Horkheimer, *Kants Kritik der Urteilskraft als Bindeglied zwischen theoretischer und praktischer Philosophie* (Stuttgart, 1925).

10. Letter from Pollock to me, March 24, 1970.

11. Hans Cornelius, "Leben und Lehre," in *Die Philosophie der Gegenwart in Selbstdarstellungen*, ed. Raymund Schmidt, vol. 11 (Leipzig, 1923), p. 6.

12. Letter from Pollock to me, March 24, 1970.

13. Cornelius, *Die Elementargesetze der bildenden Kunst* (Leipzig, 1908).

14. Letter from Pollock to me, March 24, 1970.

15. Cornelius, "Leben und Lehre," p. 19.

16. *Ibid.*, p. 65. Interestingly, when Horkheimer wrote about Kant in 1962 ("Kants Philosophie und die Aufklärung," in *Zur Kritik der instrumentellen Vernunft* [Frankfurt, 1967], p. 210), he praised Kant for the antiharmonistic, critical elements in his philosophy.

17. So it has been interpreted in an anonymous article in the *Times Literary Supplement*, "From Historicism to Marxist Humanism" (June 5, 1969), p. 598. The article is by George Lichtheim. For a discussion of Hegel's importance to Critical Theory, see Friedrich W. Schmidt, "Hegel in der Kritischen Theorie der Frankfurter Schule," in *Aktualität und Folgen der Philosophie Hegels.*

18. Horkheimer [Heinrich Regius], *Dämmerung* (Zurich, 1934), p. 86.

19. Horkheimer, "Zum Problem der Wahrheit," *ZfS* IV, 3 (1935), p. 333.

20. Horkheimer, "Ein neuer Ideologiebegriff?," *Grünbergs Archiv* XV, 1 (1930), p. 34.

21. Horkheimer, "Hegel und die Metaphysik," in *Festschrift für Carl Grünberg: Zum 70. Geburtstag* (Leipzig, 1932).

22. *Ibid.*, p. 197.

23. *Ibid.*, p. 192.

24. G. Lukács, *History and Class Consciousness*, p. xxiii.

25. Horkheimer, "Gedanke zur Religion," *Kritische Theorie*, ed. Alfred Schmidt (Frankfurt, 1968), 2 vols., originally "Nachbemerkung," *ZfS* vol. IV, 1 (1935).

26. *Ibid.*, p. 375. See also Horkheimer [Regius], *Dämmerung*, p. 55.

27. Horkheimer, "Zum Rationalismusstreit in der gegenwärtigen Philosophie," *ZfS* III, 1 (1934), p. 9.

28. Horkheimer, "Materialismus und Metaphysik," *ZfS* II, 1 (1933), pp. 3–4.

29. "Zum Rationalismusstreit," p. 36.

30. *Ibid.*

31. Horkheimer, "Der neueste Angriff auf die Metaphysik," *ZfS* VI, 1 (1937), p. 9.

32. Karl Mannheim had made the same point in his essay, "Conservative Thought," in *From Karl Mannheim*, ed. Kurt H. Wolff (New York, 1971), pp. 213f. But this was written in 1925, well before the Nazi takeover.

33. See Lukács, *Die Zerstörung der Vernunft*, in *Werke*, vol. IX (Neuwied, 1961). Here Lukács repudiated his own origins in Dilthey, Simmel, and others, especially as they had appeared in *History and Class Consciousness.*

34. Horkheimer, "Geschichte und Psychologie," *ZfS* I, 1/2 (1932) *passim.*

35. Horkheimer, "The Relation between Psychology and Sociology in the Work of Wilhelm Dilthey," *SPSS* VIII, 3 (1939) *passim.*

36. See Horkheimer, *Anfänge der bürgerlichen Geschichtsphilosophie* (Stuttgart, 1930), for a discussion of Vico.

37. "Zum Problem der Wahrheit," p. 361.
38. Horkheimer, "Bemerkungen zu Jaspers' 'Nietzsche,' " *ZfS* VI, 2 (1937).
39. "Zum Problem der Wahrheit," p. 357.
40. "Zum Rationalismusstreit," p. 44.
41. Theodor Adorno, in a review of Ernest Newman's biography of Wagner (*Kenyon Review*, vol. IX, 1 [Winter, 1947]), made a similar point. Nietzsche's negativism, he wrote, "expressed the humane in a world in which humanity had become a sham." His "unique demonstration of the repressive character of occidental culture" was what set him apart from Wagner (p. 161).
42. See Horkheimer, "Zu Bergsons Metaphysik der Zeit," *ZfS* III, 3 (1934), and his review of Bergson's *Les deux sources de la morale et de la religion* in *ZfS* II, 2 (1933).
43. Review of *Les deux sources*, p. 106.
44. Quoted in Horkheimer, *Kritische Theorie*, vol. I, p. 175, from a letter to Celestin Bouglé (January 24, 1935).
45. He did not, however, ignore its origins in the Reformation. See, for example, his discussion of Luther in Horkheimer, "Montaigne und die Funktion der Skepsis," *ZfS* VII, 1 (1938), pp. 10–13.
46. Horkheimer, "Materialismus und Moral," *ZfS* II, 2 (1933), p. 165.
47. Adorno, *Minima Moralia* (Frankfurt, 1951), p. 80.
48. "Materialismus und Moral," pp. 183–184.
49. *Ibid.,* p. 186.
50. Horkheimer, "Materialismus und Metaphysik," *ZfS* II, 1 (1933).
51. *Ibid.,* p. 14.
52. Karl Marx, "Theses on Feuerbach," *Marx and Engels, Basic Writings on Politics and Philosophy*, ed. Lewis S. Feuer (New York, 1959), p. 243.
53. Adorno, *Zur Metakritik der Erkenntnistheorie* (Stuttgart, 1956), p. 82.
54. Lukács, *History and Class Consciousness*, p. 162 (italics in the original).
55. For an example of this consideration in the Institut's work, see Adorno, "Veblen's Attack on Culture," *Prisms*, trans. Samuel and Shierry Weber (London, 1967), where he discusses the concept of "conspicuous consumption" (p. 87).
56. For a discussion of Marx's attitude towards the state, which makes this point, see Avineri, *Social and Political Thought of Marx*, pp. 202f.
57. *Dämmerung*, p. 18.
58. Horkheimer, "Bemerkungen zur philosophischen Anthropologie," *ZfS* IV, 1 (1935), p. 5.
59. Adorno, *Zur Metakritik der Erkenntnistheorie*; Marcuse, "The Concept of Essence," *Negations: Essays in Critical Theory*, trans. Jeremy J. Shapiro (Boston, 1968) (originally in *ZfS* V, 1 [1936]).
60. Anon., "From Historicism to Marxist Humanism," p. 598.
61. See interview with Horkheimer in *Der Spiegel* (January 5, 1970), entitled "Auf das Andere Hoffen."
62. See, for example, "Montaigne und die Funktion der Skepsis," pp. 21, 45, and "Zum Problem der Wahrheit," p. 363.
63. *Dämmerung*, p. 116.
64. Jürgen Habermas, "Der deutsche Idealismus der jüdischen Philosophen," *Philosophisch-politische Profile* (Frankfurt, 1971), p. 41. Horkheimer made a similar point in "Über die deutschen Juden," *Zur Kritik der instrumentellen Vernunft,* p. 311.
65. See H. Marcuse, *An Essay on Liberation* (Boston, 1969), pp. 6f.

66. Avineri, *Social and Political Thought of Marx*, p. 85.

67. *Dämmerung*, p. 181.

68. Walter Benjamin, *Illuminations*, trans. Harry Zohn, with an intro. by Hannah Arendt (New York, 1968), p. 261.

69. Horkheimer, "Egoismus und Freiheitsbewegung," *ZfS* V, 2 (1936).

70. Marcuse was to make the same point in his article "The Affirmative Character of Culture," *Negations*, p. 119 (originally *ZfS* VI, 1 [1937]).

71. Horkheimer, "Egoismus und Freiheitsbewegung," p. 171. Marcuse was later to expand this idea in psychoanalytic terms with his concept of "repressive desublimation."

72. *Ibid.*, pp. 174–215 *passim.*

73. Marcuse, "On Hedonism," *Negations* (originally "Zur Kritik der Hedonismus," *ZfS* VI, 1 [1938]).

74. *Ibid.*, p. 160.

75. *Ibid.*, p. 168.

76. *Ibid.*, p. 190.

77. "The Concept of Essence," p. 191.

78. *Ibid.*, p. 193.

79. (Boston, 1964).

80. *Ibid.*, p. 199.

81. For a discussion of "positive freedom," see Franz Neumann, "The Concept of Political Freedom," *The Democratic and the Authoritarian State*, ed. Herbert Marcuse (New York, 1957), and Isaiah Berlin, *Four Essays on Liberty* (Oxford, 1969).

82. See, for example, Horkheimer's *Eclipse of Reason* (New York, 1947).

83. Marcuse, "Philosophy and Critical Theory," *Negations*, pp. 135–136 (originally *ZfS* VI, 3 [1937]). Further amplification of the distinction between the two types of reason can be found in his *Reason and Revolution*, pp. 44–46.

84. For a discussion of the importance of identity theory in Marcuse's work, see my article "The Metapolitics of Utopianism," *Dissent* XVII, 4 (July–August, 1970).

85. "Zum Rationalismusstreit," p. 1; "Der neueste Angriff auf die Metaphysik," p. 6.

86. "Zum Problem der Wahrheit," p. 354.

87. *Ibid.*, p. 357.

88. For a discussion of the Vienna Circle's emigration to the United States, see Herbert Feigl, "The *Wiener Kreis* in America," in *The Intellectual Migration: Europe and America, 1930–1960*, ed. Donald Fleming and Bernard Bailyn (Cambridge, Mass., 1969).

89. See *Eclipse of Reason, passim.*

90. "Der neueste Angriff auf die Metaphysik," *ZfS* VI, 1 (1937).

91. *Ibid.*, p. 13.

92. For an expansion of this point by a second generation Frankfurt School thinker, see Habermas, *Knowledge and Human Interests, passim.*

93. "Der neueste Angriff auf die Metaphysik," p. 27.

94. *Ibid.*, p. 49.

95. *Ibid.*, p. 29.

96. "Zum Problem der Wahrheit," pp. 337–338.

97. "Philosophy and Critical Theory," *Negations*, pp. 147–148.

98. "Ein neuer Ideologiebegriff?"

99. *Ibid.*, p. 50.

100. *Ibid.*, p. 56.

101. *Ibid.,* p. 55. Marcuse, in his article on Mannheim ("Zur Wahrheitsproblematik der soziologischen Methode," *Die Gesellschaft* VI [October, 1929]), makes the same point (pp. 361–362). Marcuse was a bit kinder to Mannheim than Horkheimer, arguing that Mannheim's reduction of Marxism to the consciousness of a specific class pointed to a valid connection between theory and *praxis.* He did, however, criticize Mannheim for missing "the intentional moment of all occurrences" (p. 362) and for his relationism, with its quietistic implications. Adorno, when he wrote on the sociology of knowledge, was harsher still; see his "The Sociology of Knowledge and Its Consciousness," *Prisms.*

102. *Reason and Revolution,* p. 322.

103. Hannah Arendt, "What is Authority?," *Between Past and Future* (Cleveland and New York, 1961).

104. Adorno, *Kierkegaard: Konstruktion des Aesthetischen* (Tübingen, 1933), and *Zur Metakritik der Erkenntnistheorie* (Stuttgart, 1956).

105. Letter from Adorno to Lowenthal, July 6, 1934.

106. For Benjamin's review, see *Vossische Zeitung* (April 2, 1933). Tillich, newly appointed to the faculty of the Union Theological Seminary in New York, wrote a review in the *Journal of Philosophy,* XXXI, 23 (November 8, 1934). Karl Löwith wrote another in the *Deutsche Literatur-Zeitung,* V, 3F, 5 (1934).

107. "Notiz" in the third edition of *Kierkegaard: Konstruktion des Aesthetischen* (Frankfurt, 1966), p. 321.

108. Quoted in *Kierkegaard* (1966 ed.), p. 29.

109. *Ibid.,* p. 29.

110. *Ibid.,* p. 46.

111. *Ibid.,* p. 135.

112. *Ibid.,* p. 111.

113. *Ibid.,* p. 62.

114. *Ibid.,* p. 67.

115. *Ibid.,* p. 90.

116. *Ibid.,* p. 97.

117. In *SSPS,* VIII, 3 (1939–1940), Adorno wrote an article "On Kierkegaard's Doctrine of Love."

118. This was the word Adorno used when I spoke with him in March, 1969, in Frankfurt.

119. *Kierkegaard,* p. 137.

120. Adorno, *Zur Metakritik der Erkenntnistheorie,* pp. 24–25.

121. *Ibid.,* p. 79.

122. *Ibid.,* p. 82.

123. Adorno, "Husserl and the Problem of Idealism," *Journal of Philosophy* XXVII, 1 (January 4, 1940), p. 11.

124. *Zur Metakritik,* p. 43.

125. "Husserl and the Problem of Idealism," p. 7.

126. *Zur Metakritik,* p. 47.

127. *Ibid.,* p. 55.

128. *Ibid.,* p. 79.

129. *Ibid.,* p. 88.

130. *Ibid.,* p. 90.

131. *Ibid.,* p. 146.

132. *Ibid.,* p. 151.

133. In his article on the decline of story-telling ("The Storyteller: Reflections on

the Works of Nikolai Leskov," *Illuminations*), Benjamin wrote: "Experience has fallen in value. . . . Never has experience been contradicted more thoroughly than strategic experience by tactical warfare, economic experience by inflation, bodily experience by mechanical warfare, moral experience by those in power" (pp. 83–84).

134. *Zur Metakritik*, p. 180.

135. *Ibid.*, p. 221.

136. *Ibid.*, pp. 28–29. Marcuse was to state this even more forcefully in his article "The Concept of Essence," *Negations.*

137. Adorno, "A Portrait of Walter Benjamin," *Prisms*, p. 235.

138. Georg Picht entitled his article on Adorno's death "Atonale Philosophie" (*Merkur*, XXIII, 10 [October, 1969]).

139. For one recent example, see Jerry Cohen, "The Philosophy of Marcuse," *New Left Review* (September–October, 1969).

140. Habermas, "Zum Geleit," in *Antworten auf Herbert Marcuse*, ed. Jürgen Habermas (Frankfurt, 1968), pp. 11–12.

141. See, for example, Alfred Schmidt, "Existential-Ontologie und historischer Materialismus bei Herbert Marcuse," *Antworten auf Herbert Marcuse*; and Paul Piccone and Alex Delfini, "Marcuse's Heideggerian Marxism," *Telos* (Fall, 1970).

142. Marcuse, "Beiträge zu einer Phänomenologie des historischen Materialismus," *Philosophische Hefte* I, 1 (1928).

143. *Ibid.*, p. 52.

144. *Ibid.*, p. 55. According to Schmidt ("Existential-Ontologie," pp. 28–29), there were elements of an expressionistic action for action's sake in all of this. In general, Schmidt is very critical of Marcuse's efforts to combine Marxism and phenomenology.

145. Marcuse, "Beiträge," p. 46.

146. *Ibid.*, p. 68.

147. *Ibid.*, p. 59.

148. *Ibid.*, p. 65.

149. *Ibid.*, p. 60.

150. Marcuse, "Zum Problem der Dialektik," *Die Gesellschaft* VII, 1 (January, 1930), p. 26.

151. "Das Problem der geschichtlichen Wirklichkeit," *Die Gesellschaft* VIII, 4 (April, 1931).

152. Marcuse, *Hegels Ontologie und die Grundlegung einer Theorie der Geschichtlichkeit* (Frankfurt, 1932).

153. For a discussion of both Hegel books, see Alain de Libera, "La Critique de Hegel," *La Nef* (January–March, 1969).

154. *Hegels Ontologie*, p. 368.

155. Marcuse, "Neue Quellen zur Grundlegung des Historischen Materialismus," *Die Gesellschaft* IX, 8 (1932).

156. *Ibid.*, p. 151.

157. *Ibid.*, p. 167.

158. *Ibid.*, p. 147.

159. *Ibid.*, p. 173. Marcuse also wrote an entire article on the ontological centrality of labor, "Über die philosophischen Grundlagen des Wirtschaftswissenschaftlichen Arbeitsbegriff," *Archiv für Sozialwissenschaft und Sozialpolitik* LXIX, 3 (June, 1933).

160. "Neue Quellen," p. 158.

161. *Reason and Revolution*, p. 78.

162. Habermas, *Technik und Wissenschaft als "Ideologie"* (Frankfurt, 1968).

163. *Reason and Revolution*, p. 75.

164. See Marcuse, *Eros and Civilization* (Boston, 1955), pp. 170–179, for his discussion of the "play drive."

165. See, for example, Marcuse, "The Struggle against Liberalism in the Totalitarian State," *Negations* (originally *ZfS* III, 1 [1934]).

166. "The Concept of Essence," p. 44.

167. *Ibid.*, p. 69.

168. *Ibid.*, p. 78.

169. Marcuse, "Philosophy and Critical Theory," *Negations*, p. 147.

170. *Ibid.*, pp. 149–150.

171. *Ibid.*, p. 156.

172. *Ibid.*, p. 155. Marcuse was to develop the importance of fantasy in his later works, especially *Eros and Civilization.*

173. New York, 1941. Part of the book appeared in the *SPSS* as Marcuse, "An Introduction to Hegel's Philosophy," VIII, 3 (1939).

174. Ironically in the light of his later stance, Marcuse flattered his American audience in his introduction by quoting Hegel's belief that America's rational spirit made it the "land of the future" (*Reason and Revolution*, p. xv.)

175. *Ibid.*, p. 60.

176. *Ibid.*, pp. 313–314.

177. *Ibid.*, p. 256.

178. *Ibid.*, p. 322.

179. See, for example, Habermas, *Knowledge and Human Interests* and *Technik und Wissenschaft als "Ideologie"*; and Albrecht Wellmer, *Critical Theory of Society* (New York, 1971).

180. *Reason and Revolution*, p. 400.

181. This was pointed out in a generally favorable review by Paul Tillich in *SPSS* IX, 3 (1941), and in a more critical one by Karl Löwith in *Philosophy and Phenomenological Research* II, 4 (1942). It is a theme that continues to reappear in assessments of the book; for example, Lucio Colletti, "Von Hegel zu Marcuse," *Alternative* 72/73 (June–August, 1970).

182. Horkheimer, "Traditionelle und kritische Theorie," *ZfS* VI, 2 (1937).

183. *Ibid.*, p. 257.

184. Horkheimer, "Zum Problem der Voraussage in den Sozialwissenschaften," *ZfS* II, 3 (1933).

185. "Traditionelle und kritische Theorie," p. 276.

186. *Ibid.*, p. 275.

187. *Ibid.*, p. 277.

188. Quoted in Adorno, *Prisms*, p. 231.

189. George Kline, "Some Critical Comments on Marx's Philosophy," in *Marx and the Western World*, ed. Nicholas Lobkowicz (Notre Dame, Ind., 1967), p. 431.

190. See, for example, Horkheimer, "Zum Problem der Wahrheit," pp. 340–343, and "Traditionelle und kritische Theorie," p. 252. The Institut tended to assimilate American pragmatism with positivism.

191. Letter from Horkheimer to Lowenthal, January 14, 1946 (Lowenthal collection).

192. "Zum Problem der Wahrheit," p. 343.

193. Conversations with Lowenthal in Berkeley (August, 1968) and Habermas in

Frankfurt (February, 1969). For Habermas's discussion of pragmatism, see his treatment of C. S. Pierce in *Knowledge and Human Interests.*

194. "Zum Problem des Wahrheit," p. 345.

195. "Traditionelle und kritische Theorie," p. 269.

196. *Ibid.,* p. 269.

197. Marcuse, "The Struggle against Liberalism in the Totalitarian State," *Negations,* p. 42.

198. Horkheimer, "Autoritärer Staat," in "Walter Benjamin zum Gedächtnis" (unpub., 1942), in Pollock's collection.

3. THE INTEGRATION OF PSYCHOANALYSIS

1. For a discussion of early attempts to merge Freud and Marx, see "When Dogma Bites Dogma, or The Difficult Marriage of Marx and Freud," *The Times Literary Supplement* (January 8, 1971).

2. For a description of Reich's plight see Paul A. Robinson, *The Freudian Left* (New York, 1969), pp. 28–59.

3. Philip Rieff, *Freud: The Mind of the Moralist* (New York, 1959), pp. 237–239.

4. See Franz Neumann, "Anxiety and Politics," in his *The Democratic and the Authoritarian State,* ed. Herbert Marcuse (New York, 1957), and H. Stuart Hughes, "Franz Neumann between Marxism and Liberal Democracy," in *The Intellectual Migration: Europe and America, 1930–1960,* ed. Donald Fleming and Bernard Bailyn (Cambridge, Mass., 1969).

5. *Zur Psychologie des Marxismus,* translated into English as *The Psychology of Marxism* (New York and London, 1928). For a discussion of de Man, see Peter Dodge, *Beyond Marxism: The Faith and Works of Hendrik de Man* (The Hague, 1966).

6. So Professor Gladys Meyer of Barnard has suggested in a letter to me. Professor Meyer, who was a student at the Institut in the pre-emigration period, has written a novel, *The Magic Circle* (New York, 1944), in which de Man is thinly disguised as Adriaan de Barenne, one of the main characters. Pollock, when I spoke with him in March, 1969, denied the idea that de Man was deliberately brought to Frankfurt for the purpose Professor Meyer claims.

7. Theodor Wiesengrund, "Der Begriff des Unbewussten in der Transzendentalen Seelenlehre" (unpub. diss., Frankfurt University, 1927).

8. *Ibid.,* p. 318.

9. Interview with Horkheimer, Montagnola, Switzerland, March, 1969.

10. It emerged out of a factional split within the German psychoanalytic movement. See Carl M. Grossman and Sylvia Grossman, *The Wild Analyst* (New York, 1965), p. 178.

11. Horkheimer interview, March, 1969.

12. Meng taught a course entitled "Einführung in die Psychoanalyse," Landauer, "Psychoanalytische Klinik," Frieda Fromm-Reichmann, "Psychoanalytische Trieblehre," and Fromm, "Die Anwendung der Psychoanalyse auf Soziologie und Religionswissenschaft." See the May–June, 1929, issue of *Die psychoanalytische Bewegung* (I, 1) for a description of the Institute's opening. See also Adolf Friedmann, "Heinrich Meng, Psychoanalysis and Mental Hygiene," *Psychoanalytic Pioneers,* ed. Franz Alexander, Samuel Eisenstein, and Martin Grotjahn (New York and London, 1966).

13. Erich Fromm, *Beyond the Chains of Illusion* (New York, 1962), p. 5.
14. See, for example, Fromm, *Marx's Concept of Man* (New York, 1961).
15. In *Fear of Freedom* (the English version of *Escape from Freedom* whose pagination will be used in these notes [London, 1942]), Fromm acknowledged the importance of Hegel and Marx for their notion of alienation (p. 103).
16. Fromm, *Beyond the Chains of Illusion*, p. 28.
17. John Schaar, *Escape from Authority: The Perspectives of Erich Fromm* (New York, 1961), has argued that Fromm fails to answer the criticisms of G. E. Moore and David Hume against the naturalistic fallacy, that he doesn't understand that society is more than nature, that one must have full knowledge of nature before judging what is natural or not, and that if evil exists, it must be part of nature too (pp. 20–24).
18. Letter from Fromm to me, May 14, 1971.
19. See Fromm's *Marx's Concept of Man* for evidence of his respect for Marx's ability as a psychologist. A more extensive statement appears in "Marx's Contribution to the Knowledge of Man," *The Crisis of Psychoanalysis* (New York, 1970).
20. *Beyond the Chains of Illusion*, p. 12. In his letter to me of May 14, 1971, Dr. Fromm said that he regretted the comparison, because it was foolish to rank one great man next to another, but his judgment about their respective merits was unchanged.
21. *Beyond the Chains of Illusion*, p. 10: "There is not a single theoretical conclusion about man's psyche, either in this or in my other writings, which is not based on a critical observation of human behavior carried out in the course of this psychoanalytic work." For a rebuttal of this assertion, see J. A. C. Brown, *Freud and the Post-Freudians* (London, 1961), p. 205.
22. Fromm, "Der Sabbath," *Imago*, XIII, Nos. 2, 3, 4 (1927).
23. Published originally in Vienna in 1931, it appeared in English as *The Dogma of Christ, and Other Essays on Religion, Psychology, and Culture*, trans. James Luther Adams (New York, 1963).
24. *Ibid.*, p. 91.
25. *Ibid.*, p. 94.
26. Fromm, "Über Methode und Aufgabe einer analytischen Sozialpsychologie," *ZfS* I, 1/2 (1932). Translated in *The Crisis of Psychoanalysis.*
27. *Ibid.*, p. 32. Reich's more recent work he approved. See his review of Reich's *Der Einbruch der Sexualmoral* in *ZfS* II, 1 (1933).
28. Fromm, "Über Methode," p. 48. See also Fromm, *The Dogma of Christ*, p. 47.
29. "Über Methode," p. 45.
30. *Ibid.*, p. 28.
31. *Ibid.*, p. 30.
32. Letter from Fromm to me, May 14, 1971.
33. "Über Methode," p. 38.
34. Fromm, "Die psychoanalytische Charakterologie und ihre Bedeutung für die Sozialpsychologie," *ZfS* I, 3 (1932). Translated in *The Crisis of Psychoanalysis.*
35. *Ibid.*, p. 265.
36. In *Eros and Civilization* (Boston, 1955), Marcuse was to write: "Reactivation of polymorphous and narcissistic sexuality ceases to be a threat to culture and can itself lead to culture-building if the organism exists not as an instrument of alienated labor but as a subject of self-realization" (pp. 191–192). "Polymorphous perversity" was a term Norman O. Brown popularized in his *Life against Death* (New York, 1959).

37. Reich differed from Fromm in arguing that *all* character "armoring" was pernicious and repressive. See Robinson, *The Freudian Left*, p. 23.

38. Interview with Fromm, New York, N.Y., December, 1968.

39. Fromm, "Die psychoanalytische Charakterologie," p. 268.

40. *Ibid.*, p. 273.

41. E. M. Butler, *The Tyranny of Greece over Germany* (Cambridge, 1935), p. 327. For a bibliography of articles written on Bachofen in the 1920's, see Adrien Turel, *Bachofen-Freud, Zur Emanzipation des Mannes vom Reich der Mutter* (Bern, 1939), pp. 209–210.

42. Quoted in Robinson, *The Freudian Left*, p. 50.

43. "Family Sentiments," *ZfS* III, 1 (1934).

44. Fromm, "Die sozialpsychologische Bedeutung der Mutterrechtstheorie," *ZfS* III, 2 (1934). Translated in *The Crisis of Psychoanalysis*.

45. The notion of nature as a dominant force to which man must passively submit played a large part in the Institut's analysis of fascism. See, for example, Marcuse's "Der Kampf gegen den Liberalismus in der totalitären Staatsauffassung," *ZfS* III, 2 (1934); and Leo Lowenthal's "Knut Hamsun. Zur Vorgeschichte der autoritären Ideologie," *ZfS* VI, 2 (1937).

46. Fromm, "Die sozialpsychologische Bedeutung der Mutterrechtstheorie," p. 221.

47. In the light of Fromm's early religiosity, his discussion of Judaism in this context is worth noting. Although acknowledging the patriarchal God at its core, he also pointed to such elements in Jewish thought as the vision of the land of milk and honey, which were clearly matriarchal. The Hasidim, he argued (once again as Buber would have done), were especially matriarchal in character (*Ibid.*, p. 223).

48. Fromm, "Die gesellschaftliche Bedingtheit der psychoanalytischen Therapie," *ZfS* IV, 3 (1935).

49. *Ibid.*, pp. 371–375.

50. Marcuse, "Repressive Tolerance," *A Critique of Pure Tolerance*, with Robert Paul Wolff and Barrington Moore, Jr. (Boston, 1965). Similarly, Adorno wrote: "The bourgeois is tolerant. His love for men as they are arises out of hate for the correct man" (*Minima Moralia* [Frankfurt, 1951], p. 27). Horkheimer made a similar point in *The Eclipse of Reason* (New York, 1947), p. 19.

51. "Die gesellschaftliche Bedingtheit," p. 393.

52. "Repressive Tolerance," p. 109.

53. For Fromm's own attitude towards radicals, see "The Revolutionary Character," included in *The Dogma of Christ and Other Essays on Religion, Psychology, and Culture* (New York, 1966). Horkheimer expressed similar doubts about Freud's view of revolutionaries as early as 1934 (Heinrich Regius [pseud.], *Dämmerung* [Zurich, 1934], p. 256).

54. "Die gesellschaftliche Bedingtheit," pp. 384–385.

55. Ernest Jones, *The Life and Work of Sigmund Freud* (New York, 1963), p. 400. Jones also accused Otto Rank of insanity. Fromm tried to set the record straight in *Sigmund Freud's Mission* (New York, 1959).

56. Grossman and Grossman, *The Wild Analyst*, p. 195. Frieda Fromm-Reichman was especially close to Groddeck and was one of the last people to see him before his death in 1934. She included him in the dedication of her first book, *Principles of Intensive Psychotherapy* (Chicago, 1950).

57. Fromm, "Zum Gefühl der Ohnmacht," *ZfS* VI, 1 (1937). This and Fromm's contribution to *Studien über Autorität und Familie* (Paris, 1936) will be treated in the next chapter.

58. See Schaar, *Escape from Authority*, and Guyton Hammond, *Man in Estrangement* (Nashville, 1965), for two discussions of the book.

59. Fromm, *Fear of Freedom*, p. 9.

60. *Ibid.*, p. 157.

61. *Ibid.*, p. 251.

62. *Ibid.*, p. 249.

63. Fromm, *Man for Himself* (New York, 1947). Fromm divided character types into "productive" and "nonproductive" orientations. The latter was subdivided into receptive, exploitative, hoarding, and marketing subtypes (p. 120).

64. *Fear of Freedom*, p. 7. In *The Sane Society* (New York, 1955), however, Fromm attacked Sullivan's notion of love as alienated (pp. 193–199).

65. Letter from Fromm to me, May 14, 1971.

66. *Fear of Freedom*, p. 239.

67. *Ibid.*, p. 18.

68. *Ibid.*, p. 130.

69. *Ibid.*, p. 136. This was a concept Fromm had not used in his discussion of sado-masochism in his article in the *Studien über Autorität und Familie*, "Sozialpsychologischer Teil."

70. *Fear of Freedom*, p. 222.

71. *Man for Himself*, pp. 225–226.

72. Fromm, *Zen Buddhism and Psychoanalysis*, with D. T. Suzuki and R. de Martino (New York, 1960).

73. Letter from Fromm to me, May 14, 1971.

74. *Ibid.*

75. Horkheimer, "Geschichte und Psychologie," *ZfS* I, 1/2 (1932), p. 141.

76. Horkheimer, "Egoismus und Freiheitsbewegung," *ZfS* V, 2 (1936), pp. 225–226.

77. Benjamin wrote an article on Bachofen in 1934. Intended for the *Nouvelle revue française*, which rejected it, it was not published until 1954, when it appeared in *Les Lettres nouvelles*; Walter Benjamin, *Briefe*, ed. Gershom Scholem and Theodor W. Adorno (Frankfurt, 1966), vol. II, pp. 614–615. When Benjamin came to write a brief history of the Institut for Thomas Mann's journal *Mass und Wert* in 1938 (I, 5, May–June), he paid special attention to Fromm's work on matriarchal theory.

78. Interview with Fromm, December, 1968 in New York.

79. Interview with Lowenthal, August, 1968 in Berkeley.

80. Horkheimer, "The Relation between Psychology and Sociology in the Work of Wilhelm Dilthey," *SPSS* VIII, 3 (1939).

81. Letter from Horkheimer to Lowenthal, October 31, 1942, from Pacific Palisades, California (Lowenthal collection).

82. Horkheimer, "Traditionelle und kritische Theorie," *ZfS* VI, 2 (1937), p. 276.

83. In *Sociologica: Aufsätze, Max Horkheimer zum sechzigsten Geburtstag gewidmet* (Frankfurt, 1955) and *New Left Review*, 46 (November–December, 1967), 47 (January–February, 1968).

84. I am indebted to Professor Lowenthal for making this paper available to me. There is a German version of it in *Sociologia II: Reden und Vorträge*, ed. Max Horkheimer and Theodor W. Adorno (Frankfurt, 1962).

85. Adorno "Social Science and Sociological Tendencies in Psychoanalysis," April 27, 1946 (unpublished), p. 4; in Lowenthal's collection.

86. Benjamin had written extensively on the importance of shocks in modern life

in "Über einige Motive bei Baudelaire," *ZfS* VIII, 1/2 (1939)), which has been translated in *Illuminations.* He explicitly used Freudian ideas to support his interpretation.

87. "Social Science and Sociological Tendencies in Psychoanalysis," p. 6.

88. *Ibid.,* pp. 6–7.

89. *Ibid.,* p. 14.

90. *Ibid.,* p. 15.

91. *Ibid.,* p. 22.

92. Walter Benjamin, *Schriften,* ed. Gershom Scholem and Theodor W. Adorno (Frankfurt, 1955), vol. I, p. 140.

93. "Social Science and Sociological Tendencies in Psychoanalysis," pp. 22–23.

94. *Minima Moralia,* p. 78.

95. For an imaginative use of Freud by a second generation Critical Theorist, see Jürgen Habermas, *Knowledge and Human Interests,* trans. Jeremy J. Shapiro (Boston, 1971). Earlier in the Institut's postemigration history, psychoanalytic categories were used in empirical studies, such as the *Gruppenexperiment,* ed. Friedrich Pollock, *Frankfurter Beiträge zur Soziologie,* vol. II (Frankfurt, 1955).

96. *Freud in der Gegenwart, Frankfurter Beiträge zur Soziologie,* vol. VI (Frankfurt, 1957). The book consisted of addresses and papers given at Frankfurt by a number of distinguished psychologists, including Erik Erikson, Franz Alexander, René Spitz, and Ludwig Binswanger.

97. Marcuse, "Autorität und Familie in der deutschen Soziologie bis 1933," in *Studien über Autorität und Familie.* Marcuse also contributed a long introductory essay on the intellectual history of the idea of authority.

98. Robinson, *The Freudian Left,* pp. 188–191.

99. Marcuse, "The Affirmative Character of Culture," *Negations: Essays in Critical Theory,* trans. Jeremy J. Shapiro (Boston, 1968), pp. 122–123 (originally *ZfS* VI, 1 [1937]).

100. *Ibid.,* p. 116. Here Marcuse expressed an attitude towards the carrying through of reification to its extreme which he later was to admire in Sartre's *Being and Nothingness* ("Existentialism: Remarks on Jean-Paul Sartre's *L'Être et le néant,*" *Philosophy and Phenomenological Research* VIII, 3 [March, 1948], p. 327).

101. Marcuse, "On Hedonism," *Negations,* p. 190.

102. Robinson, *The Freudian Left,* p. 179.

103. *Eros and Civilization,* p. 218.

104. *Ibid.,* p. 41.

105. *Ibid.,* p. 223.

106. *Ibid.,* pp. 54–55.

107. *Ibid.,* p. 231.

108. *Ibid.,* p. 235.

109. "The Oedipus complex, although primary source and model of neurotic conflicts, is certainly not the central cause of the discontents in civilization, and not the central obstacle for their removal" (*ibid.,* p. 204). Robinson, in *The Freudian Left,* notes this passage, but neglects Marcuse's discussion of the Oedipus complex in his epilogue, where he grants it greater importance. For an excellent critique of Marcuse's attitude towards the Oedipus complex, see Sidney Lipshires, "Herbert Marcuse: From Marx to Freud and Beyond" (Ph.D. diss., University of Connecticut, 1971).

110. Quoted by Marcuse, *Eros and Civilization,* p. 246, from Fromm's *Psychoanalysis and Religion* (New Haven, 1950), pp. 79ff.

111. *Eros and Civilization*, p. 247.
112. See, for example, Fromm, *Man for Himself*, p. 215.
113. *Eros and Civilization*, p. 248.
114. Sigmund Freud, *Beyond the Pleasure Principle* (New York, 1950), p. 76.
115. *Eros and Civilization*, pp. 214–215.
116. Here Marcuse did not go as far as Norman O. Brown in arguing that all sexual organization was repressive; see Brown's *Life Against Death*, pp. 122ff. Marcuse refused to accept the total breakdown of differentiations of all sorts championed by Brown. "The unity of subject and object is a hallmark of absolute idealism; however, even Hegel retained the tension between the two, the distinction. Brown goes beyond the Absolute Idea: 'Fusion, mystical, participation' " (*Negations*, p. 138).
117. The term appears in Marcuse's *One-Dimensional Man* (Boston, 1964), p. 16.
118. Horkheimer and Adorno both expressed doubts about aspects of Marcuse's reading of Freud when I spoke with them in the winter of 1968–1969.
119. Fromm, "The Human Implications of Instinctive 'Radicalism,' " *Dissent* II, 4 (Autumn, 1955), and "A Counter-Rebuttal," *Dissent* III, 1 (Winter, 1956).
120. "The Human Implications of Instinctive 'Radicalism,' " p. 346.
121. Marcuse, "A Reply to Erich Fromm," *Dissent* III, 1 (Winter, 1956). In *The Crisis of Psychoanalysis*, Fromm picked up the debate where he had put it down fifteen years earlier (pp. 14–20).
122. *Ibid.*, p. 81. This was a term Marcuse was to use extensively in *One-Dimensional Man* and his subsequent works. *Nicht Mitmachen* had been a favorite "password" of the Institut from the earliest Frankfurt days, so Lowenthal told me (letter, August 15, 1970).
123. *Fear of Freedom*, p. 158 (italics in original).
124. Fromm, *The Heart of Man* (New York, 1964), pp. 53–54.
125. Horkheimer, "Gedanke zur Religion," *Kritische die Theorie*, vol. I (Frankfurt, 1968), p. 375.

4. THE INSTITUT'S FIRST STUDIES OF AUTHORITY

1. Max Horkheimer, "Autoritärer Staat," in "Walter Benjamin zum Gedächtnis" (unpub., 1942; Collection Friedrich Pollock in Montagnola, Switzerland), p. 152.
2. Margaret Mead, "On the Institutionalized Role of Women and Character Formation," *ZfS* V, 1 (1936); Charles Beard, "The Social Sciences in the United States," *ZfS* IV, 1 (1935); Harold Lasswell, "Collective Autism as a Consequence of Culture Contact," *ZfS* IV, 2 (1935).
3. In 1935 Tönnies' rather unexceptional article on the right to work was published out of deference to his position and reputation; Ferdinand Tönnies, "Das Recht auf Arbeit," *ZfS* IV, 1 (1935).
4. 1938 unpublished mimeographed history of the Institut in Friedrich Pollock's collection in Montagnola, p. 13.
5. "Ten Years on Morningside Heights: A Report on the Institute's History 1934 to 1944" (unpub., 1944), in Lowenthal's collection. Paying honoraria for published or unpublished articles and reviews in the *Zeitschrift* was a frequently used device to make the support "more respectable" (letter from Lowenthal to me, August 15, 1970).
6. Interview with Friedrich Pollock, Montagnola, Switzerland, March, 1969.
7. Ludwig Marcuse, *Mein zwanzigstes Jahrhundert* (Munich, 1960), pp. 239–240.

8. Conversation with Professor Pachter, New York, N.Y., October 13, 1971.

9. These appeared in two special issues of a Berlin journal called *Alternative*, 56/57 (October–December, 1967) and 59/60 (April–June, 1968).

10. For a discussion of this period at Columbia, see Robert MacIver's autobiography, *As a Tale That Is Told* (Chicago, 1968). According to his account, MacIver wanted a broader, more theoretically oriented department than Lynd, who stressed a utilitarian, professional approach. The final break came over a hostile review MacIver wrote of Lynd's *Knowledge for What* (pp. 137–141).

11. Letter from Horkheimer to Lowenthal, November 8, 1942, in Lowenthal's collection.

12. Henry Pachter, "A Memoir," in *The Legacy of the German Refugee Intellectuals* (*Salmagundi*, 10/11 [Fall, 1969–Winter, 1970]), p. 18.

13. Horkheimer, "Die gegenwärtige Lage der Sozialphilosophie und die Aufgaben eines Instituts für Sozialforschung," *Frankfurt Universitätsreden* (Frankfurt, 1931), pp. 14–15.

14. Adolf Levenstein, *Die Arbeiterfrage* (Munich, 1912). Paul Lazarsfeld first brought the importance of this predecessor to my attention. His student, Anthony Oberschall, has written on Levenstein's work in *Empirical Social Research in Germany, 1846–1914* (Paris, The Hague, 1965), pp. 94ff. Fromm denies the importance of Levenstein's model (letter from Fromm to me, May 14, 1971).

15. Fromm, "Die psychoanalytische Charakterologie und ihre Bedeutung für die Sozialpsychologie," *ZfS* I, 3 (1932).

16. Fromm, *Social Character in a Mexican Village*, with Michael Maccoby (Englewood Cliffs, N.J., 1970).

17. So it was called in the *International Institute of Social Research: A Report on Its History and Activities, 1933–1938* (New York, 1938), pp. 14–15.

18. Letter from Pollock to me, March 24, 1970. Paul Massing, who was a student at the Institut in its Frankfurt days, suggested to me that the study was really not that conclusive because revolutions might well be made by authoritarian types under certain conditions (interview with Massing, New York, N.Y., November 25, 1970).

19. Letter from Fromm to me, May 14, 1971.

20. Fromm, *Fear of Freedom* (British title of *Escape from Freedom*) (London, 1942), p. 183.

21. Horkheimer, "Allgemeiner Teil," in *Studien über Autorität und Familie* (Paris, 1936), pp. 23–24.

22. See, for example, Franz Neumann's "Economics and Politics in the Twentieth Century," *The Democratic and the Authoritarian State*, ed. Herbert Marcuse (New York, 1957), written originally in 1951. Here he wrote: "Marxist theory suffers from a misunderstanding: the confusion of sociological analysis with the theory of political action" (p. 273). In a posthumously published paper entitled "Confining Conditions and Revolutionary Breakthroughs," in *Politics, Law, and Social Change: Selected Essays of Otto Kirchheimer*, ed. Frederic S. Burin and Kurt L. Shell (New York and London, 1969), Kirchheimer made a similar point.

23. For a recent discussion of this issue, see Sheldon Wolin, *Politics and Vision* (Boston, 1960).

24. Marcuse, *Negations: Essays in Critical Theory*, trans. Jeremy J. Shapiro (Boston, 1968), pp. xi–xii.

25. For a recent restatement of the Institut's stress on society, see Adorno's "Society," in *The Legacy of the German Refugee Intellectuals* (*Salmagundi*, 10/11 [Fall, 1969–Winter, 1970]).

26. Marcuse, *Negations*, pp. 31ff.
27. For a discussion of this change, see Robert V. Daniels, "Fate and Will in the Marxian Philosophy of History," in *European Intellectual History Since Darwin and Marx*, ed. W. Warren Wager (New York, 1966).
28. Horkheimer, "Vernunft und Selbsterhaltung," in "Walter Benjamin zum Gedächtnis," p. 25.
29. Fromm, *Fear of Freedom*, pp. 26, 232.
30. Marcuse, *Negations*, p. 39 (italics in the original).
31. Horkheimer, "Autoritärer Staat," p. 153.
32. Horkheimer, "Allgemeiner Teil," pp. 48–49.
33. Fromm, "Sozialpsychologischer Teil," in *Studien über Autorität und Familie*, pp. 132–133.
34. Horkheimer, "Vernunft und Selbsterhaltung," p. 29.
35. The relevant section of this work first appeared in English in 1947, in Max Weber, *The Theory of Social and Economic Organization*, trans. A. M. Henderson and Talcott Parsons (New York, 1947).
36. *Ibid.*, p. 185.
37. Horkheimer, "Allgemeiner Teil," pp. 48–49.
38. Horkheimer, "Vernunft und Selbsterhaltung," p. 56.
39. Marcuse, *Negations*, p. 19.
40. Horkheimer, "Die Juden und Europa," *ZfS* VIII, 1/2 (1939), p. 115.
41. Horkheimer, "Zum Rationalismusstreit in der gegenwärtigen Philosophie," *ZfS* III, 1 (1934), p. 36.
42. Marcuse, *Negations*, p. 18.
43. *Ibid.*, p. 13.
44. *Ibid.*, p. 23.
45. *Ibid.*, pp. 30–31.
46. *Ibid.*, p. 32.
47. *Ibid.*, p. 36.
48. *Ibid.*, p. 38.
49. *Ibid.*, p. 39.
50. Horkheimer, "Die Juden und Europa," p. 125.
51. *Ibid.*, p. 121.
52. For an analysis of fascism as middle-class extremism by a theorist very different from those of the Frankfurt School, see Seymour Martin Lipset, *Political Man* (New York, 1960).
53. Horkheimer, "Vorwort," *Studien über Autorität und Familie*, p. xii.
54. J. N. Findlay, in his *Hegel: A Reexamination* (New York, 1958), writes: "Alone among modern philosophers Hegel has an almost Freudian realization of the simple sexual and family foundations of organized group-life" (p. 116).
55. For a recent discussion of the literature on the family in the last century see René König, "Soziologie der Familie," in *Handbuch der empirischen Sozialforschung*, vol. II (Stuttgart, 1969).
56. Horkheimer, "Allgemeiner Teil," p. 19.
57. *Ibid.*, p. 49.
58. In a subsequent article in *ZfS* VI, 1 (1937), entitled "Zum Gefühl der Ohnmacht," Fromm explored the consequences and causes of the growing feeling of impotence.
59. Horkheimer, "Allgemeiner Teil," p. 66.
60. *Ibid.*, pp. 75–76.

61. Mitscherlich, a psychoanalyst connected with the University of Frankfurt and director of the Sigmund Freud Institute, was very much influenced by the Institut für Sozialforschung after the war. His *Society without the Father*, trans. Eric Mosbacher (New York, 1970), shows how indebted he was to the Frankfurt School's earlier studies of social psychology.

62. Fromm, "Sozialpsychologischer Teil," p. 84.

63. *Ibid.*, p. 101.

64. *Ibid.*, p. 110.

65. See Chapter 3, p. 99.

66. He elaborated on these symptoms of masochistic passivity in "Zum Gefühl der Ohnmacht," p. 117.

67. Marcuse, "Autorität und Familie in der deutschen Soziologie bis 1933," in *Studien über Autorität und Familie.*

68. See, for example, Alasdair MacIntyre's very harsh treatment of his work, *Herbert Marcuse: An Exposition and a Polemic* (New York, 1970).

69. Marcuse, "Ideengeschichtlicher Teil," in *Studien über Autorität und Familie,* p. 140.

70. The Institut was generally at one with German academic philosophy in concentrating on the Greeks, Descartes, Kant and Hegel, the various philosophers of life, and modern phenomenologists. Most medieval philosophy was ignored, and the empiricist tradition was usually discussed as a whole in order to be dismissed. Marcuse, however, did discuss Hobbes, Locke, and Rousseau in lectures at Columbia (letter from Lowenthal to me, August 15, 1970).

71. This quotation is taken from the English abstract at the end of the *Studien über Autorität und Familie*, p. 901.

72. Letter from Fromm to me, May 14, 1971.

73. Interview with Ernst Schachtel, New York, N.Y., June, 1970.

74. Fromm, "Geschichte und Methoden der Erhebungen," in *Studien über Autorität und Familie*, pp. 235–238.

75. *Ibid.*, p. 235.

76. Ernst Schachtel, "Zum Begriff und zur Diagnose der Persönlichkeit in den 'Personality Tests,' " *ZfS* VI, 3 (1937).

77. These included the following:

Karl A. Wittfogel, "Wirtschaftsgeschichtliche Grundlagen der Entwicklung der Familien Autorität."

Ernst Manheim, "Beiträge zu einer Geschichte der autoritären Familie."

Andries Sternheim, "Materialen zur Wirksamkeit ökonomischer Faktoren in der gegenwärtigen Familie."

Hilde Weiss, "Materialen zum Verhältnis von Konjunktur und Familie."

Gottfried Salomon, "Bemerkungen zur Geschichte der französischen Familie."

Willi Strelewicz, "Aus den familienpolitischen Debatten der deutschen Nationalversammlung 1919."

Ernst Schachtel, "Das Recht der Gegenwart und die Autorität in der Familie."

Harald Mankiewics, "Die Entwicklung des französischen Scheidungsrechts."

———, "Die Rechtslage der in nichtlegalisierten Ehen lebendenden Personen in Frankreich."

Zoltán Ronai, "Die Familie in der französischen und belgischen Sozialpolitik."

Hubert Abrahamsohn, "Die Familie in der deutschen Sozialpolitik."

Paul Honigsheim, "Materialen zur Beziehung zwischen Familie und Asozialität von Jugendlichen."

Kurt Goldstein, "Bemerkungen über die Bedeutung der Biologie für die Soziologie anlässlich des Autoritätsproblems."

Fritz Jungmann, "Autorität und Sexualmoral in der freien bürgerlichen Jugendbewegung." (Jungmann was a pseudonym for Franz Borkenau, who was living in London at the time. This was his last contribution to the Institut.)

Marie Jahoda-Lazarsfeld, "Autorität und Erziehung in der Familie, Schule und Jugendbewegung."

Curt Wormann, "Autorität und Familie in der deutschen Belletristik nach dem Weltkrieg."

78. Interview with Pollock, March, 1969.

79. Horkheimer, "Die Juden und Europa."

80. Hans Speier, review of "Studien über Autorität und Familie," *Social Research* III, 4 (November 1936), pp. 501–504.

81. Among Wittfogel's articles in the thirties, which were all part of his more ambitious project to write a series of books on Chinese history and society, were the following: "The Foundations and Stages of Chinese Economic History," *ZfS* IV, 1 (1935), and "Die Theorie der orientalischen Gesellschaft," *ZfS* VII, 1 (1938). In much of his work he was helped by his second wife, Olga Lang, whose book *Chinese Family and Society* (New Haven, 1946) appeared under the auspices of the Institute of Pacific Relations and the Institute of Social Research. Like his work, it did not really employ the methodology of Critical Theory, as Professor Lang admitted to me in conversation (New York, N.Y., June, 1970).

82. Felix Weil, *The Argentine Riddle* (New York, 1944).

83. Mirra Komarovsky, *The Unemployed Man and His Family* (New York, 1940). Originally, this was to be part of a comparative study of unemployment and the family in European cities as well, but the Institut's European branches were all closed by 1938.

84. For a discussion of Lazarsfeld's Research Center, see his article "An Episode in the History of Social Research: A Memoir," in *The Intellectual Migration: Europe and America, 1930–1960*, ed. Donald Fleming and Bernard Bailyn (Cambridge, Mass., 1969), pp. 285f.

85. Paul Lazarsfeld, "Some Remarks on the Typological Procedures in Social Research," *ZfS* VI, 1 (1937).

86. Komarovsky, *The Unemployed Man and His Family*, p. 122.

87. *Ibid.*, p. 3.

88. Adorno, "Fragmente über Wagner," *ZfS* VIII, 1/2 (1939). This was a condensation of several chapters of the book he later published entitled *Versuch über Wagner* (Frankfurt, 1952).

89. Leo Lowenthal, *Erzählkunst und Gesellschaft; Die Gesellschaftsproblematik in der deutschen Literatur des 19. Jahrhunderts* with an intro. by Frederic C. Tubach (Neuwied and Berlin, 1971).

90. *Ibid.*, p. 83.

91. *Ibid.*, p. 132.

92. In addition to the opening essay and the piece on Meyer, which were printed in the *Zeitschrift*, a shortened version of the Goethe essay appeared in Lowenthal's *Literature and the Image of Man* (Boston, 1957), and a similarly abbreviated version of the chapter on Freytag was included in a Festschrift for Georg Lukács, *George Lukács zum achtzigsten Geburtstag*, ed. Frank Benseler (Neuwied, 1965).

93. Lowenthal, "Zur gesellschaftlichen Lage der Literatur," *ZfS* I, 1 (1932).

94. *Ibid.*, p. 90.

95. Lowenthal, "Conrad Ferdinand Meyers heroische Geschichtsauffassung," *ZfS* II, 1 (1933).

96. *Ibid.*, p. 61.

97. Lowenthal, "Die Auffassung Dostojewskis im Vorkriegsdeutschland," *ZfS* III, 3 (1934). A version of the paper in English is contained in *The Arts in Society*, ed. Robert N. Wilson (Englewood Cliffs, N.J., 1964).

98. Benjamin wrote him a very appreciative letter from Paris on July 1, 1934, calling it a breakthrough in studies of this type (Lowenthal collection).

99. Lowenthal in *The Arts in Society*, p. 125.

100. *Ibid.*, p. 368.

101. Lowenthal, "Das Individuum in der individualistischen Gesellschaft. Bemerkungen über Ibsen," *ZfS* V, 3 (1936). The article appeared with minor changes in translation in Lowenthal's *Literature and the Image of Man.* All quotations refer to the English version.

102. *Ibid.*, p. 170.

103. *Ibid.*, p. 175.

104. *Ibid.*, p. 179.

105. *Ibid.*, p. 184.

106. Lowenthal, "Knut Hamsun. Zur Vorgeschichte der autoritären Ideologie," *ZfS* VI, 3 (1937). This also was republished with a few changes in *Literature and the Image of Man*, from which the following quotations are taken.

107. So Lowenthal told me in conversation, Berkeley, Calif., August, 1968.

108. *Literature and the Image of Man*, p. 198.

109. *Ibid.*, p. 202.

110. They were also to be found, Adorno added in a footnote (written pseudonymously as Hektor Rottweiler), in the music of Jan Sibelius. (Page 338 in the original article in *ZfS*, omitted in the English version in *Literature and the Image of Man.*)

111. *Ibid.*, p. 218.

5. THE INSTITUT'S ANALYSIS OF NAZISM

1. Interview with Alice Maier, New York, N.Y., May, 1969.

2. Franz Neumann, *Behemoth: The Structure and Practice of National Socialism, 1933–1944* (rev. ed.; New York, 1944).

3. Neumann *et al.*, *The Cultural Migration: The European Scholar in America* (Philadelphia, 1953), p. 18.

4. Herbert Marcuse, Preface to *The Democratic and the Authoritarian State: Essays in Political and Legal Theory*, by Franz Neumann (New York, 1957), p. vii. See also H. Stuart Hughes, "Franz Neumann between Marxism and Liberal Democracy," in *The Intellectual Migration: Europe and America, 1930–1960*, ed. Donald Fleming and Bernard Bailyn (Cambridge, Mass., 1969).

5. Most frequently he appeared in *Die Arbeit* and *Die Gesellschaft.*

6. Franz Neumann, "Der Funktionswandel des Gesetzes im Recht der bürgerlichen Gesellschaft," *ZfS* VI, 3 (1937), reprinted in English as "The Change in the Function of Law in Modern Society," in *The Democratic and the Authoritarian State*, from which the following quotations are taken.

7. *Ibid.*, p. 39.

8. *Ibid.*, p. 42.

9. *Ibid.*, p. 52.

10. *Ibid.*, p. 65.

11. Neumann made the same point in *Behemoth*, p. 451.

12. *The Democratic and the Authoritarian State*, p. 66.

13. Herbert Marcuse, "The Struggle against Liberalism in the Totalitarian State," *Negations: Essays in Critical Theory*, trans. Jeremy J. Shapiro (Boston, 1968) (originally in *ZfS* III, 1 [1934]).

14. Neumann, "Types of Natural Law," *SPSS* VIII, 3 (1939). The *Studies in Philosophy and Social Science* were a continuation of the *Zeitschrift für Sozialforschung*. This was its first issue. Neumann's article was reprinted in *The Democratic and the Authoritarian State*, from which the following quotations are taken.

15. *Ibid.*, p. 72.

16. *Ibid.*, p. 75. Neumann was later to change his opinion of Rousseau and positive freedom in general.

17. *Ibid.*, p. 79.

18. Even in his later, more liberal period, Neumann could write, "I cannot agree that the state is always the enemy of freedom" ("Intellectual and Political Freedom," *The Democratic and the Authoritarian State*, p. 201).

19. For biographical material on Kirchheimer, see John H. Herz and Erich Hula, "Otto Kirchheimer: An Introduction to His Life and Work," in Otto Kirchheimer, *Politics, Law, and Social Change*, ed. Frederic S. Burin and Kurt L. Shell (New York, 1969).

20. Otto Kirchheimer, "The Socialist and Bolshevik Theory of the State," reprinted in *Politics, Law, and Social Change*, p. 15. Later, Kirchheimer abandoned Schmitt's ideas about emergency situations. See "In Quest of Sovereignty," reprinted in *Politics, Law, and Social Change*, p. 191.

21. Kirchheimer, *Weimar — und Was Dann?* (Berlin, 1930), reprinted in *Politics, Law, and Social Change*.

22. Kirchheimer, "Constitutional Reaction in 1932," originally in *Die Gesellschaft* IX (1932), reprinted in *Politics, Law, and Social Change*, p. 79.

23. In their introduction, Herz and Hula remark: "In this respect Kirchheimer clearly underestimated the advantages which even an authoritarian rule of civil servants and military entailed as contrasted with what was to come: Nazi totalitarianism" (*Politics, Law, and Social Change*, p. xvi). Although not wishing to embark on a full-scale discussion of the point, I think Kirchheimer's position had more merit than they allow. I have tried to develop the reasons why in a review of Istvan Deak's *Weimar Germany's Left-Wing Intellectuals* in *Commentary* XLIV, 4 (October, 1969).

24. Kirchheimer also wrote an analysis of the French attempts to establish an authoritarian government above politics in "Decree Powers and Constitutional Law in France under the Third Republic," originally in *American Political Science Review* XXXIV (1940), and reprinted in *Politics, Law, and Social Change*. Here he wrote: "The French example, coming eight years after the German *Präsidialregierung* of Brüning and Papen, shows that the unlimited decree-rule of a constitutional government with a dubious popular or parliamentary basis serves only as an intermediate station on the road to complete authoritarianism" (p. 130).

25. Kirchheimer had articles in the *Archives de Philosophie du droit et de Sociologie juridique* IV (1934), and the *Revue de Science criminelle et de Droit penal comparé* I (1936).

26. *Staatsgefüge und Recht des Dritten Reiches* (Hamburg, 1935), written under the name of Dr. Hermann Seitz and smuggled into Germany as underground literature.

27. Kirchheimer and George Rusche, *Punishment and Social Structure* (New York, 1939).

28. *Ibid.*, p. 5.

29. Kirchheimer, "The Legal Order of National Socialism," *SPSS* IX, 2 (1941).

30. *Punishment and Social Structure*, p. 179.

31. A. R. L. Gurland, *Produktionsweise-Staat-Klassendiktatur* (Leipzig, 1929). The director of the thesis was Hans Freyer of the philosophy faculty.

32. Gurland, "Die Dialektik der Geschichte und die Geschichtsauffassung Karl Kautskys," *Klassenkampf* (Berlin, Sept. 1, 1929).

33. Gurland, "Die K.P.D. und die rechte Gefahr," *Klassenkampf* (Berlin, Dec. 1, 1928). Gurland also wrote a discussion of the SPD's situation, stressing the need for *praxis,* entitled *Das Heute der proletarischen Aktion* (Berlin, 1931).

34. For a discussion of Grossmann's career, see Walter Braeuer, "Henryk Grossmann als Nationalökonom," *Arbeit und Wissenschaft*, vol. VIII (1954).

35. Henryk Grossmann, "Marx, die klassische Nationalökonomie und das Problem der Dynamik," (mimeographed, 1940). Braeuer refers to a manuscript entitled "Marx Ricardiensis?," which Pollock feels may be another title for the same work, although according to Braeuer, it was over three hundred pages long, rather than 113 pages like the one in Pollock's possession (letter to me from Friedrich Pollock, April 16, 1970). The work was finally published with an afterword by Paul Mattick in Frankfurt in 1969.

36. Henryk Grossmann, "The Evolutionist Revolt against Classical Economics," *Journal of Political Economy* LI, 5 (1943); "W. Playfair, the Earliest Theorist of Capitalist Development," *Economic History Review* XVIII, 1 (1948).

37. In our interviews, Lowenthal, Pollock, and Marcuse all mentioned Grossmann's growing distrust of the Institut's members during the forties. The Lowenthal-Horkheimer correspondence confirms their assertions in a number of letters.

38. The same might be said of another old Institut acquaintance, Ernst Bloch, who was refused financial support from the Institut because of his politics (interview with Leo Lowenthal, Berkeley, Calif., August, 1968).

39. Interview, New York, May, 1969.

40. Gerhard Meyer, "Krisenpolitik und Planwirtschaft," *ZfS* IV, 3 (1935); Meyer also contributed several bibliographical essays, "Neuere Literatur über Planwirtschaft," *ZfS* I, 3 (1932), and "Neue englische Literatur zur Planwirtschaft," *ZfS* II, 2 (1933). With Kurt Mandelbaum, he wrote "Zur Theorie der Planwirtschaft," *ZfS* III, 2 (1934).

41. Under the pseudonym Kurt Baumann, Mandelbaum wrote "Autarkie und Planwirtschaft," *ZfS* II, 1 (1933). Under his own name, he wrote "Neuere Literatur zur Planwirtschaft," *ZfS* IV, 3 (1935), and "Neuere Literatur über technologische Arbeitslosigkeit," *ZfS* V, 1 (1936).

42. Erich Baumann was also a pseudonym for Mandelbaum. The article appearing under this name was "Keynes' Revision der liberalistischen Nationalökonomie," *ZfS* V, 3 (1936). "Sering's" piece was entitled "Zu Marshalls neuklassischer Ökonomie," *ZfS* VI, 3 (1937).

43. Felix Weil, "Neuere Literatur zum 'New Deal,'" *ZfS* V, 3 (1936); "Neuere Literatur zur deutschen Wehrwirtschaft," *ZfS* VII, 1/2 (1938).

44. Marcuse, "Some Social Implications of Modern Technology," *SPSS* IX, 3 (1941); in this piece Marcuse first expressed some of the ideas he was to develop in *One-Dimensional Man.* Gurland, "Technological Trends and Economic Structure under National Socialism," *SPSS* IX, 2 (1941).

45. Conversation with Karl August Wittfogel, New York, N.Y., June 21, 1971.

46. Conversation with Gerhard Meyer, Meredith, N.H., July 19, 1971.

47. Friedrich Pollock, *Die planwirtschaftlichen Versuche in der Sowjetunion (1917–1927)*, (Leipzig, 1929).

48. Pollock, "Die gegenwärtige Lage des Kapitalismus und die Aussichten einer planwirtschaftlichen Neuordnung," *ZfS* I, 1/2 (1932). In the following year, he continued his discussion of the Depression in "Bemerkungen zur Wirtschaftskrise," *ZfS* II, 3 (1933).

49. Pollock, "State Capitalism: Its Possibilities and Limitations," *SPSS* IX, 2 (1941).

50. *Ibid.*, p. 207.

51. James Burnham, *The Managerial Revolution* (New York, 1941). Burnham had originally been a Trotskyist. Although Trotsky himself rejected the notion of state capitalism, at least as it applied to the Soviet Union, a number of his followers did not. There is no evidence, however, of Pollock's having gotten the idea from this source.

52. Pollock, "Is National Socialism a New Order?," *SPSS* IX, 3 (1941), p. 447.

53. *Ibid.*, p. 449.

54. *Ibid.*, p. 450. Neumann was to use the same term in *Behemoth*; Willi Neuling had coined it in "Wettbewerb, Monopol und Befehl in der heutigen Wirtschaft," *Zeitschrift für die gesamte Staatswissenschaft*, LXXXXIX (1939).

55. For a recent discussion of the same issue, see T. W. Mason, "The Primacy of Politics: Politics and Economics in National Socialist Germany," in *The Nature of Fascism*, ed. S. J. Woolf (New York, 1968).

56. Max Horkheimer, "Philosophie und Kritische Theorie" *ZfS* VI, 3 (1937), p. 629.

57. Pollock, "State Capitalism," p. 207.

58. For a discussion of this point, see Robert C. Tucker, "Marx As a Political Theorist," in *Marx and the Western World*, ed. Nicholas Lobkowicz (Notre Dame, Ind., 1967).

59. Marcuse, *Reason and Revolution*, rev. ed. (Boston, 1960), p. 410. Earlier, in his article on "Der Kampf gegen den Liberalismus in der totalitären Staatsauffassung," *ZfS* III, 1 (1934), Marcuse also talked solely of "monopoly capitalism." At this early date, however, the other members of the Institut agreed.

60. Horkheimer, "Autoritärer Staat," in "Walter Benjamin zum Gedächtnis" (unpub., 1942), pp. 124–125, in Pollock's collection.

61. Horkheimer, Preface to *SPSS* IX, 2 (1941), p. 195.

62. Horkheimer, "Vernunft und Selbsterhaltung," in "Walter Benjamin zum Gedächtnis," p. 66.

63. Kirchheimer, "In Quest of Sovereignty," pp. 178–180. Here Kirchheimer related rackets to the technological ethos of modern society: "Rackets seem to correspond to a stage of society where success depends on organization and on access to appropriate technical equipment rather than on special skills" (p. 179).

64. Horkheimer, Preface to *SPSS* IX, 2 (1941), p. 198.

65. Horkheimer, "Die Juden und Europa," *ZfS* VIII, 1/2 (1939), p. 115. This essay was one of the last predominantly Marxist pieces Horkheimer wrote. Not insignificantly, it was excluded from the collection of his work published as *Kritische Theorie*, 2 vols., ed. Alfred Schmidt (Frankfurt, 1968).

66. "Autoritärer Staat," p. 151.

67. Walter Benjamin, *Illuminations*, ed. Hannah Arendt, trans. Harry Zohn (New York, 1968), p. 263.

68. "Autoritärer Staat," p. 143.

69. *Ibid.*, pp. 148–149.

70. For a more serious discussion of the function of terror and coercion by an Institut member, see Leo Lowenthal, "Terror's Atomization of Man," *Commentary* I, 3 (January, 1946). In a later article on "The Lessons of Fascism," in *Tensions That Cause Wars*, ed. Hadley Cantril (Urbana, Ill., 1950), Horkheimer argued that the authoritarian character was not so widespread until the Nazis began using terror and massive propaganda to atomize the population (p. 223).

71. "Die Juden und Europa," p. 125.

72. "Autoritärer Staat," p. 138.

73. "Vernunft und Selbsterhaltung," p. 59.

74. "Autoritärer Staat," p. 160.

75. So Lowenthal told me during one of our interviews, in Berkeley, August, 1968.

76. Kirchheimer, "Criminal Law in National Socialist Germany," *SPSS* VIII, 3 (1939). Kirchheimer also published another article on German criminal practice, entitled "Recent Trends in German Treatment of Juvenile Delinquency," *Journal of Criminal Law and Criminology* XXIX (1938).

77. Compare Kirchheimer's critique of phenomenological law with Marcuse's article "The Concept of Essence," *Negations*, and Adorno's more extensive attack on Husserl in his *Zur Metakritik der Erkenntnistheorie* (Stuttgart, 1956). The source of the Kiel School's phenomenology was Scheler's materialist eidetics rather than Husserl's idealistic variety.

78. Kirchheimer, "The Legal Order of National Socialism," *SPSS* IX, 3 (1941), reprinted in *Politics, Law, and Social Change*, from which the following quotations are taken (p. 93).

79. *Ibid.*, p. 99.

80. *Ibid.*, p. 108.

81. Kirchheimer, "Changes in the Structure of Political Compromise," *SPSS* IX, 2 (1941), also reprinted in *Politics, Law, and Social Change*, from which the following quotations are taken.

82. *Ibid.*, p. 131.

83. *Ibid.*, p. 155.

84. *Ibid.*, pp. 158–159.

85. Gurland, "Technological Trends and Economic Structure under National Socialism," *SPSS* IX, 2 (1941).

86. *Ibid.*, p. 248.

87. *Ibid.*, p. 261.

88. Conversations with Marcuse and Lowenthal are the major source of this observation. When *Behemoth* came to be published in German, it was not included in the Institut's series of *Frankfurter Beiträge zur Soziologie*.

89. In discussing Emil Lederer's *State of the Masses: The Threat of the Classless Society* (New York, 1940), Neumann wrote, "Were Lederer's analysis correct, our earlier discussion would be completely wrong. . . . Racism would not be the concern of small groups alone but would be deeply imbedded in the masses" (*Behemoth*, p. 366).

90. *Behemoth*, p. 121.

91. *Studies* IX, 1 (1941), p. 141. The prospectus was dated 1939.

92. *Behemoth*, p. 465.

93. *Ibid.*, p. 476.

94. In *Behemoth* Kehr is mentioned several times and called "extremely gifted" (p. 203). Kehr's estimation of psychoanalysis can be found in his essay "Neuere deut-

sche Geschichtsschreibung," *Der Primat der Innenpolitik*, ed. Hans-Ulrich Wehler (Berlin, 1965).

95. *Behemoth*, pp. 403–413.

96. *Ibid.*, p. 224.

97. *Ibid.*, p. 227.

98. *Ibid.*, pp. 228–234.

99. *Ibid.*, p. 260.

100. Quoted by John M. Cammett, "Communist Theories of Fascism, 1920–1935," *Science and Society* XXXI, 2 (Spring, 1967).

101. *Behemoth*, p. 261.

102. *Ibid.*, p. 298.

103. *Ibid.*, p. 305.

104. *Ibid.*, p. 185.

105. *Ibid.*, p. 354.

106. *Ibid.*, p. 366.

107. *Ibid.*, p. 449. David Schoenbaum's "revision" of Neumann in *Hitler's Social Revolution* (Garden City, N.Y., 1966), which is based on the importance of the Nazi status revolution, was thus in part anticipated by Neumann himself.

108. *Behemoth*, p. 278.

109. *Ibid.*, p. 472.

110. *Ibid.*, p. xii.

111. *Ibid.*, p. 471.

112. Horkheimer, Foreword to *SPSS* VIII, 3 (1939), p. 321. This was actually dated July, 1940.

113. On the board of directors of the Social Studies Association were Charles Beard, Robert MacIver, Robert Lynd, Morris Cohen, and Paul Tillich, all old friends of the Institut. ("Supplementary Memorandum on the Activities of the Institute from 1939 to 1941," mimeographed; Friedrich Pollock's collection in Montagnola).

114. Of the new research associates, Karsen had contributed the most to the *Zeitschrift*, with two bibliographical pieces, "Neue Literatur über Gesellschaft und Erziehung," *ZfS* III, 1 (1934), and "Neue amerikanische Literatur über Gesellschaft und Erziehung," *ZfS* VIII, 1 (1939).

115. Interviews with Marcuse (May, 1968) in Cambridge, Mass. and Lowenthal (August, 1968). One ought not to make too much out of Neumann's friction with other members of the Institut. Pollock, with whom he was most clearly at odds on theoretical matters, delivered a eulogy at his funeral in Switzerland in December, 1954.

116. Gurland, Neumann, and Kirchheimer, *The Fate of Small Business in Germany* (Washington, D.C., 1943). This was partially financed by a grant from the Carnegie Foundation. Pepper's subcommittee was designed to study problems of American small business. The book's conclusion that small business in Weimar and Nazi Germany had been caught in the squeeze between big business and labor fitted well with the goals of the subcommittee.

117. "Cultural Aspects of National Socialism," in Lowenthal's collection in Berkeley. Another abortive project which the Institut tried to get sponsored was a study of the postwar reconstruction of German society.

118. *Ibid.*, p. 51.

119. The dissertation was a study of the agrarian situation in France after World War I. Massing did much of the research at the Sorbonne and spent eighteen

months in Moscow at the Agrarian Institute after its completion in 1929. (This and the subsequent biographical information comes from an interview with Dr. Massing in New York, November 25, 1970).

120. Massing [pseud: Karl Billinger], *Schutzhäftling 880* (Paris, 1955); Wittfogel [pseud: Klaus Hinrichs], *Staatliches Konzentrationslager VII* (London, 1936). The information about the pseudonym comes from my interview with Massing in New York.

121. See Wittfogel's testimony on August 7, 1951, Internal Security Subcommittee of the Senate Judiciary Committee, 82nd Congress, 1951–1952, vol. III, p. 276.

122. For a description of the trip, see Hede Massing, *This Deception* (New York, 1951), pp. 244f.

123. Conversation with Wittfogel, New York, June 21, 1971.

124. This was the reason Marcuse mentioned during our interview.

125. "Ten Years on Morningside Heights," (unpub., 1944), in Lowenthal's collection.

126. Horkheimer, "Egoismus und Freiheitsbewegung," *ZfS* V, 1 (1936), p. 219. Marcuse wrote an article "Über den affirmativen Charakter der Kultur," *ZfS* VI, 1 (1937), which we shall examine in the following chapter.

6. AESTHETIC THEORY AND THE CRITIQUE OF MASS CULTURE

1. George Steiner, "Marxism and the Literary Critic," *Language and Silence* (New York, 1967).

2. Georg Lukács, *The Historical Novel*, trans. Hannah and Stanley Mitchell (Boston, 1963), pp. 30–63.

3. With his *Wider den missverstandenen Realismus* (Hamburg, 1958), after Stalin's death, Lukács lessened his hostility somewhat. See Roy Pascal's essay in *Georg Lukács: The Man, His Work, and His Ideas*, ed. G. H. R. Parkinson (New York, 1970).

4. See his lengthy polemic against "irrationalism" in Lukács, *Die Zerstörung der Vernunft* (Berlin, 1954).

5. Herbert Marcuse's critique of socialist realism in his *Soviet Marxism: A Critical Analysis* (New York, 1958) stresses this fallacy.

6. Walter Benjamin, *Briefe*, ed. Gershom Scholem and Theodor W. Adorno (Frankfurt, 1966), vol. I, pp. 350, 355.

7. Theodor Adorno, "Erpresste Versöhnung," *Noten zur Literatur II* (Frankfurt, 1961), p. 152.

8. See Adorno, "The George-Hofmannsthal Correspondence, 1891–1906," *Prisms*, trans. Samuel and Shierry Weber (London, 1967), p. 217.

9. For a description of Cornelius's artistic background, see his essay "Leben und Lehre," in *Die Philosophie der Gegenwart in Selbstdarstellungen*, ed. Raymund Schmidt (Leipzig, 1923), vol. II. Among his works on aesthetics were *Elementargesetze der bildenden Kunst: Grundlagen einer praktischen Ästhetik* (Leipzig and Berlin, 1911), and *Kunstpädagogik* (Erlenbach-Zurich, 1920).

10. In a letter to Horkheimer on October 27, 1942, Lowenthal refers to a novel that Horkheimer had begun to write (Lowenthal collection).

11. Samuel and Shierry Weber have an interesting essay on the difficulties of translating Adorno at the beginning of *Prisms*.

12. Adorno, *Prisms*, p. 225.

13. *Ibid.*, p. 150.

14. *Ibid.*, p. 246.
15. *Ibid.*, p. 229.
16. This was similar to the task Norman O. Brown seems to have set himself in *Love's Body* (New York, 1966), where much of the text consists of quotations.
17. See his letter to Max Rychner, in Benjamin, *Briefe*, vol. II, p. 524.
18. Quoted in Adorno, *Prisms*, p. 232.
19. Benjamin, *Briefe*, vol. II, pp. 726, 727.
20. "Ten Years on Morningside Heights: A Report on the Institute's History, 1934–1944" (unpub., 1944) (Lowenthal collection).
21. *Prisms*, p. 71.
22. Benjamin, *Illuminations*, ed. with an intro. by Hannah Arendt, trans. Harry Zohn (New York, 1968), p. 258.
23. Max Horkheimer, "Art and Mass Culture," *SPSS* IX, 2 (1941), p. 291.
24. This was a transition the young Lukács had made as well. See Lucien Goldmann, "The Early Writings of Georg Lukács," *Tri-Quarterly* IX (Spring, 1967).
25. *Prisms*, p. 184. "Force-field" *(Kraftfeld)*, it will be recalled, was the term Adorno also used in his critique of Husserl.
26. *Ibid.*, p. 262.
27. *Ibid.*, p. 262.
28. This point is made by Ilse Müller-Strömsdörfer in "Die 'helfende Kraft bestimmter Negation,'" *Philosophische Rundschau* VIII, 2/3 (Jan. 1961), p. 98.
29. Adorno, "Über den Fetischcharakter in der Musik und die Regression des Hörens," *ZfS* VII, 3 (1938), p. 321; Leo Lowenthal, *Literature, Popular Culture, and Society* (Englewood Cliffs, N.J., 1961), p. 12.
30. *Prisms*, p. 30.
31. Benjamin, *Briefe*, vol. II, p. 785; Adorno, *Prisms*, p. 236.
32. Horkheimer, "Art and Mass Culture," p. 292. For an expansion of the connection between religion and art, see Adorno's "Theses upon Art and Religion Today," *Kenyon Review* VII, 4 (Autumn, 1945).
33. Nietzsche was the first to pick up this phrase and use it against Kant's definition of beauty as the object of disinterested desire. Marcuse first used it in "The Affirmative Character of Culture," *Negations: Essays in Critical Theory*, trans. Jeremy J. Shapiro (Boston, 1968), p. 115.
34. So Horkheimer argued (under the pseudonym Heinrich Regius) in *Dämmerung* (Zurich, 1934), p. 60, and Adorno in *Prisms*, p. 32.
35. *Prisms*, p. 32.
36. *Ibid.*, p. 171.
37. *Ibid.*, p. 32.
38. Adorno, "Theses on Art and Religion Today," p. 678.
39. Marcuse, "The Affirmative Character of Culture," p. 117. This was to be a major theme of his *Eros and Civilization* (Boston, 1955).
40. *Prisms*, p. 87.
41. *Ibid.*, p. 230.
42. Marcuse "On Hedonism," *Negations*, p. 198.
43. In one of the last articles he wrote, Adorno returned to the centrality of mediation for a genuine aesthetic theory. In criticizing the notion of communications in the work of the sociologist of music Alphons Silbermann, Adorno wrote: "Mediation is . . . in the object itself, not something between the object and that to which it is brought. What is contained in communications, however, is solely the relationship between producer and consumer" ("Thesen zur Kunstsoziologie," *Kölner Zeitschrift für Soziologie und Sozialpsychologie* XIX, 1 [March, 1967], p. 92).

44. *Prisms*, p. 33.

45. Benjamin, *Briefe*, vol. II, pp. 672, 676. Several of Adorno's letters to Benjamin are included in the volume.

46. *Prisms*, p. 85.

47. *Ibid.*, p. 84.

48. "Music did not 'represent' anything outside of itself; it was on the order of prayer and play, not painting and writing. The decay of this reality of music by its becoming an image of itself tends to break the spell" (Adorno, "Currents of Music: Elements of a Radio Theory" [unpub. prospectus for the Princeton Radio Research Project, 1939], p. 72). I am indebted to Professor Lazarsfeld for making this available to me.

49. Many of his early articles appeared in the journal he edited, *Anbruch*, and in others such as *Musik, Pult und Taktstock, Scheinwerfer*, and *23*.

50. Several of these articles have been reprinted in Adorno, *Moments Musicaux* (Frankfurt, 1964).

51. Adorno, "Zur gesellschaftlichen Lage der Musik," *ZfS* I, 1/2, and I, 3 (1932).

52. *Ibid.*, 1/2, p. 106.

53. Adorno, *Philosophie der neuen Musik* (Frankfurt, 1949).

54. Adorno, "Zur gesellschaftlichen Lage der Musik," 1/2, p. 112.

55. *Prisms*, p. 166.

56. Adorno, "Zur gesellschaftlichen Lage der Musik," 1/2, p. 116. The relationship between neoclassical objectivism and fascism is not that farfetched. Stephen Spender has suggested a similar connection in the work of T. E. Hulme; see his *The Struggle of the Modern* (Berkeley and Los Angeles, 1963), p. 49.

57. Adorno, "Zur gesellschaftlichen Lage der Musik," 1/2, p. 119.

58. *Ibid.*, 3, p. 359.

59. *Ibid.*, p. 365.

60. *Ibid.*, p. 368.

61. Adorno [Hektor Rottweiler], "Über Jazz," *ZfS* V, 2 (1936).

62. Adorno, *Moments Musicaux*, p. 9.

63. In his *Essay on Liberation* (Boston, 1969), Marcuse was to include blues and jazz among the artifacts of "the new sensibility," which he considered critical of the prevailing affirmative culture (p. 38).

64. Adorno, "Oxford Nachträge," *Dissonanzen: Musik in der verwalteten Welt* (Frankfurt, 1956), p. 117. This was originally written in 1937 during Adorno's stay at Merton College, Oxford.

65. Adorno [Rottweiler], "Über Jazz," p. 238.

66. *Ibid.*, p. 242.

67. "Perennial Fashion — Jazz," *Prisms*, p. 122.

68. Hans Mayer, *Der Repräsentant und der Märtyrer* (Frankfurt, 1971), pp. 156–157.

69. A review of Wilder Hobson's *American Jazz Music* and Winthrop Sargeant's *Jazz Hot and Hybrid*, written with the assistance of Eunice Cooper, in the *SPSS* IX, 1 (1941), p. 169. Adorno was enthusiastic about Sargeant's interpretation of jazz, which he took as a native confirmation of his own ideas. Hobson, on the other hand, he criticized for trying to abstract the music from its commodity character.

70. *Ibid.*, p. 177.

71. "Oxford Nachträge," p. 119.

72. *Ibid.*, p. 123.

73. *Ibid.*, p. 123.

74. *Prisms*, pp. 199f.

75. Adorno, "Scientific Experiences of a European Scholar in America," in *The Intellectual Migration: Europe and America, 1930–1960*, ed. Donald Fleming and Bernard Bailyn (Cambridge, Mass., 1969), p. 341. Curiously, Adorno writes, "I actually still considered jazz to be a spontaneous form of expression," which seems scarcely to have been the case.

76. Marcuse's mid-1960's enthusiasm for the "counterculture," however, has begun to wane in the 1970's; see, for example, his review of Charles Reich's *The Greening of America* (*The New York Times*, Nov. 6, 1970, p. 41), and his *Counterrevolution and Revolt* (Boston, 1972).

77. Adorno, "Scientific Experiences of a European Scholar in America," p. 340.

78. *Ibid.*, p. 341, and Paul Lazarsfeld, "An Episode in the History of Social Research: A Memoir," in *The Intellectual Migration*, pp. 322f.

79. Lazarsfeld, "An Episode in the History of Social Research," p. 301.

80. "Über den Fetischcharakter in der Musik und die Regression des Hörens," *ZfS* VII, 3 (1938).

81. Benjamin, "L'Oeuvre de l'art à l'époque de sa reproduction mécanisée," *ZfS* V, 1 (1936).

82. Adorno, "Über den Fetischcharakter," p. 327.

83. *Ibid.*, p. 330.

84. More orthodox Marxist critics were always quick to point to this as an inadequacy of Adorno's work. See, for example, Konrad Boehmer, "Adorno, Musik, Gesellschaft" in *Die neue Linke nach Adorno*, ed. Wilfried F. Schoeller (Munich, 1969), p. 123.

85. "Über den Fetischcharakter," p. 355.

86. Adorno acknowledged the importance of Simpson's help in his essay "Scientific Experiences," in *The Intellectual Migration*, pp. 350–351. Simpson had been a student of Robert MacIver. His major work was as translator and critic of Durkheim's sociology.

87. Adorno, "A Social Critique of Radio Music," *Kenyon Review* VII, 2 (Spring, 1945).

88. Ernst Křenek, "Bemerkungen zur Rundfunkmusik," *ZfS* VII, 1/2 (1938). Adorno later wrote a tribute to Křenek in *Moments Musicaux*, entitled "Zur Physiognomik Křeneks."

89. Adorno, "A Social Critique of Radio Music," pp. 210–211.

90. See his discussion of their genesis in *The Intellectual Migration*, p. 351.

91. Adorno, "On Popular Music," *SPSS* IX, 1 (1941).

92. *Ibid.*, p. 48.

93. Professor Lazarsfeld has graciously made the original manuscript available to me. It was entitled "Currents of Music: Elements of a Radio Theory." A shortened version appeared as "The Radio Symphony," in *Radio Research 1941*, ed. Paul Lazarsfeld and Frank Stanton (New York, 1941).

94. *Ibid.*, p. 14.

95. Benjamin, "Theses on the Philosophy of History," *Illuminations*, p. 262.

96. Adorno, "Currents of Music," p. 26.

97. *Ibid.*, p. 79.

98. "Scientific Experiences," p. 352

99. Adorno, "Fragmente über Wagner," *ZfS* VIII, 1/2 (1939).

100. In a letter to Lowenthal, in June, 1941, Horkheimer spoke enthusiastically of his new friendship with the past greats of German letters.

101. Horkheimer, "Die philosophie der absoluten Konzentration," *ZfS* VII, 3 (1938).

102. Interview with Pollock, March, 1969, in Montagnola. The study's results, which indicated that conservatives and Catholics had done more for the Jews than other groups in society, was never published.

103. Thomas Mann, *The Story of a Novel: The Genesis of Doctor Faustus*, trans. Richard and Clara Winston (New York, 1961), pp. 94–95.

104. *Ibid.*, p. 103.

105. *Ibid.*, p. 46.

106. *Ibid.*, p. 48.

107. *Ibid.*, p. 150.

108. *Ibid.*, p. 222.

109. See *Letters of Thomas Mann, 1889–1955*, selected and trans. Richard and Clara Winston, intro. Richard Winston (New York, 1971), pp. 546–547, 587–588.

110. Hanns Eisler, *Composition for the Film* (New York, 1947). For a discussion of Adorno's role in its creation, see Helmut Lück, "Anmerkungen zu Theodor W. Adornos Zusammenarbeit mit Hanns Eisler," in *Die neue Linke nach Adorno*. Eisler's brother Gerhart was under serious attack at the time for his involvement in Communist activities, and Adorno wanted no part of the association the book might have suggested.

111. Adorno, "Gegängelte Musik," in *Dissonanzen.*

112. Adorno, *Minima Moralia* (Frankfurt, 1951); and Adorno and Horkheimer, *Dialektik der Aufklärung* (Amsterdam, 1947).

113. Adorno et al., *The Authoritarian Personality* (New York, 1950). Adorno's paper on Martin Luther Thomas was never published.

114. Adorno and Bernice T. Eiduson, "How to Look at Television" (paper read at the Hacker Foundation in Los Angeles, April 13, 1953) (Lowenthal collection).

115. Adorno, "The Stars Down to Earth: *The Los Angeles Times* Astrology Column: A Study in Secondary Superstition," *Jahrbuch für Amerikastudien*, vol. II (Heidelberg, 1957).

116. Adorno, "Thesen gegen den Okkultismus," *Minima Moralia*, pp. 462f.

117. Adorno used this work as the basis of his discussion in an article he wrote at approximately the same time, "Freudian Theory and the Pattern of Fascist Propaganda," in *Psychoanalysis and the Social Sciences*, ed. Geza Roheim (New York, 1951).

118. Adorno, "The Stars Down to Earth," p. 82.

119. *Prisms*, p. 98.

120. See, for example, his letter to Horkheimer in the fall of 1934 (Benjamin, *Briefe*, vol. II, p. 625f.). Benjamin also resisted invitations to move to Denmark, Palestine, and the Soviet Union.

121. Adorno, "Interimbescheid," *Über Walter Benjamin* (Frankfurt, 1970), p. 95.

122. Benjamin, *Briefe*, vol. II, p. 834. The rest of the history of Benjamin's life comes from the Introduction to *Illuminations* by Hannah Arendt and the biographical sketch by Friedrich Pollock in Benjamin's *Schriften*, ed. Theodor W. Adorno and Gershom Scholem, vol. II (Frankfurt, 1955).

123. Arthur Koestler, *The Invisible Writing* (London, 1954), p. 512.

124. *Ibid.*, p. 513.

125. Horkheimer, "Autoritärer Staat" and "Vernunft und Selbsterhaltung"; Adorno, "George und Hofmannsthal"; and Benjamin, "Thesen zur Geschichtsphilosophie," in "Walter Benjamin zum Gedächtnis" (unpub., 1942) (Friedrich Pollock's collection in Montagnola).

126. Rolf Tiedemann, *Studien zur Philosophie Walter Benjamins* (Frankfurt, 1965).

127. See, especially, *Alternative*, 56/7 (Oct.–Dec., 1967) and 59/60 (April–June, 1968), and Hannah Arendt, intro. to *Illuminations*. Other contributions to the debate include Siegfried Unseld, "Zur Kritik an den Editionen Walter Benjamins," *Frankfurter Rundschau* (January 24, 1968); Rolf Tiedemann, "Zur 'Beschlagnahme' Walter Benjamins, oder Wie Man mit der Philologie Schlitten fährt," *Das Argument* X, 1/2 (March, 1968); Friedrich Pollock, "Zu dem Aufsatz von Hannah Arendt über Walter Benjamin," *Merkur*, XXII, 6 (1968); Hannah Arendt, "Walter Benjamin und das Institut für Sozialforschung — noch einmal," *Merkur*, XXII, 10 (1968); and Hildegaard Brenner, "Theodor W. Adorno als Sachwalter des Benjaminschen Werkes," in *Die neue Linke nach Adorno*. Adorno's own reply, "Interimbescheid," is reprinted in his *Über Walter Benjamin*. For a summary of the debate, see "Marxistisch Rabbi," *Der Spiegel*, XXII, 16 (April 15, 1968).

128. See Benjamin's article, "Unpacking My Library," *Illuminations*.

129. Benjamin, *Berliner Kindheit um Neunzehnhundert* (Frankfurt, 1950) *passim*. In 1940 Benjamin wrote to Adorno: "Why should I hide from you that I find the root of my 'Theory of Experience' in a childhood memory?" (*Briefe*, vol. II, p. 848).

130. So Gershom Scholem has suggested in "Walter Benjamin," *Leo Baeck Institute Yearbook* (New York, 1965).

131. Adorno, *Über Walter Benjamin*, p. 97.

132. Benjamin, *Briefe*, vol. II, p. 655.

133. Gretel Adorno has denied the effect of his marriage's failure on his turning away from Zionism (letter to me, November 4, 1970), but Hannah Arendt has suggested otherwise in her Introduction to *Illuminations*, p. 36.

134. Max Rychner, "Erinnerungen an Walter Benjamin," *Der Monat*, XVIII, 216 (September, 1966), p. 42. *Ursprung des deutschen Trauerspiels* was published in Berlin in 1928.

135. *Briefe*, vol. II, p. 524.

136. Adorno, "A Portrait of Walter Benjamin," *Prisms*, p. 234.

137. See Benjamin, "The Task of the Translator," *Illuminations*; Hans Heinz Holz, "Philosophie als Interpretation," *Alternative*, 56/57 (October–December, 1967); and "Walter Benjamin: Towards a Philosophy of Language," *The Times Literary Supplement* (London, August 22, 1968). Although anonymous, this last article is almost certainly by George Steiner.

138. *Illuminations*, p. 263. Miss Arendt adds a footnote to the English translation in which she argues that Benjamin meant a mystical *nunc stans* rather than the more prosaic *Gegenwart* (the normal German word for the present). Ernst Bloch in his "Erinnerungen an Walter Benjamin," *Der Monat*, XVIII, 216 (September, 1966), suggested that *Jetztzeit* meant a break in the continuity of the temporal flow, in which the past suddenly became present (p. 40).

139. "Theses on the Philosophy of History." *Illuminations*, p. 255.

140. Letter from Lowenthal to Horkheimer, June 18, 1942.

141. Benjamin, *Briefe*, vol. II, p. 786. This would seem to contradict Hildegaard Brenner's assertion that Adorno sought to encourage the theological elements in Benjamin's work; see her article, "Die Lesbarkeit der Bilder: Skizzen zum Passagenentwurf," *Alternative*, 59/60 (April–June, 1968), p. 56.

142. One possible reason for Benjamin's distance from Marxism directly after the war was that it was often connected with an expressionist aesthetic, which he strongly disliked. On the merging of radicalism and expressionism, see Lewis D. Wurgaft, "The Activist Movement: Cultural Politics on the German Left, 1914–

1933" (Ph.D. diss., Harvard University, 1970). On Benjamin's hostility to expressionism, see Adorno, *Über Walter Benjamin*, pp. 96–97.

143. Bloch, "Erinnerungen an Walter Benjamin," p. 38. According to Adorno, Benjamin's social conscience was also aroused during the same year by the beginning of the inflation (*Über Walter Benjamin*, p. 57).

144. Benjamin quoted from *The Theory of the Novel* (Berlin, 1920) in his piece on Nikolai Leskov, "The Storyteller," *Illuminations*, p. 99.

145. Scholem, in his article on "Walter Benjamin" (p. 18), called Brecht's influence "baleful, and in some respects disastrous." Adorno frequently warned Benjamin against Brecht; see, for example, his letter in the Benjamin *Briefe*, vol. II, p. 676.

146. Tiedemann, *Studien zur Philosophie Walter Benjamins*, p. 89.

147. See the excerpts in Iring Fetscher, "Bertolt Brecht and America," in *The Legacy of the German Refugee Intellectuals* (*Salmagundi*, 10/11 [Fall, 1969–Winter, 1970]). For example, on May 12, 1942, Brecht wrote in his diary: "With Eisler at Horkheimer's for lunch. After that, Eisler suggests for the Tui novel: the story of the Frankfurt Institute for Social Research. A wealthy old man dies, worried over the suffering in the world, leaves in his will a substantial sum of money establishing an institute that shall search for the source of misery — which of course was he himself" (p. 264).

148. *Briefe*, vol. II, p. 594.

149. Introduction to *Illuminations*, p. 15. The phrase (*das plumpe Denken*) is Brecht's own description of his style of thought. Benjamin picked it up in his discussion of Brecht's *Dreigroschenroman* (Benjamin, *Versuche über Brecht*, ed. Rolf Tiedemann [Frankfurt, 1966], p. 90).

150. Introduction to *Illuminations*, p. 15.

151. See, for example, Hildegaard Brenner's essay in *Die neue Linke nach Adorno*, *passim.*

152. Benjamin, *Versuche über Brecht.*

153. *Briefe*, vol. II, p. 657. Benjamin cited the Bibliothèque Nationale as the reason why he could not leave Paris for Svendborg permanently.

154. Bertolt Brecht, "An Walter Benjamin, der sich auf der Flucht vor Hitler Entleibte" and "Zum Freitod der Flüchtlings W.B.," *Gedichte VI* (Frankfurt, 1964).

155. Benjamin, *Der Begriff der Kunstkritik in der deutschen Romantik* (Bern, 1920).

156. *Briefe*, vol. II, p. 857.

157. Benjamin, "Über das Programm der kommenden Philosophie," *Zur Kritik der Gewalt und andere Aufsätze* (Frankfurt, 1965), pp. 15–16.

158. Quoted in Adorno, *Prisms*, p. 232.

159. *Briefe*, vol. II, pp. 726, 727.

160. Adorno, *Alban Berg: Der Meister des kleinsten Übergangs* (Vienna, 1968), p. 32.

161. Benjamin, "The Author as Producer," *New Left Review*, 62 (July–August, 1970).

162. *Illuminations*, p. 265. In a letter to me, Gretel Adorno emphatically denied an analogical moment in her late husband's thinking (January 27, 1970).

163. Quoted in Adorno, *Prisms*, p. 234.

164. *Ibid.*, p. 240.

165. It was published in Hofmannsthal's *Neue Deutsche Beiträge*, II, 1 (April, 1924).

166. See Hannah Arendt's discussion in her introduction to *Illuminations*, pp. 8–9.

167. *Briefe*, vol. I, p. 379.

168. With Franz Hessel, Benjamin translated *À l'ombre des jeunes filles en fleurs* and two volumes of *Le Côté de Guermantes* during the twenties.

169. Letter to me from Gretel Adorno (November 4, 1970).

170. Benjamin, *Berliner Kindheit um Neunzehnhundert* (Frankfurt, 1950).

171. What Benjamin once wrote of Kafka might have been applied to himself: "Kafka's work is an ellipse with foci that are far apart and are determined, on the one hand, by mystical experience (in particular, the experience of tradition) and, on the other, by the experience of the modern big-city dweller" (*Illuminations*, pp. 144–145).

172. Benjamin [Detlef Holz], *Deutsche Menschen: Eine Folge von Briefen* (Lucerne, 1936).

173. As Adorno remembers it, they met either through Siegfried Kracauer or in a sociological seminar run by Gottfried Salomon-Delatour in Frankfurt. See "Erinnerungen an Walter Benjamin," *Der Monat*, XVIII, 216 (September, 1966). Benjamin was also close friends with Marguerite (Gretel) Karplus, later Adorno's wife, whom he met in 1928. Many of his letters in the *Briefe* are addressed to "Felizitas," as he called her. In 1928, so Adorno wrote (*Über Walter Benjamin*, p. 98), Benjamin became part of the Institut's circle. If so, he certainly was not a very close member. In fact, he did not actually meet Horkheimer in person until 1938.

174. Benjamin, "Zum gegenwärtigen gesellschaftlichen Standort des französischen Schriftstellers," *ZfS* III, 1 (1934). In his discussion of French writers from Barrès to Gide, Benjamin showed his distance from the Leninist strain in Marxist aesthetics. For example, he contended that surrealism, although beginning apolitically with Apollinaire, was moving towards reconciliation with political *praxis*, in the work of Breton and Aragon (p. 73).

175. *Briefe*, vol. II, p. 652.

176. *Ibid.*, p. 685.

177. These changes and others are pointed out by Helga Gallas, "Wie es zu den Eingriffen in Benjamins Texte kam oder über die Herstellbarkeit von Einständnis," *Alternative*, 59/60, p. 80.

178. Horkheimer [Regius], *Dämmerung*, p. 178.

179. Benjamin, "Eduard Fuchs, der Sammler und der Historiker," *ZfS* VI, 2 (1937), and "L'Oeuvre de l'art à l'époque de sa reproduction mécanisée," *ZfS* V, 1 (1936).

180. Hildegaard Brenner has argued that the changes were substantial, according to the original copy in the *Potsdam Zentralarchiv* in East Germany; see her piece in *Die neue Linke nach Adorno*, p. 162.

181. *Briefe*, vol. II, p. 742.

182. This was at least one possible plan for the work; see the *Briefe*, vol. II, p. 774.

183. *Briefe*, vol. II, pp. 671–683.

184. *Ibid.*, p. 678.

185. *Ibid.*, pp. 681–682. Benjamin's lack of interest in the subjective individual has often been noted. He once confided to Adorno that "I am interested not in men, but only in things" (Adorno, Introduction to Benjamin's *Schriften*, vol. I, p. 17).

186. *Briefe*, vol. II, pp. 782–790.

187. *Ibid.*, p. 786.

188. *Ibid.*, p. 788.

189. *Ibid.*, pp. 790–799.

190. *Ibid.*, pp. 794–795.

191. A translation has appeared as "Paris: Capital of the Nineteenth Century," in *Dissent*, XVII, 5 (September–October, 1970). A more complete version finally appeared in 1969 in German as *Charles Baudelaire: Ein Lyriker im Zeitalter des Hochkapitalismus* (Frankfurt, 1969).

192. "Über einige Motive bei Baudelaire," *ZfS* VIII, 1/2 (1939), trans. in *Illuminations*, p. 159.

193. To Baudelaire, so Benjamin argued, the creative process was like a duel with the traumas of shocks, in which the artist tried to parry with all his powers (*Illuminations*, p. 165).

194. *Ibid.*, p. 174.

195. Miss Arendt's introduction to *Illuminations*, for example, is rooted in this view of Benjamin.

196. *Illuminations*, p. 184.

197. See Benjamin, *Ursprung des deutschen Trauerspiels.* Tiedemann comments extensively on Benjamin's *Umfunktionierung* (changing the function) of Goethe's *Urphänomene* in his *Studien zur Philosophie Walter Benjamins*, p. 59f.

198. Horkheimer, "Zu Bergsons Metaphysik der Zeit," *ZfS* III, 3 (1934).

199. *Illuminations*, p. 187.

200. *Studien zur Philosophie Walter Benjamins*, p. 69.

201. *Illuminations*, p. 263.

202. On Kraus's concern for origins, see Hans Mayer, *Der Repräsentant und der Märtyrer*, pp. 51–52.

203. Fredric Jameson entitled his article in *The Legacy of the German Refugee Intellectuals* (*Salmagundi*, 10/11 [Fall, 1969–Winter, 1970]), "Walter Benjamin, or Nostalgia," and Peter Szondi wrote an article called "Hoffnung im Vergangenen," in *Zeugnisse: Theodor W. Adorno zum Sechzigsten Geburtstag* (Frankfurt, 1963), in which he suggests that Benjamin sought his utopia in the past.

204. "On Certain Motifs in Baudelaire," *Illuminations*, p. 189.

205. *Ibid.*, p. 224.

206. *Ibid.*, p. 223.

207. *Ibid.*, p. 225.

208. *Ibid.*, p. 226.

209. Brecht had been disappointed in 1931 with the film version of the *Dreigroschenoper.* From this experience, he argued that intellectuals had themselves been proletarianized, a theme that Benjamin picked up in "Der Autor als Produzent," written in 1934 and published in his *Versuche über Brecht.* Here Benjamin attacked as reactionary the notion of an independent intellectual *Logokratie*, of the type proposed by Kurt Hiller and the Activists. By implication, Benjamin also questioned the tendency in Adorno's aesthetics to oppose avant-garde art to the popular culture of the working class. "The revolutionary struggle," he wrote at the end of the essay, "occurs not between capitalism and *Geist* [which was the key word of the Activists], but between capitalism and the proletariat" (*Versuche über Brecht*, p. 116).

210. *Illuminations*, p. 236.

211. *Ibid.*, p. 242.

212. *Ibid.*, p. 244.

213. *Briefe*, vol. II, p. 798. Adorno remained skeptical about the validity of Benjamin's position, calling it "identification with the aggressor" in his Introduction to the *Briefe*, vol. I, p. 16. "Identification with the aggressor" was one of the classic psy-

choanalytic defense mechanisms. See Anna Freud, *The Ego and the Mechanisms of Defense*, rev. ed. (New York, 1966), pp. 109f.

214. The remark was made in Benjamin's study of Goethe's *Wahlverwandtschaften* in *Neue Deutsche Beiträge*, II, 1 (April, 1924), and is quoted in *One-Dimensional Man* (Boston, 1964), p. 257.

215. Herta Herzog, "On Borrowed Experience: An Analysis of Listening to Daytime Sketches"; Harold Lasswell, "Radio as an Instrument of Reducing Personal Insecurity"; Charles A. Siepmann, "Radio and Education"; and Adorno, with the assistance of George Simpson, "On Popular Music," all in *SPSS*, IX, 1 (1941).

216. Horkheimer, "Art and Mass Culture," *SPSS*, IX, 1 (1941).

217. Leo Lowenthal, "German Popular Biographies: Culture's Bargain Counter," in *The Critical Spirit: Essays in Honor of Herbert Marcuse*, ed. Kurt H. Wolff and Barrington Moore, Jr. (Boston, 1967).

218. Lowenthal, "Biographies in Popular Magazines," in *Radio Research: 1942–1943*, ed. Paul F. Lazarsfeld and Frank Stanton (New York, 1944); later republished in Lowenthal's *Literature, Popular Culture, and Society* as "The Triumph of Mass Idols."

219. Adorno, *Prisms*, pp. 103–104. This serves to contradict the analysis of such critics as Edward Shils ("Daydreams and Nightmares: Reflections on the Criticism of Mass Culture," *Sewanee Review* LXV, 4 [Autumn, 1957]), who call the Institut puritanical because of its attack on escapism.

220. Quoted in *Prisms*, p. 109.

221. See Chapter 3, p. 102.

222. Marcuse, *Eros and Civilization*, p. ix.

223. Adorno, "Resumé über Kulturindustrie," *Ohne Leitbild* (Frankfurt, 1967), p. 60.

224. The term was originally Nietzsche's. It is quoted in Adorno and Horkheimer, *Dialektik der Aufklärung* (Amsterdam, 1947), p. 153.

225. *Ibid.*, p. 187.

226. *Ibid.*, pp. 166–167.

227. *Ibid.*, p. 170. Marcuse had used the same example in his article on affirmative culture, *Negations*, p. 116, where he says that "in suffering the most extreme reification man triumphs over reification." This was an idea he also found in Sartre, as his article "Existentialism: Remarks on Jean-Paul Sartre's *L'Être et le néant*," *Philosophy and Phenomenological Research* VIII, 3 (March, 1948) indicates.

228. For an expanded discussion of this point, see my article, "The Frankfurt School in Exile," *Perspectives in American History*, vol. VI (Cambridge, 1972).

229. For a history of the critique of mass culture, see Leon Bramson, *The Political Context of Sociology* (Princeton, 1961); William Kornhauser, *The Politics of Mass Society* (Glencoe, Ill., 1959); Bernard Rosenberg and David Manning White, *Mass Culture: The Popular Arts in America* (London, 1957); and Lowenthal's essays in *Literature, Popular Culture, and Society.*

230. See, for example, David Riesman, *The Lonely Crowd*, written in collaboration with Reuel Denny and Nathan Glazer (New Haven, 1950). The authors expressly acknowledge the impact of Lowenthal's study of popular biographies (p. 239).

231. Richard Hoggart, *The Uses of Literacy* (London, 1957). Several of Dwight Macdonald's essays on mass culture are collected in his *Against the American Grain* (New York, 1962).

232. Adorno termed his own life a *"beschädigten"* existence in the subtitle of *Minima Moralia.*

7. THE EMPIRICAL WORK OF THE INSTITUT IN THE 1940'S

1. The years in New York, he wrote, were by no means entirely negative, but they had forced the Institut to become a *Betrieb* (a research enterprise) with all the attendant problems (Horkheimer letter to Lowenthal, May 3, 1941) (Lowenthal collection).

2. For a discussion of its creation, see Paul F. Lazarsfeld, "An Episode in the History of Social Research: A Memoir," in *The Intellectual Migration: Europe and America, 1930–1960*, ed. Donald Fleming and Bernard Bailyn (Cambridge, Mass., 1969).

3. In the issue of the *SPSS* devoted to mass communications (IX, 1, 1941), Lazarsfeld contributed a very optimistic appraisal of the future cross-fertilization of the two research styles.

4. The results of the content analysis, which included all the Institut's publications, were reported in an accompanying memorandum and are worth repeating here:

Books	16
Articles and monographs	91
Manuscripts used as basis for lectures and seminars	38
Research reports	2
TOTAL	147

PUBLICATIONS BY FIELD OF INTEREST	NUMBER OF PUBLICATIONS	PERCENTAGE OF TOTAL
Studies in authority	76	40
Philosophy	43	22
Studies in literature, music and art	38	18
Social prejudices	17	9
Miscellaneous	22	11
TOTAL	196	100

5. Letter from Horkheimer to Lazarsfeld, June 10, 1946 (Lowenthal collection).

6. Letter from Horkheimer to Lowenthal, October 31, 1942 (Lowenthal collection).

7. *SPSS* IX, 1 (1941). the prospectus was dated two years earlier.

8. Theodor W. Adorno, "Scientific Experiences of a European Scholar in America," in *The Intellectual Migration*, p. 343.

9. *Ibid.*, p. 347.

10. Letter from Lazarsfeld to Adorno, undated (Lazarsfeld collection). Lazarsfeld remembers it as being written at some time during the summer of 1939. All the subsequent quotations are from the letter.

11. Lazarsfeld, "An Episode in the History of Social Research: A Memoir," p. 325.

12. *Ibid.*

13. Interview with Massing in New York, November 25, 1970.

14. Letter from Paul Massing to Leo Lowenthal, May 31, 1953 (Lowenthal collection).

15. Memorandum of December 1, 1944. I am indebted to Paul Lazarsfeld for making this and other memoranda on the Labor Project available to me.

16. Interview with Friedrich Pollock, Montagnola, Switzerland, March 28, 1969.

17. Letter from Horkheimer to Lowenthal, July 26, 1944 (Lowenthal collection).

18. Interview with Massing in New York, November 25, 1970.

19. Massing to Lowenthal, May 31, 1953.

20. Memorandum attached to Massing letter, initialed by Alice Maier.

21. Adorno *et al., The Authoritarian Personality*, vol. II, p. 605.

22. See Iring Fetscher, "Bertolt Brecht and America," *The Legacy of the German Refugee Intellectuals, Salmagundi*, 10/11 (Fall, 1969–Winter, 1970).

23. *The Authoritarian Personality*, vol. I, p. vii. This passage should be compared with Adorno's discussion of the "education rather than social change" syndrome characteristic of certain high scorers on the F Scale (vol. II, pp. 700f.).

24. *Ibid.*, vol. I, p. vii.

25. Herbert H. Hyman and Paul B. Sheatsley, "*The Authoritarian Personality* — a Methodological Critique," in *Studies in the Scope and Method of "The Authoritarian Personality,"* ed. Richard Christie and Marie Jahoda (Glencoe, Ill., 1954), p. 109.

26. The spread of ego psychology, Adorno suggested in a later essay, was a reflex of society in which individuals mirror objective trends like automatons; Adorno, "Sociology and Psychology," pt. 2, *New Left Review*, 47 (January–February, 1968), p. 95.

27. For this critique, see above, Chapter 3, pp. 103ff.

28. *The Authoritarian Personality*, vol. II, p. 747.

29. Horkheimer, "Sociological Background of the Psychoanalytic Approach," *Anti-Semitism: A Social Disease*, ed. E. Simmel (New York, 1946), p. 3.

30. Letter from Horkheimer to Lowenthal, October 2, 1946.

31. *The Authoritarian Personality*, vol. II, p. 671.

32. Memorandum from Adorno on the Labor Project, November 3, 1944, pp. 43–44 (Lazarsfeld collection).

33. Marx, "On the Jewish Question," *Karl Marx: Early Writings*, trans. and ed. T. B. Bottomore, foreword by Erich Fromm (New York, 1964).

34. Horkheimer and Adorno, *Dialektik der Aufklärung* (Amsterdam, 1947), p. 204.

35. *Ibid.*, p. 228.

36. *Ibid.*, p. 230.

37. *Ibid.*, p. 233.

38. Adorno, "Note on Anti-Semitism," September 30, 1940 (Lowenthal collection).

39. *Ibid.*, p. 1. Here it sounds as if Adorno had projected the condition of the Jews after the Diaspora back to a far earlier period. He offered no concrete evidence of this as a historical reality.

40. *Ibid.*, p. 1.

41. Horkheimer to Lowenthal, July 24, 1944 (Lowenthal collection).

42. Horkheimer and Adorno, *Dialektik der Aufklärung*, p. 234.

43. *Ibid.*, p. 199.

44. Horkheimer to Lowenthal, July 5, 1946 (Lowenthal collection).

45. In English, the word "atonement" captures some of this in the sense that it can be understood as "at-one-ment." Yom Kippur, of course, is known as the "Day of Atonement."

46. In a letter to Lowenthal on November 17, 1945, Horkheimer supported alternatives to the creation of Israel "to prevent Judaism, as a whole, being held morally responsible for the fallacies of Zionism."

47. *Dialektik der Aufklärung*, p. 236.

48. Adorno, "Scientific Experiences of a European Scholar in America," p. 356.

49. Bruno Bettelheim and Morris Janowitz, *Dynamics of Prejudice: A Psychological and Sociological Study of Veterans* (New York, 1950).

50. Nathan W. Ackerman and Marie Jahoda, *Anti-Semitism and Emotional Disorder: A Psychoanalytic Interpretation* (New York, 1950).

51. Leo Lowenthal and Norbert Guterman, *Prophets of Deceit* (New York, 1949).

52. Paul Massing, *Rehearsal for Destruction* (New York, 1949).

53. *Die Arbeitlosen von Marienthal* (Leipzig, 1932).

54. Among the better known of these are *Love Is Not Enough* (Glencoe, Ill., 1950), *Symbolic Wounds* (Glencoe, Ill., 1954), *The Empty Fortress* (New York, 1967), *The Informed Heart* (Glencoe, Ill., 1968), and *The Children of the Dream* (New York, 1969).

55. Bettelheim and Janowitz, *Dynamics of Prejudice*, p. 171.

56. Bruno Bettelheim and Morris Janowitz, *Social Change and Prejudice* (New York, 1964), pp. 74f. This was a reedition of *Dynamics of Prejudice*, with considerable new material added.

57. Nathan Glazer, "*The Authoritarian Personality* in Profile: Report on a Major Study of Race Hatred," *Commentary*, IV, 6 (June, 1950).

58. Lowenthal and Guterman, *Prophets of Deceit*, p. xvi. Horkheimer, "Egoismus und Freiheitsbewegung," *ZfS*, V, 2 (1936).

59. *Ibid.*, p. xii.

60. *Ibid.*, p. 140.

61. Adorno "Freudian Theory and the Pattern of Fascist Propaganda," in *Psychoanalysis and the Social Sciences*, ed. Geza Roheim (New York, 1951). The Freudian text on which Adorno primarily based his argument was *Group Psychology and the Analysis of the Ego*. He also referred to Erikson's work on fascism (see the following note).

62. Erik Erikson, "Hitler's Imagery and German Youth," *Psychiatry* V, 4 (November 1942); reprinted in *Childhood and Society* (New York, 1950), from which the following quotation comes.

63. *Ibid.*, pp. 332–333.

64. Leon Bramson, *The Political Context of Sociology* (Princeton, 1961).

65. So Adorno reports in "Scientific Experiences of a European Scholar in America," p. 358.

66. Mrs. Frenkel-Brunswik was herself a refugee from Vienna and the wife of the distinguished psychologist Egon Brunswik. For further information on their contribution to American psychology, see Jean Matter Mandler and George Mandler, "The Diaspora of Experimentalist Psychology: The Gestaltists and Others," in *The Intellectual Migration*, pp. 411–413. Levinson later became professor of psychology at Yale Medical School and Sanford went on to Stanford as professor of psychology and education.

67. R. Nevitt Sanford and H. S. Conrad, "Some Personality Correlates of Morale," *Journal of Abnormal and Social Psychology* XXXVIII, 1 (January, 1943).

68. *The Authoritarian Personality*, p. xii.

69. *Ibid.*, p. ix.

70. Roger Brown points out the similarity in *Social Psychology* (New York and London, 1965).

71. Part of *Anti-Semite and Jew* appeared in *The Partisan Review* in 1946, but it was not fully translated until 1948, by G. J. Becker.

72. Wilhelm Reich, *The Mass Psychology of Fascism* (New York, 1946), and Abraham H. Maslow, "The Authoritarian Character Structure," *Journal of Social Psychology* 18 (1943).

73. Horkheimer, "The Lessons of Fascism," *Tensions That Cause War* (Urbana, Ill., 1950), p. 230.

74. Adorno, "Scientific Experiences of a European Scholar in America," p. 363.

75. Horkheimer, "Notes on Institute Activities," *SPSS* IX, 1 (1941), p. 123.

76. Ernst Schachtel, it will be recalled, had criticized personality tests in the *Zeitschrift* for similar reasons ("Zum Begriff und zur Diagnose der Persönlichkeit in den 'Personality Tests,' " *ZfS* VI, 3, 1937).

77. *The Authoritarian Personality*, p. 15.

78. *Ibid.*, p. 18.

79. For a discussion of the two scales, see Marie Jahoda, Morton Deutsch, and Stuart W. Cook, *Research Methods in Social Relations*, vol. I (New York, 1951), pp. 190–197.

80. *Ibid.*, p. 196.

81. *The Authoritarian Personality*, vol. I, chap. 7.

82. *Ibid.*, p. 228.

83. Herbert H. Hyman and Paul B. Sheatsley, "*The Authoritarian Personality* — a Methodological Critique."

84. Lazarsfeld, "Problems in Methodology," in *Sociology Today*, ed. Robert K. Merton, Leonard Broom, Leonard S. Cottrell, Jr. (New York, 1959), p. 50.

85. Brown, *Social Psychology*, p. 523.

86. *Ibid.*, p. 515.

87. *Ibid.*, p. 506.

88. Hyman and Sheatsley, "*The Authoritarian Personality*," p. 65.

89. Paul Kecskemeti, "The Study of Man: Prejudice in the Catastrophic Perspective," *Commentary* II, 3 (March, 1951).

90. Part of it was published as Else Frenkel-Brunswik, "A Study of Prejudice in Children," *Human Relations* I, 3 (1948). One of the conclusions of the project modified the findings of *The Authoritarian Personality*, as Adorno was to admit in "Scientific Experiences of a European Scholar in America," p. 364. The results of Mrs. Frenkel-Brunswik's work, he wrote, "refined the conception of the distinction between conventionality and the authoritarian temperament. It emerged that precisely the 'good,' i.e., conventional, children are *freer* from aggression and therefore from one of the fundamental aspects of the authoritarian personality, and vice versa." This would seem to indicate empirical confirmation of Bettelheim and Janowitz's argument more than that of the Berkeley group, at least if adult behavioral patterns are understood in the same way as children's.

91. *The Authoritarian Personality*, p. 359.

92. Bramson, *The Political Context of Sociology*, p. 137.

93. *The Authoritarian Personality*, pp. 759f.

94. Fromm himself had abandoned the sexual interpretation of the sado-masochistic character, which he had used in the *Studien* for a more "existential" approach. See above, Chapter 3, p. 99.

95. *The Authoritarian Personality*, p. 759.

96. *Ibid.*, p. 760.

97. Horkheimer, "Authoritarianism and the Family Today," *The Family: Its Function and Destiny*, ed. Ruth Nanda Anshen (New York, 1949).

98. *Ibid.*, p. 367.

99. *The Authoritarian Personality*, p. 371.

100. Ralf Dahrendorf, *Society and Democracy in Germany* (London, 1968), p. 371; and Hannah Arendt, *Between Past and Future* (Cleveland, 1963), p. 97.

101. Edward Shils, "Authoritarianism: 'Right' and 'Left,' " in *Studies in the Scope and Method of the "The Authoritarian Personality."* Bramson repeats this criticism in *The Political Context of Sociology*, pp. 122f.

102. Kecskemeti, "The Study of Man: Prejudice in the Catastrophic Perspective," p. 290.

103. Bettelheim and Janowitz, *Social Change and Prejudice*, p. 75.

104. *The Authoritarian Personality*, p. 676.

105. *Ibid.*, p. 976.

106. *Ibid.*, p. 182. The notion of "pseudo-conservatism" was picked up by other scholars in the 1950's. See, for example, Richard Hofstadter, "The Pseudo-Conservative Revolt," in *The Radical Right*, ed. Daniel Bell (New York, 1963).

107. *The Authoritarian Personality*, p. 176.

108. *Ibid.*, p. 771.

109. Interview with Adorno, Frankfurt, March 7, 1969.

110. M. Rokeach, *The Open and Closed Mind* (New York, 1960). Rokeach tried to develop a "Dogmatism (D) Scale" to measure leftist authoritarianism. On the basis of this and other studies, Seymour Martin Lipset argued that authoritarianism and neurosis might well be inversely related in the working class; Lipset, *Political Man* (New York, 1960), p. 96.

111. Adorno, "Scientific Experiences of a European Scholar in America," p. 361.

112. J. F. Brown's review of the *Studies in Prejudice* in *Annals of the American Academy of Political and Social Science*, CCVXX (July, 1950), p. 178.

113. For a summary of the earlier efforts see Richard Christie, "Authoritarianism Reexamined," in *Studies in the Scope and Method of "The Authoritarian Personality."* For later additions, see Roger Brown's bibliography in *Social Psychology*.

114. Friedrich Pollock, ed., *Gruppenexperiment: Ein Studienbericht* (Frankfurt, 1955). This was published as vol. II in the Institut's *Frankfurter Beiträge zur Soziologie*, ed. T. W. Adorno and Walter Dirks.

115. Adorno, "Zur gegenwärtigen Stellung der empirischen Sozialforschung in Deutschland," *Empirische Sozialforschung* (Frankfurt, 1952), p. 31.

116. See, for example, Adorno's article, "Contemporary German Sociology," *Transactions of the Fourth World Congress of Sociology*, vol. I (London, 1959).

117. For a cross-section of the views expressed by participants in the debate, see Ernst Topitsch, ed., *Logik der Sozialwissenschaften* (Cologne and Berlin, 1965). Adorno's contributions have been posthumously collected in *Aufsätze zur Gesellschaftstheorie und Methodologie* (Frankfurt, 1970). A summary of the recent literature in English appeared in "Dialectical Methodology: Marx or Weber," *The Times Literary Supplement* (London, March 12, 1970) published anonymously but actually written by George Lichtheim.

8. TOWARD A PHILOSOPHY OF HISTORY: THE CRITIQUE OF THE ENLIGHTENMENT

1. So Adorno reported to Benjamin by letter on November 10, 1939; Theodor W. Adorno, *Über Walter Benjamin* (Frankfurt, 1970), p. 143.

2. Max Horkheimer and Theodor W. Adorno, *Dialektik der Aufklärung* (Amsterdam, 1947). The house was Querido.

3. I have been able to locate two reviews in professional journals: J. D. Mabbott in *Philosophy*, XXIII, 87 (October, 1948), which was generally favorable, and John R. Everett in *Journal of Philosophy*, XLV, 22 (October 21, 1948), which was less enthusiastic. Lowenthal told me during one of our interviews that the sales of the book were disappointing.

4. Horkheimer, *Kritik der instrumentellen Vernunft*, trans. Alfred Schmidt (Frankfurt, 1967).

5. Göran Therborn's assertion to the contrary seems to me clearly erroneous. See his "Frankfurt Marxism: A Critique," *New Left Review*, 63 (September–October, 1970), p. 76, where he writes that the nonmastery of nature "was not present in Frankfurt thinking from the start. Moreover, it is shared by their archenemy, Heidegger."

6. Adorno, *Kierkegaard: Konstruktion des Aesthetischen*, rev. ed. (Frankfurt, 1966), p. 97.

7. In an early essay on *Der Freischütz*, Adorno said that salvation (*Rettung*) could be found only in reconciled nature; see his *Moments Musicaux* (Frankfurt, 1964), p. 46.

8. Horkheimer [Heinrich Regius], *Dämmerung* (Zürich, 1934), pp. 185f. on animals, and p. 181 on the work ethic. In *Dialektik der Aufklärung* Horkheimer and Adorno included a long aphorism on "Mensch und Tier," pp. 295f.

9. Leo Lowenthal, *Literature and the Image of Man* (Boston, 1957), p. 197.

10. Erich Fromm, "Die sozialpsychologische Bedeutung der Mutterrechtstheorie," *ZfS* III, 2 (1934), p. 206. Here Fromm cited Bachofen as saying that the victory of patriarchal society corresponded to the break between spirit and nature, the triumph of Rome over the Orient.

11. Horkheimer, *Die Anfänge der bürgerlichen Geschichtsphilosophie* (Stuttgart, 1930).

12. Horkheimer, "Vernunft und Selbsterhaltung," in "Walter Benjamin zum Gedächtnis" (unpub., 1942), p. 43 (Friedrich Pollock collection, Montagnola).

13. Only on rare occasions did the Institut attempt to relate a thinker's work to his life. One example was Adorno's discussion of Kierkegaard's role as a *rentier* in *Kierkegaard: Konstruktion des Aesthetischen*, p. 88.

14. Letter from Horkheimer to Lowenthal, May 23, 1942 (Lowenthal collection).

15. Horkheimer, *Eclipse of Reason* (New York, 1947), p. 104.

16. Therborn has made the astute observation that whereas Lukács stressed reification as the essential meaning of capitalism, and others such as the early Marcuse emphasized alienation (Fromm could also be included here), Horkheimer and Adorno regarded the exchange principle as its essence. See his "Frankfurt Marxism: A Critique," p. 79.

17. Friedrich Nietzsche, *Genealogy of Morals*, trans. Francis Golffing (New York, 1956), p. 202.

18. Much later, one of the younger members of the second generation of the Frankfurt School extended this argument considerably; see Albrecht Wellmer, *Critical Theory of Society* (New York, 1971).

19. This phrase is used by Hannah Arendt in her critique of Marx in *The Human Condition* (Chicago, 1958). She draws a distinction between man as *animal laborans* and as *homo faber* (man the maker), which the Frankfurt School did not make.

20. This was the phrase that Adorno used during our interview on March 15, 1969, in Frankfurt.

21. In 1913–1914, Lukács had been part of Weber's circle in Heidelberg. For a

discussion of his relationship with Weber, see George Lichtheim, *George Lukács* (New York, 1970), *passim*.

22. Horkheimer, "Vernunft und Selbsterhaltung," p. 33.

23. *Ibid.*, p. 34.

24. Horkheimer, *Eclipse of Reason*, p. 174.

25. Horkheimer and Adorno, *Dialektik der Aufklärung*, p. 41.

26. *Ibid.*, p. 35.

27. Marcuse, *Negations*, trans. Jeremy J. Shapiro (Boston, 1968).

28. See his article "Über Sprache überhaupt und über die Sprache des Menschen," in Walter Benjamin, *Schriften*, ed. Theodor W. Adorno and Gershom Scholem, vol. II (Frankfurt, 1955). Discussions of his theory of language can be found in Hans Heinz Holz, "Philosophie als Interpretation," *Alternative*, 56/57 (October–December, 1967), and Anon., "Walter Benjamin: Towards a Philosophy of Language," *The Times Literary Supplement* (London, August 23, 1968).

29. Benjamin, "The Task of the Translator," *Illuminations*, ed. with an introduction by Hannah Arendt, trans. Harry Zohn (New York, 1968), p. 80.

30. *Ibid.*, p. 77.

31. Jürgen Habermas made this point to me in an interview in Frankfurt, March 7, 1969.

32. Anon., "Walter Benjamin: Towards a Philosophy of Language," uses this phrase to describe Benjamin. In "The Task of the Translator" Benjamin wrote that the transparency of pure language might be approached "above all, by a literal rendering of the syntax which proves words rather than sentences to be the primary element of the translator" (p. 79).

33. See the letter from Horkheimer to Lowenthal quoted on page 233, Chapter 7, above.

34. *Eclipse of Reason*, p. 179.

35. *Ibid.*, p. 180.

36. *Ibid.*, p. 183.

37. Walter Benjamin, *Briefe*, ed. Theodor W. Adorno and Gershom Scholem (Frankfurt, 1966), vol. II, p. 786.

38. *Dialektik der Aufklärung*, p. 195.

39. Herbert Marcuse has an extensive discussion of the "closing of the Universe of Discourse" in *One-Dimensional Man* (Boston, 1964), pp. 85f.

40. *Dialektik der Aufklärung*, p. 71. In *Eros and Civilization*, Marcuse wrote that "the predominant culture-hero is the trickster and (suffering) rebel against the gods, who creates culture at the price of perpetual pain" (p. 146). He used Prometheus rather than Odysseus as its prototype.

41. *Dialektik der Aufklärung*, pp. 76f.

42. *Ibid.*, pp. 117–118.

43. This point was developed in the aphorism on "Mensch und Tier," *ibid.*, pp. 297f.

44. *Dialektik der Aufklärung*, p. 218. Horkheimer discussed this point at greater length in *Eclipse of Reason*, pp. 121f.

45. Alfred Schmidt has tried to distinguish between Adorno as a "real humanist" and other conventional humanists. The term "real humanist" first appeared in Marx's *The Holy Family* in 1845 in opposition to the abstract, ahistorical humanism of Feuerbach. Adorno himself liked to be called an "antihumanist," not only for the reason Schmidt cites — his dislike of the positive connotations of any static definition of human nature — but also because of his fear that anthropocentricity would

mean the concomitant denigration of nature. For Schmidt's argument, see his "Adorno — ein Philosoph des realen Humanismus," *Neue Rundschau*, LXXX, 4 (1969). See also my article "The Frankfurt School's Critique of Marxist Humanism," *Social Research* XXXIX, 2 (Summer, 1972).

46. *Dialektik der Aufklärung*, p. 267.

47. *Eclipse of Reason*, p. 184.

48. There is a considerable critical literature on Bloch which stresses this point. For one example, see Jürgen Habermas, "Ernst Bloch — A Marxist Romantic," in *The Legacy of the German Refugee Intellectuals, Salmagundi*, 10/11 (Fall, 1969–Winter, 1970).

49. *Dialektik der Aufklärung*, p. 223.

50. *Ibid.*, p. 305.

51. In *Eros and Civilization* Marcuse wrote that "the restoration of remembrance to its rights, as a vehicle of liberation, is one of the noblest tasks of thought. In this function, remembrance (*Erinnerung*) appears at the conclusion of Hegel's *Phenomenology of the Spirit*: in this function, it appears in Freud's theory" (p. 212). In Marcuse's work, the importance of "re-membering" what has been split asunder was closely related to the identity theory he never fully abandoned. Habermas has also stressed the liberating function of memory in his brilliant chapters on psychoanalysis in *Erkenntnis und Interesse* (Frankfurt, 1968), pp. 262f.

52. *Dialektik der Aufklärung*, p. 274.

53. Benjamin, *Berliner Kindheit um Neunzehnhundert* (Frankfurt, 1950).

54. Letter from Adorno to Benjamin, February 29, 1940, in Adorno, *Über Walter Benjamin*, p. 159.

55. Adorno's defense of some reification as a necessary element of all culture appeared in his article on Huxley. See above, Chapter 6, p. 178. In another context, Horkheimer had criticized Dilthey and his followers for reducing history to the *Nacherleben* of past events. His reasoning was similar: the complete identity of historian as subject and historical event as object was unattainable. See above, Chapter 2, p. 49.

56. Lecture at Columbia University, April 17, 1945. There were three other lectures in the following weeks. These were similar, but not the same as the 1944 lectures on which *Eclipse of Reason* was based (Lowenthal collection).

57. *Karl Marx: Early Writings*, trans. and ed. T. B. Bottomore (New York, 1963), p. 155.

58. Marx himself had hoped for one science: "Natural science will one day incorporate the science of man, just as the science of man will incorporate natural science; there will be a *single* science" (*Early Writings*, p. 164). His followers had forgotten the second clause of his sentence and also ignored the fact that Marx had said "one day" there will be a unified science of nature and man.

59. Marcuse, "Zum Problem der Dialektik," *Die Gesellschaft* VII, 1 (January, 1930), p. 26.

60. See, for example, Louis Althusser, *For Marx*, trans. Ben Brewster (New York, 1969). Göran Therborn, whose article on the Frankfurt School is mentioned above, is an Althusserian.

61. Emile Durkheim, *Suicide*, trans. John A. Spaulding and George Simpson (New York, 1951), pp. 123–142. Tarde's major work was *Les Lois de l'imitation* (Paris, 1890).

62. Sigmund Freud, *Group Psychology and the Analysis of the Ego*, trans. James Strachey (New York, 1960), p. 27.

63. "Research Project on Anti-Semitism," *SPSS* IX, 1 (1941), p. 139.

64. Horkheimer, *Eclipse of Reason*, p. 115.

65. *Ibid.*, p. 116.

66. Leo Lowenthal and Norbert Guterman, in *Prophets of Deceit* (New York, 1949), mentioned the frequency with which anti-Semitic agitators mimic Jews (p. 79).

67. April 24, 1945 (Lowenthal collection).

68. *Eclipse of Reason*, p. 179.

69. *Ibid.*, pp. 105–107.

70. *Ibid.*, p. 122.

71. See, for example, Marcuse, *Negations: Essays in Critical Theory*, trans. Jeremy J. Shapiro (Boston, 1968), pp. 32, 47.

72. Interview with Habermas, Frankfurt, March, 1969.

73. Fritz Ringer, *The Decline of the German Mandarins* (Cambridge, Mass., 1969).

74. Max Scheler, *Die Wissensformen und die Gesellschaft* (Leipzig, 1926), pp. 234–235.

75. The most extensive recent defenses of this position can be found in Rolf Ahlers, "Is Technology Intrinsically Repressive?," *Continuum* VIII, 1/2 (Spring–Summer, 1970), and Paul Piccone and Alexander Delfini, "Marcuse's Heideggerian Marxism," *Telos* 6 (Fall, 1970).

76. The essay is reprinted in Michael Oakeshott, *Rationalism in Politics and Other Essays* (London, 1962). Oakeshott equated rationalism with its instrumental variant, and was thus able to write: "This assimilation of politics to engineering is, indeed, what may be called the myth of rationalist politics" (p. 4).

77. *Eclipse of Reason*, pp. 122–123.

78. *Ibid.*, p. 125.

79. *Ibid.*, p. 123. The book contained an extensive critique of the work of Sidney Hook and John Dewey.

80. Benjamin, "Eduard Fuchs, der Sammler und der Historiker," *ZfS* VI, 2 (1937), p. 364.

81. *Eclipse of Reason*, p. 127.

82. *Ibid.*, p. 87.

83. *Ibid.*, p. 90.

84. Horkheimer, "Bemerkungen zu Jaspers 'Nietzsche,'" *ZfS* VI, 2 (1937). In a letter to Lowenthal on May 2, 1946, he made other disparaging remarks about Jaspers (Lowenthal collection).

85. Marcuse, *Negations*, p. 41.

86. *Ibid.*, pp. 31–42.

87. Letter from Horkheimer to Lowenthal, August 19, 1946 (Lowenthal collection).

88. Marcuse, "Existentialism: Remarks on Jean-Paul Sartre's *L'Être et le néant*," *Philosophy and Phenomenological Research* VIII, 3 (March, 1948).

89. Sartre was to repudiate much of *Being and Nothingness* in his *Critique de la raison dialectique* (Paris, 1960). Marcuse's appraisal of this work was far more favorable; see his added paragraph to the German version of his essay on *Being and Nothingness* in *Kultur und Gesellschaft*, vol. II (Frankfurt, 1965), pp. 83–84.

90. Marcuse, "Existentialism," p. 322.

91. *Ibid.*, p. 323.

92. For a later discussion of the existentialists' alienation from nature, see Albert William Levi, "The Concept of Nature," in *The Origins of Modern Consciousness*, ed. John Weiss (Detroit, 1965), pp. 57f.

93. Paul Robinson, *The Freudian Left* (New York, 1969), pp. 192f.
94. Marcuse, "The Affirmative Character of Culture," *Negations*, p. 116.
95. *Ibid.*
96. This occurred not in *Being and Nothingness*, but in a separate article entitled "Materialisme et révolution," *Les Temps modernes* I, 1 and I, 2 (1946). In the article, Sartre tried to reject the materialist premises of Marxism, but still be a revolutionary.
97. Marcuse, *Eros and Civilization*, pp. 40f.
98. *Dialektik der Aufklärung*, pp. 280–281.
99. Benjamin, *Briefe*, vol. II, pp. 681–682.
100. More orthodox Marxist critics of the Frankfurt School always pointed to the continuation of contradictions under capitalism. See, for example, Paul Mattick, "The Limits of Integration," in *The Critical Spirit: Essays in Honor of Herbert Marcuse*, ed. Kurt H. Wolff and Barrington Moore, Jr. (Boston, 1967).
101. *Eclipse of Reason*, p. 186.
102. Adorno, *Minima Moralia*, p. 10.
103. *Ibid.*, p. 13.
104. *Ibid.*, p. 80. In the same spirit, he wrote, "the task of art today is to bring chaos into order" (p. 428).
105. Adorno, "Reflexionen," *Aufklärung* IV, 1 (June, 1951), p. 86.
106. *Minima Moralia*, p. 7.
107. *Ibid.*, p. 80.
108. *Ibid.*, p. 480.
109. *Ibid.*, p. 481.
110. Benjamin, *Illuminations*, p. 256.
111. Adorno, *Negative Dialektik* (Frankfurt, 1966).
112. Horkheimer, "Schopenhauer Today," in *The Critical Spirit*, p. 70.
113. Letter from Horkheimer to Lowenthal, December 2, 1943 (Lowenthal collection).
114. A recent student of utopias and of Rousseau, Judith N. Shklar, has made this point in *Men and Citizens: A Study of Rousseau's Social Theory* (Cambridge, 1969), p. 2.
115. Quoted in *Die Süddeutsche Zeitung* (April 26–27, 1969), p. 10.
116. Adorno, *Negative Dialektik*, p. 12.
117. Adorno's recent critics have discussed this theme at length. See, for example, Manfred Clemenz, "Theorie als Praxis?," *Neue politische Literatur* XIII, 2 (1968).

EPILOGUE

1. Letter from Leo Lowenthal to Max Horkheimer, May 12, 1946 (Lowenthal collection).
2. The first contact was made in letters to Felix Weil and Friedrich Pollock, so Lowenthal reported in a letter to Horkheimer on October 19, 1946 (Lowenthal collection).
3. Letter from Horkheimer to Lowenthal, April 12, 1947 (Lowenthal collection).
4. In a letter to Paul Lazarsfeld written on August 4, 1947, Horkheimer mentioned possibilities at the University of California at Los Angeles, the University of Southern California, and Occidental College. (Lowenthal collection.)
5. Interview with Horkheimer, Montagnola, Switzerland, March 12, 1969.

6. Letter from Horkheimer to Lowenthal, February 18, 1950 (Lowenthal collection).

7. Letter from Horkheimer to Lowenthal, April 8, 1950 (Lowenthal collection).

8. Conversation with Everett Hughes, Cambridge, Mass., July 21, 1971.

9. In his first letter to me on November 22, 1968, Horkheimer wrote of Butler's "great kindness and understanding," adding, "I met him the first time a few weeks after my arrival in New York and I shall never forget what we owe to him."

10. This was a phrase Pollock used during a conversation in Lugano, March, 1969.

11. This was also extended to Werner Richter. A description of the bill exists in a clipping in Horkheimer's scrapbooks, which he graciously allowed me to see during my stay in Montagnola.

12. Theodor W. Adorno, "*Auf die Frage*: Was ist deutsch," *Stichworte: Kritische Modelle 2* (Frankfurt, 1969), p. 110. Elsewhere in the article Adorno wrote: "At no time during the emigration did I give up the hope of return" (p. 107).

13. Herbert Marcuse, *Soviet Marxism* (New York, 1958).

14. Records of the Senate Judiciary Committee, 82nd Congress, 1951–1952, vol. III.

15. Conversation with Wittfogel in New York, June 21, 1971.

16. The petition is in the Lowenthal collection.

17. Letter from Weil to me, March 30, 1971.

18. The description of the Institut's return is derived from clippings in Horkheimer's scrapbooks.

19. *Sociologica I* (Frankfurt, 1955).

20. His addresses on academic affairs were published as Horkheimer, "Gegenwärtige Probleme der Universität," *Frankfurt Universitätsreden* VIII (Frankfurt, 1953).

21. Horkheimer's rectoral address was entitled "Zum Begriff der Vernunft," *Frankfurt Universitätsreden* VII (Frankfurt, 1952).

22. Horkheimer, *Survey of the Social Sciences in Western Germany* (Washington, D.C., 1952).

23. The letter, which was an open letter published as well in the German press, is included in Horkheimer, *Kritische Theorie*, ed. Alfred Schmidt (Frankfurt, 1968), vol. II.

24. A twenty-volume edition of Adorno's works is now being planned by the Suhrkamp Verlag. At this writing, volume VII, a posthumously published fragment on *Ästhetische Theorie*, has appeared (Frankfurt, 1970), as has volume V, *Zur Metakritik der Erkenntnistheorie* (Frankfurt, 1971).

25. For one treatment of this question, see Paul Breines, "Marcuse and the New Left in America," *Antworten auf Herbert Marcuse*, ed. Jürgen Habermas (Frankfurt, 1968). I have attempted a more extensive analysis of the post-1950 influence of the Institut in America in "The Frankfurt School in Exile," *Perspectives in American History*, vol. VI (Cambridge,.1972).

26. The Horkheimer scrapbooks contain many articles about his appearances in the mass media.

27. Letter from Horkheimer to Lowenthal, February 2, 1943 (Lowenthal collection).

28. Adorno, *Prisms*, trans. Samuel and Shierry Weber (London, 1967), p. 166.

29. See, for example, Claus Grossner, "Frankfurter Schule am Ende," *Die Zeit* (Hamburg, May 12, 1970), p. 5.

30. In 1966 Horkheimer expressed alarm about the Chinese Communist threat by

saying that Kaiser Wilhelm II's warning about "the menace of the yellow race should be taken very seriously today"; "On the Concept of Freedom," *Diogenes*, 53 (Paris, 1966). In the following year, he appeared at a celebration of German-American Friendship Week on the Romerplatz in Frankfurt, which prompted anti-Vietnam War students to shout "*Horkheimer Raus*" in an effort to persuade him to dissociate himself from American policy. They failed.

31. Edward Shils, "Tradition, Ecology, and Institution in the History of Sociology," *Daedalus* LXXXXIX, 4 (Fall, 1970).

32. Interview with Marcuse, Cambridge, Mass., June 18, 1968.

33. The term is used by Lazarsfeld. See his "An Episode in the History of Social Research: A Memoir," in *The Intellectual Migration: Europe and America, 1930–1960*, ed. Donald Fleming and Bernard Bailyn (Cambridge, Mass., 1969), p. 286.

34. Conversation with Lazarsfeld, New York, N.Y., January 3, 1971.

35. Interview with Pollock, Montagnola, Switzerland, March 14, 1969.

36. Interview with Paul Massing, New York, N.Y., November 25, 1970.

37. On November 12, 1943, Lowenthal wrote to Horkheimer that "if you look up in the Encyclopedia of Social Sciences you will find that this [George Herbert] Mead apparently was a philosopher and sociologist with genuine problems." This, however, is the only mention of Mead in the Institut's writings I've been able to find. Location: Lowenthal collection.

38. Letter from Horkheimer to Lowenthal, July 17, 1946 (Lowenthal collection). Part of this quotation reappears in Horkheimer, *Eclipse of Reason* (New York, 1970), p. 160.

39. Hans Mommsen, "Historical Scholarship in Transition: The Situation in the Federal Republic of Germany," *Daedalus*, C, 2 (Spring, 1971), p. 498.

40. Adorno, *Prisms*, p. 48.

41. Horkheimer, "Traditionelle und kritische Theorie," *ZfS* VI, 2 (1937), p. 269.

42. Walter Benjamin, "Zeitschrift für Sozialforschung," *Mass und Wert* I, 5 (May–June, 1938), p. 820.

43. Adorno noted this in one of his essays on Benjamin: "The predominance of spirit extremely alienated his psychical and even psychological existence. . . . He considered animal warmth tabu; a friend could scarcely dare to lay a hand on his shoulder."; *Über Walter Benjamin* (Frankfurt, 1970), p. 50.

44. Fritz Ringer, *The Decline of the German Mandarins* (Cambridge, Mass., 1969).

45. Carl Grünberg, "Festrede gehalten zur Einweihung des Instituts für Sozialforschung an der Universität Frankfurt a.M. am 22 Juni 1924," *Frankfurter Universitätsreden*, XX (Frankfurt, 1924), p. 4.

46. Ringer, *Decline of the German Mandarins*, p. 5.

47. *Ibid.*, p. 106.

48. *Ibid.*, p. 90.

49. "I have encountered only one favorable comment upon Freud's work in the academic literature of this period, and that was written by the radical critic Ernst von Aster," Ringer wrote (*ibid.*, p. 383).

50. Adorno, *Prisms*, p. 22.

51. This is not to say that the Frankfurt School denied the continued existence of class struggle entirely. "Society remains class struggle, today just as in the period when that concept originated," Adorno later wrote; "Society," *The Legacy of the German Refugee Intellectuals, Salmagundi* 10/11 (Fall, 1969–Winter, 1970), p. 149. It was, however, no longer the focal point of their analysis.

52. See, for example, Hans Heinz Holz, *Utopie und Anarchismus: Zur Kritik der kritischen Theorie Herbert Marcuses* (Cologne, 1968), pp. 60f.

53. This comment is mentioned in one of the clippings in Horkheimer's scrapbooks.

54. Quoted in a letter from Weil to me, January 31, 1971.

55. Harold Poor, *Kurt Tucholsky and the Ordeal of Germany, 1914-1935* (New York, 1968) p. 137.

56. This was the figure Pollock mentioned during one of our conversations in Montagnola in March, 1969.

57. Adorno, *Minima Moralia* (Frankfurt, 1951), p. 98.

58. Göran Therborn has written that "understandably, fascism became a Medusa's head for the Frankfurt School. The result was that the initial attitude of revulsion was *frozen*, instead of developing into a scientific analysis and participation in revolutionary political practice"; "Frankfurt Marxism: A Critique," *New Left Review*, 63 (September–October, 1970), p. 94. His criticism was made from the left, but liberals also have pointed to the Institut's obsession with fascism. See, for example, Leon Bramson, *The Political Context of Sociology* (Princeton, 1961), p. 129, and David Riesman, *Individualism Reconsidered and Other Essays* (Glencoe, Ill., 1954), p. 477.

59. Martin Jay, review of *The Intellectual Migration*, ed. Donald Fleming and Bernard Bailyn, and *The Bauhaus*, by Hans Wingler, in *Commentary*, XXXXIX, 3 (March, 1970).

60. Horkheimer [Heinrich Regius], *Dämmerung* (Zurich, 1934), p. 216.

61. Marcuse indicated this during our interview in Cambridge, Mass. on June 18, 1968.

62. Adorno, *Prisms*, p. 34.

Bibliography

The following abbreviations are used:

Grünbergs Archiv: *Archiv für die Geschichte des Sozialismus und der Arbeiterbewegung*
SPSS: *Studies in Philosophy and Social Sciences*
ZfS: *Zeitschrift für Sozialforschung*

PUBLICATIONS OF THE INSTITUT

The Institut was associated with or published the following journals:

Archiv für die Geschichte des Sozialismus und der Arbeiterbewegung, vols. I–XV (1910–1930).
Zeitschrift für Sozialforschung, vols. I–VIII, 2 (1932–1939).
Studies in Philosophy and Social Science, vol. VIII, 3–IX, 3 (1939–1941).
Individual *Beihefte* of *Grünbergs Archiv* are listed below next to their authors' names.

The collective works of the Institut included the following:

Studien über Autorität und Familie (Paris, 1936).
"Anti-Semitism within American Labor: A Report to the Jewish Labor Committee." 4 vols. Unpublished, 1945; in Pollock's collection.

The Institut's own histories included:

Institut für Sozialforschung an der Universität Frankfurt am Main (Frankfurt, 1925).
International Institute of Social Research: A Short Description of Its History and Aims (New York, 1935).
International Institute of Social Research: A Report on Its History and Activities, 1933–1938 (New York, 1938).
"Institute of Social Research (Columbia University), Supplementary Memorandum on the Activities of the Institute from 1939 to 1941." Unpublished, 1941; in Pollock's collection.
"Supplement to the History of the Institute of Social Research." Unpublished, 1942; in Pollock's collection.

"Ten Years on Morningside Heights: A Report on the Institute's History, 1934 to 1944," Unpublished, 1944; in Lowenthal's collection and in Pollock's collection.

Institut für Sozialforschung an der Johann Wolfgang Goethe-Universität Frankfurt am Main; Ein Bericht über die Feier seiner Wiedereröffnung, seiner Geschichte, und seine Arbeiten (Frankfurt, 1952).

Collections of documents, letters, unpublished papers, memoranda, and lectures in the possession of Leo Lowenthal, Friedrich Pollock, and Paul Lazarsfeld were also used. So too were the various clippings in Max Horkheimer's scrapbooks, which were collected primarily after 1950. Since the time I examined them, the letters in Lowenthal's collection have been deposited in the Houghton Library at Harvard.

THE WRITINGS OF INDIVIDUAL FIGURES IN THE INSTITUT'S HISTORY

Nathan W. Ackerman and Marie Jahoda

Anti-Semitism and Emotional Disorder: A Psychoanalytic Interpretation (New York, 1950).

Theodor W. Adorno

At this writing, Adorno's *Gesammelte Schriften* are being collected by the Suhrkamp Verlag. Volume VII, *Ästhetische Theorie*, (Frankfurt, 1970), and Volume V, *Zur Metakritik der Erkenntnistheorie* (Frankfurt, 1971), have already appeared. (The earlier version of *Zur Metakritik* [Stuttgart, 1956], has been quoted in the text). Specific works consulted:

Alban Berg: Der Meister des kleinsten Übergangs (Vienna, 1968).

"*Auf die Frage*: Was ist deutsch," *Stichworte: Kritische Modelle 2* (Frankfurt, 1969).

Aufsätze zur Gesellschaftstheorie und Methodologie (Frankfurt, 1970).

The Authoritarian Personality, with Else Frenkel-Brunswik, Daniel J. Levinson, and R. Nevitt Sanford (New York, 1950).

"Der Begriff der Unbewussten in der Transzendentalen Seelenlehre." Unpublished, 1927; in University of Frankfurt library.

"Contemporary German Sociology," *Transactions of the Fourth World Congress of Sociology*, vol. I (London, 1959).

"Currents of Music: Elements of a Radio Theory." Unpublished, 1939; in Lazarsfeld's collection.

Dialektik der Aufklärung, with Max Horkheimer (Amsterdam, 1947).

Dissonanzen: Musik in der verwalteten Welt (Frankfurt, 1956).

"Erpresste Versöhnung," *Noten zur Literatur II* (Frankfurt, 1961).

"Fragmente über Wagner," *ZfS* VIII, 1/2 (1939).

"Freudian Theory and the Pattern of Fascist Propaganda," in *Psychoanalysis and the Social Sciences*, ed. Geza Roheim (New York, 1951).

Der getreue Korrepetitor (Frankfurt, 1963).

"How to Look at Television," with Bernice T. Eiduson. Paper read at Hacker Foundation, Los Angeles, April 13, 1953; in Lowenthal's collection.

"Husserl and the Problem of Idealism," *Journal of Philosophy* XXVII, 1 (January 4, 1940).

Kierkegaard: Konstruktion des Aesthetischen (Tübingen, 1933), rev. ed. (Frankfurt, 1966).
Minima Moralia: Reflexionen aus dem beschädigten Leben (Frankfurt, 1951).
Moments Musicaux (Frankfurt, 1964).
Negative Dialektik (Frankfurt, 1966).
Ohne Leitbild (Frankfurt, 1967).
"On Kierkegaard's Doctrine of Love," *SPSS* VIII, 3 (1939).
"On Popular Music," with the assistance of George Simpson, *SPSS* IX, 1 (1941).
Philosophie der neuen Musik (Frankfurt, 1949).
Prismen (Frankfurt, 1955); in English as *Prisms*, trans. Samuel and Shierry Weber (London, 1967).
"Reflexionen," *Aufklärung* IV, 1 (June, 1951).
"Scientific Experiences of a European Scholar in America," in *The Intellectual Migration: Europe and America, 1930–1960*, ed. Donald Fleming and Bernard Bailyn (Cambridge, Mass., 1969).
"A Social Critique of Radio Music," *Kenyon Review* VII, 2 (Spring, 1945).
"Social Science and Sociological Tendencies in Psychoanalysis." Unpublished, Los Angeles, April 27, 1946; in Lowenthal's collection.
"Sociology and Psychology," *New Left Review*, 46 (November–December, 1967) and 47 (January–February, 1968).
"The Stars Down to Earth: *The Los Angeles Times* Astrology Column: A Study in Secondary Superstition," *Jahrbuch für Amerikastudien*, vol. II (Heidelberg, 1957).
"Thesen zur Kunstsoziologie," *Kölner Zeitschrift für Soziologie und Sozialpsychologie*, XIX, 1 (March, 1967).
"Theses upon Art and Religion Today," *Kenyon Review* VII, 4 (Autumn, 1945).
"Über den Fetischcharakter in der Musik und die Regression des Hörens," *ZfS* VII, 3 (1938).
(Under the pseudonym Hektor Rottweiler), "Über Jazz," *ZfS* V, 2 (1936).
Über Walter Benjamin (Frankfurt, 1970).
"Veblen's Attack on Culture," *SPSS* IX, 3 (1941).
Versuch über Wagner (Frankfurt, 1952).
"Wagner, Hitler, and Nietzsche," *Kenyon Review* IX, 1 (1947).
"Zur gegenwärtigen Stellung der empirischen Sozialforschung in Deutschland," in *Empirische Sozialforschung, Schriftenreihe des Instituts zur Förderung Öffentlichen Angelegenheiten e.v.*, vol. XIV (Frankfurt, 1952).

WALTER BENJAMIN

Berliner Kindheit um Neunzehnhundert (Frankfurt, 1950).
Briefe, ed. Gershom Scholem and Theodor W. Adorno. 2 vols. (Frankfurt, 1966).
Charles Baudelaire: Ein Lyriker im Zeitalter des Hochkapitalismus (Frankfurt, 1969).
Deutsche Menschen: Eine Folge von Briefe, under the pseudonym "Detlef Holz," (Lucerne, 1936).
"Eduard Fuchs, der Sammler und der Historiker," *ZfS* VI, 2 (1937).
Illuminations: Essays and Reflections, ed. with introduction by Hannah Arendt, trans. Harry Zohn (New York, 1968).
"L'Oeuvre d'art à l'époque de sa reproduction mécanisée," *ZfS* V, 1 (1936).
"Paris, Capital of the Nineteenth Century," *Dissent* XVII, 5 (September–October, 1970).
"Probleme der Sprachsoziologie," *ZfS* IV, 3 (1935).
Schriften, ed. Theodor W. Adorno and Gershom Scholem. 2 vols. (Frankfurt, 1955).

Versuche über Brecht, ed. Rolf Tiedemann (Frankfurt, 1966).
"Zeitschrift für Sozialforschung," *Mass und Wert* I, 5 (May–June, 1938).
"Zum gegenwärtigen gesellschaftlichen Standort des fransözischen Schriftstellers," *ZfS* III, 1 (1934).
Zur Kritik der Gewalt und andere Aufsätze (Frankfurt, 1965).

BRUNO BETTELHEIM AND MORRIS JANOWITZ

Dynamics of Prejudice: A Psychological and Sociological Study of Veterans (New York, 1950).
Social Change and Prejudice (New York, 1964).

FRANZ BORKENAU

Der Übergang vom feudalen zum bürgerlichen Weltbild (Paris, 1934).
"Zur Soziologie des mechanistischen Weltbildes," *ZfS* I, 3 (1932).

ERICH FROMM

Beyond the Chains of Illusion: My Encounter with Marx and Freud (New York, 1962).
"A Counter-Rebuttal," *Dissent* III, 1 (Winter, 1956).
The Crisis of Psychoanalysis (New York, 1970).
The Dogma of Christ, and Other Essays on Religion, Psychology, and Culture (New York, 1963).
Fear of Freedom (London, 1942). (English version of *Escape from Freedom.*)
"Die gesellschaftliche Bedingtheit der psychoanalytischen Therapie," *ZfS* IV, 3 (1935).
The Heart of Man (New York, 1964).
"The Human Implications of Instinctive 'Radicalism,'" *Dissent* II, 4 (Autumn, 1955).
Sigmund Freud's mission (New York, 1963).
Man for Himself (New York, 1947).
Marx's Concept of Man (New York, 1961).
"Die psychoanalytische Charakterologie und ihre Bedeutung für die Sozialpsychologie," *ZfS* I, 3 (1932).
"Der Sabbath," *Imago* XIII, 2, 3, 4 (1927).
The Sane Society (New York, 1955).
Social Character in a Mexican Village, with Michael Maccoby (Englewood Cliffs, N.J., 1970).
"Die sozialpsychologische Bedeutung der Mutterrechtstheorie," *ZfS* III, 2 (1934).
"Sozialpsychologischer Teil," in *Studien über Autorität und Familie* (Paris, 1936).
"Über Methode und Aufgabe einer analytischen Sozialpsychologie," *ZfS* I, 1/2 (1932).
Zen Buddhism and Psychoanalysis with D. T. Suzuki and R. de Martino (New York, 1960).
"Zum Gefühl der Ohnmacht," *ZfS* VI, 1 (1937).

HENRYK GROSSMANN

Das Akkumulations-und Zusummenbruchsgesetz des kapitalistischen Systems (Leipzig, 1929).

"Die gesellschaftlichen Grundlagen der mechanistischen Philosophie und die Manufaktur," *ZfS* IV, 2 (1935).
Marx, die klassische Nationalökonomie und das Problem der Dynamik, afterword by Paul Mattick (Frankfurt, 1969).
"Die Wert-Preis-Transformation bei Marx und das Krisisproblem," *ZfS* I, 1/2 (1932).

CARL GRÜNBERG

"Festrede gehalten zur Einweihung des Instituts für Sozialforschung an der Universität Frankfurt a.M. am 22 Juni 1924," *Frankfurter Universitätsreden*, vol. XX (Frankfurt, 1924).

JULIAN GUMPERZ

"Zur Soziologie des amerikanischen Pa. teiensystems," *ZfS* I, 3 (1932).
"Recent Social Trends," *ZfS* II, 1 (1933).

ARCADIUS R. L. GURLAND

"Die Dialektik der Geschichte und die Geschichtsauffassung Karl Kautskys," *Klassenkampf* (Berlin, September 1, 1929).
The Fate of Small Business in Nazi Germany, with Franz Neumann and Otto Kirchheimer (Washington, D.C., 1943).
"Die K.P.D. und die rechte Gefahr," *Klassenkampf* (Berlin, December 1, 1928).
"Technological Trends and Economic Structure under National Socialism," *SPSS* IX, 2 (1941).

MAX HORKHEIMER

Most of Horkheimer's essays in the *ZfS* are collected in *Kritische Theorie*, 2 vol., ed. Alfred Schmidt (Frankfurt, 1968). Other works and individual *Zeitschrift* essays:

"Allgemeiner Teil," *Studien über Autorität und Familie* (Paris, 1936).
Anfänge der bürgerlichen Geschichtsphilosophie (Stuttgart, 1930).
"Art and Mass Culture," *SPSS* IX, 2 (1941).
"Auf das Andere Hoffen," Interview in *Der Spiegel* (January 5, 1970).
"Authoritarianism and the Family Today," in *The Family: Its Function and Destiny*, ed. Ruth Nanda Anshen (New York, 1949).
"Autoritärer Staat," in "Walter Benjamin zum Gedächtnis." Unpublished 1942; in Pollock's collection.
"Bemerkungen über Wissenschaft und Krise," *ZfS* I, 1/2 (1932).
"Bemerkungen zu Jaspers 'Nietzsche,'" *ZfS* VI, 2 (1937).
"Bemerkungen zur philosophischen Anthropologie," *ZfS* IV, 1 (1935).
Dämmerung, written under the pseudonym "Heinrich Regius," (Zurich, 1934).
Dialektik der Aufklärung, with Theodor W. Adorno (Amsterdam, 1947).
Eclipse of Reason (New York, 1947).
"Egoismus und Freiheitsbewegung," *ZfS* V, 2 (1936).
"Die Gegenwärtige Lage der Sozialphilosophie und die Aufgaben eines Instituts für Sozialforschung," *Frankfurter Universitätsreden*, vol. XXVII (Frankfurt, 1931).
"Geschichte und Psychologie," *ZfS* I, 1/2 (1932).

"Hegel und die Metaphysik," *Festschrift für Carl Grünberg: zum 70. Geburtstag* (Leipzig, 1932).
"Die Juden und Europa," *ZfS* VIII, 1/2 (1939).
Kants Kritik der Urteilskraft als Bindeglied zwischen theoretischer und praktischer Philosophie (Stuttgart, 1925).
"The Lessons of Fascism," in *Tensions That Cause Wars*, ed. Hadley Cantril (Urbana, Ill., 1950).
"Materialismus und Metaphysik," *ZfS* II, 1 (1933).
"Materialismus und Moral," *ZfS* II, 2 (1933).
"Montaigne und die Funktion der Skepsis," *ZfS* VII, 1 (1938).
"Ein neuer Ideologiebegriff?," *Grünbergs Archiv* XV, 1 (1930).
"Der neueste Angriff auf die Metaphysik," *ZfS* VI, 1 (1937).
"Notes on Institute Activities," *SPSS* IX, 1 (1941).
"On the Concept of Freedom," *Diogenes* 53 (Paris, 1966).
"Die Philosophie der absoluten Konzentration," *ZfS* VII, 3 (1938).
"Philosophie und kritische Theorie," *ZfS* VI, 3 (1937).
Preface, *SPSS* IX, 2 (1941).
"The Relation between Psychology and Sociology in the Work of Wilhelm Dilthey," *SPSS* IX, 3 (1939).
"Schopenhauer Today," *The Critical Spirit; Essays in Honor of Herbert Marcuse*, ed. Kurt H. Wolff and Barrington Moore, Jr. (Boston, 1967).
"The Social Function of Philosophy," *SPSS* VIII, 3 (1939).
"Sociological Background of the Psychoanalytic Approach," in *Anti-Semitism: A Social Disease*, ed. Ernst Simmel (New York, 1946).
Survey of the Social Sciences in Western Germany (Washington, D.C., 1952).
"Traditionelle und kritische Theorie," *ZfS* VI, 2 (1937).
"Vernunft und Selbsterhaltung," in "Walter Benjamin zum Gedächtnis." Unpublished, 1942; in Pollock's Collection.
"Zu Bergsons Metaphysik der Zeit," *ZfS* III, 3 (1934).
"Zum Begriff der Vernunft," *Frankfurter Universitätsreden*, vol. VII (Frankfurt, 1952).
"Zum Problem der Voraussage in den Sozialwissenschaften," *ZfS* II, 3 (1933).
"Zum Problem der Wahrheit," *ZfS* IV, 3 (1935).
"Zum Rationalismusstreit in der gegenwärtigen Philosophie," *ZfS* III, 1 (1934).
Zur Kritik der instrumentellen Vernunft (Frankfurt, 1967).

Otto Kirchheimer

"Criminal Law in National Socialist Germany," *SPSS* VIII, 3 (1939).
The Fate of Small Business in Nazi Germany, with Arcadius R. L. Gurland and Franz Neumann (Washington, D.C., 1943).
"Franz Neumann: An Appreciation," *Dissent* IV, 4 (Autumn, 1957).
Political Justice: The Use of Legal Procedure for Political Ends (Princeton, 1961).
Politics, Law, and Social Change: Selected Essays of Otto Kirchheimer, ed. Frederic S. Burin and Kurt L. Shell (New York and London, 1969). Contains a selected bibliography.
Punishment and Social Structure, with George Rusche (New York, 1939).

Mirra Komarovsky

The Unemployed Man and His Family (New York, 1940).

ERNST KRĚNEK

"Bemerkungen zur Rundfunkmusik," *ZfS* VII, 1/2 (1938).

OLGA LANG

Chinese Family and Society (New Haven, 1946).

PAUL LAZARSFELD

"An Episode in the History of Social Research: A Memoir," in *The Intellectual Migration: Europe and America, 1930–1960*, ed. Donald Fleming and Bernard Bailyn (Cambridge, Mass., 1969).
"Problems in Methodology," in *Sociology Today*, ed. Robert K. Merton, Leonard Broom, and Leonard S. Cottrell, Jr. (New York, 1959).
"Remarks on Administrative and Critical Communications Research," *SPSS* IX, 1 (1941).
"Some Remarks on the Typological Procedures in Social Research," *ZfS* VI, 1 (1937).

LEO LOWENTHAL

"Die Auffassung Dostojewskis in Vorkriegsdeutschland," *ZfS* III, 3 (1934); an English version can be found in *The Arts in Society*, ed. Robert N. Wilson (Englewood Cliffs, N.J., 1964).
"Conrad Ferdinand Meyers heroische Geschichtsauffassung," *ZfS* II, 1 (1933).
"Das Dämonische," in *Gabe Herrn Rabbiner Dr. Nobel zum 50. Geburtstag* (Frankfurt, 1921).
Erzählkunst und Gesellschaft: Die Gesellschaftsproblematik in der deutschen Literatur des 19. Jahrhunderts, with an intro. by Frederic C. Tubach (Neuwied and Berlin, 1971).
"German Popular Biographies: Culture's Bargain Counter," in *The Critical Spirit: Essays in Honor of Herbert Marcuse*, ed. Kurt H. Wolff and Barrington Moore, Jr. (Boston, 1967).
"Historical Perspectives of Popular Culture," in *Mass Culture: The Popular Arts in America*, ed. Bernard Rosenberg and David Manning White (Glencoe, Ill. and London, 1957).
Literature and the Image of Man (Boston, 1957).
Literature, Popular Culture, and Society (Englewood Cliffs, N.J., 1961).
Prophets of Deceit, with Norbert Guterman (New York, 1949).
"Terror's Atomization of Man," *Commentary*, I, 3 (January, 1946).
"Zugtier und Sklaverei," *ZfS* II, 1 (1933).
"Zur gesellschaftlichen Lage der Literatur," *ZfS* I, 1/2 (1932).

RICHARD LÖWENTHAL [PAUL SERING]

"Zu Marshals neuklassischer Ökonomie," *ZfS* VI, 3 (1937).

KURT MANDELBAUM

(Under the pseudonym Kurt Baumann), "Autarkie und Planwirtschaft," *ZfS* II, 1 (1933).
(Under the pseudonym Erich Baumann), "Keynes Revision der liberalistischen Nationalökonomie," *ZfS* V, 3 (1936).

"Neuere Literatur über technologische Arbeitslosigkeit," *ZfS* V, 1 (1936).
"Zur Theorie der Planwirtschaft," with Gerhard Meyer, *ZfS* III, 2 (1934).

HERBERT MARCUSE

For a complete bibliography of Marcuse's works until 1967, see *The Critical Spirit: Essays in Honor of Herbert Marcuse*, ed. Kurt H. Wolff and Barrington Moore, Jr. (Boston, 1967) p. 427–433. Works consulted in this study:

"Beiträge zu einer Phänomenologie des historischen Materialismus," *Philosophische Hefte* I, 1 (1928).
"Der Einfluss der deutschen Emigranten auf das amerikanische Geistesleben: Philosophie und Soziologie," *Jahrbuch für Amerikastudien*, vol. X (Heidelberg, 1965).
Eros and Civilization (Boston, 1955).
An Essay on Liberation (Boston, 1969).
"Existentialism: Remarks on Jean-Paul Sartre's *L'Être et le néant*," *Philosophy and Phenomenological Research* VIII, 3 (March, 1949).
Five Lectures, trans. Jeremy J. Shapiro and Shierry M. Weber (Boston, 1970).
Hegels Ontologie und die Grundlegung einer Theorie der Geschichtlichkeit (Frankfurt, 1932).
"Ideengeschichtlicher Teil," in *Studien über Autorität und Familie* (Paris, 1936).
"An Introduction to Hegel's Philosophy," *SPSS* VIII, 3 (1939).
"Der Kampf gegen den Liberalismus in der totalitären Staatsauffassung," *ZfS* III, 1 (1934).
Kultur und Gesellschaft, 2 vols. (Frankfurt, 1965).
Negations: Essays in Critical Theory, trans. Jeremy J. Shapiro (Boston, 1968).
"Neue Quellen zur Grundlegung des historischen Materialismus," *Die Gesellschaft* IX, 8 (August, 1932).
"The Obsolescence of Marxism," in *Marx and the Western World*, ed. Nicholas Lobkowicz (Notre Dame, Indiana, 1967).
One-Dimensional Man: Studies in the Ideology of Advanced Industrial Society (Boston, 1964).
"Philosophie und kritische Theorie," *ZfS* VI, 3 (1937).
"Das Problem der geschichtlichen Wirklichkeit," *Die Gesellschaft* VII, 4 (April, 1931).
Psychoanalyse und Politik (Frankfurt, 1968).
Reason and Revolution: Hegel and the Rise of Social Theory, rev. ed. (Boston, 1960).
"A Reply to Erich Fromm," *Dissent* III, 1 (Winter, 1956).
"Repressive Tolerance," *A Critique of Pure Tolerance*, with Robert Paul Wolff and Barrington Moore, Jr. (Boston, 1965).
"Some Social Implications of Modern Technology," *SPSS* IX, 3 (1941).
Soviet Marxism: A Critical Analysis (New York, 1958).
"Über den affirmativen Charakter der Kultur," *ZfS* VI, 1 (1937).
"Über die philosophischen Grundlagen des wirtschaftswissenschaftlichen Arbeitsbegriff," *Archiv für Sozialwissenschaft und Sozialpolitik*, LXIX, 3 (June, 1933).
"Zum Begriff des Wesens," *ZfS* V, 1 (1936).
"Zum Problem der Dialektik," *Die Gesellschaft* VII, 1 (January, 1930).
"Zur Kritik des Hedonismus," *ZfS* VII, 1 (1938).
"Zur Wahrheitsproblematik der soziologischen Methode," *Die Gesellschaft* VI, 10 (October, 1929).

PAUL MASSING

Rehearsal for Destruction (New York, 1949).
(Under the pseudonym Karl Billinger), *Schutzhaftling 880: Aus einem deutschen Konzentrationslager* (Paris, 1935); trans. as *Fatherland*, intro. by Lincoln Steffens (New York, 1935).

GERHARD MEYER

"Krisenpolitik und Planwirtschaft," *ZfS* IV, 3 (1935).
"Neue englische Literatur zur Planwirtschaft," *ZfS* II, 2 (1933).
"Neuere Literatur über Planwirtschaft," *ZfS* I, 3 (1932).
"Zur Theorie der Planwirtschaft" (with Kurt Mandelbaum), *ZfS,* III, 2 (1934).

FRANZ NEUMANN

Behemoth: The Structure and Practice of National Socialism, 1933–1944, rev. ed. (New York, 1944).
The Democratic and the Authoritarian State: Essays in Political and Legal Theory, ed. with a preface by Herbert Marcuse (New York, 1957). Contains a selected bibliography.
The Fate of Small Business in Nazi Germany, with Arcadius R. L. Gurland and Otto Kirchheimer. (Washington, 1943).
"The Social Sciences," *The Cultural Migration: The European Scholar in America*, with Henri Peyre, Erwin Panofsky, Wolfgang Köhler, and Paul Tillich, intro. by W. Rexford Crawford (Philadelphia, 1953).

FRIEDRICH POLLOCK

The Economic and Social Consequences of Automation, trans. W. O. Henderson and W. H. Chalmer (Oxford, 1957).
"Die gegenwärtige Lage des Kapitalismus und die Aussichten einer planwirtschaftlichen Neuordnung," *ZfS* I, 1/2 (1933).
Ed., *Gruppenexperiment: Ein Studienbericht; Frankfurter Beiträge zur Soziologie,* vol. II (Frankfurt, 1955).
"Is National Socialism a New Order?," *SPSS* IX, 3 (1941).
Die planwirtschaftlichen Versuche in der Sowjetunion, 1917–1927 (Leipzig, 1929).
Sombarts "Widerlegung" des Marxismus (Leipzig, 1926).
"Sozialismus und Landwirtschaft," in *Festschrift für Carl Grünberg: zum 70. Geburtstag* (Leipzig, 1932).
"State Capitalism: Its Possibilities and Limitations," *SPSS* IX, 2 (1941).
"Zu dem Aufsatz von Hannah Arendt über Walter Benjamin," *Merkur* XXII, 6 (1968).

ERNST SCHACHTEL

"Zum Begriff und zur Diagnose der Persönlichkeit in den 'Personality Tests,' " *ZfS* VI, 3 (1937).

ANDRIES STERNHEIM

"Zum Problem der Freizeitgestaltung," *ZfS* I, 3 (1932).

FELIX J. WEIL

The Argentine Riddle (New York, 1944).
"Neuere Literatur zum 'New Deal,'" *ZfS* V, 3 (1936).
"Neuere Literatur zur deutschen Wehrwirtschaft," *ZfS* VII, 1/2 (1938).
Sozialisierung: Versuch einer begrifflichen Grundlegung (Nebst einer Kritik der Sozialisierungspläne). (Berlin-Fichtenau, 1921).

KARL AUGUST WITTFOGEL

Das Erwachende China (Vienna, 1926).
"The Foundations and Stages of Chinese Economic History," *ZfS* IV, 1 (1935).
Geschichte der bürgerlichen Gesellschaft (Vienna, 1924).
Oriental Despotism: A Comparative Study of Total Power (New Haven, London, and New York, 1957).
Testimony in front of the Internal Security Subcommittee of the Senate Judiciary Committee (August 7, 1951), 82nd Congress, 1951–1952, vol. III.
"Die Theorie der orientalischen Gesellschaft," *ZfS* VII, 1 (1938).
Wirtschaft und Gesellschaft Chinas (Leipzig, 1931).
Die Wissenschaft der bürgerlichen Gesellschaft (Berlin, 1922).

WORKS DIRECTLY RELATING TO THE INSTITUT OR ONE OF ITS MEMBERS

Arendt, Hannah, Introduction to *Illuminations: Essays and Reflections* (New York, 1968); reprinted in Hannah Arendt, *Men in Dark Times* as "Walter Benjamin: 1892–1940" (New York, 1968).
Axelos, Kostas, "Adorno et l'école de Francfort," *Arguments*, III, 14 (1959).
Bernsdorf, Wilhelm, *Internationalen Soziologen Lexikon* (Stuttgart, 1965).
Bloch, Ernst, "Erinnerungen an Walter Benjamin," *Der Monat* XVIII, 216 (September, 1966).
Boehmer, Konrad, "Adorno, Musik, Gesellschaft," in *Die neue Linke nach Adorno*, ed. Wilfried F. Schoeller (Munich, 1969).
Braeuer, Walter, "Henryk Grossman als Nationalökonom," *Arbeit und Wissenschaft*, VIII (1954).
Bramson, Leon, *The Political Context of Sociology* (Princeton, 1961).
Braunthal, Alfred, "Der Zusammenbruch der Zusammenbruchstheorie," *Die Gesellschaft* VI, 10 (October, 1929).
Brecht, Bertolt, *Gedichte VI* (Frankfurt, 1964).
Breines, Paul, ed., *Critical Interruptions: New Left Perspectives on Herbert Marcuse* (New York, 1970).
Brenner, Hildegaard, "Die Lesbarkeit der Bilder: Skizzen zum Passagenentwurf," *Alternative* 59/60 (April–June, 1968).
———, "Theodor W. Adorno als Sachwalter des Benjaminschen Werkes," in *Die neue Linke nach Adorno*, ed. Wilfried F. Schoeller (Munich, 1969).
Brown, Roger, *Social Psychology* (New York, 1965).
Christie, Richard, and Marie Jahoda, *Studies in the Scope and Method of "The Authoritarian Personality"* (Glencoe, Ill., .954).
Claussen, Detlev, "Zum emanzipativen Gehalt der materialistischen Dialektik in Horkheimers Konzeption der kritischen Theorie," *Neue Kritik* 55/56 (1970).

Clemenz, Manfred, "Theorie als Praxis?," *Neue Politische Literatur* XIII, 2 (1968).

Cohen, Jerry, "The Philosophy of Marcuse," *New Left Review*, 57 (September–October, 1969).

Colletti, Lucio, "Von Hegel zu Marcuse," *Alternative*, 72/73 (June–August, 1970).

Continuum VIII, 1/2 (Spring-Summer, 1970).

Dahrendorf, Ralf, *Society and Democracy in Germany* (London, 1968).

Deakin, F. W., and G. R. Storry, *The Case of Richard Sorge* (London, 1966).

"Dialectical Methodology; Marx or Weber; the New *Methodenstreit* in Postwar German Philosophy," *The Times Literary Supplement* (London, March 12, 1970).

Fermi, Laura, *Illustrious Immigrants* (Chicago, 1968).

Fetscher, Iring, "Asien im Lichte des Marxismus: Zu Karl Wittfogels Forschungen über die orientalischen Despotie," *Merkur* XX, 3 (March, 1966).

———, "Ein Kämpfer ohne Illusion," *Die Zeit* (Hamburg, August 19, 1969).

———, "Bertolt Brecht and America," in *The Legacy of the German Refugee Intellectuals, Salmagundi,* 10/11 (Fall, 1969–Winter, 1970).

Fingarette, Herbert, "Eros and Utopia," *The Review of Metaphysics* X, 4 (June, 1957).

Fleming, Donald, and Bernard Bailyn, eds., *The Intellectual Migration: Europe and America, 1930–1960* (Cambridge, Mass., 1969).

Friedenberg, Edgar, "Neo-Freudianism and Erich Fromm," *Commentary* XXXIV, 4 (October, 1962).

"From Historicism to Marxist Humanism," *The Times Literary Supplement* (London, June 5, 1969).

Gay, Peter, *Weimar Culture: The Outsider as Insider* (New York, 1968).

Giltay, H., "Psychoanalyse und sozial-kulturelle Erneuerung," *Psychoanalytische Bewegung* IV, 5 (September–October, 1932).

Glazer, Nathan, "*The Authoritarian Personality* in Profile: Report on a Major Study of Race Hatred," *Commentary* IV, 6 (June, 1950).

Goldmann, Lucien, "La Pensée de Herbert Marcuse," *La Nef*, 36 (January–March, 1969).

Graubard, Allen, "One-dimensional Pessimism," *Dissent*, XV, 3 (May–June, 1968).

Grossner, Claus, "Frankfurter Schule am Ende," *Die Zeit* (Hamburg, May 12, 1970).

Gruchot, Piet, "Konstruktive Sabotage: Walter Benjamin und der bürgerlichen Intellektuelle," *Alternative* 56/57 (October–December, 1967).

Habermas, Jürgen, ed., *Antworten auf Herbert Marcuse* (Frankfurt, 1968).

———, *Philosophisch-politische Profile* (Frankfurt, 1971).

Hammond, Guyton B., *Man in Estrangement* (Nashville, 1965).

Heise, Rosemarie, "Der Benjamin-Nachlass in Potsdam," interview with Hildegaard Brenner, *Alternative* 56/57 (October–December, 1967).

———, "Nachbemerkungen zu einer Polemik oder Widerlegbare Behauptungen der frankfurter Benjamin-Herausgeber," *Alternative* 59/60 (April–June, 1968).

Herz, John H., and Erich Hula, "Otto Kirchheimer: An Introduction to his Life and Work," in *Politics, Law, and Social Change: Selected Essays by Otto Kirchheimer*, ed. Frederic S. Burin and Kurt L. Shell (New York and London, 1969).

———, "Otto Kirchheimer," *The Legacy of the German Refugee Intellectuals, Salmagundi* 10/11 (Fall, 1969–Winter, 1970).

Holz, Hans Heinz, "Philosophie als Interpretation," *Alternative* 56/57 (October–December, 1967).

———, *Utopie und Anarchismus: Zur Kritik der Kritischen Theorie Herbert Marcuses* (Cologne, 1968).

Howard, Dick, and Karl Klare, ed. *The Unknown Dimension: European Marxism Since Lenin* (New York and London, 1972).

Hughes, H. Stuart, "Franz Neumann between Marxism and Liberal Democracy," in *The Intellectual Migration: Europe and America, 1930–1960*, ed. Donald Fleming and Bernard Bailyn (Cambridge, Mass., 1969).

Jameson, Fredric, "T. W. Adorno, or Historical Tropes," *Salmagundi* II, 1 (Spring, 1967).

———, "Walter Benjamin, or Nostalgia," *The Legacy of the German Refugee Intellectuals, Salmagundi*, 10/11 (Fall, 1969–Winter, 1970).

Jay, Martin, "The Frankfurt School in Exile," *Perspectives in American History*, vol. VI (Cambridge, 1972).

———, "The Frankfurt School's Critique of Marxist Humanism," *Social Research* XXXIX, 2 (Summer, 1972).

———, "The Metapolitics of Utopianism," *Dissent* XVII, 4 (July–August, 1970) reprinted in *The Revival of American Socialism*, ed. George Fischer et al. (New York, 1971).

———, "The Permanent Exile of Theodor W. Adorno," *Midstream* XV, 10 (December, 1969).

Kecskemeti, Paul, "The Study of Man: Prejudice in the Catastrophic Perspective," *Commentary* XI, 3 (March, 1951).

Kettler, David, "Dilemmas of Radicalism," *Dissent* IV, 4 (Autumn, 1957).

Kittsteiner, Heinz-Dieter, "Die 'geschichtsphilosophischen' Thesen," *Alternative* 56/57 (October–December, 1967).

Koestler, Arthur, *Arrow in the Blue* (New York, 1952).

———, *The Invisible Writing* (London, 1954).

König, René, "Soziologie der Familie," in *Handbuch der empirischen Sozialforschung*, vol. II (Stuttgart, 1969).

———, "On Some Recent Developments in the Relation Between Theory and Research," in *Transactions of the 4th World Congress of Sociology*, vol. II (London, 1959).

Laplanche, Jean, "Notes sur Marcuse et le Psychoanalyse," *La Nef* 36 (January–March, 1969).

Lefebvre, Henri, "Eros et Logos," *La Nef* 36 (January–March, 1969).

Leibowitz, René, "Der Komponist Theodor W. Adorno," *Zeugnisse: Theodor W. Adorno zum sechzigsten Geburtstag* (Frankfurt, 1963).

Lethen, Helmut, "Zur materialistischen Kunsttheorie Benjamins," *Alternative* 56/57 (October–December, 1967).

Libera, Alain de, "Le Critique de Hegel," *La Nef* 36 (January–March, 1969).

Lichtheim, George, "From Marx to Hegel: Reflections on Georg Lukács, T. W. Adorno, and Herbert Marcuse," *Tri-Quarterly*, 12 (Spring, 1968).

Lipshires, Sidney S., "Herbert Marcuse: From Marx to Freud and Beyond," Ph.D. diss., University of Connecticut, 1971.

Lück, Helmut, "Anmerkungen zu Theodor W. Adornos Zusammenarbeit mit Hanns Eisler," *Die neue Linke nach Adorno*, ed. Wilfried F. Schoeller (Munich, 1969).

MacIntyre, Alasdair, *Herbert Marcuse: An Exposition and a Polemic* (New York, 1970).

———, "Herbert Marcuse," *Survey* 62 (January, 1967).

———, "Modern Society: An End to Revolt?," *Dissent* XII, 2 (Spring, 1965).

Mann, Thomas, *The Story of a Novel: The Genesis of Doctor Faustus*, trans. Richard and Clara Winston (New York, 1961).
———, *Letters of Thomas Mann, 1889–1955*, selected and trans. Richard and Clara Winston, intro. by Richard Winston (New York, 1971).
Marks, Robert W., *The Meaning of Marcuse* (New York, 1970).
Massing, Hede, *This Deception* (New York, 1951).
Mayer, Gustav, *Erinnerungen* (Zurich and Vienna, 1949).
Mayer, Hans, *Der Repräsentant und der Märtyrer: Konstellationen der Literatur* (Frankfurt, 1971).
Müller-Strömsdörfer, Ilse, "Die 'helfende Kraft bestimmter Negation,'" *Philosophische Rundschau* VIII, 2/3 (January, 1961).
Oppens, Kurt, et al., *Über Theodor W. Adorno* (Frankfurt, 1968).
Piccone, Paul, and Alexander Delfini, "Marcuse's Heideggerian Marxism," *Telos* VI (Fall, 1970).
Picht, Georg, "Atonale Philosophie. Theodor W. Adorno zum Gedächtnis," *Merkur* X, 13 (October, 1969).
Pross, Helge, *Die deutsche akademische Emigration nach den Vereinigten Staaten, 1933–1941* (Berlin, 1955).
Radkau, Joachim, *Die deutsche Emigration in den USA: Ihr Einfluss auf die amerikanische Europapolitik, 1933–1945* (Düsseldorf, 1971).
Riesman, David, and Nathan Glazer, *Faces in the Crowd* (New Haven, 1952).
———, *Individualism Reconsidered and Other Essays* (Glencoe, Ill., 1954).
———, and Reuel Denney and Nathan Glazer, *The Lonely Crowd* (New Haven, 1950).
Robinson, Paul, *The Freudian Left* (New York, 1969).
Rosenberg, Bernard, and David Manning White, eds., *Mass Culture: The Popular Arts in America* (London, 1957).
Rusconi, Gian Enrico, *La Teoria Critica della Societa* (Bologna, 1968).
Rychner, Max, "Erinnerungen an Walter Benjamin," *Der Monat* XVIII, 216 (September, 1966).
Schaar, John H., *Escape from Authority: The Perspectives of Erich Fromm* (New York, 1961).
Schmidt, Alfred, "Adorno — ein Philosoph des realen Humanismus," *Neue Rundschau* LXXX, 4 (1969).
———, "Nachwort des Herausgebers: Zur Idee der kritischen Theorie," in *Kritische Theorie*, vol. II (Frankfurt, 1968).
———, *Die "Zeitschrift für Sozialforschung": Geschichte und gegenwärtige Bedeutung* (Munich, 1970).
Scholem, Gershom, "Erinnerungen an Walter Benjamin," *Der Monat* XVIII 216 (September, 1966).
———, "Walter Benjamin," *The Leo Baeck Institute Yearbook* (New York, 1965).
Sedgwick, Peter, "Natural Science and Human Theory," *The Socialist Register* (London, 1966).
Shils, Edward, "Daydreams and Nightmares: Reflections on the Criticism of Mass Culture," *Sewanee Review*, LXV, 4 (Autumn, 1957).
———, "Tradition, Ecology, and Institution in the History of Sociology," *Daedalus* LXXXIX, 4 (Fall, 1970).
Silbermann, Alphons, "Anmerkungen zur Musiksoziologie," *Kölner Zeitschrift für Soziologie und Sozialpsychologie* XIX, 3 (September, 1967).
Stourzh, Gerald, "Die deutschsprachige Emigration in den Vereinigten Staaten:

Geschichtswissenschaft und Politische Wissenschaft," *Jahrbuch für Amerikastudien* X (Heidelberg, 1965).

Sweezy, Paul, "Paul Alexander Baran: A Personal Memoir," *Monthly Review* XVI, 11 (March, 1965).

Szondi, Peter, "Hoffnung im Vergangenen," in *Zeugnisse: Theodor W. Adorno zum sechzigsten Geburtstag* (Frankfurt, 1963).

———, "Nachwort," Städtebilder, by Walter Benjamin (Frankfurt, 1963).

Therborn, Göran, "Frankfurt Marxism: A Critique," *New Left Review*, 63 (September–October, 1970).

"Theodor Adorno," *The Times Literary Supplement* (London, September 28, 1967).

Tiedemann, Rolf, *Studien zur Philosophie Walter Benjamins* (Frankfurt, 1965).

———, "Zur 'Beschlagnahme' Walter Benjamins, oder Wie Man mit der Philologie Schlitten fährt," *Das Argument* X, 1/2 (March, 1968).

Trottman, Martin, *Zur Interpretation und Kritik der Zusammenbruchstheorie von Henryk Grossmann* (Zurich, 1956).

Unseld, Siegfried, "Zur Kritik an den Editionen Walter Benjamins," *Frankfurter Rundschau* (January, 1968).

"Walter Benjamin: Towards a Philosophy of Language," *The Times Literary Supplement* (London, January 8, 1971).

Wellmer, Albrecht, *Critical Theory of Society* (New York, 1971).

Werckmeister, O. K., "Das Kunstwerk als Negation; Zur Kunsttheorie Theodor W. Adornos," *Die Neue Rundschau* LXXIII, 1 (1962).

"When Dogma Bites Dogma, or The Difficult Marriage of Marx and Freud," *The Times Literary Supplement* (London, January 8, 1971).

Wilden, Anthony, "Marcuse and the Freudian Model: Energy, Information, and *Phantasie*," *The Legacy of the German Refugee Intellectuals, Salmagundi*, 10/11 (Fall, 1969–Winter, 1970).

Wolff, Kurt H., and Barrington Moore, Jr., eds., *The Critical Spirit: Essays in Honor of Herbert Marcuse* (Boston, 1967).

OTHER WORKS

Althusser, Louis, *For Marx*, trans. Ben Brewster (New York, 1969).

Arendt, Hannah, *Between Past and Future* (Cleveland and New York, 1961).

———, *The Human Condition* (Chicago, 1958).

———, *The Origins of Totalitarianism* (Cleveland, 1958).

Aron, Raymond, *German Sociology* (Glencoe, Ill., 1964).

Avineri, Shlomo, *The Social and Political Thought of Karl Marx* (Cambridge, 1968).

Berlin, Isaiah, *Four Essays on Liberty* (Oxford, 1969).

Bottomore, T. B., trans. and ed., *Karl Marx: Early Writings* (New York, 1963).

Brown, Norman O., *Life Against Death* (New York, 1959).

Butler, E. M., *The Tyranny of Greece over Germany* (Cambridge, 1935).

Cornelius, Hans, "Leben und Lehre," in *Die Philosophie der Gegenwart in Selbstdarstellungen*, ed. Raymund Schmidt, vol. II (Leipzig, 1923).

Deak, Istvan, *Weimar Germany's Left-Wing Intellectuals: A Political History of the Weltbühne and Its Circle* (Berkeley and Los Angeles, 1968).

Dodge, Peter, *Beyond Marxism: The Faith and Works of Hendrik de Man* (The Hague, 1966).

Duggan, Stephen, and Betty Drury, *The Rescue of Science and Learning* (New York, 1948).
Erikson, Erik, *Childhood and Society* (New York, 1950).
Findlay, J. N., *Hegel: A Reexamination* (New York, 1958).
Friedemann, Adolf, "Heinrich Meng, Psychoanalysis and Mental Hygiene," *Psychoanalytic Pioneers*, ed. Franz Alexander, Samuel Eisenstein, and Martin Grotjahn (New York and London, 1966).
Goldmann, Lucien, "The Early Writings of George Lukács," *Tri-Quarterly*, 9 (Spring, 1967).
Grossman, Carl M., and Sylvia Grossman, *The Wild Analyst: The Life and Work of Georg Groddeck* (New York, 1965).
Hoggart, Richard, *The Uses of Literacy* (London, 1957).
Jahoda, Marie, Paul F. Lazarsfeld, and Hans Zeisel, *Die Arbeitslosen von Marienthal* (Leipzig, 1932).
Jahoda, Marie, Morton Deutsch, and Stuart W. Cook, *Research Methods in Social Relations*, vol. I (New York, 1951).
Habermas, Jürgen, *Knowledge and Human Interests*, trans. Jeremy J. Shapiro (Boston, 1971).
———, *Technik und Wissenschaft als "Ideologie"* (Frankfurt, 1968).
———, *Theorie und Praxis* (Neuwied, 1963).
———, *Toward a Rational Society*, trans. Jeremy J. Shapiro (Boston, 1970).
Honigsheim, Paul, "Reminiscences of the Durkheim School," *Emile Durkheim, 1858–1917*, ed. Kurt H. Wolff (Columbus, Ohio, 1960).
Hughes, H. Stuart, *Consciousness and Society* (New York, 1958).
Kockelmans, Joseph J., ed., *Phenomenology* (New York, 1967).
Kornhauser, William, *The Politics of Mass Society* (Glencoe, Ill., 1959).
Korsch, Karl, *Marxismus und Philosophie*, ed. and intro. by Erich Gerlach (Frankfurt, 1966).
Kracauer, Siegfried, *From Caligari to Hitler* (Princeton, 1947).
Leser, Norbert, *Zwischen Reformismus und Bolschewismus: Der Austromarxismus als Theorie und Praxis* (Vienna, Frankfurt, and Zurich, 1968).
Lichtheim, George, *The Concept of Ideology* (New York, 1967).
———, *George Lukács* (New York, 1970).
———, *Marxism: An Historical and Critical Study* (New York and London, 1961).
———, *The Origins of Socialism* (New York, 1969).
Lipset, Seymour M., *Political Man* (New York, 1960).
Lobkowicz, Nicholas, ed., *Marx and the Western World* (Notre Dame, Ind., 1967).
———, *Theory and Practice: History of a Concept From Aristotle to Marx* (Notre Dame, Ind., 1967).
Lorei, Madlen, and Richard Kirn, *Frankfurt und die goldenen zwanziger Jahre* (Frankfurt, 1966).
Löwith, Karl, *From Hegel to Nietzsche* (New York, 1964).
Lukács, Georg, *Essays on Thomas Mann*, trans. Stanley Mitchell (New York, 1964).
———, *History and Class Consciousness*, trans. Rodney Livingston (Cambridge, Mass., 1971).
———, *The Historical Novel*, trans. Hannah and Stanley Mitchell (Boston, 1963).
———, *Die Zerstörung der Vernunft*, in *Werke*, vol. IX (Neuwied, 1961).
Macdonald, Dwight, *Against the American Grain* (New York, 1962).
MacIver, Robert M. *As a Tale That Is Told* (Chicago, 1968).
Marcuse, Ludwig, *Mein zwanzigstes Jahrhundert* (Munich, 1960).

Maslow, Abraham H., "The Authoritarian Character Structure," *The Journal of Social Psychology* XVIII, 2 (November, 1943).
Mason, T. W., "The Primacy of Politics: Politics and Economics in National Socialist Germany," *The Nature of Fascism*, ed. S. J. Woolf (New York, 1968).
Maus, Heinz, "Bericht über die Soziologie in Deutschland 1933 bis 1945," *Kölner Zeitschrift für Soziologie und Sozialpsychologie* II, 1 (1959).
Merton, Robert, *Social Theory and Social Structure*, rev. ed. (Glencoe, Ill., 1957).
Meyer, Gladys, *The Magic Circle* (New York, 1944).
Mitscherlich, Alexander, *Society without the Father*, trans. Eric Mosbacher (New York, 1970).
Negt, Oskar, ed. *Aktualität und Folgen der Philosophie Hegels* (Frankfurt, 1970).
Oakeshott, Michael, *Rationalism in Politics and Other Essays* (London, 1962).
Oberschall, Anthony, *Empirical Social Research in Germany* (Paris and The Hague, 1965).
Parkinson, G. H. R., ed., *Georg Lukács: The Man, His Work, and His Ideas* (New York, 1970).
Popper, Karl, *The Poverty of Historicism* (London, 1957).
Reich, Wilhelm, *The Mass Psychology of Fascism* (New York, 1946).
Rieff, Philip, *Freud: The Mind of the Moralist* (New York, 1959).
———, ed., *On Intellectuals* (New York, 1970).
Riemer, Svend, "Die Emigration der deutschen Soziologen nach den Vereinigten Staaten," *Kölner Zeitschrift für Soziologie und Sozialpsychologie* II, 1 (1959).
Ringer, Fritz, *The Decline of the German Mandarins* (Cambridge, Mass., 1969).
Rokeach, M., *The Open and Closed Mind* (New York, 1960).
Sanford, Nevitt, and H. S. Conrad, "Some Personality Correlates of Morale," *Journal of Abnormal and Social Psychology* XXXVIII, 1 (January, 1943).
Scheler, Max, *Die Wissensformen und die Gesellschaft* (Leipzig, 1926).
Schmidt, Alfred, *Der Begriff der Natur in der Lehre von Marx* (Frankfurt, 1962).
Schoenbaum, David, *Hitler's Social Revolution* (Garden City, N.Y., 1966).
Shklar, Judith N., *Men and Citizens: A Study of Rousseau's Social Theory* (Cambridge, 1969).
Speier, Hans, "The Social Condition of the Intellectual Exile," *Social Order and the Risks of War: Papers in Political Sociology* (New York, 1952).
Steiner, George, *Language and Silence: Essays on Language, Literature, and the Inhuman* (New York, 1967).
Werk und Wirken Paul Tillichs: Ein Gedenkbuch (Stuttgart, 1967).
Topitsch, Ernst, *Logik der Sozialwissenschaften* (Cologne and Berlin, 1965).
Turel, Adrien, *Bachofen-Freud: Zur Emanzipation des Mannes vom Reich der Mutter* (Bern, 1939).
Weber, Max, *The Theory of Social and Economic Organization*, trans. A. M. Henderson and Talcott Parsons (New York, 1947).
Wolin, Sheldon, *Politics and Vision* (Boston, 1960).
Wurgaft, Lewis D., "The Activist Movement: Cultural Politics on the German Left, 1914–1933." Ph.D. diss., Harvard University, 1970.

Index